Modern
Scottish
Writers

Energy is Eternal Delight.

William Blake
The Marriage of Heaven and Hell, 1790

About

Edwin

Morgan

edited by
Robert Crawford
and
Hamish Whyte

Edinburgh University Press

© 1990 Edinburgh University Press
22 George Square, Edinburgh

Set in Linotron Garamond 3 by
Photoprint Limited, Torquay
and printed in Great Britain by
Redwood Press Limited
Melksham, Wilts

British Library Cataloguing in
   Publication Data
About Edwin Morgan.
   1. Poetry in English. Morgan,
   Edwin, 1920–
I. Crawford, Robert, 1959–
   II. Whyte, Hamish, 1947–
821.914

ISBN 0 7486 0158 9
   0 7486 0182 1 pbk

Carcanet's permission to quote Edwin Morgan's poetry in this volume
is gratefully acknowledged.

Robert Crawford wishes to thank the British Academy for the award
of a post-doctoral fellowship, during which he wrote his chapter and
did much of the co-editing of this volume.

The publisher acknowledges subsidy from the Scottish Arts Council
towards the publication of this volume.

Contents

           Hamish Whyte

                                    About the Contributors   256
                                                    Index   258

Preface

About Edwin Morgan is the first full-length book on the work of one of Scotland's most distinguished and distinctive poets. He has won honours for his literary achievement in Britain, Europe, and the United States; he is one of the most popular contemporary Scottish writers, as well as the poet whose verse is most widely taught in schools. His influence on Scottish writing has been crucial.

This book is intended as a helpful prelude to further reading, and further critical reflection. Our aim has been to present Morgan's *oeuvre* in the round, demonstrating his versatility and scope, placing him in relevant Scottish as well as in international perspectives. While the majority of the contributors concentrate on Morgan's original poetry, the book also provides new biographical information, a scholarly and comprehensive checklist of his published writings, and essays on facets of Morgan's work which are both important in themselves and integral to his complex achievement: his criticism, his translations, his place in Scottish education.

Because it is ground-breaking, this book cannot be definitive. It does not try to be so; it is intended to stimulate. Aware of Morgan's creative eminence, the contributors steer clear of hagiography. The individual essayists write from their own critical perspectives, but they demonstrate a degree of consensus which may contribute to a clearer understanding of Morgan's output. As editors, we have attempted to provide useful starting points for readers approaching the work of a poet whose name so often seems to be writ in mercury. If this book serves as an intelligent point of reference, it fulfils its function.

The contributors include both writers and academics, both older and younger critics, writing from a variety of environments from Scotland to

New Zealand. This is as it should be, for Morgan's work continues to extend its direct, yet sophisticated appeal. Attending to Morgan's poems about Glasgow as well as his poems about quantum physics, the essays avoid such fashionable but facile labels as 'the Glasgow Writer'. In exploring the exciting range of his work, this book aims to avoid dealing with mere stereotypes. Instead, it tries more accurately and more usefully to be about Edwin Morgan.

ROBERT CRAWFORD, St Andrews
HAMISH WHYTE, Glasgow

Abbreviations

Akros 'Edwin Morgan: an interview'. Interview with EM by Marshall
Walker. *Akros* 11:32, December 1976. Published separately in 1977
(Preston: Akros Publications). Reprinted in *Nothing Not Giving
Messages* (Edinburgh: Polygon, 1990).

B *Beowulf: A Verse Translation into Modern English* (Aldington, Kent:
Hand and Flower Press, 1952).

E *Essays* (Cheadle Hulme: Carcanet New Press, 1974).

FR *Fifty Renascence Love-Poems*, translated by Edwin Morgan (Reading:
Whiteknights Press, 1975).

Gairfish 'An Alphabet of Morgan'. Interview with EM by W.N. Herbert. *The
Gairfish* 1:2, Autumn 1988. Reprinted in *Nothing Not Giving
Messages.*

MPP *Master Peter Pathelin: An Anonymous 15th Century French Farce*,
translated by Edwin Morgan (Glasgow: Third Eye Centre 1983).

P *Poems of Thirty Years* (Manchester: Carcanet Press, 1982).

PP *Provenance and Problematics of 'Sublime and Alarming Images' in Poetry*
(London: The British Academy, 1979. The Warton Lecture).

RP *Rites of Passage: Translations* (Manchester: Carcanet New Press, 1976).

SP *Selected Poems* (Manchester: Carcanet Press, 1985).

SSV *Scottish Satirical Verse: An Anthology*, edited by Edwin Morgan
(Manchester: Carcanet New Press, 1980).

TV *Themes on a Variation* (Manchester: Carcanet Press, 1988).

Verse Interview with EM by Robert Crawford. *Verse* 5:1, February 1988.
Reprinted in *Nothing Not Giving Messages.*

WHV *Wi the Haill Voice: 25 poems by Vladimir Mayakovsky*, translated by
Edwin Morgan (Oxford: Carcanet Press, 1972).

One

Edwin Morgan: Lives and Work

Kevin McCarra

As a teenager Edwin Morgan made a list, in the pages of an old diary, of the books he had read. Within that record of his childhood interests we can detect some of the crucial enthusiasms which have shaped his writing as an adult. Predictably, the titles of vivid adventure stories by writers like G.A. Henty, Jules Verne, Edgar Rice Burroughs, and Jack London appear beside more 'literary' but equally colourful works by Dickens, Scott and Thackeray. Morgan has spoken of this enthusiasm for writing which offered access to other worlds, recalling that it was strong enough to conjure parental disapproval, once driving his father to cast a copy of the pulp magazine *Amazing Stories* onto the fire. Adoption of the hallowed practice of reading under the bedclothes with the aid of a torch meant that this particular taste continued to be satisfied.

A recourse to daydream, and to books which provide the material for it, is unsurprising in an only child but Morgan's reading list also points to a contrasting strain in his character, for titles such as *The Wonder Book of Science* and *The Book of Why and What* also crop up. In this his father's influence might be detected, for Stanley Morgan possessed a practical turn of mind. A Sunday walk could be given over to an explanation of some such topic as the making of iron and steel and Morgan remembers that even in fiction his father's tastes ran to books with a political dimension, which seemed to promise an explanation of the way things actually were. A summer's day excursion might blend pleasure and instruction:

> . . . when we went on a Clyde steamer he would make a bee-line
> for the engine-room, dragging me with him: to me, as a boy, the
> engines would have only a sort of hypnotic functional beauty, the

sleek well-oiled movements, the various parts that always miraculously avoided hitting each other, but my father knew how the parts were made, how they fitted together, he could tell me how the boat actually moved, and somehow the whole industrial process remained human, despite all its problems, and I was never able to become a Luddite.[1]

Practical knowledge and exuberant fantasy: Morgan has always had a great appetite for both and in his best writing has succeeded in finding each in the other. He is in every sense a dramatic poet and his cast of characters favours the exotic: the movie star, the gangster, the astronaut (and occasional alien), the political rebel, but less commonly anyone who might be regarded as representative of the 'common man'. And yet despite this the reader of these poems is surprised to find that something is being suggested about the chances and choices of everyone's life. He argues that life only appears ordinary when it is unexamined. In the light of his poems everything appears as an exception and ideas of the norm belong to statistics rather than to experience.

In Morgan's best-known poems the search for transformation takes place in and against the setting of Glasgow's steady poverty and intermittent violence. The city is home ground for Morgan. He was born in Glasgow's West End in 1920 but the family later settled in Pollokshields and Rutherglen and it was there that Morgan grew up.

His father was first a clerk and ultimately a director of Arnott, Young & Co., a small firm of iron and steel merchants. Morgan recalls him as an anxious and conscientious man whose alert sense of morality went hand in hand with the charitable instincts which led him to help former employees who had fallen on hard times. Political conservatives (though with views so ingrained that they would have disclaimed the term) and Presbyterian church-goers, the Morgans created a loving but rigorous home life for their son. As an only child, Morgan felt the force of his parents' hopes and fears with particular intensity. On one occasion he raided the threepenny bits saved for family funds with the intention of buying a racy Sexton Blake thriller. The misdemeanour was regarded as an act of grand larceny by his parents and produced emotions and recriminations of operatic proportions.

More serious apprehensions concerned his solitary nature. Morgan's mother was particularly concerned by the degree to which books and his own imaginings satisfied him. Although a successful pupil, he was unhappy at Rutherglen Academy. Indeed, he gave serious consideration to the idea of leaving school at fifteen and becoming a trainee carpet designer with Templetons. The fact that his great-grandfather on his mother's side had worked in the trade in Aubusson added to the notion's plausibility but instead he took bursary exams and completed his schooling with three years at Glasgow High.

So omnivorous was Morgan's reading that any number of literary influences can be proposed, but insufficient attention has been paid to the effect of the decade in which he passed through adolescence. It is habitual to associate the 1930s with economic depression (the Morgans had to move to a smaller house) but the process of re-arming did promote something of a revival in the years immediately before the Second World War. There was a resurgence in both public and private building. More importantly, the architectural concern with simple geometrical shapes promised a clean break with the ornamentation of traditional styles.

Morgan remembers particularly the strong impression made by the Beresford Hotel (now Strathclyde University's Baird Hall of Residence) in Glasgow's Sauchiehall Street. Its opening came only weeks before that of the Empire Exhibition of 1938. By and large (ignoring the odious Highland Clachan) the various elements of that exhibition held the promise of a streamlined future, underpinned by science and modern engineering, only a few years distant. It was therefore with particular regret that Morgan viewed the timid nostalgia of the Garden Festival in the same city all of fifty years later.

Even before the Empire Exhibition, notions of the futuristic city had already taken root in Morgan's mind. Glasgow being Glasgow, the cinema had to play its part in his life. Fritz Lang's *Metropolis* (first released in 1926) exercised the same power over him as it has over most viewers since; its theme of class oppression is readily forgotten but its vision of urban life bewitches. If literary influences are also sought, one might point to Auden, whose early work draws on the industrial landscape of the Midlands, and those who imitated him.

Childhood and adolescence left Morgan with the conviction that the future should be something more than a continuation of the past. In a 1987 interview he remarked, 'I don't think we should just be curators, tending the buildings erected in the past. Each generation ought to have a chance of fulfilling its ambitions and shaping the world in its own way. I don't like to think of people in the future wondering why we never achieved anything.' It is a line of thought he applies to more than just buildings. Despite his reading in a host of languages, he is on record as disliking ideas of history and tradition. Writers are to be regarded as individual cases and when chatting about favourites he is quite likely to pass from a twentieth century sound poet to the fourteenth-century writer of *Sir Gawain and the Green Knight*. What he rejects in notions of heritage is the implication that the past is forcing the poet in a particular direction. The restless variety of Morgan's work serves as a demonstration that, in writing at least, tomorrow need have no connection with today.

As a schoolboy, Morgan had thought of trying to go to Art School but was eventually reconciled to the fact that his talents did not really lie in that direction. Instead, he entered Glasgow University in 1937. Morgan found it difficult to settle there and recalls, as late as 1940, ignoring the questions in an English Language Anglo-Saxon exam and writing instead a fairly depressed essay about his life.

He was not, however, entirely given over to introspection and the events of the age, in any case, made that impossible. Arguments raged amongst students about the events in Europe, with much debate about the significance of the Spanish Civil War. Morgan was in sympathy with the aims of the Peace Pledge Union, although he was never a member. The outbreak of the Second World War forced him, as it did everyone else in the appropriate age group, to test their convictions in their own lives. When called up in 1940 Morgan registered as a Conscientious Objector.

His parents were horrified and arranged for Morgan to visit the family solicitor to see if he could be dissuaded. The solicitor was forced to report that their son was cogent in defence of his views. None the less, in the period before his case was to be considered by a tribunal, Morgan's attitude did change. He began to believe that there was, by that time, no real alternative to war with Germany but his lingering sympathy with pacifism drove him to an uneasy compromise and he asked that he might serve in the Royal Army Medical Corps. His request was granted.

Morgan spent the war with the 42nd General Hospital in Egypt, the Lebanon, and Palestine. He was a private and the fact that he could type saw him working as a Quartermaster's clerk, maintaining records of medical stores. It was not until *The New Divan* (1977) that Morgan turned to his war-time experiences and even then they are treated in an opaque and tangential manner.

Occasionally, though, the sequence coalesces into horrible clarity. Aside from his clerical duties Morgan was often called upon to work as a stretcher carrier. On those occasions he was filled with dread that his strength might give out and the injured man be dropped. The physical weakness, as he saw it, which made that a possibility provoked self-disgust. In fact, the feared event never happened. Poem 99 of 'The New Divan' draws on those memories while recalling the 'easiest trip' he ever had when amputation had lightened the weight of the man being carried. The recollection of the devastation caused by Rommel's break-out to Alexandria in 1942 has also stayed with him.

He was de-mobbed in 1946 and returned to Glasgow University. In 1947 he graduated with a first class Honours in English Language and English Literature but his studies had also included courses in Political Economy, French, History and Russian. There was the chance of a scholarship to Oxford but at the age of twenty-seven Morgan was naturally keen to be done with his studies and instead accepted the offer of a lectureship in the Department of English at Glasgow University.

Morgan continued, by his own admission, to be a troubled person and the poetry of his which began to be published reflected the fact. The reader familiar with the stringent optimism of his maturity is likely to be puzzled by the early work. One is struck first of all by how mannered it is. The tone of 'Dies Irae' (1952), for example, echoes that of great Anglo-Saxon poetry like 'The Wanderer' and 'The Seafarer', which he had also translated, with, perhaps, a touch of Dylan Thomas added as a concession to modernity. It and 'The Cape of Good Hope' (1955) contain large measures of guilt, despair and self-loathing. Through the metaphor of the journey they deal with personal problems but they conceal more than they communicate.

In common with many other servicemen, he felt somewhat estranged from the world he returned to but his unhappiness had more to do with private matters. While at school Morgan had become aware of his homosexuality. Given the nature of the times, his sex life required a large degree of discretion, if not absolute secrecy. His suspicion that any disclosure would have meant the ruin of his career was surely well-founded. In addition, there was the disquieting knowledge that private activities could constitute a breach of the law. In themselves these facts militated against an harmonious, integrated life but Morgan in any case tended to find the affairs in which he was involved a cause of misery.

All of that changed in 1963 when he met John Scott. Scott came from a working-class Catholic family and earned his living as a storeman. For the first time Morgan had found a relationship of romantic, enduring, reciprocated love. In the year before Scott's death in 1978 they had been to some extent estranged but it was he who gave Morgan the capacity for joy which inspires his work. *Poems of Thirty Years* is dedicated to John Scott.

If there has been no formal declaration on the subject, only a wilful misreading of the poetry could blind the reader to Morgan's homosexu-ality. 'Christmas Eve' could scarcely be clearer on the subject and the nature of the excitement in one section of 'Glasgow Green' is unmistakeable. 'The New Divan' tells of an affair ended when suspicious authorities posted the other man elsewhere. By the 1980s even the titles ('Dear man, my love goes out in waves') announce the news. Any lingering reticence stems from his fear that he will be confined in the role of 'gay poet'. He would prefer to remain unrestricted by adjectives. Before the overtly homosexual poetry, Morgan was inclined, in the autobiographical pieces, to displace the eroticism. The sensuality is transferred to objects connected with the lover – a cigarette and a bowl of strawberries in two of the best-known poems. The writing is lushly romantic but the objects it enshrines are mostly mundane. Ordinary life had become worthy of wonder.

Despite his importance, John Scott was not the sole cause of all this. Between the end of the 1950s and the middle of the 1960s the world seemed to be conspiring to turn Morgan into an important poet. For one thing, his reading in that period revealed a whole range of approaches that were open to him. He was greatly impressed by Black Mountain poets like Olson and Creeley, Beats like Ginsberg and Kerouac, and older poets like William Carlos Williams whose work was beginning to become known in Britain. The strain of Russian modernism from Mayakovsky to Voznesensky excited him too, as did the Brazilian and Portuguese concrete poets he came across in 1962. He was conscious of the Beatles and the sense of liberation to be found in pop music. In its playfulness or immediacy all of this work made it clear that writing flourished away from the universities, in the streets.

And what interesting streets there were for Morgan to write about. As his life changed so, too, did the city in which it was set. Glasgow was bent on refashioning itself, solving its problems with headlong solutions such as motorways, tower-blocks and housing estates. When the dust cleared, the very skyline had altered. The scale of the ambition delighted Morgan and it continues to do so now, when nostalgia for a fictitious past grips Glasgow. By drastic means the city had attracted his attention and, in the 1960s above all, his own fascination produced fascinating poems about motorway lights, snack-bars, slum landlords, gang leaders, drunks, and tough children.

Most of this work was collected in the 1968 volume *The Second Life*. The title requires no explanation but one might conjecture that Morgan's was, in fact, one life resumed after a long hiatus. As we have seen, the 1930s appeared to offer a gleaming new world. The war put paid to that vision but as Morgan saw Glasgow being re-created at the beginning of the 1960s did it feel as if the intervening decades had been annulled and promises were at last to be kept? In a similar manner, the satisfying relationships that are supposed to come with manhood had been withheld. In his imagination at least adolescence occurred in the 1930s and maturity in the 1960s. If his life was paralysed between times, he has scarcely stopped moving since.

It would be easy to lapse into a recitation of the successes: the OBE, the literary prizes, the acclaimed books, the travel and the international reputation he now enjoys. All of it deserved. His influence on the Scottish scene has always been refreshing. There was nothing seigneurial, for instance about the approval he gave younger writers like Liz Lochhead and Tom Leonard. He simply enjoyed their work and thought you might too. Incidentally, he was doing a reading with them not next Thursday but the one after – why not go?

Yet there is something elusive about Morgan. A list of facts is useless if it only obscures that fact. His defences have been long and well prepared. He retired from his University position, a professor by then, in 1980 but there had been opportunities for him to leave before that and devote himself to full-time writing. It would not have suited. His poetry is immensely popular but there is an intimate, driven quality about it; the stuff of vocation rather than career.

He liked to have the salary and status of an academic position. The security of routine was vital in order that he might be all the more free in his poetry. Morgan was an industrious member of staff and students even tended to regard him as a martinet (he required that they complete the tutorial assignments they were given). Only occasionally was the touch of impishness allowed to show. The Department's expert on Milton was perennially aggrieved by the lectures Morgan would give proposing Satan as the hero of *Paradise Lost*.

He is very far from being a recluse and in company he is genial and entertaining. Despite that, though, he would agree that he is at heart a loner. Morgan has many friends but it must be said that he is much likelier to communicate with them by postcard or letter (highly entertaining) than by telephone. It can look as if the separation is as important as the contact to him. He and John Scott never actually lived together, although they saw one another frequently.

His activities resemble excursions in which the return to base is the most important element. Despite the attraction to other countries, he has, with the compulsory exception of the war, never chosen to live abroad. Home is, as it has been for over twenty-five years, a flat in Anniesland. Tom Leonard captured the impenetrability of it all when he wrote the following programme note:

> Cultural attaché to the legendary city of Morganiana, said to exist
> behind a door marked 'Morgan' in an unobtrusive block of flats off
> Great Western Road. From here translations and original poems

go out daily to magazines all over the world, while the city director converses by golden telephone with the spirits of some dead but perky Russian Futurists.[2]

Perhaps Morgan is concerned with maintaining a constant setting: himself alone in habitual surroundings. He agrees that he has always thought of a solitary life as a necessity if he were to succeed as a writer. The determination with which he has pursued that course tells us something about the act of will required to create his poetry.

In interview Morgan has remarked that he would have wished, had he been a parent, to have had a family of more than one child (*Verse*, 27). If that reflection contains a sense of regret about his own youth, the reader, selfish as always, can scarcely wish that Morgan's life had been different. One returns to thoughts of the boy who alarmed his mother with his self-absorption. It could be said that Morgan has continued to associate the origins of imagination with that state. If he makes sure that the path is always open for a return to that solitary, intense condition it may be because it is there that poetry began for him.

However it might be explained, he has always known how to renew himself. He has avoided the obvious traps: superannuated beatnikdom, grand old mannerism. In the writing, he always gets clean away.

NOTES

1. *Noise and Smoky Breath: Glasgow Poems and Visual Images 1900–1983* (Glasgow: Third Eye Centre and Glasgow District Libraries Publications Board, 1983), pp. [2–3]. Text of address given by EM to launch book and exhibition, 5 May 1983.

2. Poster for POETSOUND '84, Third Eye Centre, Glasgow, 23–25 March, 1984.

CHRONOLOGY

1920	27 April: born at 60 York Drive (now Novar Drive), only child of Stanley and Madge (née Arnott).
1922	At 245 Nithsdale Road, Pollokshields.
1928	Family moves to Rutherglen, finally settling at 12 Albert Drive, a semi-detached villa.
1928–34	At Rutherglen Academy.
1934–37	At High School of Glasgow.
1937	Writes poem on Coronation of George VI. School trip to Germany.
1937–40	At Glasgow University.
1940	Registers as Conscientious Objector. Enlists in the Royal Army Medical Corps.

1940–46	Serves at El Ballah, Sidon, Haifa and Murrayfield.
1946–47	Returns to Glasgow University, takes First Class Honours Degree in English Language and Literature.
1947	Turns down chance of scholarship to Oxford.
1947–50	Assistant Lecturer, Department of English, Glasgow University.
1952	*The Vision of Cathkin Braes* and translation of *Beowulf* published (the latter becomes a standard translation in USA).
1955	Trip to Russia, first of many to East Europe.
1962	Leaves parental home and moves to modern flat in Anniesland between Christmas and New Year. Corresponds with Brazilian concrete poets.
1963	Meets John G. Scott.
1965–71	Senior Lecturer, Department of English, GU.
1965	Father dies.
1968	*The Second Life* published. Receives Cholmondeley Award for poetry.
1968–74	Co-editor and Editorial Adviser of *Scottish International*.
1969	Scottish Arts Council Award (others in 1973, 1975, 1977, 1978, 1983).
1970	Mother dies.
1971–75	Reader, Department of English, GU.
1972	Awarded the Hungarian P.E.N. Memorial Medal.
1973	*From Glasgow to Saturn* published (Poetry Book Society Choice).
1975–80	Titular Professor, Department of English, GU.
1976	Selected translations, *Rites of Passage*, published.
1977	*The New Divan* published.
1980	Takes early retirement from Glasgow University. Receives Hon.D.Litt. from Loughborough University.
1982	*Poems of Thirty Years* published. Receives OBE.
1983	Shares Saltire Society Award for Best Scottish Book of the Year (for *Poems of Thirty Years*).
1984	*Sonnets from Scotland* published.
1985	Wins Soros Translation Award for translations from Attila József. Blows prize money on day trip by Concorde to North Pole. Meets Santa Claus.
1987	Appointed Visiting Professor of English at Strathclyde University.
1988	*Themes on a Variation* published. Visits Albania.
1989	D.Univ. from Stirling University.

Two

'to change / the unchangeable' –
The Whole Morgan

Robert Crawford

His unpublished poems of the late 1930s and those which had a limited circulation reveal that Edwin Morgan, an adolescent reader of Eliot and Pound, savoured most the diction of Romanticism in its nineteenth-century, Hopkinsian, and Dylan Thomas incarnations. These first poems (written long before Morgan put himself to school as a translator to learn a modern voice) are also shot through with Old English accents. A 1940 poem, one of a series of erotic pieces, is entitled 'Drihten Dryhtna, Gemiltsa Me' ('Lord of Lords, Have Pity on Me'), while his scrapbooks from the 1930s contain alongside cuttings about robots, primitive poeples, and monsters a quotation (in the original Anglo-Saxon) of the lament over change and transience from the poem 'The Wanderer'.[1] Morgan was clearly stimulated by his study of Old English under Ritchie Girvan at Glasgow University. His 1952 translation of *Beowulf*, dedicated to Girvan, appeared in the same year as the first collection of his own poems, and formed part of his search for a modern idiom. The bulk of the introduction, with its epigraph from the Russian Revolutionary poet Vladimir Mayakovsky, pinpoints lasting concerns. It opens with the provocative question, 'What literary activity is more powerful than translation?' and, after mentioning Pound, stresses the need for a genuinely modern tone. Morgan notices similarities between medieval metrics and those of Eliot and Auden. In language which anticipates some of his later poetic concerns, he assures the reader that in good translation

> Communication must take place; the nerves must sometimes tingle and the skin flush, as with original poetry; is there not an attitude of mind, a backward and elusive faculty to be encouraged; is there not an art or science of translation, still in its crudest stages, to be developed? (*B*, viii)

Morgan's early work on *Beowulf* was seminal; there is also a strong medieval presence at the core of the first published collection of his own poems, *The Vision of Cathkin Braes*. Throughout his career he has continued to admire the visionary quality of medieval works such as *Sir Gawain and the Green Knight, Pearl*, and *The Vision of Piers Ploughman*. The idea of the modern poet as medievalist was scarcely new. Translating 'The Seafarer' (*P*, 15) in 1954, Morgan followed cheekily in Pound's footsteps. He shared this enthusiasm with his first poet friend, W.S. Graham, who (like Morgan) would write constantly of language's peculiarities and of voyages, knowing as he wrote that he had 'read Pound's translation of the Seafarer.'² Auden, another poet admired by the young Morgan and Graham, had drawn on Anglo-Saxon sound-effects in his early verse, and when living on Clydeside had employed some of the paraphernalia of the medieval vision poem in works such as 'A Happy New Year' (1932).

In translating not only 'The Ruin' and the heroic-elegiac poems 'The Seafarer' and 'The Wanderer' (*P*, 18) but also Anglo-Saxon riddles (*P*, 21) as well as the whole of *Beowulf*, Morgan outdid Pound and Auden. A medieval legacy keeps resurfacing in his later work, whether in the poem 'Grendel' (*P*, 435) or in the 'Newspoems' collected in *Themes on a Variation* (1988) which (drawing on cut-up techniques perfected in the scrapbooks Morgan kept from 1931–66) include 'Caedmon's Second Hymn' (*TV*, 92) and two 'New English Riddles' (*TV*, 93–4). 'Harrowing Heaven, 1924' (*P*, 13; first published in 1954) in its title and opening lines with their heavy alliteration and caesurae shows that Morgan has fused medieval heroic poetry with another of his early and continuing enthusiasms, the heroic and adventurous work of Mayakovsky. Morgan invokes 'Vladimir!', linking him with an ironic upending of the medieval harrowing of Hell: 'Tell the archangels in their cells of divinity / They must levitate like larks, for LENIN is coming.' The energy and some of the imagery of this poem look forward to Morgan's later work, as does the fact that, drawing on medieval roots, it is a heroic poem. 'The Old Man and the Sea' (*P*, 125), the opening poem of his first widely published collection, *The Second Life* (1968), with 'The Death of Marilyn Monroe' (*P*, 126) and 'Je ne regrette rien' (*P*, 127) show, like other well-known Morgan poems, from 'King Billy' (*P*, 148) through 'Che' (*P*, 248) to 'Cinquevalli' (*P*, 440) and beyond, his interest in developing a poetry of heroic elegy and, more generally a heroic poetry. Part of his interest in science fiction verse is surely bound up with space travel as a heroic endeavour. Morgan the modern, Morgan the futurist, and Morgan the medievalist are united.

Nor was the sense of humour that we associate with much of

Morgan's work absent from his early uses of the medieval. This is manifest in the comic 'The Vision of Cathkin Braes' (*P*, 27) which glances towards Auden, but looks more firmly to medieval dream poems, pageants, and processions of the sort that come out of the Middle Ages into Spenser. This poem's choreography unites Scottish and non-Scottish elements and employs a degree of specifically Scots vocabulary — 'gloaming', 'mavis', and 'mutch', not to mention the rather more aureate term 'makariferous'. The emergent Morgan was clearly interested in linguistic choices facing Scottish poets, as his 1954 article 'Modern Makars Scots and English'[3] shows. But the poet's keen interest in language is most apparent in this period in the only sustained piece of criticism of medieval writing which Morgan has published, the 1952 essay on 'Dunbar and the Language of Poetry' (*E*, 81–99).

Most obviously, this essay is about a medieval subject, and a Scottish one at that. The young Morgan clearly felt a strong urge to make contact with remote, non-Scottish cultures. His translations from Russian are part of this, as is his early and continuing attraction to Middle Eastern verse, stimulated by reading Fitzgerald's *Rubáiyát* and the translations by E. Powys Mathers in *An Anthology of World Poetry* (1930) edited by Mark van Doren. Perhaps Morgan's early medievalism was also a movement away from his own immediate environment, but when he literally left Scotland for North Africa, he became more aware of what it meant to him to be Scottish, experiencing 'a kind of revelation' when he read M.M. Gray's anthology *Scottish Poetry from Barbour to James VI*, in which Dunbar figured prominently (*Verse*, 30).

If Morgan's 'Vision of Cathkin Braes' culminates in an absurd dance, then in so doing it bears a clear relation to his study of Dunbar, from whose 'Dance in the Quenis Chalmer' Morgan singles out the lines 'Than cam in Dunbar the mackar, / On all the flure thair was nane frackar' commenting that they 'might well describe his [Dunbar's] equally nimble and lively entry into poetry' (*E*, 89). Liveliness and nimbleness are surely among the most striking features of Morgan's own work. He goes on to set this 'free and hilarious' dancing poem beside Dunbar's more sombre 'Dance of the Sevin Deidly Sinnis', contending that 'one of Dunbar's greatest pleasures' is 'the approach towards' a scene 'where either dancing or some other vivid movement is described.' Morgan adds in a footnote that this is 'A recurrent pleasure in Scots verse, as witness *Colkelbie Sow*, *Tam o'Shanter*, and *The Witch's Ballad*' (*E*, 89). This 'recurrent pleasure' clearly recurs in 'The Vision of Cathkin Braes'. Consciously or not, Morgan is supplying a Scottish poetic background against which his own work may be read.

At least as striking, in view of Morgan's later career, is the problem

which the young poet sees being posed by Dunbar's *oeuvre*: the problem
of apparently outrageous diversity. Morgan points out that Dunbar did
not have Burns's talent for intimate erotic lyrics, but that

> Lacking this gift, he disturbs us by a startling indifference to
> theme in poetry; we are uneasy as we watch him turn from the
> Rabelaisian endearments of 'In secreit place' to a religious *Nativitie*
> or *Resurrection*, from a mocking address to a Negro lady to his
> 'Quhat is this lyfe bot ane straucht way to deid', from fantasy to
> ethics, from ethics to satire, and from satire to stately elegy and
> eulogy . . . (*E*, 97)

In describing Dunbar, Morgan is describing the sort of poet he would
himself become. Reading between (and perhaps beyond) the medieval
poet's lines, he presents Dunbar as having 'restless and nervous force'
and a 'darting quick-silver personality' (*E*, 97). Morgan's own verse
delights in presenting such figures. His long dialogue-poem 'The
Whittrick' (*P*, 67) begun in the 1950s celebrates an elusive, mercurial
essence imaged in Scots as the 'whittrick' or weasel − the spirit of
creativity. Each of 'The Whittrick' 's dialogues is like a temporal and
geographical translation of the preceding dialogue as the creative energy
represented by the whittrick is charted, but never caged. Such an
uncatchable essence recurs later in, for example, 'Adventures of the Anti-
Sage' (*P*, 368) and it is celebrated in the endlessly 'displaced person' of
the juggler Cinquevalli in the poem of that title. In his poetry and his
person, Morgan not only celebrates but embodies something of this
whittrick-energy. He has always liked energy in poetry − an energy that
lets poet and reader travel far and fast − 'what I love about poetry is its
ion engine' ('A View of Things', *P*, 187). To him, as 'On the Water'
(*P*, 422) (with its interested swipe at Ashbery) suggests, energy not
lazing is basic. When asked if he was particularly attracted to mercurial
figures, Morgan replied strongly in the affirmative, adding that for him
such a quality of energy had always been represented by MacDiarmid,
Burns, and Dunbar (*Verse*, 33).

'Dunbar and the Language of Poetry' shows that what most attracted
the young Morgan to Dunbar was a controlled poetic energy which
could manifest itself verbally as 'a continuous inevitability of movement
from word to word' (*E*, 81). This essay appeared three years before
Donald Davie's *Articulate Energy*, but Morgan too is interested in how
energy may be articulated in verse. Dunbar's poetry, for Morgan, is an
example of energy 'as order', that is energy which is manifested through
verbal arrangement and connections. While this apparently inevitable
movement from word to word may take mysterious, hidden forms,

the poets who are attracted by the 'energy as order' mode try to

make of such half-felt and unanalysed word-linkages something
concrete, basic, and sustaining, by opening up the way to them
more externally and consciously (E, 82).

Though it might describe 'The Computer's First Christmas Card'
(P, 159), all this sounds very sober; but Morgan makes it clear that the
tradition which influenced Dunbar was also a ludic one, producing in
Scottish verse a 'disequilibriating infusion of forthright zestful topsyturvydom'. This topsyturvydom and exposed inevitability of movement
from word to word are present in 'The Flyting of Dunbar and Kennedie'
from which Morgan quotes in his essay (E, 90). That flyting's huge
outpouring of language might be related to the effect of Morgan's 'Soho'
(P, 240), with its cumulatively powerful yet defiling flood where, as
often in his mature work, we are aware of literary learning worn lightly.
Yet, while this outpouring might seem to have evolved from the
technique of flyting, Morgan's interest in Dunbar extends further.

Sometimes in Morgan's early poetry there is a sense of great energy,
but it is not clear that he knows exactly what to do with it. 'The Cape of
Good Hope' (P, 47) shows him, like W.S. Graham, a determined
voyager, yet one who spends more time praising the energy of other
artists than getting on with his own job. Sometimes, as in a surging
cumulative energy of the twenty-five-line sentence near the opening of
the poem (synthesising Auden and medieval acoustics) he gives the verse
its head and we hear a strong alliteration, a repetition of vowels, and
even a curious repetition of whole words knitting the energy together
and powering it outwards:

> Out from the landfall smell of law, the landmarks
> Of wedding and fidelity, pylon, aerial, radar-ear,
> Hangar and customs-shed, junction and terminal, the handclasp
> Handclasp and kiss that stave off the shrieking whistles
> As the train steams in its pit, and the streaming face
> As the window darkens and dwindles; from departures
> Out by the last (except the departure of death),
> Out from the heart and the spirit and humanity and love
> Over matter alone, and into that sea of matter
> Moves out, till everything that is is nature.   (P, 47)

Among many things that are going on here, we can see the effort to
manifest poetic energy through alliteration's internal rhymes, and
through a run of word-linkages (Out . . . landfall . . . landmarks . . .
handclasp / Handclasp . . . steams . . . streaming . . . departures / Out
. . . departure . . . Out . . . matter . . . matter . . . out . . . is is) as if
Morgan had been attending to his own counsel (with regard to Dunbar)

that 'Like sounds draw the ear forward, sometimes before it has
assimilated the sense.' Morgan had experimented with such effects from
his early poetry of the late 1930s. But a much more developed
deployment of this verbal energy is to be found in his mature work:

> I am not here to talk about a scratch
> video I am here to make a scratch I am
> here to make a scratch video to make
> tape recorder on *a young man of mysterious*
> *appearance coming towards me* fore-edge
> painting flip a friend did this flip of me
> jumping flip from bank to flip bank
> *like the force of enchantment* miniature home video
> watch it miniature home video I am bounding
> into fields and woods back back I am
> bounding from the door towards the fields   (*TV*, 118)

Here in a poem involving energy and containment, collaged together
out of various materials including Hogg's *Memoirs and Confessions of a
Justified Sinner*, Morgan manifests that use of sounds to 'draw the ear
forward' which he had admired in Dunbar. Morgan's sounds more
accurately draw the ear back *and* forward, and owe a considerable debt
to pop-music techniques, yet even that ties in exactly with his
enthusiasm for the Dunbar whose 'poems were produced by co-
operating with and transforming the linguistic trends of his age rather
than by relying (as Henryson did) on the ancient common fund of
human situation and story from which poetic feeling can be summoned
with less expenditure of the specifically poetic verbal gift' (*E*, 89).
Morgan's willingness to collaborate with and transform the linguistic
materials of his own age can put off readers who want something more
traditionally 'poetic'. Yet referring Morgan's techniques to features
which he specifically praised in Dunbar gives them a clear base in
tradition.

If the 'scratch video' poem explicitly opens up the kind of word
linkages which, Morgan argued in the Dunbar essay, contribute to
poetic energy, its technique has evolved from his own earlier work. A
calmer, lyrical instance comes in the poem 'Oban Girl' (*P*, 225), where
the linkage between lines becomes utterly explicit through repetition as
one line is translated into the next. Moving in their linked dance, then
poignantly interrupted, the lines of that poem look back towards the
Dunbar essay's interest in word-linkages. In a different but related way,
Morgan makes explicit hidden links when he playfully, riddlingly
generates out of Wittgenstein's sentence 'the world is everything that is

the case' a wide variety of linked sentences hidden in it, while also translating Wittgenstein himself into an unexpected location in 'Wittgenstein on Egdon Heath' (*P*, 354). Here, as often in Morgan's work, there is a conflict between order and wildness. There is also what he drew attention to in the Dunbar essay as 'the *display* of *poetic energy* in forms that have considerable technical and craftsmanly interest, rather than the *distillation* of *poetic situation*, in personal emotional encounters.' Morgan in poems like 'Levi-Strauss at the Lie-Detector' (*P*, 353), the Newspoems, sound poems, and concrete poems, is picking up secret messages generated by language, making explicit normally hidden aspects of the wordscape. In doing this, he is also continuing one of his earliest verbal activities – the activity seen in his 1952 *Beowulf* – that of the translator, the decoder of an alien message.

Themes of translation and decoding run through his work and are closely linked to the control of energy. The Dunbar poems he seems to like best manifest energy through controlled, rapid movement – whether the rapid acoustic change that uses rhyme to move 'Mauchmuttoun' to 'byt-buttoun', to 'peilit gluttoun' all within one flyting line, or the larger thematic display of energy as stationary figures are set in motion in an accelerating dance. Energy in Dunbar is manifested as controlled change also through the way the poet is able to deploy form after form, genre after genre.

A poem in the 1940 erotic series ('Those clouds are drunken with unearthly light') suggests that verse is built out of storm and strife, beauty resulting from often painful change. Poetry for Morgan is frequently like a release of energy, of force for change which seems to have been pent up like the water to be located by his dowser in the desert or the power of suns whose energy, in the words of the 1940 erotic sequence, could be used for 'Wakening flowerless acres into light'. Significantly, the scrapbooks crammed with homoerotic images, articles about art, poetry, natural history, monsters, robots, astronauts – a whole private hoard and energy-bank – cease in the mid-1960s, at the very stage when Morgan was able publicly to acknowledge many of his hitherto private concerns in his own increasingly successful poetry of change. Morgan found the 1960s a liberating decade; they were after all a decade when public discussion of wideranging changes in sexual, economic, religious, and technological living patterns came to be taken for granted. They were also in linguistics the decade of Chomsky, whose ideas about the constantly changing generation of verbal patterns out of certain deep structures shared by all humanity were becoming common intellectual currency, and surely relate not only to international movements with which Morgan was associated, such as concrete poetry and sound poetry, but also to other areas of his own apparently more idiosyncratic interest in linguistic change.

In Old English poetry the most celebrated refrain (þæs ofereode; þisses sþa mæʒ – 'that passed away; so may this') is one which sees change as a remedy, a relief from melancholy or oppression. Morgan's poem 'The Change' is like this when, addressing tyrannies and over-rigid systems, the poet mocks:

> Straighten up and pat your holsters.
> Self-righteousness and a ramrod back
>
> will not help. The sun goes down with you,
> other fruits ripen for other lips.   (*TV*, 57)

Such sentiments are in line with the celebration in an unpublished 1939 poem 'Sculptures' of a Zadkine sculpture which seems 'to change / The unchangeable'. In reading Dunbar, Morgan's response is to a rapid, mercurial manifestation of change as energy, and in his own poetry change is similarly displayed in a way that often carries a strong charge of optimism.

Love of change and changing is present most obviously in his accurate work as a translator from that battery of languages including Old English, Dutch, French, German, Hungarian, Italian, Russian, and Spanish. Some writers view poetry as untranslatable simply because translation changes the original. For Morgan poetry (as his career demonstrates) is constantly and energetically translatable because his own attitude to poetry appears to be that it, like life, is bound up with translation, with change. His poem 'Shaker Shaken' (*P*, 351) performs a series of metamorphoses, ending with the 'translating' of a nineteenth century sound poem into a strange English. Translation is a crossover, a change, a rite of passage into something other. Perhaps this is seen most clearly in the poem 'The First Men on Mercury' (*P*, 259), which opens with English-speakers confronting aliens

> – We come in peace from the third planet.
> Would you take us in your leader?
>
> – Bawr stretter! Bawr. Bawr. Stretterhawl?

As the poem develops the languages converge and are exchanged, each translated into the other, so that the conclusion has the Earthmen speaking Mercurian, while the people of Mercury bid farewell in English. What happens here parallels what happens in 'Memories of Earth' where alien experience changes the speaker ('She's changed. / I'm changing', *P*, 333), and may even change utterly. 'The First Men on Mercury' wittily models cultural crossover, the moving from one language community and the assumptions which it invites into another different one – a theme that is strong, for instance, in Scott's *Waverley*, and very relevant to any multicultural, multilinguistic society, not least Scotland. As its flick of the tail reminds us, 'The First Men on Mercury' epitomizes change in general – 'nothing is ever the same, / now is it?' (*P*, 260). Linguistic translation is bound up with physical translation – travelling from earth to Mercury. Another version of the translation that changes, and of the mercurial energy involved, is seen clearly in the poem 'In Sobieski's Shield' (*P*, 181) where the survivors of a dying world are translated across the galaxy, and changed in the process. Moving from the 'end' of its first line to the 'let's go' of its conclusion, the poem also suggests that change itself translates ends into beginnings. 'Dies Irae' (*P*, 3) and 'Stanzas of the Jeopardy' (*P*, 7) are both fuelled by the terrible energies released when worlds end and this apocalyptic, darker side of Morgan's imagination has continued. From these early poems through 'Era' (*P*, 389) to the poems of the late 1980s, where many poets might contemplate the end of human life as we know it with simple horror, Morgan does so with curiosity to see what will come after. The sonnet 'Computer Error: Neutron Strike' (*TV*, 161) sees destruction visited on a Scotland which is changed utterly, not extinguished. As usual, Morgan's imagination sides with the energy of change and what it may bring, rather than with the wailings of prophets and criers of doom.

It is this which connects Morgan's poems of outer space with his poems of Glasgow. For the city too is a text for translation, site of 'endless . . . interchange' (*P*, 413); Morgan is for translating, changing the city rather than embalming a *status quo*. The 'Glasgow Sonnets' depict vividly the problems of his city in the early 1970s, but go on to show that while 'Environmentalists, ecologists / and conservationists are fine no doubt' (*P*, 285), he sides with the bulldozer, with the energy of metamorphosis which will make it new in ways that might 'displease the watchers from the grave' yet still delight Charles Rennie Mackintosh (*P*, 285). For Morgan, hope and energy always lie in change, in translation. What he dislikes most are the forces which impede change – like the speakers repeating proverbial platitudes in 'The Clone Poem' (*P*, 392) or like those responsible for the death of the foetus in the 'Stobhill' sequence which also ends with verbal ossification (*P*, 282). Opposed to petrification is constant verbal translation, of the sort that we hear energetically buzzing in Morgan's 'Bees' Nest' (*P*, 141) a piece whose shape emphasises that we are dealing with a wild, if contained energy in a poem charged-up like a small, high voltage battery. Such works resist verbal (and, by implication, other forms of) ossification, and so resemble the computer poems where line is constantly translated into line as the poem moves towards what may or may not be an eventual 'correct answer'. The computer which ends, translates or changes one line into another to end up wishing us

```
m  e  r  r  y  C  h  r  i  s
a  m  m  e  r  r  y  a  s  a
C  h  r  i  s  m  e  r  r  y
a  s  M  E  R  R  Y  C  H  R
Y  S  A  N  T  H  E  M  U  M        (P, 159)
```

is to be celebrated for the same reason as the semi-literate pioneers of the Channel Tunnel, who may not be able to spell, but are able to change, and, as inscription translates into inscription eventually record '10880. Brigde bugn' (*P*, 172). Morgan's early poems such as 'The Cape of Good Hope' had begun to connect physical translation with metamorphic energy, but had tended to do it rather longwindedly, vaguely, namedroppingly. As he develops, he is able to manifest more clearly his celebration of changes, changers, and the energy on which they can draw. So Morgan praises MacDiarmid for placing man 'with all the world he changes as it changes him' (*P*, 134). Ian Hamilton Finlay (*P*, 135) and Joan Eardley (*P*, 144), like MacDiarmid, are seen as sharing with Morgan a certain creative impatience, making things new with the converter's hurry of a Columba who appreciates the beauty of nature, but hastens on to use his particular power for change (*P*, 221). Such figures energetically translate us into the new. Morgan celebrates them as he celebrates bridges, spacemen, remakers of Glasgow, persevering computers, because they can allow all with whom they communicate to 'Make, and take, your crossing' (*P*, 134), translating us through a rite of passage into a fresh experience or (to use one of Morgan's favourite expressions) a 'second life'.

   Prefacing his 1974 collection of *Essays*, Morgan declared punningly, CHANGE RULES is the supreme graffito. Gathering up the shards – 'performances, assortments, résumés' – can hope perhaps to scatter values through a reticulation that surprises thought rather than traps it.

'Thought' here seems whittrick-like, something that might be 'surprised' but should not be trapped. 'CHANGE RULES' is a *credo* appropriate to the poet of 'The Gourds' (*P*, 252) where, by linking the poem's head to its tail, Morgan gives us a poem that endlessly makes itself new. This

poem, like his computer poems, seems to gloss the assertion made in
'The Whittrick' that 'the created may create' (*P*, 109). Fascination with
change connects those apparently *outré* parts of Morgan's work with the
documentary 'Instamatic Poems' which, however much they may appear
random snapshots, are carefully selected to reveal moments when the
mundane is translated into the strange. All are poems of change, be it
the change that comes with snow in Nice (*P*, 204), or the arrival of the
whittrick-like 'Fox Man' at U.S. Steel (*P*, 204). These poems attend to
moments when energy is focused, to destroy a plate glass window
(*P*, 203), to dedicate a building (*P*, 210), to recreate a concerto
(*P*, 217). Elsewhere, in 'Itinerary' (*P*, 262) verbal and physical translation are again linked. In 'A Jar Revisited' (*P*, 266) an apparently
random variation (a typographical slip) gives birth to the theme of a
whole poem, as it had done in 'An Addition to the Family' (*P*, 136).
These poems are expressions of interest in the possibility of any change.
The poet who selects the material for his 'Instamatic Poems' has gone
out, like 'The Dowser' (*TV*, 11) of a later poem, in search of spots where
metamorphic energy is let out. The same poet locates the force of 'Three
Trees' (*P*, 348) in a series of poems where Morgan, like an Old English
poet, has objects speak in their own right. Each tree, the 'Lightning
Tree', the 'Water-skier's Tree', and the 'Impacted Windscreen Tree' is a
pattern created by a moment when energy was suddenly released and
each is in the process of change – even the windscreen tree which
concludes 'I feel evergreen till the crusher'. In giving these objects
voices, Morgan is developing a pattern established earlier in his career.
He has responded at some length to the suggestion that the idea of
translation is central to his work as a whole, and pointed out

> If I write a poem called 'The Apple's Song', the apple is being
> translated if you like into *human* language . . . I like the idea
> particularly that in a sense we're surrounded by messages that
> we perhaps ought to be trying to interpret. (*Verse*, 35)

Morgan lets us hear 'The Loch Ness Monster's Song' (*P*, 237), leaving
the reader to translate it from the original. The poet who began as a
translator of Anglo-Saxon and other languages had moved on to wider
kinds of translating by the time of 'Unscrambling the Waves at
Goonhilly' (*P*, 174), and has continued to grow. The alien is not to be
fended off, but to be decoded, scanned. 'Deplore what is to be deplored,
and then find out the rest' (*P*, 148) ends 'King Billy', another poem
focused on a strange energy, a disrupting force. For Morgan that finding
out, the act of imaginative translation which as in 'Memories of Earth'
(*P*, 327–38) may well change the translator, is of paramount importance.
His 'Reconstruction' poems (*TV*, 42–8) are remakings of older verse

which is translated into modern idiom and Morgan's own poetic voice. In his reconstruction of a famous passage from Pope's 'Essay on Criticism', Morgan's remaking involves contradicting the original (*TV*, 46). Yet this is surely an extreme version of his extensions of the idea of translation. Morgan, always fascinated by energy and control, is well aware that small verbal 'translations' can change our perception totally. 'Rules for Dwarf-Throwing' (*TV*, 51) concludes with a hint of how a slight translation could transform reactions:

> 10. It is strictly forbidden, in dwarf-throwing literature and publicity, to refer to dwarfs as 'persons of restricted growth' or 'small people'.

So ends a poem presented as a set of rules. Morgan likes to experiment with such clearly articulated structural devices, manifestations of energy as order where the structure may help generate the poem. He writes 'An Alphabet of Goddesses' (*SP*, 123) a 'Dictionary of Tea' (*SP*, 120) and the dictionary-like 'Nineteen Kinds of Barley' (*TV*, 30); he provides a poem structured like a computer printout (*P*, 269) or a map in a linguistic atlas (*P*, 161). But Morgan is also concerned with what destroys or evades systems. This relates to the strong interest in monsters and mutants seen in his early scrapbooks and in the unpublished 1954 story 'Dr Tampelius', about a werewolf in a Scottish village. Monsters in Morgan's work, condemned (like homosexuals) to exist outside social norms, can show strangely creative potential, as well as manifesting darker threats through their perceived system-breaking wildness. Such issues surface in 'The Third Day of the Wolf' (*P*, 132). Delight in system-disruption leads Morgan to compile 'A Hantle of Howlers' (*E*, 255–76) out of diverting slips of the pen in students' exam papers, and to write the sequences 'Interferences' (*P*, 243–8) and 'Unfinished Poems' (*P*, 374–82) where language crashes like a computer, veers off-course into the alien, or suddenly dies into silence. Competing pulls of uncontrollable energies and systems of management, explored in the Dunbar essay, continue to obsess Morgan, whether in 'Glasgow Green' (*P*, 149) where desperate homoerotic violence is set against mundane orderliness, or 'Grendel' (*P*, 435) or 'Jack London in Heaven' (*P*, 438) where each protagonist inhabiting an unchanging atmosphere (one of darkness, the other of celestial routine) is fascinated by the changeable world of men. Morgan clearly likes the closely structured form of the sonnet, yet he also recalls thinking of shuffling his *Sonnets from Scotland* on index cards in order to arrive at an unsystematic final arrangement. His distinguished long poem, 'The New Divan' (1977), hovers between structure and the lack of it, designed to imitate Arabic

and Persian models, allowing the reader to 'move around . . . cast your
eye here and there' (*Verse*, 38). Yet Morgan does point to the beginning,
middle and end of that poem as important. He seems to wish to unite in
it both structure and freedom from structure and in doing so returns his
readers to the familiar theme of change, at the poem's start not only
involving Hafiz, maker of the most famous *Divan*, but also stressing the
importance of Proteus, the Old Man of the Sea.

> Go on then, dance yourself into the masks.
> The Old Man of the Sea has all the gales
> within his heaving pack, get deep within
> his folds, he's on your back, get deep
> within gale-weary Sinbad, be the driver
> of tritons and the triton, be before
> the mast and be the aftermath, what might
> be, what could never be, and keep
> no form but water. Let matter
> envy you the metamorphoses a
> dancer steals and cannot say.   (*P*, 289)

Here again is the explicit knitting of verbal and acoustic linkages
(within . . . pack . . . deep within . . . back . . . deep / within . . .
tritons . . . triton . . . before . . . mast . . . aftermath . . . be . . . be
. . . water . . . matter) which had fascinated him from at least the time
of the Dunbar essay.

Verbal and thematic linkages net across this work's hundred sections
as thoughts and sensations fade and revive over a mysterious territory
that is visited and revisited. Dealing with war and ruin, the shifting
sands of history and the tidal wash of memory, the poem is also strongly
(homo)erotic. It again hymns change as sometimes painful, yet scintil-
latingly positive since 'man in his restlessness is really / making,
making' (*P*, 299). 'The New Divan' returns to the poetic terrain of that
unpublished 1940 erotic series which seems to draw on Fitzgerald and
E. Powys Mathers. Revisiting the scene of wartime destruction, all the
speaker finds is 'the winged / seed of a sycamore, all / their memorial,
oh our loved and fated!' (*P*, 306). But the seed, with its promise of the
future, is enough in the work of this poet, for whom even the most
destructive change leads towards some form of positive evolution. As in
'The Dowser', what Morgan celebrates is the ability to find sweetness in
the desert. For the dowser the question is how to release energy and
sweetness through an apparently unorderable barren flux:

> But how to quarter such shifting acres
> when the wind melts their shapes, and shadows

> mass where all was bright before,
> and landmarks walk like wraiths at noon?   (*TV*, 11)

'The New Divan''s conclusion suggests that it is from flux, apparently meaningless change, that the valuable is to be extracted. The flux may be both inner and outer, and is likely to involve considerable pain. Morgan has always had a sharp sense of human suffering, as poems such as 'In the Snack-bar' (*P*, 152) and 'The Coals' (*P*, 428) demonstrate. Arguably, this sense of suffering has developed as his work progressed. Yet it is typical of Morgan's imagination that in the third of the *Video Box* poems the destruction of the new British Library (*TV*, 116) should yield material for new creation. Ideas of creation and destruction, war and art, are bound together in his verse whether in 'Vereshchagin's Barrow' (*TV*, 58) or 'Pictures Floating from the World' (*P*, 340). Presented more lyrically and in more powerfully resonant language, the fundamentally optimistic concluding section of 'The New Divan' parallels the contention of the British Library videopoem. For in 'The New Divan' a scrap of damaged sailcloth from the end of the literal voyage becomes what holds together the book at the start of its publication, its going abroad.

'The New Divan', one of Morgan's most substantial achievements, is impressive not least for its lyrical eroticism. His concentration on the transitory, often fugitive aspects of love in poems such as 'After the Party' (*P*, 228) and 'The Milk-cart' (*P*, 230) fits in with his fascination with change. The subtly homoerotic love poems deploy such images as smoke, burning cigarettes, drifting and floating, as if impermanence were accepted as a vital part of love. So it is that these poems too, more tender but no less generally applicable than Auden's, form part of Morgan's *oeuvre* in which 'CHANGE RULES is the supreme graffito'.

Morgan pointed out in his 1952 essay that Dunbar lacked 'heartfelt immediacy' (*E*, 97). If his own range extends in some ways beyond that of Dunbar, this confirms that he is an unusually diffuse writer. A reviewer once remarked that Morgan had the ability to write whole themes on a variation, and Morgan liked this so much that he made it the title of his 1988 collection.[4] All this is true, yet the themes and the variations are related because throughout Morgan's work whether at the level of individual words, forms, or topics change, variation is the guiding theme. Seeing Morgan whole reveals that the fascination for change produces in his work a decoding, encoding, translating power which manifests itself through displays of energy whose variety rivals that of his admired Dunbar. Whether he is seen against the background of John Davidson and Hugh MacDiarmid, or against the wider background of Dunbar, Burns and MacDiarmid, Morgan's metamorphic vitality is in keeping with that of the most distinguished Scottish tradition. His own main interest is not in tradition but in change. A poet-academic (rather than an academic poet), his verse choreographs many preoccupations of the Structuralists, while gesturing towards the ludic aspect of Post-structuralism. Lively, nimble, protean, that poetry's cumulative power sets Morgan in a position of sparky distinction amongst his contemporaries and alongside the most outstanding individual voices in the course of Scottish poetry. If the whittrick flashes through Dunbar's many modes then, exactly because of the contention that CHANGE RULES, it also flashes through the whole poetry of Edwin Morgan.

NOTES

1. The unpublished works and scrapbooks cited are all among the Edwin Morgan Papers in the Special Collections Department, Glasgow University Library.
2. W.S. Graham, letter to Tony Lopez, 30 March 1981, cited in Tony Lopez, *The Poetry of W.S. Graham* (Edinburgh: Edinburgh University Press, 1989), p.63.
3. *Saltire Review* I:2, August 1954, pp.75–81.
4. Nicholas Jacobs, 'Divided by One Language?' *Balliol College Annual Record*, 1985, p.80.

Three

A Declaration of Independence: Edwin Morgan and Contemporary Poetry

Robyn Marsack

How is Edwin Morgan's protean poetry to be usefully located amidst the decorous and the rancorous, the ring-masters and the historians of empire, those who have unleashed animals, and those who have unleashed anecdotes, who have been writing British poetry during the last four decades? Does it go against the grain to put it in a British context at all? 'You have a passport which says you're UK or British, and you obviously have to acknowledge that in a purely official sense, but I don't feel British. I don't feel, certainly, English' (*Verse*, 41). This tendency towards separatism shows up, less positively, in the public perception of – or public presentation of – post-war poetry in the United Kingdom, if we are to judge by the anthologies. Naturally enough, given the ratio of population, they are dominated by the English, with a leavening of the Irish over the last twenty years – itself a well-established tradition in the canon of English literature – while the Scots, and indeed the Welsh, are confined to the cabinets of national specimens. If these cabinets were a recognition of profoundly different cultural experiences, of linguistic forms and possibilities quite other than those found south of the border, even of a different climate and physical landscape, then the labelling would be acceptable. Instead, it is difficult to see in this confinement much beyond a lazy indifference, resting on dusty notions of Scott and Burns: a label makes a challenge easy to ignore, and removes the need to re-assess boundary lines.

   Other contributors to this volume will be meditating on Morgan's place in the Scottish tradition. My brief, to place him in a wider context, has produced some unexpected juxtapositions, and some poetic models that are not usual among Morgan's contemporaries. He has looked beyond the United Kingdom: in particular to Central Europe,

well before its poets were in vogue as they are today, and to the west
coast of America.

Edwin Morgan and Charles Tomlinson, for instance, seem an
unlikely pair, yet their very different poems have been nourished by the
same youthful reading. Both men found their way out of the pervasive
atmosphere of Dylan Thomas by a combination of French and
American escape-routes. In Morgan's case, there was also the strong
attraction of Old English crossed with W.H. Auden, and their varying
degrees of melancholy, heroism and menace. One of the salutary lessons
the Americans offered was their openness to poetry in other languages, a
sense of the necessity to explore other traditions:

> . . . they have simply got to read French poetry, whereas so many
> English poets are so pleased with the parish pump it doesn't seem
> to concern them that they ought to know what happened in French
> Symbolism from, say, 1870 to round about 1920: from Rimbaud
> to Valéry.[1]

The result of Tomlinson's absorbed reading was specifically the poem
'Antecedents' in *Seeing is Believing* (1960), and less specifically, a way of
seeing a 'moral landscape', a way of conveying a 'mental climate' that
was elegant, aesthetically delicate, and perceptibly un-English in its
ambitiousness. Yet Tomlinson has also said that he takes himself to be
writing 'a phenomenological poetry, with roots in Wordsworth and
Ruskin'.

Morgan looks through oddly similar, unfashionable, Romantic and
Symbolist spectacles; but the objects of his gaze are not the fugitive
natural phenomena that Tomlinson, like Ruskin, so often takes as his
material. His Wordsworth, too, is not the poet of landscape and
weather that seems most to have influenced Tomlinson; the 'real'
Wordsworth has a vision of 'unaccommodated man' that speaks to
Morgan's darkest perceptions (*E*, 131). Nevertheless, he looked in the
same direction, beyond the parish pump.

> It was the whole of the French Symbolist movement that really got
> under my skin when I was a student, Baudelaire and Rimbaud, but
> Verlaine too, and others. . . . I particularly admired what
> Baudelaire was doing because it was classical. If you want a
> classical poetry, that's it. He had an extraordinary command of
> regular modes of writing, and yet at the same time he's got a very
> deep infusion of something you could only call Romantic, even
> decadently so. . . . [Rimbaud] is also able to combine that formal
> control with the most extraordinary adventurousness of ideas and
> language. (*Verse*, 31)

Tomlinson took this as a lesson in poise: Morgan sought a more obvious tension between his subject-matter and the chosen disciplines of form. Unlike Eliot and his generation, it was not a tonal nuance, Laforgue's mastery of gesture, that he sought; it was something altogether more robust. He wanted a kind of Whitmanesque inclusiveness without Whitman's gorgeous egotism – or indeed, Dylan Thomas's; like his contemporaries, Morgan was backing off from self-display.

His English contemporaries, it is perhaps surprising to realise, were the celebrated Movement poets. They wrote in 'regular modes', unobscured by bardic gestures, untroubled by the feverish or chilly dreams of surrealism. Not all of them were philistine – Barbara Everett has made a persuasive case for a post-Symbolist reading of Larkin's poetry, for instance – and yet they are fixed in the aspic of Kingsley Amis's ban on foreign cities, philosophy and art galleries as fit subjects for poetry. Where were the ideas to come from, where the sense of linguistic adventure? Perhaps, having come through the war, the crudest impulse to adventure was crushed. 'No ideas but in things', then.

And yet William Carlos Williams's dictum was not adopted either. Williams was not adopted *tout court*, except by Tomlinson; I shall return to Morgan's reaction. Donald Davie, looking back deliberately in anger on the Movement, remarked that all the poets shared

> a hatred for writing as self-expression: but all we put in its place was writing as self-adjustment, a getting on the right terms with our reader (that is, with our society), a hitting on the right tone and attitude towards him. . . . how difficult we find it to conceive of or approve any 'tone' that isn't ironical, and ironical in a limited way, defensive and self-deprecating, a way of looking at ourselves and our pretensions, not a way of looking at the world.[2]

Thus the classical forms in Movement hands were not a way of articulating an energy of perception; they sealed off instead of opening out; the poetry was, generally, insular in the most profound sense.

Davie, two years Morgan's junior, was perhaps the least typical of the Movement poets: his adaptation of Mickiewicz's epic poem *Pan Tadeusz* as *The Forests of Lithuania* (1959) has an exotic specificity when set beside the titles of contemporaneous collections: D.J. Enright's *Bread Rather than Blossoms*, Elizabeth Jennings's *A Sense of the World*, or John Wain's *A Word Carved on a Sill*. An advocate and critic of Pound and Basil Bunting (for whom Morgan has recently published an elegy of great charm), Davie also turned to a study of Boris Pasternak in the 1960s.

Poets and critics of today – particularly Seamus Heaney, but also A. Alvarez and Tom Paulin – have so publicly adopted the poetry of Eastern Europe as a kind of litmus test for poetry, that it is as though these exemplars are peculiar to the 1970s and are quite a new resource. Certainly the increase in translation is a phenomenon of the last twenty years, though tapering off now; so the work of poets such as Zbigniew Herbert, Osip Mandelstam, and Czeslaw Milosz is available to a wide audience who can read them only in English. Heaney is explicit about the value of these poets from the Eastern bloc to a poet formed by Irish experience: 'There is an unsettled aspect to the different worlds they inhabit, and one of the challenges they face is to survive amphibiously, in the realm of "the times" and the realm of their moral and artistic self-respect . . .'.[3] The work of the lyric poet, in these terms, is justified in a suffering world: his fidelity to his song – a faithfulness unto death, in Mandelstam's case – is his way of serving humanity. Poetry is seen not as a refuge from the truth of facts but as pure truth in itself, not a luxury but a necessity to the human community. This is high ground, and poets had of course found their way to it before the last decade.

Earlier than that, a Russian writer had become emblematic in the West: in the uproar created by the first publication of *Dr Zhivago* in Italy, in 1957, and the subsequent offer and refusal of the Nobel Prize. Pasternak was emblematic because he persistently refused the kind of public or civic role the Russians had long regarded as proper to their poets. His witness was private and lyrical: for this Davie honoured him; he went to the Russian for lessons that were poetical rather than political. And he contrasted Pasternak unfavourably with his friend and predecessor, Vladimir Mayakovsky, whose death Davie could just remember – Morgan, more clearly:

> It must have been widely reported in the newspapers. I don't recall anything about it, except that somehow it was a 'public' event, a writer in history, of interest all over the world. . . . The writer as himself a 'fact': that is very much the European spirit – from Pushkin to Brecht, from Dostoevsky to Lorca – and I admire it. (*Gairfish*, 57)

This is what post-war Western poets have found seductive: the Eastern European writers suffer, but they are indisputably important in the life of the nation, unignorable by the authorities because valued by their readers – a massive number of readers, not confined to the educated middle-class. Davie points out in this context that 'British and American poets are, as it were, condemned to the private life; and many of them have worried, so far to no purpose, about how to break into the public realm, to take on that civic responsibility which their societies indulgently deny them'.[4]

For Morgan, who admits that Mayakovsky wrote too much and indulged in 'tedious rhetoric and breast-beating' (*E*, 64), the older

Russian poet nevertheless offers a model of public modernity in direct, illuminating contrast to Pasternak. The younger poet, consciously and unconsciously, abandoned the 'notion of biography as spectacle . . . inherent in my time' in favour of the poet 'as living personality absorbed in moral cognition'.[5] Davie sees this as pertinent and appealing to his own generation, who had backed off from the 'biography as spectacle' that had characterised the extravagances of their predecessors; he himself returned to an Augustan sense of decorum in diction, and with others began to apprehend what Thomas Hardy might teach them.

This road was not taken by Morgan: it was the extraordinary vigour of Mayakovsky and his embrace of everything new that exerted its fascination. Not retreat but engagement, and 'an attempt to incorporate into verse something of the urban, industrial and technical dynamism of the modern world' (*E*, 61). New facts require new forms. What British poet had managed to contemplate scientific and social upheavals without despair — leaving aside the contaminated idealism of the 1930s and the naïvetés of pylon poetry? Although he had his reservations, Morgan saw in Mayakovsky an undimmed modernist, with his

> determination to refresh and revive language, not only in the post-Revolution sense of a newly liberated popular speech which must find its way into art . . . but also at the aesthetic level of mind-bending imagery and juxtaposition, and an acutely inventive use of word and sound in every device of onomatopoeia, alliteration, assonance and dissonance, pun and palindrome, and perhaps above all (and in the spirit of the highly inflected Russian language) morphological play and dislocation. (*E*, 61)

These are Morgan's own strategies, and he could not find a British model for them — apart from the dangerously fluent example of Hugh MacDiarmid. In these apparently divergent European styles — the French classicism of form that nevertheless accommodated a new language; the frenetic Russian experimentalism in form to carry its revolutionary message — Morgan saw a way, or rather, ways, forward that we discern in his poetry of the 1960s.

From Mayakovsky's innovations it was not a long way to the concrete poetry of the Brazilians and Czechs, especially since it was allied in them with political and social comment. Here the interest in sound and in the appearance of poems on the page removed the poet from the foreground as effectively as any self-deprecating strategies. Davie considered Pasternak's early poetry to have at its centre a concern for the Presence of Art, not for objects nor for autobiography: in its different — but not entirely unrelated — way, this is also the lesson of concrete poetry. Morgan was typically optimistic when he stated in his 1972 essay on concrete poetry that everyone had to accept 'that a revolt in perception, or more properly a jolt into perception, has occurred, and that this will increasingly affect publishing, education, art training and many forms of design, quite apart from the impact on aesthetics itself' (*E*, 32); it has certainly provided a source of pleasure in his own work, as in Ian Hamilton Finlay's. The challenges of concrete poetry, aural and visual, offered an alternative to the constrictions of the 'well-made' poem – the mildly erotic, faintly speculative, conversational, 'witty', metropolitan (or week-end rural) English poetry that those without the resources of Davie, say, or perhaps Enright, produced in the 1950s and 1960s. In the same essay, Morgan suggested that writing concrete poetry was both a critical and a positive gesture:

> Finlay's 'Acrobats' is certainly not swept under the table by (for example) Ted Hughes's *Crow*. Those who think that it is might ask themselves the question, whether they would prefer their children to go to a school where one external wall was carved with the poem 'Acrobats', or to a school where they were taught to admire either the view of life or the deployment of language we find in *Crow*?
> (*E*, 24–5)

This was very much apropos the question articulated by A. Alvarez in his notorious introduction to *The New Poetry*, the Penguin anthology first issued in 1962 and revised in 1966, concerning the direction of British poetry: could it reconcile the psychological insights of D.H. Lawrence with the formal intelligence of T.S. Eliot? Could it admit that life was disordered and violent, that emotions were often uncontrollable, with messy or – remembering the war – all-too-organized consequences? Alvarez looked to the Americans, especially to Lowell, Berryman and Plath, as the exemplars of such reconciliation, and he compared Larkin unfavourably with Ted Hughes, the latter being the English poet least susceptible to any charge of gentility.

This Larkin/Hughes divide – ancestrally, the Hardy/Lawrence divide, perhaps even reaching back to Cowper and Blake – is something Morgan bypasses in an unexpected fashion. Davie and Tomlinson, in their cultural scope and in their poetic ambitions, are very different from Larkin, but clearly belong also to the tradition that takes some bearings from Hardy. For all that they write of Stoke-on-Trent and Barnsley, of Mexico and of California, Tomlinson and Davie share with Hughes a profound feeling for rural landscapes. Hughes's and Davie's sense of England draws on a knowledge of ancient pieties – it is hard to find a more accurate word, though it may seem to sort ill with Hughes's violence – which connect the inhabitants of England to their physical environment; Larkin has lost those connections, and laments the loss.

Like Morgan, Larkin is a poet of urban life. Larkin's 'unsentimental, unsmart charity' (a quality in which he judged Auden to be deficient) is exercised at a distance from the life he observes, and the perspective in which he places this life opens on to an infinity unburdened by the observer's presence – something both longed for ('Such attics cleared of me! Such absences!'), and deeply feared ('Not to be here, / Not to be anywhere, / And soon; nothing more terrible, nothing more true'). All those half-familiar phrases and tones of voice in Larkin's poems seem to come from overheard conversations: 'loneliness clarifies' might be his motto. The poet on the margin, indecisive, regretful, seeing into a distance that renders the present already too late – these are elements that make him peculiarly susceptible to the power of photography: 'as no art is, / Faithful and disappointing!' There is a quality of the photograph album about Larkin's volumes of poems: a succession of stills where the commonplace unexpectedly becomes witness to some profounder emotion; where some detail becomes poignant because it no longer exists outside the words; where some rites are preserved. The sense of failed connections in these contexts, domestic and national, is something to which Morgan is also alert, but his aim is much more deliberately documentary; and his context is sometimes more precisely erotic.

The *Instamatic Poems* (1972) are Morgan's way of preserving the particulars of a period, events reported in newspapers or on television that are then lost because never 'fixed', except perhaps by novelists with a similar sense of the often violent underside of British society, of the people whose only means of articulation may be a nonchalantly brutal act (Paul Theroux's *Family Arsenal*, 1976, comes to mind). He has said that it is always the human story that attracts him, and that although tempted to work up these snaps into a larger comment on the early 1970s, in the end he left it for each poem to provide the context for the others. This is also the strategy of *From the Video Box*, 1986, a roughly parallel collection.

What he does provide in the *Instamatic Poems*, as in various of the *Glasgow to Saturn* poems (notably 'Stobhill' and the 'Glasgow Sonnets') are the voices of the urban dispossessed. Morgan's academic and middle-class circumstances would seem to create a great distance between them; Douglas Dunn and Tony Harrison, poets who have dealt with similar themes, have explicitly written out of just this sense of uneasy and guilty distance. The strength of Morgan's poems of human relations is, however, his inwardness with his subjects; I take this to be based on two factors. Morgan's slightly oblique stance towards the society he depicts may be conditioned by his homosexuality, and an inability to express

openly the terms of his intimate relationships, an example being the
series of love poems in *The Second Life*; twenty years later, this discretion
has been modified in *Themes on a Variation*. Unlike Larkin, however, he
is not without such relationships, which broaden the scope of his
observations, as they fuel his despairs.

Like Morgan, Harrison makes use of classical forms and introduces
language that has not been acceptable in poetry; in Harrison's case
obscenities as much as dialect, in Morgan's, the language spoken on the
west coast of Scotland. But the 'Them and Uz' division which Harrison
has exposed with such memorable clarity is quite differently weighted
in Glasgow. Harrison speaks directly from his family experience, as,
interestingly, Morgan does not. His 'Uz' is a community with a
particular, often perversely expressed, rueful pride in Scottish working-
class traditions. Thus its sense of urban life is not entirely defensive, and
at times the London/south-east/BBC mould is disregarded with perfect
ease. Dunn refers to his speaker, in 'St Kilda's Parliament', as 'A
suitably ashamed/Observer of the poor', and risks the charge of
exploiting these same people as material for his art. Morgan escapes this
by his position in the poems: there is no patronising because there is
often no observing 'I', simply the voices of others speaking. His skill is
such that they have a natural inevitability; there are no false notes,
though plenty of discords. Morgan wants to give everything a voice –
animals, inanimate objects and machines equally with humans – and in
denying no one, except the powerful whose voices too readily find their
channels, he expresses the humanity that is the constant pulse of his art.
We warm to his indignation, that has nothing of rhetoric or self-
deception in it:

> But stalled lives never budge.
> They linger in the single-ends that use
> their spirit to the bone, and when they trudge
> from closemouth to laundrette their steady shoes
> carry a world that weighs us like a judge.
>
> 'Glasgow Sonnets', x

The political passion, again, was a spirit that Morgan found
congenial in Mayakovsky, and later he discovered Attila József
(1902–37)

> . . . in Italian translation, and made my own translations from
> that, out of sheer excitement and delight at coming across a poetry
> of such deep urban pathos and concern – it was almost like finding
> a kind of poetry I had been half-searching for (in Baudelaire, in
> 'B.V.' Thomson, in early Eliot) but never truly experienced until
> then. Budapest and Glasgow! (*Gairfish*, 59)

József, John Pilling has suggested, may be the greatest Socialist poet of the century[6]: given the scarcity of translations into English, it is impossible to reach a conclusion. What Morgan was seeking was a modernism that yielded nothing to the Right, that avoided propaganda and retained its sense of poetic adventure, what he saw as Mayakovsky's struggle in the 1920s not to 'dilute your poetry for the popular market just because you were left-wing'. Both József and Mayakovsky paid the price of their struggle in suicide.

Set against the long, bitter haul of Central Europe – with the Prague Spring as reminder – the Utopian politics of the 1960s flower children look merely self-indulgent. The sub-Blakean poetry that emerged from the 'Underground' in Britain, anthologised by Michael Horowitz in *Children of Albion* (1969), or from 'The Liverpool Poets' (*Penguin Modern Poets 10*, 1968) has scarcely survived its performance. Still, it had tenuous connections with sterner revolutions in trying to make poetry a popular and internationalist art, and it caught fire from the Beats in America, where the single issue of the Vietnam War gave political coherence to a range of protesting poets.

> In Ginsberg it was equally a freedom of spirit and of form. I am thinking of *Howl* in particular, which was the first poem of his I read. The long, swinging lines, the extraordinary juxtapositions of imagery, the sexual explicitness – all these appealed, not separately but as part of a new amalgam of liberation . . .
>
> WNH: Ginsberg demands a dimension of social responsibility, of direct comment: does that appeal?
>
> EM: Yes – even if it is only his claim (in 'America') that he is putting his queer shoulder to the wheel. It is probably the 'direct comment' that guards and guarantees the 'social responsibility'. That is what the Americans have to give us, peculiarly. From the Beats I got into Williams, and Creeley, and Bukowski. I learned, really learned for the first time . . . that you can write poetry about anything. . . . The world, history, society, everything in it, pleads to become a voice, voices. (*Gairfish*, 58)

The immediate effect of the long lines may be seen in a poem like 'The Unspoken' (*P*, 164), or in 'Flowers of Scotland' (*P*, 188), Morgan's grimly accurate reply to the sentimental view of Scottish landscape and Scottish working life. There is a kind of liberation, a secular redemption perhaps, in human gestures in the here-and-now, like the joyful Christmas shopping expedition of 'Trio' (*P*, 154). If the 1960s opened the gates for some writers on Eastern mysticism, this was not part of Morgan's release in those years: nor has his poetry been concerned with the religious themes that have perplexed Davie, obviously, and Geoffrey Hill, notably, in the next generation. Again Morgan did not pick up on the element in American poetry that was the most obvious: the return to centre-stage of the biographical element, the rage for confession – however imperially handled and set against the backdrop of a raging history, as in Lowell's case. At last he could make some sense of Williams, for whose work he had not cared much in the 1950s.

The importance of Williams for Morgan has not been his metrics, nor the pared-down vocabulary: Morgan's linguistic exuberance – a richer mixture than the plums provided in recent Martian pies – places him at some distance from Williams and his Black Mountain successors. Rather, it lies in the way the American has found to anchor his larger vision in the quiddities of everyday life, without trivialising them. He often celebrates a quality of stubborn endurance, in humanity as in nature, with an optimism akin to Morgan's own. Morgan found in *Paterson* a 'sharp, stinging, splintery immediacy, sensuous, cinematic and human' (*E*, 12) – a description that might be applied to *Sonnets from Scotland*. While he admired *Paterson* and Hart Crane's *The Bridge*, his way of approaching such sustained meditation has been the method of accretion seen in 'The New Divan', and the *Sonnets*: 'secret narrative' *avant la lettre*, perhaps. *Paterson* has also the specific sense of place and of confronting urban existence with which Morgan's poetry has obvious affinities; later American poets such as John Ashbery, with whom Morgan would seem to have much in common, nevertheless do not provide the earthbound-ness he relishes in the older man.

In these long American poems Morgan finds an eagerness to embrace the new, poets leaning forward into the future instead of using the past as prop and stay: a Scottish poet might be particularly wary of that. This is the focus of Morgan's quarrel with high modernism, in which the poet is always tugged at, judged by, the past. When he uses texts, they are likely to be newspaper cuttings or recalcitrant facts from old encyclopedias: 'the found material should be minor, and preferably prose, so that there is a challenge to engage in some sturdy or subtle metamorphosis' (*Gairfish*, 60). His movement into the far future of science fiction is nevertheless earthed by contemporary detail: the poem floats in space but has a long lead back to a solid structure. This does not mean a dismissal of history, but Morgan's approach to it is very different from Dunn's, or Paulin's, or Jeffrey Wainwright's. His perspective on it is often geological: not the landscape as worked by man, rather what was given, and what might be left when the race has destroyed itself. MacDiarmid's *On a Raised Beach* has clearly been influential here; a poet of Morgan's generation could not be deaf to such a voice. Political desire and scepticism informs Morgan's work – see the poem 'On John MacLean' (*P*, 349) for example – but not the desire to narrate one particular struggle, or to meditate on the dissolution of a community or an empire.

Auden, in his provocative notes on 'The Poet and the City', remarked that anyway it was not the politicians and statesmen who transformed the world today, but the scientists. 'Unfortunately poetry cannot celebrate them because their deeds are concerned with things, not persons, and are, therefore, speechless'.[7] Obviously Morgan could not concur with Auden: what is more, he would surely find the statement symptomatic of that distance widening between the poet and his modern audience, who need the poets to mediate the bewildering facts of science as much as they need them to reinterpret history or renew the language – indeed, the whole enterprise is inextricable, although not every poet can undertake all of it. Miroslav Holub (b. 1923), the Czech poet and biologist, is such a mediator, and one whom Morgan admires. Morgan is passionate on this score in his essay 'A Glimpse of Petavius', where he argues for the combined strengths of MacDiarmid's intellectual curiosity and Williams's humanity as urgently necessary to modern poetry:

> It is here that our Lawrences and Leavises take the wrong turning. To go on 'asserting human values' in terms that are isolated from the world of rockets and computers and television sets, as if they did not exist within the same frame of reality at all, will in the end make these values less and less convincing . . . (*E*, 14)

The concept of 'two cultures' may be hoary, but it has remarkable staying power. Again we have to look to a poet of the Eastern bloc, Czeslaw Milosz (b. 1911), to see this dilemma clarified – in terms with which the West remains uncomfortable:

> He has no patience with what has been called the 'Two Truths' theory of knowledge, according to which scientific language does not have to be reconciled with lyrical language, since each is true 'in its own terms', in terms of the universe of discourse which each inhabits and appeals to, two universes which are held not to be in competition since at no point do they touch or overlap. By refusing to sign this amiable treaty of non-intervention, Milosz sets himself at odds with most Anglo-American opinion . . .[8]

Donald Davie's pessimistic conclusion is that once the poet steps outside the lyric framework that is his popularly conceived place, then he will 'fail to find readers, or else lose those he has already found'. Morgan's ambitions cannot be compared with those of Milosz, yet his wrestle with the lyrical and the scientific languages might be more honourably placed in that tradition than amidst the simpler ironies and narrow perspectives that prevail in contemporary British poetry.

Still, if Morgan has found his *confrères* and exemplars across Europe
and the Atlantic, he should not appear entirely isolated within Great
Britain. In the flourishing small-press world of the 1960s and 1970s, a
few names – Northern House, Fulcrum and Carcanet – stand out as
publishing the kind of poetry more congenial to his ambitions than that
of the larger houses, many of which had substantial poetry lists in those
years. Carcanet, which has outgrown the small-press label, in fact
became Morgan's publisher in 1973 (*From Glasgow to Saturn*), incidentally the same year as it published József's *Selected Poems and Texts*; the
previous year it had issued Morgan's translations of Mayakovsky into
Scots. The late 1960s was a particularly strong period for Stuart
Montgomery's Fulcrum Press, based in London but hospitable to non-
metropolitan voices: he published Basil Bunting's *Collected Poems* in
1968 and Roy Fisher's in 1969, along with Lee Harwood's *The White
Room*, Christopher Middleton's *Our Flowers and Nice Bones*, and a revised
edition of Ian Hamilton Finlay's *The Dancers Inherit the Party*. These
poets form a constellation that could not be included in the galaxy of
more conventional post-Movement poets, any more than their technical
concerns could be assimilated to the free-flow of the Liverpool poets –
though they might admire some of the same artists, Tzara, for example.
Leaving aside Bunting, whose age and clearly Poundian allegiance
separates him from the younger men, perhaps the most serviceable
generalisation about these poets is that they demand a particular kind of
collaboration from the reader: a willingness to accept irresolution, to
work hard with the eye as well as the ear, to take part in the game of the
poem. Everything is seen as chaotic and the poet uses the elements of
chaos, the pleasures of hazard, as part of his verbal construction. In this
company, Morgan's poems of sound patternings, for instance, begin to
look less *sui generis*.

Of this group, Middleton (b. 1926) is now also on Carcanet's list,
and is closest to Morgan in terms of his technical range, his linguistic
curiosity – fuelled by his fine work as a translator – his syntactical
innovations and frequently surreal imagination. A reviewer has called
him 'an avant-garde poet we can actually *read*'; another has said of
Morgan that he represents the acceptable face of modernism. This may
be merely a reflection of low reviewing standards; on the other hand, it
may be a more positive comment on these poets' ability not to sacrifice
adventurousness for the sake of accessibility. Middleton's *oeuvre* has an
individual waywardness and a quality of detachment – which by no
means precludes a sensual appreciation of the world, and of women –
that may stem from his position as an expatriate at home only in
language, or languages; Morgan's rootedness in Scottish culture is an

obvious contrast. Both poets show a quirky sense of humour that is otherwise rare among their contemporaries, whose humour is less playful and more satirical.

It is not the hallmark of Roy Fisher's poetry, certainly, but he shares to some extent the surrealist vision of the older poets (he was born in 1930), and Morgan's concern with the passing urban moment that will be lost without the poet's witness. In Fisher's long poem *City*, it was not the particularity of Birmingham in the late 1950s that he wanted to 'fix', but the whole phenomenon of 'having a perceptual environment which was taken as read . . . not a thing for which any vocabulary needed to exist . . . Seeing this life ending . . . made you realize more than usually how much the place was dependent upon very evanescent, temporal, subjective renderings of it, which might never *be* rendered'.[9] Fisher's poetic Cubism, in which there was an edge of desperation, has been succeeded by poems of multiple perspectives – like Morgan, he favours sequences rather than a single extended work – in which the views may be disconcerting but the multiplicity itself a sign for rejoicing.

What separates Morgan from these poets, finally, is not only his extensive use of dramatised speech – all the clamorous voices, from starlings to Shakespeare – but the unembarrassed, true voice of feeling, the life of the community beating in his poems.

> – Although a poem is
> undoubtedly a 'game'
> it is not a game.
> And although now it is even
> part of the game to say so,
> making it a " 'game' "
> is spooky, and we'll
> not play that.   (*P*, 270)

Can Morgan have it both ways? Uniquely, among contemporary poets, I think he can.

NOTES

1. Charles Tomlinson, interview in *The Poet Speaks*, edited by Peter Orr (London: Routledge and Kegan Paul, 1966), p.252.
2. Donald Davie, *The Poet in the Imaginary Museum: essays of two decades*, edited by Barry Alpert (Manchester: Carcanet New Press, 1977), p.74.
3. Seamus Heaney, *The Government of the Tongue* (London: Faber and Faber, 1988), p.xx.

4. Donald Davie and Angela Livingstone, *Pasternak* (London: Macmillan, Modern Judgements Series, 1969), p.29.

5. Quoted by Davie in *Pasternak*, p.21.

6. John Pilling, 'Attila József' in *An Introduction to 50 Modern European Poets* (London: Pan Books, 1982), p.332.

7. W.H. Auden, *The Dyer's Hand and other essays* (London: Faber and Faber, 1975), p.81.

8. Donald Davie, *Czeslaw Milosz and the Insufficiency of Lyric* (Cambridge: Cambridge University Press), pp.27–8.

9. Ian Gregson, 'Roy Fisher: *A Furnace* and Before' in *Verse* 6:1, March 1989, p.61.

Four

The Public and Private Morgan

Iain Crichton Smith

1

Edwin Morgan is a very private person. Yet he reads often in public and reads well, with vigour and humour. He is witty in a quiet way: he is learned in an encyclopaedic way. I have been with him, and with him often, but I cannot say that I know him. This may be part of the academic ethos: I have met many academics who have the same reticence, the same shyness. It may be, however, an inner modesty and decorum.

MacCaig talks as he writes, with the same sensuous love of words, the same wit and paradox. It was said of Henry James that he talked in round, intricate, meditative paragraphs. Spender tells the story of having dinner with T.S. Eliot and the latter saying, 'Do I dare to eat this cheese?'.

Morgan isn't like that. The creative part of him is mysterious, secret. Outwardly one might not expect him to be an ardent glutton of the present, of what is and what is to be. One would not expect him to be an admirer of Mayakovsky, and rather doubtful about Eliot.

He is not at all what one might expect according to the Scottish paradigm of what a Scottish poet should be. He does not drink much, he is not extravagantly theatrical, aggressive, wasteful. He has his railway timetable which he consults. He moves about easily in our technological world.

He loves words yet he is puzzled by my passion for difficult crosswords. He is obviously adept at languages yet when I asked him why he didn't learn Gaelic, he smiled. Perhaps he thinks of Gaelic as belonging slightly to the past. He doesn't seem particularly interested in the past, even his own past: I haven't seen much autobiography by him.

He has what Robin Fulton called 'an efficient intelligence'.[1] This is shown particularly by his craftsmanship which is of a high order and, I think, Audenesque. There are poets who are obsessive and poets who are not. Morgan has an incurable virtuosity. Thus he plays on language as an instrument. 'When Morgan fails,' according to Fulton, 'it is as if his efficient intelligence were planning a space shot and calculating the chances down to the minimum.'[2] Fulton worries that Morgan's different modes of expression are ways of staying in hiding.

He is endlessly inventive, poetry is form as well as serious content. His concrete poetry is part of an incessant playfulness and inquisitiveness. He creates personas like a Browning and he has much of Browning's love of language. But he is willing to be playful. There is play in the sense of fun, and also in the sense of theatre.

And yet and yet there is more than this . . .

2

Edwin Morgan has written a great deal; his *Poems of Thirty Years* runs to over four hundred pages and he has written more since their publication. In some of his poetry he speaks through masks, in some he is playful as in the concrete poems, in some he writes space fiction, in some he writes non-committal Instamatic poems.

His early work has an Anglo-Saxon feel to it. It is about storms, about the sea. His *Beowulf* is the best translation I know of the poem. He writes a lot about people he admires, for example Lenin, Hemingway. In *The Vision of Cathkin Braes* he refers to Jenny Geddes, John Knox, Lauren Bacall (who looks odd in such company but perhaps Morgan is laying down markers that he is not going to be introvertedly Scottish), Mary Queen of Scots, MacGonagall, Mungo Park, Wordsworth: all in all, a curious mélange. In *The Cape of Good Hope* he writes about Leonardo da Vinci, Michelangelo, Newton, Beethoven, Melville, Mayakovsky (whom of course he was to translate). In *The Whittrick* he conducts conversations between MacDiarmid and Joyce, Faust and Bosch, Charlotte and Emily Brontë, Marilyn Monroe and Ulanova, the Brahan Seer and Lady Seaforth, and others.

Many of these poems are inescapably literary, though in fact they are always high-spirited and witty and at times reveal a powerful imagination. However, at no point do we find ourselves in touch with Morgan, this presently suffering individual, who orchestrates these odd tableaux; what is lacking is some individual humanity to animate the puppets. The vocabulary is intensely rich, as if words were all-important. The endless conversations are interesting but it is as if they were taking place in an echoing study. Is this, one asks, the case of a poet who wants to write poetry but has not yet found his subject matter?

Of these early poems, the one that engages my attention the most is called 'The Sleights of Darkness', though I am not wholly sure that I could paraphrase it. It seems to be about love and loneliness but the language is oddly slant and obscure, though vivid and energetic.

> One nightmare after cinderfall
> Idiocy in a slumber took me aside
> To see my friend in his golden fell
> Stumble at the handle of fiends'-hovel
> By the feral riverside. (P, 10)

It has a curious wrought ornamentation, rather like Dunbar, but beating through it is a very serious energy and curious imagery:

> Bitter vision, not of wishes!
> Let me not find his heart at bay
> Or laid with innocence in ashes,
> Or if I must, let our lost riches
> Of trust be all we must pay! (P, 10)

Among so much that is intelligent, scholarly and learned, this poem has a haunting humanity that is stronger than many of his later, more explicitly personal poems.

Emergent Poems (1967) introduces his concrete poems where gaps and single words stutter their way to more understandable phrases.

The Second Life (1968) reveals the Morgan with whom we must reckon. He was forty-seven years old when this book was published. It has been said of Scottish poets that for some reason they develop late. But it is interesting to consider how important this second life was to Morgan. It was like a renewal, a resurrection. He seems much more in charge of his work; a personal energy begins to inform it. The forms become more varied, more adroit, more contributory to the sense. One would not go so far as to say that a caterpillar becomes a butterfly (that is not quite it) but in some sense the poetry takes wing. It belongs less to the intellect than to the intellect and feelings combined. Poetic hypotheses become reality in a new way. It is as if Morgan, like Keats, had entered the room where human poetry is created. I think that this sense of a gift bestowed, of a music descended, is conveyed very much by Morgan's tone of wonderment.

The book has some interesting poems in it about Hemingway, Monroe and Piaf. These are poems about people who have lived their lives and who regretted nothing. From these poems and from such a poem as 'The Domes of Saint Sophia' (P, 129), there emerges a curiously optimistic humanism. Man and his works are important.

> The earth is my fortress
> and the meanest broch
> has that moving presence
> of imperfection . . .   (P, 130)

Ruins are often more moving than perfect domes. Man's effort to live
and to live fully is important. Man is valuable and indomitable. At the
same time he can be dangerous. Little moments, tremulous and
vulnerable, take on tremendous importance as in 'Aberdeen Train'
(P, 133). A drunken man enters a bus on Good Friday. He knows little
about Christ except that he swears by him. Two girls run along a street
laughing, carrying linoleum. Incomplete words on the wall of a shop
point to some more poignant world, incomplete, imperfect. Something
can be said for the world of King Billy. A dangerous, threatening
language inhabits 'Glasgow Green' (P, 149). 'In the Snack-Bar' (P, 152)
shows a man as victim.

What happens is that in these public poems Morgan himself has
entered the world of the deprived. He can still play games but his best
poems are poems of involvement. They are not poems of ideas but of
empathy and suffering. The poet lives in a harsh but beautiful world
from which the glow of God is absent. It is this humanism which
demands a gallery of the great who have shown the possibilities of man.
But there is a qualitative difference in the way in which he handles his
heroes in his early poems and in his later. Newton, da Vinci and
Michelangelo were really ideas. Monroe, Piaf and Hemingway are
examples of suffering humanity who belong to our own recognisable
time. They live life abundantly and recklessly. Their deaths are in some
way resurrections.

That intense feeling which has entered his poetry is also applied to
himself and in this book we have a batch of interesting love poems
which reveal, though not in a wholly penetrating way, something of the
private Morgan.

These love poems form an interesting group. They include 'The
Unspoken', 'From a City Balcony', 'When You Go', 'Strawberries',
'One Cigarette', 'The Picnic', 'Absence', 'The Welcome' (P, 164, 165,
166, 166, 168, 169, 169, 171).

What is common to all these poems is an intense poignancy, though
the choice of language and imagery sometimes seems curiously romantic.
'I stole a glance' (from 'The Unspoken') is a phrase that does not have
Morgan's usual diamond freshness. A poem like 'Strawberries', too, has
an initial attractiveness and transient poignancy, but there is again a
romanticism about it, with phrases like 'eager mouth'. In 'One
Cigarette' the phrase 'tobacco lips' seems un-Morganlike. Yet in spite of

the failures of local detail, the poems have a piercing quality which saves them. There is not much that we can fasten on as to the appearance of the loved one. We read of 'dark wet hair' (in 'The Picnic') but the poems do not give away much. There is a curious ambivalence. The lovers could be men, could be women. There is a certain generality about them, a certain expectedness in the imagery.

A number of the less happy love poems seem more authentic. Thus I find 'The Witness' (*P*, 167) more interesting than some of the others because of the language.

> No, there is no spirit standing in the sun,
> only a great light and heat, that instantly
> surround us when we meet.
> The cold of solitude was
> an effigy in a trance – (*P*, 167)

This seems to me more imaginative and real than, for instance,

> you lay
> with one arm in the rain, laughing
> shaking only your dark wet hair ('The Picnic', *P*, 169)

Love itself has to be transformed by the imagination and it seems to me that the language makes the pain of loneliness sound more genuine. Then again, a poem like 'Without It' is animated by language and not by simple romantic furniture as in the section:

> Grinding rotor! Grave of dreams! Children
> play on the sands you plunge through,
> a desolation without dimension.
> The swallow builds in your invisible eaves,
> and poppies linger blowing long,
> the smell of miles of acrid iron seems far away.
> But everything is in its place, the pinch of clover
> from a summer field could break the heart.
> Subsist in iron, and wait. (*P*, 171)

This poem seems to me to deal with ultimate loneliness in an authentic manner, recalling in the last line the enduringness of Anglo-Saxon poems. The language is rich and imaginative, a mixture of the technological and the pastoral. In another poem, 'The Sheaf', Morgan writes:

> Let this rain
> be on the children of my heart,
> I have no other ones. (*P*, 163)

It is a strange quest, pursuing this poet through thicket after thicket like a precious mythical animal. We see that he has all the right qualifications – he is on the side of the deprived, he is forceful and often optimistic, he has control over a large and splendid vocabulary, yet when we think we have caught him he is not there at all. Even his love poems do not give him away. Who is this loved one, man or woman? The unhappy poems convince more by their language than do the happy ones. Morgan, however, is no confessional poet. Playfulness, other voices, technology hide him from us.

One criticism I have seen made of Morgan is: how can he as a lecturer from a privileged environment speak for the deprived? I must say this criticism has never impressed me. Did Shakespeare have to be an old mad king to write *King Lear*? But there is also I suppose a curiosity about poets (all public figures) which may not be healthy. We ask, but what is he really like? We ask, what is this competent, knowledgeable poet, really like?

Like so many Scottish poets of recent years, he is not given to making public statements. He is not a political animal, though we gather that he is a Scottish Nationalist. The poets he admires are ones like Mayakovsky, extravagant and life-enhancing. He has reservations about Eliot, whose pessimism is not to his taste. He is an urban poet, one of the few genuinely urban poets that we have had. In this he is different from MacDiarmid, who was horrified by the tubercular light of Glasgow. Morgan, however, seems perfectly content in the city. He is at the very opposite pole from someone like George Mackay Brown who remains stationary in Orkney. Morgan on the other hand has travelled much and read his poetry in European venues.

After *The Second Life* we find *Instamatic Poems* (1972). These latter are meant to be objective recordings of reality. Some are violent, some bizarre, but when we compare them with the poems in *From Glasgow to Saturn* (1973) we realise that Morgan is not at his best when he is being realistic. He needs a certain slantness, a certain imaginative freedom and oddness, a certain amplification of his linguistic resources, to be the poet that he truly is. We see this clearly in a large number of poems in the later volume which is, I think, his most consummate. It is of course humanist in its references, as in 'Where's Brude? Where's man?' ('Columba's Song', *P*, 221), and 'There is no other life, and this is it' ('London', *P*, 241). Here too there are private allusions to love, as when someone touches him at a party or when he writes of 'your hand / lying lightly on my thigh' ('At the Television Set', *P*, 229) or 'I bore the darkness lying still, thinking / you were against my heart' ('The Milk-Cart', *P*, 230).

One of the most powerful poems in this book is 'Estranged' with its lines

> beyond the mist of Jupiter
> was the longest look
> we took at love. (*P*, 230)

There is much wit as in 'The Fifth Gospel' (*P*, 249), eeriness as in 'The Barrow' (*P*, 255), cleverness as in 'The First Men on Mercury' (*P*, 259). 'A Jar Revisited' (*P*, 266), on a misprint in a poem by Norman MacCaig, varies the word 'space' till the poem arrives at a poignant conclusion. Much riches here. Yet again the realistic poems like 'Death in Duke Street' (*P*, 276), and 'Stobhill' (*P*, 278) are dull and lack the linguistic resonance that we find in so many of the other poems, although I would make an exception of the 'Glasgow Sonnets' (*P*, 283).

It is becoming clear the more we read Morgan that the strength of his poetry is partly in his language, partly in his ingenuity, partly in a suppressed and sometimes overt playfulness which runs through his work and resonates below his cleverness. It does not lie, I think, in the sometimes too obvious images of love which he creates. It emerges more clearly from a sense of loss, of unreasoning possibilities. This sense of loss sits uneasily with the technological knowingness. It comes back time and time again in a poignant cry, below the optimism, as in 'The Milk-cart':

> Come back to me – from anywhere come back!
> I'll see you standing in my door,
> though the whistling fades to air. (*P*, 230)

and (from 'London')

> Close to me, closer! You are not afraid
> of a few icy trees, but we are both afraid
> of what is happening to us . . . (*P*, 239)

and (from 'Christmas Eve'),

> As the bus jerked, his hand fell on my knee,
> stayed there, lay heavily and alive
> with blue carvings from another world
> and seemed to hold me like a claw,
> unmoving. . . . (*P*, 277)

Much as behind the apparently comic screen of Garioch's poetry we see the uncharted distortions of madness, so beyond Morgan's apparent optimism there are strange movements of solitude, random messages of love.

Certainly his gaze into the abyss is often unflinching, but there is nevertheless the whiff of mortality here. There is the apple which the Oban girl carelessly eats but there is also 'the cancer and white hair' (from 'At the Television Set', P, 229). There is jauntiness but also

> sit like chairs
> in unforgiving air
> whatever is said or not said
> of how or where   ('Estranged', P, 231)

Fragments, obscure messages, emerge from the world; and strange resonances. Morgan himself is interesting in setting up enigmas and puzzles: how curious that our attempt to crack the code should arrive at a partially desolate solution. Yes, indeed there is intellectual power, brilliant arguments, but behind all this there is the darkness which we all share. One is reminded inescapably of Auden in the playfulness, technical expertise, the intimations of horror, except that Auden's voice is harder, less implicated, more that of someone looking at a specimen on a slide. It was Auden, however, who wrote:

> Private faces in public places
> are wiser and nicer
> than public faces in private places.[3]

As Morgan's poetry proceeds it becomes more mysterious, more enigmatic. 'The New Divan' considered in detail, is difficult though it astonishes. Morgan's interest in the exotic is shown in earlier poems such as 'Shantyman' (P, 224). This long poem arises from his knowledge of the Middle East during the Second World War. It has images of caravans, camels, cedars, lateens, as one would expect, but the arguments are complex. Each stanza has a strange intensity which at times becomes personal:

> You came under my mosquito-net
> many times, till you were posted far off.
> I was innocent enough
> to think the posting was accidental.
> When you left, it was my studious
> avoidance of you that said goodbye . . .   (P, 325)

From the point of view of identifying the private Morgan, poems like 'The Divide' (P, 370), 'Smoke' (P, 371) and part of 'Unfinished Poems' (P, 374) are important. As if through battery smoke lifting from a battlefield involved with intellectual and linguistic flashes, we now and again catch glimpses of the private Morgan in lines like:

> I keep thinking of your eyes, your hands.
> There is no reason for it, none at all.
> You would say I can't be what I'm not,
> yet I can't not be what I am.   ('The Divide', *P*, 370)

or later in the same poem:

> when you lay on one elbow on the carpet
> I could feel nothing but that hot knife
> of pain telling me what it was,
> and I can't tell you about it, not one word.   (*P*, 371)

It is odd how, as I have already said, Morgan's poetry of the immediacy of love breeds clichés as, for instance, in that phrase 'the hot knife'. And how literary some of it is:

> Are you destroying me? Or is it a comedy?
> To get together naked in bed, was that all?
> To say you had done it? And that we did nothing
> was what you had done. Iago and Cassio
> had a better night. It must be a laugh
> to see us both washed out with lying there.
> It doesn't feel like laughing, though,
> it feels like gasping, shrieking, tearing, all in silence
> as I leave your long curved back
> and go through to the kettle and the eggs.
>   ('Smoke', *P*, 371)

More true to the real Morgan that is the poet are these lines from 'Unfinished Poems';

> Pain to know,
>   pain not knowing.
> Pain to love,
>   pain not loving.
> Pain on the rack
>   and in the rocking-chair.
> Wrong to meet,
>   wrong not to.
> Wrong to be barren
>   wrong to bear.   (*P*, 379)

The more one reads Morgan the more extraordinary he appears. His variety is exceptional, though there are repetitions when one sees the poems on a larger scale. His range of vocabulary is startling, copious; he has his space poems, his plain poems about ordinary people, his playful enigmas.

This variety is unusual, almost Victorian, in its amplitude. And permeating all these poems is the love poetry which, though also confronting us with enigmas as to protagonists, vibrates at times with an almost ungovernable pain. And this provides us with a more realistic being than one might perhaps have expected from the poet's curriculum vitae. If one had expected the protected bourgeois poet one doesn't get it, and if one had expected the academic poet one doesn't get that either. Morgan becomes a puzzle such as might perhaps interest himself.

Cinquevalli, who appears in the last poem of the *Poems of Thirty Years*, is a juggler but he is more than that: he is also 'half faun' (*P*, 441). If Morgan were to be mistaken for Cinquevalli that would be true, for this is a Cinquevalli who falls into the audience, who cannot keep his aesthetic distance – hinted at by his miraculous monocle. This is a Cinquevalli whose coffin sways like that of a King Billy. Morgan is like Cinquevalli but only if one pays attention to the whole text. For this Cinquevalli is a very complex being. He is much more different than you might expect. As Morgan is.

Since the *Poems of Thirty Years* Morgan has published *Themes on a Variation* (1988). This book has the usual variety of subject matter and style. There is a poem in the manner of Lord Byron; there are a number of ingenious rewritings of famous poems by well known authors; there is the sequence *From the Video Box*: and *Sonnets from Scotland*. In a sense this book is a continuation of the kind of material that we find in the *Collected Poems*. Morgan is not the sort of poet who works through a style towards a more refined development of that style. On the contrary he chooses a style to suit his subject matter. Thus he may choose the sonnet and play variations on it. The masks, the ingenuity, continue as before, especially in the video poems which are at times moving, at times eerie and mysterious.

Also in the book is a long poem called 'Stanzas' (*TV*, 16), which seems to be a private love poem and which gives tantalising glimpses of the Morgan concealed behind the mask. This poem has a nakedness which resonates with real pain. It begins with a typical rewriting of a line from Elizabeth Barrett Browning: 'How can I love you, is there any way?' The weather in the poem is dull and rainy and this suits the melancholy content and tone. The lover enters the boredom of 'The relentless quartz [that] hums on the mantelpiece.' The lover too is much younger:

> I was thirty-eight when you were born.
> You think I want a son? Of course I do –
> or daughter – but that's not it.
> not it at all . . .   (*TV*, 17)

The images of dull wet weather haunt the love affair, which seems doomed though impassioned:

> They are not good, thoughts of the shortest day.
> A vicious intermittent frequent sleet
> turning to rain, not snow,
> thickens . . .   (*TV*, 19)

Here too are urban images of buses hissing through slush and mud. The love affair is inimical to the reason itself. It generates an almost helpless desperation: 'I clutch the flying shrouds of reason, but / I need you more and more . . .' (*TV*, 20). It is a powerful naked poem almost tragic in its depth of feeling: 'How the story will end I cannot see' (*TV*, 21). The protection that Morgan felt was necessary to him has been torn away: 'You have peeled off some covering, some coat, / I thought I needed . . .' but in spite of that the poem ends with the poet's credo: 'the truth's in feeling' (*TV*, 21). There is a grave, convincing, open sonority in this poem which needs the metrical form and gains from the desolate rhymes. It shows an apparently self-sufficient, self-contained poet being shaken by the tempest which he thought he was adequately dressed up against.

Another poem, 'Dear man, my love goes out in waves' (*TV*, 23), has the same desolation: 'Terrible the cage / to see all life from . . .', and

> Press close to me at midnight as
> you say goodbye; that's what it has
> to offer, life
> I mean . . .   (*TV*, 23)

'Waking on a Dark Morning' has the same darkness, the same hopeless urban images:

> Memory threw up streaks of something dark.
> I found I did not even want to know.
> How quick the deadly shades are, to crowd back
> As if they could not stand a waking man!   (*TV*, 26)

We have, therefore, an interesting, paradoxical poet here. The public poet is welcoming to the ideas of technology, the private poet is on the other hand at times agonised, lonely, isolated. It is a poet who wears masks, who is playful, ingenious, witty, but beyond the masks there persists the human being who reveals himself in flashes, who, as in the poems we have examined, is at times naked and desolate.

This desolate Morgan is not the poet we think of most often: on the contrary we tend to think of him in terms of, for instance, these lines from 'The Second Life' (*P*, 162):

But does every man feel like this at forty —
I mean it's like Thomas Wolfe's New York, his
heady light, the stunning plunging canyons, beauty —
pale stars winking hazy downtown quitting-time,
and the winter moon flooding the skyscrapers . . .   (*P*, 162)

We think of him in terms of acceptance; space ships setting out to far
universes. And from this point of view the public Morgan is surely
unique in his optimism and in his acceptance of the technology that the
twentieth century has brought us. It might be thought that MacDiarmid
was too, but MacDiarmid never really accepted the urban. One can
hardly think of any Scottish poet who has such energetic, contemporary
hopefulness. It is possible that one would have to go to some of the
Russian poets, such as Mayakovsky, for such hopefulness, though he
died in despair. Eliot certainly doesn't have this hopefulness. Nor
does Yeats set himself in an urban world. (It should be remembered,
though, how often Morgan is attracted to twentieth-century casualties,
suicides such as Hemingway, Monroe, Mayakovsky.)

Neither the public nor the private Morgan is religious. He is, I
would say, a humanist. He would probably agree with the saying that
'nothing human is alien to me'. He is not particularly interested in
Scotland's dark history. He is more likely to exploit the landscape of
Scotland for linguistically comic effects.

It could be argued that there is something naïve in accepting our
world as it is, except that one might agree with Carlyle who, when
asked by some woman whether we should accept the universe, is said to
have replied along the lines of, 'Madam, you had better'. The grim
predestinarian is present in that remark. Morgan is not so predestinarian.
His universe is open and fluid, subject to change, and he welcomes
change. What we have to remember, however, is the cost to the private
person of the public persona. To live in this century one has to pay a cost
which Piaf, Monroe and others paid. Morgan pays it too. Thus he is
attracted to the endurance of the Seafarer and the Wanderer:

> So I in my grief gone from my homeland
> Far from my kinsmen have often to fetter
> The images of the heart in iron chains . . .
>
> ('The Wanderer', *P*, 18)

Then again he writes in the persona of Mayakovsky:

> My solitude
> Returns in the midst of millions, bearing

> In this intolerable life its death.
> Soviet, city, and friend, remember
> My voice and verse, and pardon in the hope
> The despair, for by the despair I spoke. (*P*, 59)

And then there are the terrible voices of 'Glasgow Green' (*P*, 149), the human desolation as in 'In the Snack-Bar' (*P*, 152), the blood that streams down the screen in one of the Video Poems (*TV*, 120), and there is also much violence in the *Instamatic Poems*.

Nevertheless, the public Morgan is seen, I think, as hopeful and joyful, in spite of these tragedies, these sadnesses. They are, I suppose he would say, part of the price one must pay for the excitements of the twentieth century. There must be casualties: history moves and lives and has its being. The present and the future are more important than the past. Here we live and from here we project ourselves. To be alive is good in spite of everything. Morgan is not a Greek: he would never say 'Not to have been born is the best'.

In a curious way, the very range of his linguistic resources is positive and affirmative. In this sense I can think of few poets comparable to him except MacDiarmid. A plethora of riches is certainly here: God's plenty. MacDiarmid too had this interest in language, in geological and other specialised vocabulary, for example. So the large magnanimity of language relates to an affirmative curiosity. And this too is clearly part of the public persona, the energy, the upward and outward thrust.

This confidence, however, shown in so many different ways does not seem, as it does in MacDiarmid, to be implicated with any particularly overt political stance. It seems to be more a matter of temperament. It is not that such a poetry will move us towards perfection. It is more a personal attitude.

On the other hand this public persona, this affirmation of the present and the future, is sustained at a cost. It does not seem willed and yet it is under threat, as we can see from what we have gleaned of the private Morgan. We have already quoted from 'The Sheaff':

> Let this rain
> be on the children of my heart,
> I have no other ones. (*P*, 163)

The early love poems have a certain joy, as in 'Strawberries', 'the strawberries glistening / in the hot sunlight' (*P*, 167), and a certain bravado, as in the same poem, 'let the storm wash the plates'. Nevertheless there are also many goodbyes:

> But in the dream I woke from, you

came running through the traffic, tugging me, clinging
to my elbow, your eyes spoke
what I could not grasp –
Nothing, if you were here!   ('Absence', *P*, 170)

and from 'Without It', 'Subsist in iron, and wait' (*P*, 171).

The darkness strengthens, I think, as the love poems proceed, as in
'At the Television Set': 'What can you bear that would last / like a rock
through cancer and white hair?' (*P*, 229), and in 'The Milk-Cart': 'How
can I bear the darkness empty / and how can the darkness bear love?'
(*P*, 230). Thus we proceed to 'Stanzas', and its extraordinary desolation:
'I'd rather have your scorn / than you should never know what runs me
through . . .' (*TV*, 17).

Morgan, as has already been said, works on a roughly similar scale to
MacDiarmid, though he has retained his lyrical powers to a later age.
He is not, however, a polemicist nor a controversialist. He does not
have MacDiarmid's abrasive public stance. His background too is very
different. He has not, as far as we know, starved or suffered poverty.
Nevertheless, on the level of the imagination, he is comparable.
Whatever poetry is, it can inhabit the most paradoxical of bodies; and it
probably feeds on apparent contradictions. Morgan has, I think, greater
warmth than MacDiarmid. He is not fanatical and is not a believer in
dogma. As he says in a poem called 'Variations on Omar Khayyám':
'Ideology / makes good dust, fills in mass graves' (*TV*, 13). The private
poet does not wear political armour or defend himself by ideology.
Consequently we can see a gap opening between the private and the
public which no theory or theology can heal. Endurance is all in a
present that one can only accept. The hopeful epic is confronted by a
poignant lyricism. And above all, the feelings must not be betrayed.

Is it surprising then when we have tracked this myriad-minded poet
to his secret study that we have come face to face with desolate love and
often loneliness? And is it surprising that in spite of these he has still
embraced the twentieth century with optimism? No, I don't think it is
surprising. It is the condition, after all, of most of us. Technology as
such, the intricate mysteries of our century, cannot by themselves
absolve us from pain. One cannot but admire Morgan's enduring
courage, for in a world without theology one must rely at last on oneself
and the comradeship of humanity. Perhaps one solution is to live life to
the full as Edith Piaf did. To regret nothing. Another solution may be
to endure like the Seafarer and the Wanderer. Morgan has not betrayed
the truth of his feelings by taking refuge in dogmas of any kind. He has
remained open to the terrors and wonders of his century in a wholly

admirable way. He doesn't whine or retreat into an ivory tower of elaborate irony. His enterprise has been serious and he has given much pleasure to his readers. He is an entertaining poet. He has not thrown his confessional box wide open to the public. His admired poets are energetic, outward-going like Dunbar, Mayakovsky, Whitman, MacDiarmid. These are all expansive poets who have not built shells around themselves of devious intricacy.

I think the following quotation from his *Essays* sums him up admirably. He is writing about Mayakovsky but he could be writing about himself:

> What gives Mayakovsky's work its peculiar character, and I think also its peculiar value, is its unusual combination of wild avant-garde leanings and flashes and something of central human concern. A grotesque and vivid comic fantasy is never lost; neither is the sense of pain, of loneliness, of longing, sometimes misguided by creative exhilaration; neither is the sense of history and the role and duty of the poet (*E*, 64).

NOTES

1. Robin Fulton, *Contemporary Scottish Poetry* (Edinburgh: Macdonald, 1974), p.37.
2. *Ibid.*
3. W.H. Auden, *Collected Shorter Poems 1927–1957* (London: Faber and Faber, 1966), p.43.

Five

The Voyage Out and the Favoured Place:
Edwin Morgan's Science Fictions

Marshall Walker

The appeal of science fiction today can be seen as a symptom of concern about the future of the planet. In Kurt Vonnegut's novel, *God Bless You, Mr Rosewater*, Eliot Rosewater drunkenly compliments a convention of science fiction writers:

> I love you sons of bitches . . . You're all I read any more. You're the only ones who'll talk about the *really* terrific changes going on . . . You're the only ones with guts enough to *really* care about the future, who *really* notice what machines do to us, what wars do to us, what tremendous misunderstandings, mistakes, accidents and catastrophes do to us.[1]

Given the chance and a taste for verse, Eliot Rosewater would presumably have read Morgan and maybe loved him too. The sense of change is there, a *geist* of the *oeuvre*. The attention to machines is there, machines we've got – space stations, modules, computers, videos – and machines yet to come, like the de-/re-materialisation technique used in 'In Sobieski's Shield' (*P*, 181–3), or the 'demagnification banks' in 'Memories of Earth' (*P*, 327–8). Morgan's poetry knows about war, studies cities, continually probes and plays with ideas. But if Mr Rosewater had sobered up and looked more closely at Scotland's most prodigious body of poetry since MacDiarmid, he might have found a quality to stay his glad hand: Morgan's optimism. For Morgan, as for William Burroughs, science fiction is essentially a mode of hope. Machines may malfunction or be mischievous but they are not the bad guys of Morgan's world. His cities are savoured, far from the 'unreal' urban landscapes or T.S. Eliot's waste land. This buoyant poetical intelligence, connoisseur of the present, believes positively in the future, holding 'a hopeful of even a *very* hopeful long-term view of the possibilities of the human race' (*Akros*, 22).

Like H.G. Wells, the best writers of science fiction use their genre realistically to make guesses about a future from whose vantage point a critical eye may be cast over the present. Vonnegut himself, John Brunner, Philip K. Dick and Samuel R. Delany employ the conventions in various ways to create moral landscapes like Lewis Carroll's Wonderland or Swift's Lilliput and the country of the Houyhnhnms. The genre is not easy to define, but usually implies fantasy in which the imagination, unconstrained by mundane reality, operates within the limits of what might be scientifically possible. In Morgan's science fictions the conservative end of the imaginative bandwidth is 'A Home in Space' (*P*, 390), and the furthest and fullest reach of fantasy and fable the masterpiece, 'Memories of Earth'.

In the first of his collected *Essays*, 'A Glimpse of Petavius', Edwin Morgan argues for greater sensitivity among poets towards human experience in its total modern environment, particularly recognising that this is, in large part, inescapably technological. He disapproves of the tendency among poets to recoil from their environment: Edwin Muir was wrong to want to wrench the world back to a pre-atomic Eden. The poet should not regress into the organic world of nature, desperately abjuring the machine, but pursue the new envelope of circumstances, finding in it a *plenum* increasingly rich and full. In the second piece reprinted in *Essays*, 'The Poet and the Particle', Morgan observes that we 'seem to live, today, in many worlds rather than in one' (*E*, 16). There are the separately definable but to some degree overlapping worlds of common sense and experience, of metaphysics, and of international politics. Most separate of all is the world of modern science. Morgan recalls in his essay C.P. Snow's famous Rede Lecture on *The Two Cultures and the Scientific Revolution* (CUP, 1959): 'It is bizarre how very little of twentieth-century science has been assimilated into twentieth-century art'.[2] If the poet is 'the man who traditionally finds links and resemblances, dissolves rather than erects barriers, moves among the various worlds of his time' (*E*, 17), how can the contemporary poet, writing his time, responsibly compound the cultural felony by endorsing, even widening the gap between common life and the technological facts, implications and possibilities that characterise the era? As shaman, the artist has a duty to 'record what is happening, telling the tribe's history' (*Akros*, 11). Human beings go up in rockets, land on the moon, dock and link vehicles in space. It is time poetry rose to such occasions, and the problem of technological language is no excuse for not trying.

Two kinds of poetry might be produced by the responsible poet:

It may be that there could be a simple, even perhaps romantic kind of poetry of space exploration where things would not be described

in technical terms but where something of the epic adventure of
exploration would come into it — a kind of carry-over from an
earlier poetry; but there might also be a different kind of poetry
which was more willing to use the specifics in the situation as far as
possible and therefore to have to use technological language.
(*Akros*, 11)

In 'A Home in Space' (from *Star Gate*, 1979; *P*, 390) Morgan fuses
these two kinds. The language is as technical as it has to be: lift-off,
key-ins, food-tubes, screens, lenses, station, capsule. It is also exactly
expressive when it needs to convey the feelings of the astronauts, who
live for so long in the 'flight and nest' of their 'soaring metal' that they
become creatures of space and agree to sever their connection with earth:

> . . . — and it must be said they were —
> were cool and clear as they dismantled the station and —
> and gave their capsule such power that —
> that they launched themselves outwards —
> outwards in an impeccable trajectory, that band —
> that band of tranquil defiers, not to plant any —
> any home with roots but to keep a —
> a voyaging generation voyaging . . .

The astronauts are 'tranquil defiers' — tranquil in an access of mental
clarity induced by life in space, and defiers because they value a
collective life of continued voyaging in their perpetually mobile home
more than the safety of earth and, supposedly, more than the duty to
report on the work they were sent out to do. They prefer to follow to the
full the injunction given in 'Islands' (*P*, 180): 'Take the voyage out
then! Drink the milk of space!' The sense of excitement in the astronauts
as they reach agreement to launch themselves outwards is made vivid by
the run-on effect of repeating the last word or words of one line at the
beginning of the next. The romantic or epic assertion with which the
poem ends, affirming the life of quest, takes its authority not only from
the accelerating movement of the lines or the incantatory pressure of the
repetitions, but also, crucially, from the use of technical language by
which the experience is rendered plausible, even recognisable, to any
reader with an average knowledge of the history of space exploration. 'A
Home in Space' is a perfectly judged poem in which an ancient theme is
made totally new, in terms that might ingratiate it with the front page
of tomorrow's newspaper.

A newspaper provided the material for the 'Instamatic' poem 'Translunar Space 1972' (*P*, 211) which records the crewless two-year voyage
to Jupiter of Pioneer-10.

Aboard the capsule there is pictorial information about human life for the benefit of extra-terrestrial intelligence: a plaque shows a 'deodorized American man' and a woman 'obviously an inferior sort of the same species'. It is the method of the 'Instamatic' poems (*P*, 201–17) that the hand of the poet scarcely interferes with the given material, but here Morgan slips in:

> the male chauvinist pig
> has a sullen expression, and the woman
> is faintly smiling, so
> interplanetary intelligences may still have homework.

The scope for humour in space expands in 'The First Men on Mercury' (*P*, 259–60), which sets an astronaut as pompous, prejudiced and inadequate as the plaque on Pioneer-10, against a quizzically contemptuous Mercurian. The close-encounters situation opens with the earthman's stiff greeting: '– We come in peace from the third planet. / Would you take us to your leader?' Earthly self-importance vapourises to comedy when the Mercurian forces the earthling to swap languages:

> – I am the yuleeda. You see my hands,
> we carry no benner, we come in peace.
> The spaceways are all stretterhawn.

In a precociously rapid mastery of English – much better English than his stuffy visitor's – the Mercurian tells the earthman to push off home, a sadder and wiser man now ironically fluent in Mercurian. The moral itself – don't condescend to the natives – is less striking than the way in which Morgan dramatises it in the comic interplay of languages. Already in the sequence of nine poems called 'Interferences' (*P*, 243–48) he had experimented with language in relation to alien existence. In these poems the earthly and the alien do not confront each other; instead, the alien presence impacts on a selection of earthly moments and causes sudden deformations of language. The idea for the sequence seems to have come from the phenomenon of tektites, small glassy objects of unexplained origin found mainly in Czechoslovakia, Central Russia, Africa, Southeast Asia and Australia. In the poems of 'Interferences' the science fiction element is in the analogously small, inexplicable linguistic disruption that occurs usually at the end of each poem. The moments of interference include the flight of an arrow ('straight to its/targjx'), the conception of Christ ('I am your virgian bride'), the discovery of the 'Marie Celeste' ('where their ship is/the Mar Celste'), and a failed lift-off for a mission to Saturn ('wo de nat hove loft-iff').

When seven of the poems in 'Interferences' were originally published

in pamphlet form as *Poetry Glasgow 3* (Glasgow: Midnight Press, 1970)
they were accompanied by a note from the author:

> I hope the general idea of the poems is clear enough – it's the
> conception of 'other eyes watching' or intersecting worlds or planes
> of existence, each spot of intersection / interference being indicated
> by the spelling of a word suddenly going wrong.

These poems are more successful as quirkily original views of recognisable situations than as indicators of brief collisions with other worlds.
Like Morgan's *Newspoems* (*TV*, 61–112), they are a species of light
verse, whimsy from an unexpected source. (Language is more effective
in dramatising science fiction incident in 'Spacepoem 3: Off Course'
[*P*, 260] in which the scrambling of phrases associated with well-
regulated space flight enacts the disorder of a flight gone wrong.) The
key idea of the poems, however – the impact of the alien or the
intersection of different worlds – is the central notion in Morgan's three
most haunting science fiction narrative poems: 'In Sobieski's Shield'
(*P*, 181–3), 'From the Domain of Arnheim' (*P*, 183–4) and 'Memories
of Earth' (*P*, 327–38).

In a lecture entitled 'Scientific Thought in Fiction and in Fact',
Professor John Taylor gives a scientist's eye view of science fiction,
defining it as 'the art of making a scientific "if" interesting, a scientific
"if" being a postulate or a proposition of scientific form'.[3] 'In Sobieski's
Shield' is based on the postulate that it is possible to beam a person
through space by the method familiar to viewers of the television series,
Star Trek. If the recent miracles of satellite television and fax technology
bring such a process nearer credibility, it is scientifically still at least as
fantastic a proposition as a trip to the moon was in H.G. Wells's time.
Morgan uses the idea to trigger a meditation on change, identity and
the relationship between past and present. His fantasy is immediately
involving because he begins the first-person narrative *in medias res*, with
matters of fact simply told by the man who, with his wife and son, has
been dematerialised at source and rematerialised on a minor planet of a
sun in Sobieski's Shield (otherwise known as *Scutum Sobieskii*, a small
constellation in the Milky Way situated in the vicinity of the celestial
equator). The opening lines not only present a credible and engaging
scene in a plausible future setting but compel the reader into the matter
of the poem by making it necessary to infer. (The science fiction novelist
must do the same thing to hook his reader into believing the far-
fetched, but has more space and may adopt a more leisurely pace, as, for
example, Philip K. Dick in the opening scene of *Do Androids Dream of
Electric Sheep?* [1969].)[4] By the time we have inferred that there were
'prophets' on earth who foretold calamity, that the sun withdrew from

earth and many were frozen, and that our man in Sobieski's Shield made his shocking voyage out only a day before the earth went cold, we are ready to accept:

> . . . here we are now rematerialized
> . . . in our right mind I hope
> approximately though not unshaken.

Acceptance of the scientific 'if' is further eased by the touch of wryness that domesticates the process:

> in any case molecular reconstitution is no
> sinecure even with mice and I wouldn't have been
> utterly surprised if some of us had turned out
> mice or worse.

Morgan's strategy of involvement and his choice of register exploit but overshoot the merely fantastic, carrying us quickly into a sympathetic regard for the narrator in his predicament. Is he the same person still, even with only four fingers on his left hand? (His wife is 'hardly altered' apart from an 'extraordinarily strange and beautiful crown of bright red hair'; his son has come through with only one nipple and his voice has broken.) The answer appears to be that he is, that despite the shock of such traumatic re-birth he continues, evincing in the alien context of his 'second life' the best of human qualities. There is the tenderness of heart that marvels at his wife's new beauty as he draws her head into his arms, and marks the effects of the journey on his son:

> . . . when he speaks his boy's
> treble has broken and at thirteen he is a man
> what a limbo to lose childhood in where has
> it gone between the throwing of a switch and these
> alien iron hills across so many stars his blue eyes
> are the same but there's a new graveness of the
> second life.

There is the man's courage, his curiosity about the new environment of iron hills and lakes of mercury, and there is his deepened sense of the human bond prompted by the similarity of the new 'birthmark' on his right forearm to the tattoo on the arm of a dead person in the First World War. Above all there is his resilience as he prepares to leave the protective 'dome' and fare forward into new life in the unknown world. With the earth gone, love survives, the family survives, and history itself, in a terrible reminder of the war to end war, survives to beneficent, invigorating effect. There could be nothing more resolute

than the narrator's final, 'Let's go', nothing in the way of science fiction
more profoundly, hopefully human.

In Edgar Allan Poe's story. 'The Domain of Arnheim', the exception-
ally fortunate Mr Ellison speculates:

> There *may* be a class of beings, human once, but now invisible to
> humanity, to whom, from afar, our disorder may seem order – our
> unpicturesqueness picturesque; in a word the earth-angels, for
> whose scrutiny more especially than our own, and for whose death-
> refined appreciation of the beautiful, may have been set in array by
> God the wide landscape-gardens of the hemispheres.[5]

The beings who visit Morgan's Domain of Arnheim are, apparently, an
advanced class of humans with the power to see what happens on a
different time-scale from their own. What they see is a primitive,
earthly people in a state of seeming disorder, naked, singing to drums
and trumpets, kissing, 'burning fires of trash and mammoths' bones'.
Suddenly it is clear to these visiting 'earth-angels' that it is not disorder
they are witnessing but the celebration of a birth:

> . . . The crying
> came from one just born: that was the cause
> of the song. We saw it now. What had we stopped
> but joy?

They do not stop the joy for long. To the primitive celebrants the
invisible alien visitors are no more than 'a displacement of the air',
sufficient to attract a firebrand thrown in their direction by a sweating
trumpeter, but incapable of impinging more substantially across the
time warp upon the consciousness of a vitally secular and self-sufficient
people who will not be intimidated by other-worldly interference.
These primitive men and women are, after all, the superior beings
because, as Morgan says, 'They are going to survive, not frightened by
what to them appear to be alien spirits, gods. They have no gods: in a
sense they are going to make or be themselves the gods' (*Akros*, 22). It
is the memory of individual courage in the trumpeter and collective
energy in the group that haunts the narrator when he has returned
home. Once more Morgan has used the genre of science fiction to
express a positive view of the human condition.

Visitors to earth are haunted again in 'Memories of Earth', in which
Morgan achieves both astounding science fiction and an aesthetic hat-
trick. It is a science fiction poem; it is a relatively long narrative poem;
it is written in the medium of continuous blank verse. It is the story of
another voyage out which, like the voyages in 'A Home in Space', 'In
Sobieski's Shield' and 'From the Domain of Arnheim' modifies the
travellers' consciousness by putting their value systems to a painful test.

Now, even more so than in 'From the Domain of Arnheim', it is recognisable earth which is the alien place and again it is the visitors who are chastened, haunted and enlarged by what we may call – co-opting a phrase from Poe's Mr Ellison – an extra-terrestrially refined appreciation of the beautiful. Here the beautiful is something the visitor can see in landscapes – desert, moor or ocean – or in the sight and sound of Wordsworth musing upon Snowdon in the company of Robert Jones and the shepherd with his lurcher (the reference is to *The Prelude*, Book Fourteen), or in the love that even Auschwitz cannot extinguish, or in the frailty of a white butterfly, or in a canoe of Polynesian men, women and children rowing across the Pacific.

Morgan has fun with physics in the sequence of six 'Particle Poems' in *Star Gate* (P, 386–8). In 'Memories of Earth' he uses the idea of the particle scientifically, given that even a complicated system like the earth may be treated as a particle for many purposes of astronomy. The invention of the poem begins with a shift in scale that makes the earth a sub-atomic particle, perhaps an electron in perpetual spin round the nucleus of an atom of stone. Signals emitted by the stone have been detected by the Council of a remote, cold-blooded, authoritarian society. Hlad, Kort, Hazmon, Baltaz, and the narrator Erlkon have been despatched to investigate. Their instructions are clear:

> Keep your report formal, said the Council,
> your evidence is for the memory-banks,
> not for crude wonder or cruder appraisal.

So the discredited explorers meet in secret, listen to the tapes of their expedition and 'study how to change this life', home safely but, like T.S. Eliot's Magi, no longer at ease in the old dispensation, aliens now in their own place.

The power of 'Memories of Earth' is first felt in the precision with which Morgan imagines the narrator's attempt to describe the miniaturis-ation process that shrinks the Brobdignagian travellers to micro-Lilliputian size so that they may enter first the stone, then the smaller entities inside it:

> The shrinking must be done by stages, but
> even so it comes with a rush, doesn't
> feel like shrinking. Rather it's the landscape
> explodes upwards, outwards, the waves rise up
> and loom like waterfalls, and where we stand
> our stone blots out the light above us, a crag
> pitted with caves and tunnels, immovable
> yet somehow less solid.

Once the travellers are inside the stone the real action of the narrative is the conflict between the Council's demand for drily scientific reportage and the pull of earth's gravity of value, passion and beauty. The special pleasures of the work are the ease and exactness with which Morgan describes complex processes, the fresh perspectives he provides, and the triumph over cold injunction of our spinning particle of earth, intransigently ambiguous, beautiful, violent, frail, self-tormenting and self-renewing.

In the kaleidoscopic sequence of *Sonnets from Scotland* (*TV*, 139–66) are several poems in which the malleabilities of time and space associated with science fiction are used to afford surprising perspectives of Scotland and the planet earth. The brief narrative of 'The Coin' (*TV*, 162) is told by one of an unidentified group who find a One Pound coin bearing the head of a red deer and the words *Respublica Scotorum*. How can this be? The answer is implicit in lines 12–13 of the sonnet: 'The marshy scurf crept up to our machine, / sucked at our boots.' A machine has brought space travellers to land on the earth of a remotely future Scotland, at a time when an independent Scottish state has been in existence long enough for a coin of its realm to have had its date rubbed off by successions of fingers. The race is now 'silent', which suggests that the state may have had its day, but can we be sure? The poem ends: '. . . Yet nothing seemed ill-starred. / And least of all the realm the coin contained.' A star, good or ill, suggests a destiny, a future. Perhaps the race is only silent because the people are hidden from view. The visitors will look up from the well-worn coin to face the scrutiny of Scots whose 'yuleeda' will be waiting to try languages with them in Edinburgh, not London. A less sanguine prospect presents itself in 'On Jupiter' (*TV*, 164), where what might be 'a simulacrum, a dissolving view' of Scotland is found:

> . . . as solid as a terrier
> shaking itself dry from a brisk swim
> in the reservoir of Jupiter's grim
> crimson trustless eye.

If the gods or people of Jupiter have made this Scotland, they have abandoned it: 'its launchers were asleep, or had withdrawn, / throwing their stick into a sea of doubt.' So, a brief science fiction fantasy in the form of a sonnet becomes a metaphor for questions about the reality of Scotland, its gods, its people, and the sea of self-doubt that encircles it. It is another, oblique reference to 'the strong, sick dirkless Angel' that groans and shivers in the poem 'Post-Referendum' (*TV*, 155).

In the last of the *Sonnets from Scotland*, 'The Summons' (*TV*, 166), visitors to earth are surprised that they find it difficult to leave the planet ('Despite our countdown, we were loath to go'). 'They have', says Morgan, 'become more involved than they thought they would. They don't understand their emotional reaction. They take with them perhaps a kind of love'.[6] The love, we may say, is Morgan's own love of the earth, a wondering, wise love that only a fool would call facile. If his pleasure in science and technology is evident throughout his writing, the sonnet 'Computer Error: Neutron Strike' (*TV*, 161) graphically acknowledges the supreme peril that comes with modern science. The possibility of total destruction is, after all, the nightmare distinction of our time:

> No one was left to hear the long All Clear.
> Hot wind swept through the streets of Aberdeen
> and stirred the corpse-clogged harbour. Each machine,
> each building, tank, car, college, crane, stood sheer
> and clean but that a shred of skin, a hand,
> a blackened child driven like tumbleweed
> would give the lack of ruins leave to feed
> on horrors we were slow to understand
> but did.

'Take me / out of this earth, Erlkon, take me away', cries Baltaz in 'Memories of Earth', appalled by the horrors of the Nazi concentration camp. Differently motivated, the astronauts of 'A Home in Space' agree to 'cut communication with / with the earth base'. Morgan can imagine such characters but could never be one. His science fiction poems delight in the ways and means of present and future science for their own special beauty and, fundamentally, for the expanded awareness of earth and of human potential they can provide. Space beckons – we must take the voyage out – but the return is eternal (or earth goes too, as in the haunted imagination of the narrator of 'In Sobieski's Shield'). Among 'The Moons of Jupiter' (*Star Gate*, *P*, 393–7) only Ganymede is possibly benign. For Robert Frost, swinger of birches, earth was the right place for love; for Edwin Morgan, astronaut and time-traveller, 'Earth is again the centre / and the favoured place' (*P*, 386).

NOTES

1. Kurt Vonnegut, *God Bless You, Mr Rosewater* (New York: Holt, Rinehart and Winston, 1965), p.27.
2. C.P. Snow, *The Two Cultures and the Scientific Revolution* (London: Cambridge University Press, 1959), p.16.

3. John Taylor, 'Scientific Thought in Fiction and in Fact' in P. Nicholls, ed., *Science Fiction at Large* (London: Gollancz, 1976), pp. 57–62.
4. Philip K. Dick, *Do Androids Dream of Electric Sheep?* (London: Rapp and Whiting, 1969).
5. Edgar Allan Poe, 'The Domain of Arnheim' in *Tales of Mystery and Imagination* (London and Toronto: J.M. Dent, 1908), pp. 36–7.
6. Lesley Duncan, 'Poet's place for looking out at the universe'. *Glasgow Herald*, 1 December 1984, p. 7.

Six

Morgan's Words

W.N. Herbert

Hugh MacDiarmid once had occasion to refer to the 'tenacity of Scots'. He was making a partisan point about 'the way even educated people lapse into it on convenient occasions, or when they are genuinely moved . . .' but the issue continues to be relevant, particularly in the case of Scottish poetry.[1] When we observe the fragmentation of poetic language in contemporary Scotland, it is tempting to assume that 'Scots' is more than a linguistic entity, it is an attitude towards language. How else should we explain the extremes of dialectal idiosyncrasy, formalism and anti-formalism in conventional English, and the array of experimental poets, from the page-thirled existentialism of W.S. Graham to the language of Ian Hamilton Finlay, liberated into the very landscape (indeed, attacking the 'infection' of bureaucratic English)?

No contemporary Scottish poet embodies these disparate strains to the same degree as Edwin Morgan. R.B. Kitaj might be speaking for him when he says 'Two crazy polarities introduced by modernism are that you can do anything (Picasso, Matisse) and that you must stick to a tight (stylistic) corner. I prefer the first craziness to the much safer second one.'[2] Morgan has attempted to respond to the successive waves of the communications explosion. He has created forms which mimic modern technology's mouthpieces, tape, videotape, the photograph, the headline, the computer; he has participated in the concrete poetry movement, and invented his own extra-terrestrial (and sub-aquatic) gibberish. He has even put himself in the stylistic corner of the sonnet for several extended sequences. The obvious question is: to what extent is this because he is Scottish, and how far does his work exhibit a Scottish attitude towards language?

Several of Morgan's criticial essays, interviews, introductions and so on, seem to sketch out a critical framework within which we can attempt to answer this. It is the main intention of this essay to isolate this framework, and then use it to examine Morgan's main genres.

In the Warton Lecture *Provenance and Problematics of 'Sublime and Alarming Images' in Poetry*, Morgan makes a spirited attempt to redefine eighteenth- and nineteenth-century concepts of the sublime in relation to twentieth-century poetics: 'Does the idea survive in other, possibly disguised forms or formulations?' (*PP*, 306). What is noticeable among the expected names of Wordsworth, Dickens and Hardy is the number of Scottish poets and the emphasis he gives to them. Figures like Macpherson and Thomson form important links in the chain that leads to Pound and MacDiarmid, and in isolating aspects of the sublime in these poets he can also be said to be hypothesising a Scottish sublime. He draws attention to

> . . . a reconsideration of Macpherson's achievement in terms of a Tolkein-like creation of an imaginary but self-consistent world – a world which never really existed in either Scottish or Irish history or legend but which was devised to fit the shadowy, portentous workings of the pre-Romantic imagination. (*PP*, 294–5)

When we relate this remark to his closing comments, it is possible to suggest that a critical space is being opened for his own imaginary worlds:

> Perhaps the sublime is being reborn in science fiction, and the last refuge of the sublime is in the stars. The popularity of this genre, in fact, probably indicates that it is fulfilling a need not otherwise supplied. No doubt poets have to do what they have to do, but it would be surprising if sooner or later some of them did not find ways of reintroducing a note of acceptable grandeur. (*PP*, 313)

A work like *Sonnets from Scotland*, to echo Morgan's ringing phrase, clearly reintroduces a note of acceptable grandeur, but there are other ways in which science fiction poetry has become, in his hands, a Scottish genre.

Anyone brought up in Scotland is aware of the troublesome interface between its two main vocabularies, Scots and English. The Cox report has recently created debate by suggesting that British children should be taught certain basics about the history of their language, including its many variants, but this has long been a Scottish issue.[3] The linguistic self-mutilation enacted by such illustrious Scotsmen as David Hume and Tobias Smollett, R.L. Stevenson's scrupulous creation of his 'style' and Hugh MacDiarmid's various apologies for his 'incorrigibly maladroit terminology' all suggest that a verbal supersensitivity is one continuing trait of the Scottish sensibility. It is not altogether surprising, then, to find that the social hierarchy of language, as well as the anomie of those who stand at a self-conscious remove from it, forms a major theme in Morgan's science fiction poems.

'The First Men on Mercury' has been frequently discussed, but not, I think, in terms of this particular allegory. Like Scott's introduction to *Ivanhoe*, in which there is a surreptitious invitation to read Saxon v. Norman as Scots v. English and business as usual, there is an implicit suggestion in the sound of the Mercurian dialect that it is reflecting an English prejudice as to the sound of Glaswegian, even down to a stereotypical hint of drunkenness.[4] If we compare lines of Mercurian with some from 'Good Friday' then this becomes clearer: 'Bawr stretter! Bawr, Bawr. Stretterhawl?' '– Oh tha's, tha's all right, see I've/got to get some Easter eggs for the kiddies . . .' 'Gawl horrop. Bawr, Abawrhannahanna!' '. . . the working man/has nae education, he jist canny – jist/hasny got it, know what I mean . . .' (*P*, 259–60; 145–6).

According to this reading, the poem satisfies a Scottish fantasy; the Earthmen are condescending and imperialist dolts, outwitted by some power of the enigmatic, anti-authoritarian Mercurians that they cannot even comprehend, but which seems to be inherent in their ability to appropriate and redirect language. It is this ability which is celebrated in the *Sonnets from Scotland*, not just in such *tours-de-force* as 'Colloquy in Glaschu', in which three languages (five if you count 'gallus kern') splash together. In 'The Picts', Morgan suddenly flashes the phrase '*diuperr cartait*', employing one of the very few non-Indo-European Pictish words (*cartait* = pin) whose meaning is known to us, and flashes it in a bawdy usage! As the first line of this sonnet says, 'Names as from outer space . . .' (*TV*, 145).

In his introduction to the anthology *Scottish Satirical Verse*, Morgan again attempts to define his terminology in national terms. The question raised by our 'much fragmented national consciousness' is seen as 'whether any vacuum left by its being demolished would be better than falling into the traps of replacement ideologies' (*SSV*, xii). This again places Scotland in the role of archetypal modern culture. MacDiarmid's invention of a calvinistic communism perhaps constituted a more open response to the twentieth century than Eliot's discovery of the Anglican religion. For Morgan, though, the issue raised by any replacement ideology is more complex: one must first of all square it with tradition, yes, but then it must be balanced with what seems to be his strong need for a sense of artistic freedom. He therefore makes the spirited but guarded declaration 'A vacuum can be a merry place, and the Scottish gift for satire – perhaps it is a curse, disguised by the Little People as a gift – has filled it with an extraordinary variety of raillery'

(*SSV*, xii). Principal among this variety is the flyting, and in his discussion of this genre Morgan again makes a link between national identity and attitude towards language: 'Fantasy, catalogues, and a peculiarly Scottish kind of satire called the flyting . . .' (*SSV*, xvii).

The role of fantasy in Morgan's work extends beyond the science fiction work into the realm of Landor's *Imaginary Dialogues*, from *The Vision of Cathkin Braes*, and 'Ingram Lake', through *The Whittrick* to the series of dramatic monologues from recent years, 'Instructions to an Actor', 'The Archaeopteryx's Song', 'Eve and Adam', 'Grendel', 'Tarkovsky in Glasgow', 'Jack London in Heaven' (*P*, 27, 35, 67, 406, 434, 435, 436, 438). All of these poems share a desire to give a voice to some silent thing or become someone's voice; as he said of his development in the 1960s:

> I learned, really learned for the first time, however much I may
> have thought I believed it intellectually, that you can write poetry
> about anything. You really can! The world, history, society,
> everything in it, pleads to become a voice, voices! (*Gairfish*, 58)

This concern with finding a voice for something dumb, or borrowing someone's voice in order to induce a change of perspective in the reader, forcibly recalls the elegiac anger of the essay 'Registering the Reality of Scotland' at the equation between political power and linguistic survival:

> When one lives in one of the linguistically untidy places, the
> consciousness of this attritional process is what stabs the heart.
> Everyone knows that languages, like moas and dinosaurs, do die.
> What stories did the Etruscans tell their children? Or the Easter
> Islanders? Their dumb scripts fill us with rage and pity. (*E*, 153–4)

This is a passionate declaration, and there is a great deal of passion in some of Morgan's reclamations of voice, and behind his attempts to make merry in the vacuum. In 'Byron at Sixty-Five', the device of Byron's surviving Missolonghi opens up an alternative perspective of history that re-emphasises Byron's Scottishness, hints at that as a source of his radicalism, and creates a persona that points to Morgan's decidedly unPrufrockian approach to ageing:

> Babbage and Marx – can that be what's to come?
> Machines to compute, and all the workers free?
> My dear contessa, what a maximum
> Of bliss it would be to come back and see –
> To burn the dungeons that have made men dumb,
> And wade whole rivers to the liberty tree.
> Burns said *I guess an' fear*. Ah when we do,
> Mark then and shape the new life thundering through
>   (*TV*, 41)

The formal decision to write in *ottava rima* reminds us, perhaps, that, like the Standard Habbie, this is a Scots measure, borrowed by Byron from William Tennant's poem 'Anster Fair'.[5]

Morgan and catalogues, and the comic potential therein! Perhaps the easiest way to illustrate his sense of the magical life of the list is to list his uses of it in *Themes on a Variation*.

'Nineteen Kinds of Barley' is celebratory with a kind of epic tone, playing on the gap between an individual strain's characteristics, and the associative strands it has for a layperson: '*Celt* was a harp of cobwebs; when they plucked him in the morning he yielded creaks and shivers, a scrape of pure mildew.' Of course several have strong Scottish associations, one of which, at least, would appear to be literary; *Kym*'s father Kandym 'stalked the wastelands', rather as MacDiarmid did in 'My Songs are Kandym in the Waste Land' (*TV*, 30–31).

In 'A Trace of Wings' the purpose is elegiac; again the focus is on language, this time punning on Basil Bunting's name to produce a definition of him in bird-watching terms: 'the sweetest singer; prince of finches; gone from these parts'. By placing this at the end of a list of kennings for other 'Buntings', Morgan induces a sudden shift of perspective that is both witty and profound (*TV*, 32).

'The Hanging Gardens of Babylon' is a celebratory list of absurd variations on its title that ranges the British and other isles in order to arrive at its birthday message to John Furnival, 'the halcyon galleys of furnival'. 'A Bobbed Sonnet for Code Bobber' works in a similar manner toward a similar end (*TV*, 33–5). 'Rules for Dwarf-Throwing' however, returns us to the questions of *Scottish Satirical Verse*: 'It has always been the central paradox of satire that the better it is the less unambiguous is the trajectory of attack . . .' (*SSV*, xvi–xvii). Quite so: 'If dwarfs are thrown at night, they may be painted with phosphorescent paint, so that the point of impact may be clearly established . . .' (*TV*, 51). As Morgan says,

> But what if the problem is less intellectual, and inheres more in the bizarre nature of the whole world a satire presents? Satire needs a good going fiction, but where does fantasy take over, and what gives Scottish satire its marked fondness for the grotesque? (*SSV*, xvii)

Judging from Morgan's uses of satire, one answer to this might be attention to language, and in particular a heightened awareness of those points at which normal discourse breaks down, allowing a different order of communication to take over. In 'The Starlings in George Square' the actions of the indestructible urban birds are depicted as a cloud of Morgan's beloved interferences, settling on the 'useful' language of bureaucracy and creating chaos:

At the General Post Office
the clerks write Three Pounds Starling in the savings-books.

. . .

And as for the City Information Bureau –
I'm sorry I can't quite chirrup did you twit –
No I wanted to twee but perhaps you can't cheep –   (*P*, 147)

Morgan's discussion of the flyting concludes with a reference to the
darker side of chaos, to the force of language as a destructive and not
just as a liberating agency: 'in part at least it may be regarded as a
ritualized, aestheticized survival of the belief in bardic power, anciently
shown in the superstitious conviction that an enemy could be "rhymed
to death" . . .' (*SSV*, xvii–xviii). Whilst Morgan's stance has tended to
avoid what he called in 'MacDiarmid Embattled', 'a poetry of hatred'
(*E*, 199), he certainly shares with that poet a powerful dislike of
inhibitive factors in Scottish psychology and politics, and has occasionally given vent to this dislike, as in the concise blast of 'The Flowers of
Scotland':

> . . . a Scottish National Party that refuses to discuss Vietnam and
>   is even applauded for doing so, do they think no lesson is to
>   be learned from what is going on there? –
>
> . . .
>
> and by contrast the massive indifference to the slow death of the
>   Clyde estuary, decline of resorts, loss of steamers, anaemia
>   of yachting, cancer of monstrous installations of a foreign
>   power and an acquiescent government – what is the smell of
>   death on a child's spade, any more than rats to leaded
>   lights? (*P*, 188–9)

But his most characteristic response to such abuses may be located in
language. A poem like 'Canedolia' is comic, celebratory, compendious,
'off-concrete', but it is also a kind of massive flyting, to be read as an
alternative to the frightening drabness of 'The Flowers of Scotland',
'*what is the best of the country?* / blinkbonny! airgold! thundergay!' It also
stands as a black portrait of a nation slightly out of touch with itself: '*tell
us about last night* / well, we had a wee ferintosh and we lay on the
quirang, it was pure strontian!' (*P*, 138). The level of near-pun the
poem has been operating on brings the small village on Loch Sunart
dangerously close to an ingredient in radioactive fall-out, strontium-90.

Edwin Morgan's response to his own Scottishness has always been
marked by a certain ambiguity, a refusal to play the partisan. In the
Akros interview he gave to Marshall Walker, he talks about this
question at some length:

> If you are a Scot then you are a Scot and you have certain problems
> that come with the territory and you can't entirely solve these no
> matter what you do. I think it has in the past . . . been an incubus
> in the sense that writers have often had to keep trying to prove in
> some kind of way that they are Scottish and have not written as
> freely and naturally as they ought to have been able to write.
> (*Akros*, 19)

One way in which this issue has impinged on Morgan's poetics is
certainly linguistic; at an early point he apparently took a decision to
maintain a distinction between the separate languages he used, reserving
English for all personal subjects or wherever a narrative voice was
required. Literary Scots and the Glaswegian dialect are used exclusively
for purposes of translation or in reported speech, and all experimentation
with language is encompassed in concrete or the sub-genre he has
termed off-concrete. This is not to say there are not constant intrusions
of Scots or off-concrete touches in his English poetry – on the contrary,
these are distinctive hallmarks of Morgan's atentiveness to language, as
in Jack London's irritated reaction to Heaven's routines, 'I was up at
four / for psalms, shawms, smarms, salaams, yessirs, yesmaams', or the
moving conclusion of 'Pilate at Fortingall', who 'washed his hands, and
watched his hands, and washed / his hands, and watched his hands, and
washed his hands . . .' (*P*, 438; *TV*, 144). But Morgan is a chameleon
who chooses his settings carefully, and, as his comments on *Wi the Haill
Voice* suggest, is not always to be trusted:

> The actual decision you make as to what you're going to write
> about or what technique you are going to use are not always
> recoverable afterwards. I'm not *quite* sure why I translated
> Mayakovsky into Scots. I do give reasons in the book itself and I'm
> quite sure these are true, but I'm not sure whether they're the
> whole truth. It's very hard to get at the whole truth in these
> matters and I think that probably there's a mixture of artistic and
> national or patriotic motives at work . . . (*Akros*, 20)

I'm not sure that this is the whole truth either. Morgan's impersona-
tion of MacDiarmid in *The Whittrick* may just be an attempt to claim
that elusive creature for Scotland, but it is also in a very personal and
fluid voice which sounds nothing like MacDiarmid. When Morgan
employs Scots, he not only has a very individual attitude as to what it
should be, he also displays an original and idealistic vision. The tale of
the whittricks' wake, though not the most powerful scene in that book,
certainly suggests a formula: as Henryson's Cresseid is to Chaucer's, so
should we see MacDiarmid's wake to Joyce's. Except the language
belongs to Morgan:

It wes the Schipka Pass, the gas
Wes peeferin-pufferin in and oot, blue licht
That gied a dwaiblie warsle wi the grey grekin
O fowr o' clock i the mornin. Sheddas flauchtert
Skairlike ower the stanes. I heard an unco fuffin
But it wisna fae the gaslicht, and it wisna
Fae my ain breist; it wes a whittrick-fuffin. Hoot-
Toot and hadna my steps stummelt here on a wake,
A whittricks' wake, for yonder I saw the cratur
Ligg on a peever-scartit stane as stiff's a rake!
Maist horridable wes the caunle they had set
In the deid's yin's gruntle: thon wes a tozie glim.
Aa roon aboot in their solemneezin stacher
Scampert ten jinkin hiccupin cousin-whittricks,
A queer ill-sortit sosherie of usquebaugh,
Lugubriositie, and fancy-fuddickin.   (P, 68–9)

The whittrick is, of course, the symbol of Morgan's interface, that
point between languages at which new possibilities emerge. To borrow
William Burroughs's famous (and borrowed) concept of the third mind,
it might be suggested that the whittrick speaks in a language formed
when standard English collides with spoken Scots.[6] This third language
appears to be what interested Morgan about concrete poetry:

> I think I wanted to see what concrete poetry was up to in relation
> to poetry in general. It wasn't that I just switched over to concrete
> poetry as a way of producing instantaneous images – that was part
> of it – but I think I also wanted to see if there was some kind of
> common ground between it and linear poetry. Quite a number of
> my poems are exploring that half-way house, not strictly concrete
> and not strictly linear but mixing the two . . . (Akros, 3–4)

That last sentence seems to defy the MacDiarmid of 'I'll ha'e nae
hauf-wey hoose', who saw concrete poetry as a 'very questionable
international development' despite having written an extremely off-
concrete poem ('On a Lone Shore') over forty years before.[7] In poems like
'The Loch Ness Monster's Song' and the beautiful 'Caliban Falls Asleep
in the Isle Full of Noises', Morgan seems to be stirring the same pre-
Chomskian broth that MacDiarmid tasted in 'Gairmscoile', trying to
find voices for 'scaut-heid / Skrymmorie monsters':

grobravara hollaglob / ban ban cacaliban
thargarbonder skeeloheera / ban ban cacaliban
twing fang kong-pan-lang / ban ban cacaliban
stegzerbogzer stravavoorian / ban ban cacaliban   (P, 237: 427)

There is a sense, then, in which Morgan's sound poetry is a kind of literary dialect, combining Scots sound-units – 'gar', 'skeel', 'lang', 'strav' (as in 'stravaig') – with those of other languages, principally East European I would suggest, though he has translated so much from so many languages that the mix is Joycean. Characteristically, he eschews Joyce's high culture pretensions, though this has left him open to charges of triviality, modishness, and, ironically, cerebrality. One response to these charges might be to emphasise the passionate and compassionate aspects of Morgan's play, as he himself does in recounting the genesis of one of the emergent poems:

> 'Message Clear' really forced itself on me as an experience. It was almost written involuntarily. That is most unlike the usual method of writing a concrete poem. It came to me in the old sense in which poems were said to be inspired. . . . [It] was written when my father was very ill, dying of cancer, and I was coming home from the hospital. Suddenly this line 'I am the resurrection and the life' came into my head and then the poem began to emerge from the line. I think about half of it was in my head going home on the bus and I had to come in and write down as much of it as I could right away before it disappeared . . . (*Akros*, 6)

This sets up a very Morganic relationship between 'Message Clear' and that other moment of elegiac satori, 'The Watergaw'. But his work as a whole exhibits a concern to find those messages in things which have been overlooked because of the status of those things. There's something of the cabbalist in this and something of the pop artist, but principally, I think, there's something Scottish in it, a response to a long-term oppression so insidious as to have become a sub-conscious habit in the Scots themselves. Morgan's search for voices represents an enormous freedom from that oppression.

It is in this sense, I think, that we should take his comment that 'The artist is partly there like the shaman of the tribe to record what is happening, telling the tribe's history . . .' (*Akros*, 11). His discriminations among shades of sound and meaning displays a concern to discover distinctness amongst human values, to distinguish, in both senses of that work, the identity of an important unit, be it the individual or the city, the nation or the species.

NOTES

1. C.M. Grieve, *Albyn or Scotland and the Future* (London: Kegan Paul, Trench, Trubner, 1927), p.50.
2. John Ashbery, Joe Shannon, Jane Livingstone, Timothy Hyman,

    Kitaj: Paintings, Drawings, Pastels (London: Thames and Hudson, 1983), p.45.
3. See Roger Knight, 'A utopian English'. *Guardian*, 25 July 1989, p.21.
4. *Ivanhoe* (Oxford: Oxford University Press, 1912), pp.xi–xii.
5. 'The Comic Poems of William Tennant'. *ScotLit* 1, March 1989, p.3.
6. William S. Burroughs and Brion Gysin, *The Third Mind* (London: John Calder, 1979), p.25.
7. *The Letters of Hugh MacDiarmid*, Alan Bold ed. (London: Hamish Hamilton, 1984), p.872; Hugh MacDiarmid, *Complete Poems 1920–1976*, Michael Grieve and W.R. Aitken eds, (London: Martin Brian & O'Keeffe, 1978), II, p.1232.

Seven

Morgan's Sonnets

Douglas Dunn

High Culture, in one of its most precious forms, encounters the issues of
Glasgow in Edwin Morgan's 'Glasgow Sonnets' (*P*, 283–6). Considering
the myth of Glasgow that prevailed elsewhere in 1972 (and it might
still persist), the title is almost an oxymoron. Form by itself asks
questions, makes statements, and lays down challenges; 'Inappropriate?
– But why do you think so?' Or 'Appropriate! – But why do you think it
isn't?' Or 'Here's metrical engineering for you!'

His formalism fits in with the stylistic variousness of his other poetry.
There is an obvious relish in performance and an impression of enjoying
the extent to which he can shoulder his way free of constraints while
remaining true to the correctness of octave and sestet, which his sonnets
identify fastidiously. 'Glasgow Sonnets' especially creates an atmosphere
in which each poem feels like a verbal fist in which the immediacy and
passion of his concerns squeeze the form until its pips squeak.

> A mean wind wanders through the backcourt trash.
> Hackles on puddles rise, old mattresses
> puff briefly and subside. Play-fortresses
> of brick and bric-a-brac spill out some ash.
> Four storeys have no windows left to smash,
> but in the fifth a chipped sill buttresses
> mother and daughter the last mistresses
> of that black block condemned to stand, not crash.
>
> ('Glasgow Sonnets' *i*)

Disciplined indignation and descriptive force are offered by the two
rhymes and three couplets of that octave and Morgan clearly seizes their
opportunity.

Much of his metrical writing tackles difficult forms – *ottava rima* in
'Byron at Sixty-Five' (*TV*, 37–41), the more simple intricacy of
'Stanzas' (*TV*, 16–21), as well as 'New Year Sonnets', 'Jordanstone
Sonnets', (*P*, 425–6), and 'The Bench' (*TV*, 28–9). A poetic temperament given to 'variations', to transformation and metamorphosis is one
that is also dissatisfied with sameness, stasis, the familiar and the
unexceptional. *None* of his sequences leaves the sonnet alone or fails to
use it more vigorously than it is accustomed to. In 'Glasgow Sonnets' he
enjoys the vindictive ingenuity of its concussive rhymes, the solidity of
an argumentative structure from which a tone of authority can be
borrowed or won, and, ironically, the extent to which Glaswegian
topicality disparages the sonnet's temporal affiliation with orthodoxy.
That last point might be illuminated by Hölderlin's epigram 'Advocatus
Diaboli':[1]

> Deep in my heart I abhor the nexus of rulers
> and clerics,
> Yet more deeply I loathe genius in league
> with that gang.

Form is not entirely disinterested, or not always; and if it is difficult to
prove (or disprove) the shadowy politics of poetic form, then a
contemporary poet might take care to ensure that his gift is not in
league with the taste of Hölderlin's 'nexus of rulers and clerics'.

Differentiating between Morgan's performance in his sonnets and the
ingenuity of 'Shaker Shaken' (*P*, 351), 'Particle Poems' (*P*, 386), or
'The First Men on Mercury (*P*, 259) and a number of others, involves
the drawing of fine distinctions which are difficult to sustain. It is a
question of humour, for example, only if you refuse to accept the use of
comedy for serious purposes. Clearly, the painstaking puzzle-solving
of 'Shaker Shaken' benefits from the skills that make Morgan's sonnets
feasible, and vice versa. It is shaky ground, perhaps, for only Morgan
has written in the manner of 'Shaker Shaken', but that very uniqueness
could be what adds the exceptional quality to his sonnets. For they *are*
unusual. Morgan steps into a form, uses it wilfully in a manner to which
it is unfamiliar, and then steps away from it, leaving it in a state of
revision. There are consequences here that have to be taken into
account. More than most poets, Morgan is a writer of what appear to be
self-conscious technical decisions. He is a poet of 'the good idea', often
strung out sequentially as in *From the Video Box* (*TV*, 115–38). He is a
poet of convictions as much as of strong feelings. He is compassionate,
but impatient with pity, as if it is subordinated to the *praxis* of an

ideology of optimism. He is interested in science, its imagination and fictions. There is little hospitality to nature in his work: rarely does he surrender to a landscape. There is a strong element of the histrionic to his poetry. He is altogether an extremely self-consicous poet, and most, perhaps all of the various ingredients in his poetry are at odds with prevailing orthodoxy, or it is at odds with them.

Thematically and technically, 'Glasgow Sonnets' is less distant from these other concerns than might be supposed. Although more identifiable as sonnets than much recent writing in the form – and this seems a significant aspect of his tactic – they go hand in hand with what the rest of his work means, as does *Sonnets from Scotland* (*TV*, 139–66). In that way they are experimental, exceptional and unorthodox. For example, his criticism of MacDiarmid's characteristic view of Glasgow:

> Hugh MacDiarmid forgot
> in 'Glasgow 1960' that the feast
> of reason and the flow of soul has [*sic*] ceased
> to matter to the long unfinished plot
> of heating frozen hands. ('Glasgow Sonnets' *iv*)

Or the reprimand of *v*:

> 'Let them eat cake' made no bones about it.
> But we say let them eat the hope deferred
> and that will sicken them. We have preferred
> silent slipways to the riveters' wit.
> And don't deny it – that's the ugly bit.

Some passages of 'Glasgow Sonnets' feel like revolutionary speeches delivered on the premises of a hostile institution. What he *says* is unexpected, critical. His attack on 'sticky-fingered mock-Venetianists', for example, while local to Glasgow's architecture and its defenders, strikes out towards a general meaning which would be at home in the gestural contemporaneity of his non-traditional forms.

> Prop up's the motto. Splint the dying age.
> Never displease the watchers from the grave.
> Great when fake architecture was the rage,
> but greater still to see what you can save.
> The gutted double fake meets the adage:
> a wig's the thing to beat both beard and shave.
> ('Glasgow Sonnets' *vii*)

Anachronism might be Morgan's enemy in a sense that is too

downright to sustain intellectually and empirically. It is the area of his work where he overstates. A subjective interpretation is imposed on the municipality:

> Meanwhile the flyovers breed loops of light
> in curves that would have ravished tragic Toshy –
> clean and unpompous, nothing wishy-washy.
> Vistas swim out from the bulldozer's bite
> by day, and banks of earthbound stars at night
> begin. In Madame Emé's Sauchie Haugh, she
> could never gain in leaves or larks or sploshy
> lanes what's lost in a dead boarded site –
> the life that overspill is overkill to.
>
> ('Glasgow Sonnets' *viii*)

Wholeheartedly urban, Morgan risks denigrating suburb and country-side, lark, leaf and lane. They fail to compensate for a gutted city: 'Less is not more, and garden cities are / the flimsiest oxymoron to distil to,' he states, with a conviction that underlines the urban quality of his temperament and imagination, while a spirit of advocacy seems to contradict the last line of *xi* – 'Man and the sea make cities as they must.' Urban potential, in any case, is asserted in spite of slum-life and its deformations and the economic exploitation that makes them possible.

His dismissal of 'garden city' as 'the flimsiest oxymoron' does little more than signal controversy and that one overview of urbanity (Morgan's) is confronting another (the municipality's). Utopian capital-ism, Utopian socialism and post-war town planning departments constituted a heady brew. The professional optimism of the latter proved to be misplaced when controlled by a psychology addicted to dividing society into Them and Us. Morgan's psychology is not much better – it is Them and Me; or, rather, it is still a matter of Them and Us because the reader is enlisted under the banner of a guilty third-person plural. 'And who wants to distil?' Rhetoric leads him to repeat his own interpretation, like a politician. He disregards the possibility of how a transaction between country and city, weekend and working week, attractive and unattractive, the natural and the industrial, might, for many, be preferable to monolithic architecture designed by an ideology infatuated with the new. It is not conservative to say so; it is simply to acknowledge human desire, and to insist that it be consulted, that it be not just taken into the reckoning, but that it *be* the reckoning.

> And who wants to distil? Let bus and car
> and hurrying umbrellas keep their skill to
> feed ukiyo-e beyond Lochnagar.

That is, 'ukiyo-e beyond Lochnagar' is best kept there and far from
the city walls. 'Ukiyo-e' means 'floating-world picture' and describes
the work of a school of Japanese woodblock printing that began in the
Edo period among artists who rose from the ranks of the people they
depicted. A Japanese critic writes that the phrase suggests 'the
transitory, shifting, at times treacherous existence to which man is
condemned', and that the genre portrays 'people who, although well
aware of the snares and tricks in store for them, still do their best to
snatch as much pleasure and enjoyment out of life as they can.'[2] It was
an art for the common people; and, as such, it sounds pretty attractive.
It also seems in accordance with Morgan's artistic affections. 'Lochnagar',
however, does not give that impression. It looks like his shorthand for
romantic wilderness, the country of nature poets, Byronic, or Landseer-
like, a Scotland whose reality is not harmonious with Glasgow's. If
these terms are contradictory, then the misunderstanding is mine or
Morgan's. Either way, I admit to not knowing exactly what these three
lines mean.

Similarly, it can take a while to get used to the narrative of *Sonnets
from Scotland*.

> There is no beginning. We saw Lewis
> laid down, when there was not much but thunder
> and volcanic fires . . .   ('Slates', *TV*, 141)

The speaker and his companions are witnesses from another world. They
observe the birth of geography and evolution. 'There is no beginning'
might echo Thomas De Quincey in his essay 'System of the Heavens',[3]
where he concludes a 'Dream Vision of the Infinite' with: 'The Angel
threw up his glorious hands to the heaven of heavens, saying, "End is
there none to the Universe of God? Lo! also THERE IS NO BEGINNING." '

> Diving in the warm seas around Bearsden,
> cased in our superchitin scuba-gear . . .
>   ('Carboniferous', *TV*, 141)

has about it a touch of the whimsical details to which science fiction is
perhaps prone. These inquisitive visitors watch the 'unsinister / ferocious
tenderness' of mating sharks, and fear

> . . . the force that could inter
> such life and joy, in fossil clays, for apes
> and men to haul into their teeming heads.

'Memory of men! That was to come.' To imagine the pre-human
mediated through a presumably non-human speaker calls for an
adventurous mind, which is the main integrating link between *Sonnets*

from Scotland and Morgan's more overtly experimental work. He rises to touches of tantalising poetry, when, for instance, he writes of 'stamped-out remains / of nomad Grampian fires', or says that 'Immensities / are mind, not ice, as the bright straths unfreeze.'

In 'Post-Glacial' (*TV*, 142), the voice is impersonal, which will occur again in the sequence, although 'I' or 'we' is implied by surrounding poems. It might be the occasional uncertainty of this narrative technique that contributes to the slippery and sometimes puzzling nature of the sequence as a whole. Bookish allusiveness also blurs the narrative in that it slows the reader. A poet's skull discovered on the machair seems to refer to someone like the poet of the Gilgamesh epic – 'Far off, he sang of Nineveh the blest, / incised his tablets, stalked the dhow-bright dock – ' ('In Argyll', *TV*, 142), but the reader could be left wondering what he is doing there, or what function is served by the closing allusion to MacDiarmid's 'Perfect'.

That, though, is a local puzzle. 'The Ring of Brodgar' (*TV*, 143) introduces a moment that seems to relate to the rest of the poem – and due to how one sonnet relates to another, it might be best to think of *Sonnets from Scotland* as a long poem.

> I well recall the timeprint of the Ring
> of Brodgar we discovered, white with dust
> in twenty-second century distrust
> of truth, but dustable, with truths to bring
> into the freer ages, as it did.
> A thin groan fought the wind that tugged the stones.
> It filled an auditorium with pain.
> Long was the sacrifice. Pity ran, hid.
> Once they heard the splintering of the bones
> they switched the playback off, in vain, in vain.

History seems to be presented as a 'playback' from a 'timeprint'. Poets are for ever discovering the imaginative or spiritual equivalents of 'timeprints'. Confusion, however, might arise; chronologically, he is writing about the Ring of Brodgar in the Orkney Islands, but the speaker is in what to us is the far future and unknown, and saying that everything is preserved:

> 'If those stones could speak – ' Do not wish too loud.
> They can, they do, they will. No voice is lost.
> Your meanest guilts are bonded in like frost.
> Your fearsome sweat will rise and leave its shroud.

When are we? To whom, and when, are these occult, admonitory moral objurgations addressed?

Two poems later, in 'The Mirror' (*TV*, 144), the omniscience and ubiquity of the speaker are (almost) explained. Morgan is writing about Scotland at the time of Agricola's invasion – 'Ages/drum-tap the flattened homes and slaughtered rows' – and the aftermath of Mons Graupius. He quotes from Tacitus – Atqui *'ubi solitudinem faciunt, pacem appellant'*. ('And where they make a desert, they call it peace.') Deserts are often places of beauty in Morgan's poetry, poised on the verge of fertility, or images of the barren that the good decision can will into life. His purpose here, however, is to introduce a strange device:

> There is a mirror only we can see.
> It hangs in time and not in space. The day
> goes down in it without ember or ray
> and the newborn climb through it to be free.
> The multitudes of the world cannot know
> they are reflected there; like glass they lie
> in glass, shadows in shade, they could not cry
> in airless wastes but that is where they go.
> We cloud it, but it pulses like a gem,
> it must have caught a range of energies
> from the dead.

'Back in space' introduces his allusion to the defeat of Calgacus and his people. Time, then, is seen as a purer, more refined dimension, in which the speaker and his companions live, presumably without the need for visibility. Paraphrased like that, the poem is made to look pedantic; and although I do not believe it is, it is none the less difficult to see exactly what Morgan means, unless all he is saying is that men do what they do, sometimes with unspeakable violence, because they do not share the same ethereality as his invented observers. If that is the case then there seems little point to it. How do you lose a dimension? Or does science fiction ask us to abdicate responsibility to the literal and quotidian? Is the poem's 'mirror' metaphorical and recommending a superior and pacific way of life?

'Pilate at Fortingall' (*TV*, 144) takes the legend as fact:

> They told us he sat here beneath the yew
> even in downpours; ate dog-scraps. Crows flew
> from prehistoric stone to stone all day.

Classical writers on horticulture warned against the yew as a mortiferous plant. So the touch of lore here adds to the poem's historical pathos, while its closing lines – 'and washed his hands, and watched his hands, and washed/his hands, and watched his hands, and washed his hands – '

show Morgan at his enactive best, obliging pentameters to convey the
movement of an image, as in the freer verse of 'Cinquevalli':

> He throws it
> from hand to hand, always different,
> always the same, always
> different, always the
> same.   (*P*, 441)

Personal names in 'The Picts', as well as two Pictish words, are
probably taken from Wainwright's *The Problem of the Picts*. Nothing is
known of Bliesblituth, Edarnon, Usconbuts or Canutulachama; but the
first becomes a 'wild buffoon', Edarnon is said to be 'wily', the third
'brilliant', and the last-named a reader of the stars. Like the future, the
unknown past can be invented, though this might leave justifiable
bafflement at why Columba in 'Colloquy in Glaschu' (*TV*, 145) speaks a
mixture of English, Alfred de Vigny's French (from 'Le Cor') and Latin.
Bookish poets, even when ludic, can be exasperating.

A number of sonnets commemorate and celebrate a range of presences
in Scotland: the geographer Matthew Paris, writers – Poe, De Quincey,
Hopkins, Seferis – and other figures like the birdman of Stirling Castle
(the subject of Dunbar's 'The Fenyeit Freir of Tungland'), Thomas
Young (Milton's tutor), James Hutton, Peter Guthrie Tait, Vladimir
Solovyov and G.I. Gurdjieff. Momentarily, the sonnet reverts to its role
as a form for devotions. Within the sequence's design it can be taken for
granted that these poems, too, are 'spoken' by the timeman-poet whose
constant presence enables the work as a whole, and hence, perhaps, the
energetic, passionate impersonality of Morgan's writing in this section,
as if he has imbibed the timeman's values. Of course, Morgan is the
timeman all along – he wrote the poems; but an imaginative presence
beside a poet can be supposed to have a reality of its own which neither
poet nor reader can entirely understand.

It is interesting, too, that Morgan selects – perhaps instinctively,
perhaps not – exceptional figures, who, like Lady Grange on St Kilda,
De Quincey, Hopkins or Poe, were physical outcasts, or by tempera-
mental choice located themselves in unusual ways of life.

> what but imagination could have read
> granite boulders back to their molten roots?
> And how far back was back, and how far on
> would basalt still be basalt, iron iron?

he asks in 'Theory of the Earth' (*TV*, 148), where the geologist James
Hutton is associated with Robert Burns. 'We find no vestige of a
beginning, / no prospect of an end,' which is presumably a quotation

from Hutton, connects with De Quincey, while the mention of Inversnaid in the Solovyov poem ('1983', *TV*, 151) connects with Hopkins, whose poem of that title, although not mentioned, is well known. Imaginative power underpins the entire sequence; but the power of imagination is also close to the core of Morgan's meaning. His summary of personalities – bold original thinkers or imaginers, and not always Scottish – are there in the poem in place of political or historical events, mind, imagination and intellect as, in Morgan's terminology, 'whittricks', chronological genius instead of historical vignettes. It even extends to the Scottish war poets of the North African desert – 'North Africa' (*TV*, 152) – including Morgan himself, and 'Caledonian Antisyzygy' (*TV*, 152), in which a typically high-spirited dramatisation is forced into form.

Imagination, however, particularly in science fiction, is vulnerable to absurdity, as in 'Travellers (1)' (*TV*, 153):

> The universe is like a trampoline.
> We chose a springy clump near Arrochar
> and with the first jump shot past Barnard's Star.

'Travellers (2)', however, contains these lines: 'There is no happiness in prescience, / and there is no regret in happiness' (*TV*, 153), which resonate in themselves as moral poetry. A dozen poems later 'prescience' might begin to explain itself, for the last line of 'Travellers (2)' is recalled in the closing image of 'Computer Error: Neutron Strike' (*TV*, 161). 'Happiness' seldom does, of course, not here, and not much anywhere else either.

'Post-Referendum' and 'Gangs' confront politics. In the first, Morgan's timemen listen to 'the strong sick dirkless Angel' as he delivers an angry riposte to the people he protects or represents or whom he's failed:

> 'No no, it will not do, it will not be.
> I tell you you must leave your land alone.
> Who do you think is poised to ring the phone?
> Fish your straightjacket packet from the sea
> you threw it in, get your headphones mended.
> You don't want the world now, do you? Come on,
> you're pegged out on your feathery futon,
> take the matches from your lids, it's ended.'   (*TV*, 155)

Political poetry is far from difficult to write if a writer is willing to opt for the limited satisfaction that comes from preaching to the converted. Even preaching to the unconvertible can bring the perverse rewards of catcalls and the inner, damaging knowledge of having been lonely but offensive. Political subjects become challenging only when the poet's

imagination rises to meet the demands of artistry and originality as well
as those of conviction and conscience. It was probably an awareness of
the dismal, aggressive goodwill (and malevolence; and stupidity) of
much political poetry that obliged Morgan to devise his sequence as
hyper-imaginative, enabled by science fiction, and as discrete and
diffuse. Parts, and parts within parts, are played off against each other
from Creation to Matt McGinn (celebrated with delightful tenderness),
Kentigern to Jupiter, Pontius Pilate to Poe, prehistory to post-history,
Glasgow to Clydegrad. *Sonnets from Scotland* might be a transformational
catch-all, but it is also a means to a subjective political truthfulness,
both candid and covert, and determined in its fidelity to the imaginative breadth that is the foundation of Morgan's politics. Distaste for a
political moment – the Referendum – might have started Morgan on
the sequence (see *Verse*, 41). 'You don't want the world now, do you?'
is, however, a larger complaint and disappointment than those felt by
the majority who voted 'yes'. The originating moment becomes
submerged without being swallowed in what is in effect a long poem
that deals with Past, Present and Future mediated through these
ingenious timemen. 'A coin clattered at the end of its spin' – the last
line of 'Post-Referendum' – conveys with much dramatic brilliance the
disgusting sound of bribery or purchase by 'the Tempter', or the
unhappy noise of a lost political bet. Remarkably, such un-Morganlike
properties as 'Angel' and 'Tempter' work out this poem between them,
reported by his invisible watchers.

'Gangs' is defiantly political. It picks up from the 'strong sick
dirkless Angel' of the previous poem:

> See yours, and Dan's,
> and mine's, that's three chibs. We'll soon hiv a team.
> Whit's that? *Non-Index-Linked*! Did ye hear it?
> Look! *Tiny Global Recession*! C'moan then,
> ya bams, Ah'll take ye. *Market Power frae Drum*!
> Dave, man, get up. Dave! Ach, ye're no near it.
> Ah'm oan ma tod. But they'll no take a len
> a me, Ah'm no deid yet, or deif, or dumb!   (*TV*, 155)

In the overheard impersonality of 'Gangs' the street-leader with his
knife seems almost as bad as the 'dirkless Angel'. 'Dave, man, get up.
Dave! Ach, ye're no near it' – political bevvying could account for the
sleep of one man and the outspokenness of the other. But it is hard to
tell if Morgan is introducing political violence as a possible result of

continued national frustration, or recommending it (why is the Angel 'dirkless'?), or showing it as the incitements of an outraged braggart.

Contrasts in a poet as self-aware as Morgan are likely to be more than alternating moods. 'Gangs', for example, is followed by the moving, perhaps personal, 'After a Death' (*TV*, 156). Suddenly, then, the reader is confronted with a poem of grief which is as affecting as anything Morgan has written, and its presence comes as a shock. Next there is 'Not the Burrell Collection' (*TV*, 156), which lists objects associated with cruelty, executions, torture and the Holocaust, ending with 'a lachrymatory no man can lift.' '1983' (*TV*, 157), however, contains a limerick within a sonnet and recalls a lately dead parrot that had been drawn by Edward Lear. It ends:

> 'Oho! Lear
> sketched me, delirious old man, how he
> shuffled about, his tabby on the sill,
> a stew on the stove, a brush in his ear,
> and sometimes hummed, or he buzzed like a bee,
> painting parrots and all bright brave things still!'

Four stark contrasts, then: the violence and frustration of 'Gangs', personal sorrow in 'After a Death', historical terrors in 'Not the Burrell Collection', and then the gleeful note struck in '1983' on the side of 'all bright brave things'. Moments like these in *Sonnets from Scotland* suggest it as a long poem in which Morgan — instinctively or otherwise — seeks to integrate the contrasting elements of his poetic personality.

Science fiction is one of these elements, and in *Sonnets from Scotland* it provides both persona and narrative. At times, though, it can be obtrusive; and, as a genre, it can be argued that science fiction is often implicated in unearned overviews of actual or possible states of affairs that are too important to get wrong — such as nuclear catastrophe. Unearned or undeserved feeling is the charge levelled at sentimental writers, but poetry drawn from 'prescience' (which is imagination when it claims foreknowledge) is by definition unearned because it has not been lived. Whether or not the objection is prissily theoretical or hopelessly literary will depend on what you think of science fiction on the one hand, and the status of experience in poetry on the other. In any case, it raises an ethical issue which ought not to be dodged.

Where Morgan's fiction becomes specific and descriptive it looks too close for comfort to the Special Effects departments of the movie studios:

We flew up over Perthshire, following
Christo's great-granddaughter in her swing-wing
converted crop-sprayer till plastic shot
above Schiehallion from her spinneret
Scotland-shaped and Scotland-sized, descended
silent, tough, translucent, light-attended,
catching that shoal of contours in one net.

('The Norn (1)', *TV*, 158)

That is, Scotland is 'caught' in a Scotland-sized facsimile woven by a sci-
fi spinning-machine.

'Norn (2)' (*TV*, 159) begins with a comment on human response to
the unlikely arrival of an artificial sky: 'But was it art?' the timemen ask
themselves. They ask the French who reply with a snippet of paraphrased
Baudelaire (from his 'Correspondances').

La nature est un temple où les vivants
sont les piliers, which was at least not wrong
but did it answer us?

After some business with Old Christo's head (which is taken from a box)
his great-granddaughter speaks:

'Of course it's art,' she said, 'we just use men.
Pygmalion got it inside out, poor brute.
For all they've been made art, they've not lost face.
They'll lift the polythene, be men again.'

Probably the question and answer do little more than re-state Morgan's
belief in science-as-art, or science-and-art as part of the same culture,
and that the consequences of neglecting this unity retard progress. In
which case he is probably right, but there is an air of unreality to the
wish, especially when it is associated with what might be its ethical
partner, 'his dream / of freedom with all guilts and fears unfelt', ('The
Poet in the City', *TV*, 158) which is a long way from life as it is lived.
Yet the reader probably feels uncertain here, wondering what 'Norn'
means if it is not the Fates of Norse legend (they are usually mentioned
in the plural, a trinity, Fate, Being and Necessity). That these two
sonnets have a doctrinal design on the reader is virtually certain; it is
rather more difficult to work out what it is.

It is a pity, because the next poem, 'The Target' (*TV*, 159), has the
population of Scotland

. . . running with fire in their hair,
men and women were running everywhere,

> women and children burning everywhere,
> ovens of death were falling from the air

as 'the black angel' gestures and passes.

> 'Where I am, watch;
> when I raise one arm to destroy, I save
> none; increase, multiply; vengeance is mine;
> in no universe will man find his match.'

Christian ironies and 'the black angel' look out of place here, although
they could be intended as the last vindictive gasp of the Old Order. 'A
stick-nest in *Ygdrasil*' (a phrase from line 1457 of *A Drunk Man Looks at
the Thistle*, and obviously connected with 'The Norn') is offered as the
mythical source of modified rebirth:

> Over St Kilda, house-high poppy-beds
> made forests; towering sea-pinks turned the heads
> of even master mariners with lures
> that changed their white sea-graves to scent-drenched groves.
> Fortunate Isles!

To what extent do Morgan's indestructible observers speak for him
here? Even if only to an extent, then that exclamation in 'After Fallout'
(*TV*, 160) – is it ironic? It does not seem to be – is close to damnable.
Post-Armageddon Scotland is depicted with more pictorial wonderment
than sorrow. Science fiction is addicted to this kind of thing:

> We stood in what had once been Princes Street.
> Hogweed roots thrust, throbbed underneath for miles.
> The rubble of the shops became the food
> of new cracks running mazes round our feet,
> and west winds blew, past shattered bricks and tiles,
> millions of seeds through ruined Holyrood.
>
> ('The Age of Heracleum', *TV*, 160)

The powerfully conveyed horrors of 'Computer Error: Neutron Strike'
(*TV*, 161) close on the depopulated lyricism of 'An automatic foghorn,
and its light, / warned out to none below, and none above.' 'Inward
Bound', though, on the same page, is almost playful in its depiction of
an opening, swallowing earth, and in 'The Desert' (*TV*, 162) resistant,
regenerative lives are observed. No matter what happens, he seems to be
saying, human tenacity will win through. 'The Coin' (*TV*, 162) is a
tantalising interlude for a Scottish reader:

                                                All right:
we turned it over, read easily *One Pound*,
but then the shock of Latin, like a gloss,
Respublica Scotorum, sent across
such ages as we guessed but never found
at the worn edge where once the date had been
and where as many fingers had gripped hard
as hopes their silent race had lost or gained.

'Yet nothing seemed ill-starred,' the speaker says, 'And least of all the realm the coin contained.' The poem's motive can be sympathised with and shared; but it could be argued that it is made sentimental by being set in a future that is not foreseeable from the political present, or that the context in which Scottish independence appears seems unnecessarily sly.

No sooner do we read 'The Coin' than we read in 'Outward Bound' (*TV*, 164) that Scotland becomes like a big ship on the Atlantic, and in 'On Jupiter' that Scotland travels in space. These are mischievous inventions, dramatizing Morgan's faith in the unpredictable, his cheering optimism, although the lmost casual manner in which populations are wiped out in these poems in order to allow him to state it must be considered worrying. MacDiarmid would have had the Cheka and the Red Army clear the world of his ideological opponents; Morgan is content with a nuked globe and an aftermath in which the survivors contrive 'the freer ages'. It is here that the ethics of science fiction can be called into question, as well as optimism, which in these poems strikes this reader as antic and juvenile. (Pessimism, on the other hand, is a disease.) There is such a thing as sanity and it is rather more patient than anything suggested by Morgan's admittedly adventurous narrative.

. . . and a boat
of students rowed past, slid from black to red
into the blaze. But where will they arrive
with all, boat, city, earth, like them, afloat?
                                        ('Clydegrad', *TV*, 165)

Could it be wishful-thinking? Could it be the detached poet's desire that everyone be with him in a state of moving and unknowing, eagerness, willingness, a dream of society that it is based on modernity but so impatient with present wonders that it cannot wait for the future to happen? The questions are underlined by the hedonism of his vision in 'A Golden Age' (*TV*, 165), with its vineyards on the Campsie Fells, its 'dirigible parties', the 'eagle-high' homes of the people, those 'mile-high buildings' of Clydegrad that could remind us of 'Glasgow Sonnets' *vii, viii*, and *ix*. 'Perhaps it did not last? What lasts?'

> The bougainvillea millenniums
> may come and go, but then in thistle days
> a strengthened seed outlives the hardest blasts.

Both question and answer are historical, but he has had to imagine the future – that is, step beyond history – in order to put them into a poem. It emphasises Morgan's exceptional poetic character, his originality, his inventiveness within a consistency of vision and different manners of writing that no longer ought to be compartmentalised as readily as they have been.

Sonnets from Scotland ends with the departure of Morgan's timemen.

> If it was love we felt, would it not keep,
> and travel where we travelled? Without fuss
> we lifted off, but as we checked and talked
> a far horn grew to break that people's sleep.

The *cor*, perhaps, of Vigny's poem, the slughorn of Browning's, the call that awakens the sleepers of life and legend, or that invites the challenge of self, society and imagination.

NOTES

1. Friedrich Hölderlin, *Poems and Fragments*, translated by Michael Hamburger (London: Routledge and Kegan Paul, 1966).
2. Takashi Suzuki, *Hiroshige* (London: Elek Books, [?1959]).
3. Thomas De Quincey, *The Collected Writings*, edited by David Masson (London: A & C Black, 1896–97), vol. viii, p.34.

Eight

Edwin Morgan the Translator

Peter McCarey

'He pauses in an astounding landscape, almost afraid to move. When he moves, he is no longer himself. And that is it' – Edwin Morgan, 'The Translation of Poetry'[1]

– It's unpleasantly like being drunk.
– What's unpleasant about being drunk?
– Ask a glass of water. – Douglas Adams *The Hitch-hiker's Guide to the Galaxy*

It is not just the profusion and variety of Edwin Morgan's translation work that surprises: it is the quality, the rarity of some pieces – the improbable Aigi, the trove of Hungarian poetry done into English. I have set as many of the originals as I could locate and understand against the translations, which leaves plenty of opportunity for further study, since Morgan has translated into English and Scots from Italian, Russian, German, Spanish, French, Portuguese, Anglo-Saxon, ancient Greek, Dutch, Khmer, Armenian and Hungarian – working with cribs on the last three, although he now gets by in Hungarian.

He is not unique in this respect, but the culmination of a movement in modern Scottish poetry. In the 1920s Donald MacAlister, then Principal of Glasgow University, translated from and into many classical and modern languages; he seemed to have a particular weakness for Welsh Romany. MacAlister contributed to the *Scottish Chapbook*, whose editor, C.M. Grieve, was quite a different kind of translator. Lacking MacAlister's gift for foreign languages, he was far more intimate with his own. MacAlister was followed, more or less, by Douglas Young, MacDiarmid by Goodsir Smith. Many Scottish poets then and since have produced fine versions from foreign originals, although none matches Morgan's range or excels him in quality.

The aim of this essay is to assess his translation technique, consider his theoretical statements on translation, and ask how his translation work relates to his poetry.

Morgan takes poets at their word. When it comes to a choice, as it does at every turn, he tends to let line-break, rhyme or rhythm, image or argument or syntax go rather than lose the simple sense. Consider the first four verses of a dizain by Maurice Scève in Morgan's version:

> Comme corps mort vagant en haulte Mer,
> esbat des Ventz, & passetemps des Undes,
> j'errois flottant parmy ce Gouffre amer,
> ou mes soucys enflent vagues profondes.

> Wanderer: drowned body in the open sea:
> shuttlecock, plaything and mock of wave
> and wind: bitter the gulf: waverer
> buoyed on my own unfathomed misery –   (*FR*, 46–7)

In the first verse every semantic load-bearing word has been translated ('Wanderer' does for 'vagant') but the effect is not the same. It comes as a shock in that book, after reading through poems replete with conceits on evenings and glances, woods and golden locks, to find a corpse floating in the first verse. Morgan does not use a simile to set up the effect, and he breaks it up with a colon. This is almost a caricatural illustration of the points I set out to show: the sense of the verse is kept but line-breaks, rhythm (dodgy first line), image, argument, syntax and rhyme all go by the board as Morgan uses enjambement, punctuation, and expectance of a verb that doesn't show up to make a much more choppy sea than Scève's. It should not be concluded that this is simply a bad translation. Morgan has decided to make the first four verses rough, and that has involved the (regretted) sacrifice of the powerful first line, but the continuation of his version shows he is quite capable of keeping to the shape of the original, and the last line skilfully explains the sense of the French without expanding it: 'tout estourdy point ne me congnoissoys' – 'I am dazzled, struck; I am hidden from my mind'.

These points have to be pursued with a few more examples. In Morgan's translations there are remarkably few unforced errors – by which I mean semantic distortions not made inevitable by rhyme or rhythm. The ones I found were as follows: in 'Goya', by Voznesensky (*RP*, 18), 'Voronka' is 'bomb crater' not 'raven' (*vorona*), although since both images are suggested elsewhere in this short poem, it might be simply a shift of emphasis; judging by the grammar, Quasimodo's 'morte di pietà, / morte di pudore' at the end of 'Letter to my Mother' could be either 'compassion is dead, modesty is dead' or 'compassionate

death, tactful death' – Morgan's 'Death of compassion, / death of
quietness' hardly allows the second alternative; similarly, Montale's
description of himself 'uomo che tarda / all'atto, che nessuno, poi,
distrugge' might just be 'a man perplexed, / tardy to act when no act is
destroyed' (from 'Mediterranean', *RP*, 62) or maybe he is saying that
when he gets round to doing something, no one undoes it. There are
always such nits for the picking, but in the end the only real mistake I
found was in both Morgan's versions of 'A se stesso' by Leopardi, where
Morgan has him spurn nature at the end, instead of himself.

Morgan's semantic fidelity sometimes results in too much clarification,
something he himself warns against: 'the process of trying to understand
the foreign poem always tempts us to make the translation a little
clearer or simpler than the original, and this may have a weakening
effect.'[2] A Frenchman whom I asked to check Morgan's translations of
Maurice Scève found himself returning to the translation on difficult
points in the French; Scève has a reputation for obscurity, earned by
such as the following:

> tout lieu distant, du jour et de la nuict,
> tout intervalle, ô qui par trop me nuyt,
> seront rempliz de ta doulce rigueur.

Anyone would expect a 'toi' before the 'qui', and without it the
expectation generated by this already long sentence is cranked up still
further. Morgan's version gives the game away before the end:

> regions remote from night or turned from day,
> all space, O my too rigourous friend, will be
> filled with your sweet but changeless cruelty   (*FR*, 50–51)

It is difficult to see what else could have been done there, but the
explicative instinct that irons out the grammar is the same urge that
treats semantic ambiguities, such as those mentioned above, with a
little too much decision.

Just as he is faithful to the sense of the original, Morgan is quite
determined to add nothing of his own. A search for counter-examples
produced the following: in Montale's 'Arsenio', '. . . oh troppo noto /
delirio, Arsenio, d'immobilità'[3] becomes '. . . oh delirious / memory,
Arsenio, of marmoreality' (*RP*, 65). 'Marmoreality' is a fine, original
touch. The penultimate line of Voznesensky's 'Parabolic Ballad', which
literally translates as 'he leaves tonight for Siberia' becomes 'Galoshes
flounder through a Siberian thaw', so that Voznesensky gains something
in translation.

Because he refuses to add to the original, Morgan is at times
compelled to pad. 'I've closed my balcony' ('He cerrado mi balcon') in

Lorca's 'Casida del llanto' becomes 'My balcony I've drawn, I've shut it' (*RP*, 120); 'Terribly silent' in Yevtushenko's poem 'Stalin's Heirs' becomes 'voicelessly loud with dread' (*RP*, 29); similarly, 'O znal by ja',[4] where Pasternak seems to imitate the laconic punch of Raleigh's 'On the Life of Man', with its closure 'Thus march we playing to our latest rest, / Only we dye in earnest, that's no Jest', is neither laconic nor punchy in Morgan's version:

> neither patter nor legerdemain
> nor read-out speech redeems the player
> cued for complete decease unfeigned   (RP, 35)

On rare occasions this padding distorts the argument of the poem; here is Morgan's version of Montale's 'Spesso il male' (*Ossi di Seppia*, 54) with brackets round Morgan's interpolations:

> Often I've met the wrong of the world (in my walk:)
> (there by) the strangled brook with its guttural song
> (there with) the puckerings of the (thirsty tongue
> of a) parched leaf, (there by) the horse that fell and shook.
>
> Little I knew but what I saw (in a rune)
> a vision of the divine Unconcern:
> (there by) the statue in the drowsy sun
> at noon, and the cloud, and the heaven-climbing hawk.
>
>   (RP, 59)

The concision of the first stanza has been sacrificed to make it match the second, with its fine, clinching line. To put Morgan's technique in perspective, though, we should compare it with that of William Soutar, or Robert Lowell. Of Morgan's version of 'Verses on Pushkin: Third Variation' by Pasternak, we might quibble that the ink on the manuscript mentioned is drying, not dry; as for Soutar's version, it is not immediately apparent that it is the same poem.[5] In his imitation of Montale's 'Dora Markus II', Lowell is much more exact than Morgan on the mysterious lines

> Ravenna è lontana, distilla
> veleno una fede feroce   (*Le Occasioni*, 1976)
>
> Ravenna is far away, A ferocious faith
> distils its venom   (*Imitations*, 1962)
>
> far off is Ravenna; beliefs
> are fierce and strong with death.   (RP, 68)

But Ravenna is *very* far away from Lowell's American Dora, who saunters in her aura of sugar daddies and harmonicas.

This brings us to the least quantifiable point on Morgan's translation technique — his fidelity to the tone of the original. In this field individual examples could hardly convince; we have to try from another angle. It will be admitted that a poem cannot be translated on a word-for-word basis. Something has to inform the whole translation. There are obvious mechanical ways of doing this, but Morgan often neglects them; he is quite capable, in translating a renaissance sonnet, of producing a decasyllable with twelve, thirteen, fourteen or nine syllables (*FR*, 21, 37, 39), and of more or less neglecting the rhythm of a poem for children such as Brecht's 'The Plum-Tree' ('Der Pflaumenbaum', *RP*, 141); compare Michael Hamburger's version in Bertolt Brecht, *Poems 1913–1956* (London: Methuen, 1981, 243). What he never lets go if he can help it is the tone of the original. He even faithfully renders Voznesensky's studies in cool with suitably far-out language, of beats and bums, and birds from restaurants, since he would sooner traduce his own voice than that of the original. For the same reason, he avoids hermeneutic translation: he neither naturalises his original (like Lowell's Montale) nor updates it (like Logue's Homer), nor turns it into his own poem (like Goodsir Smith's second version of Sappho). He will, on occasion, 'make it strange', as Shklovsky might have said, but this, I hope to show, is a different matter. Morgan's best translations are from poets whose formal structure can be rendered loosely — Montale, Leopardi, Mayakovsky. The perhaps surprising conclusion is that, as far as translation is concerned, Morgan is not centrally concerned with form, but rather with the sense of the word and the tone of the poem. The rest is instrumental.

Reading Morgan's books of translations after his poems can give the eerie impression of dealing with an identikit poet. He begins conventionally enough with apprenticeship in the sonnet from Petrarch et al., and essays in discursive forms from the Anglo-Saxon onwards. In the 1960s Morgan tries the more eye-catching forms of Gomringer and Braga. But he takes more than form from other poets: there is something familiar in the arbitrary exotica of the Lorca translations ('Live iguanas arrive to gnaw the insomniacs / and the heartbroken man on the run will meet at streetcorners / the quiet incredible crocodile beneath the soft protest of the stars', *RP*, 118). In fact, Lorca's 'Asesinato' looks like a blueprint for Morgan's 'The Barrow':

> Murder
> (*Two voices at Dawn in Riverside Drive, New York*)

– How did it –?
– Scratch on the cheek,
that's all. Claw
pounding on a green
shoot. Pin plunging
to meet the roots of the scream.
And the sea stops moving.
– But how – how?
– Like this.
– Get away from me! That way?
– Sure. The heart
went out alone.
– Oh no, oh god –   (*RP*, 118)

. . . The fog was really thick, but then
someone came up out of the fog
and I shouted HELP and rattled the barrow,
and he came up closer and looked at me
and felt the bars, but not a word,
and I couldn't really see his face,
and you know this is when something happened

– He robbed you, I knew it, dirty thief,
it was all a plant, it was a trap to

– No he wasn't after my money.
He had something in his hand you see

– What do you mean in his hand? his hand?

– He had something in his hand. He killed me.   (*P*, 258)

Mayakovsky's 'A Richt Respeck for Cuddies' (*WHV*, 30) leads on to a paean for the timber wolf ('The Third Day of the Wolf', *P*, 132), and in the general progression from the isolated observer of nature to the morally committed, political outsider (Leopardi to Voznesensky via Montale, Pasternak and Mayakovsky) there are facets of Morgan the poet. There is even the unpredictable formal trickster in the person of Sandor Weöres, whom Morgan has translated in abundance. It's like the king's clothes, without the king. All that's missing from the translations is the stark simplicity of some of Morgan's love poems.

On the other hand, it is Morgan who chooses what to translate:

Montale not Pasolini, Mayakovsky not Mandelstam, Aigi not Brodsky, Brecht not Rilke. Of course he was not faced with these choices in the form of alternatives, but putting it like this highlights the selections Morgan has made. There is a degree of ventriloquy in verse translation, and at times it is difficult to tell which is the operator and which the dummy. Maybe his own comments on translation policy can help us out.

In an article comparing Gavin Douglas and William Drummond as translators, Morgan says:

> Between the times of Douglas and Drummond the Renaissance ideas in Imitation are the great divide. To Douglas, Virgil was Virgil, whether in Latin or in Scots – 'Go, wulgar (i.e. vernacular) Virgill . . .' as he says at the end. But Drummond had no hesitation in publishing as his own a large number of poems which ran the gamut from close translation to loose imitation or paraphrase, taken from Italian, French, Spanish, Latin and even English. Some of his best-known poems are in fact direct translations, though the average reader who comes across them in anthologies will be unaware of the fact. A measure of moral blame has attached to Drummond for this, especially as he quite naughtily does label some poems 'translations', but never the best ones. But this is an area we today have to walk in rather warily. A property-conscious, copyright-conscious world is not the best vantage-point for understanding the subtleties of the communion of European writers, a vast web of ideals and traditions shading off in each country into finer and finer distinctions and measures of vernacular or personal variation. Drummond relished these European blueprints not simply because, as Ben Jonson claimed, he was conservative or old-fashioned, but also because the doctrine suited the subtle and delicate movement of his own mind: the making of small distinctions, the slight renewal or slewing round of established metaphors or comparisons, the infusion of a personality drop by drop into a tradition – these are what Drummond wanted and got from his habit of translation.

('Gavin Douglas and William Drummond as Translators', 198)[6]
Morgan is like Douglas in that he views the original as the touchstone, the essential constant in the practice of translation. He is like Drummond in that he likes to explore the transmutation effected when the foreign poem comes into his own language. Yet he wants neither literary monuments nor cannibalised texts; he has not tackled the translation of a celebrated classic poem, just as he has avoided hermeneutics, where the kind of fusion that can produce brilliant effects

always erodes the boundary between original and translation. Stop at this point and think of a famous translation. Or ten famous translations. The King James Bible? Constance Garnett's Dostoevsky? Urquhart? Fitzgerald? Translations tend to be famous either because the original was a famous classic and the translator was there at the right time, or because the translator left a powerful personal stamp on the work. So what's in it for Morgan? He has made a lot of translations, many of them unpublished. My own, limited experience of verse translation tells me that, given thorough knowledge of the work and its cultural and linguistic nexus, and given the luck to hit on a good approach quickly, a good translation of an eight-line poem might be made in a day. My experience of payment for verse translation is even more limited, though I am told there is not much money in it. Having considered how and what Morgan translates it is probably worth asking why he translates.

In a review of Robin Fulton's translation of Blok's 'Twelve', Morgan alludes to the totally different approach to the poem taken by Sidney Goodsir Smith in his (Scots) version, and comments that there is more than one valid route up the mountain. I have always found this a very suggestive comment and wish Morgan had developed it. Whoever has tried to translate a lyric will know the feeling of nearly getting there and having to abandon the attempt, because a crucial rhyme is missing, or a notion can't be negotiated with the materials to hand. A famous example is Pushkin's 'Ja vas ljubil' – 'I loed ye but. Aiblins intil my briest', in Morgan's version (*Voice of Scotland* VI: 1, April 1955). The first three words of the Russian have stymied all attempts: 'I loved you', 'you' in the polite form, whereas love lyrics from Petrarch onwards have used the intimate form. In those three words the author acknowledges that the intimacy is gone forever. Douglas Young, too, translated it into Scots, and not satisfied with that tried to put it into German (using 'du', for some reason, instead of 'Sie').

The comparison of poem to mountain and translation to route would also seem to suggest that a translation is radically different from a poem: ephemeral and dependent rather than substantial and rooted. This may be connected with what Walter Benjamin says in 'The Task of the Translator', which Morgan commends in a paper entitled 'The Third Tiger: The Translator as Creative Communicator' (delivered at Glasgow University on 3 June 1988). It may be connected, but since I do not understand Benjamin I turn to Morgan's comments:

> . . . Is there some interface that makes translation possible?
>
> This is what Walter Benjamin thought, in his essay, 'The Task of the Translator' (1923), and I think most translators would agree with him, although it's an elusive and difficult idea. Benjamin

wrote: 'If there is such a thing as a language of truth, the tensionless and even silent depository of the ultimate truth which all thought strives for, then this language . . . is concealed in concentrated fashion in translations . . . It is the task of the translator to release in his own language that pure language which is under the spell of another, to liberate the language imprisoned in a work in his re-creation of that work' (trans. Harry Zohn, in *Illuminations*, 1973). It is as if the translator had to get *behind* the words of the foreign poem, through his understanding of them, through his analysis of their meaning and their associations, until he is in touch with a deverbalized poem, a brain pattern (possibly) of nervous or electrical energy which he can then reverbalize into his own language. One is reminded of the search of machine translation for an interlingua, a computer language, or even perhaps a spoken language, like the South American Indian language Aymara which has been tried out because it has an extremely regular and complex grammatical structure 'capable of containing other languages as subsets'. If there is anything in Benjamin's idea, it makes for a different conception of fidelity in translation, a more creative fidelity if that is not a contradiction in terms. If you are in touch with the mysterious hidden 'real' poem underneath the surface foreign words, you will start your translation on a deeper and less conscious level; things, solutions will fly into your head suddenly and seem right without their being plodding word-for-word equivalents.

Now this is hard to follow, or swallow, accommodating as it does three radically different versions of the 'interface': Benjamin's cabalistic notion of a language of truth in the mind of God, a Chomskian view of 'a deverbalized poem, a brain pattern (possibly) of nervous or electrical energy', and an elusive interlingua, artificial or Amerindian. What this amounts to is that Morgan feels the poem is drawn out of the source langauge into some other medium, before being reconstituted in the target language. I have heard Morgan say that he doesn't like to delve too much into the sources of his poetry for fear of rationalising it out of existence. I think it's possible to go a little further into his translation technique without doing any harm. The title of his paper is drawn from a poem by Borges, 'El Otro Tigre', 'The Other Tiger' in Thomas di Giovanni's translation, which Morgan reproduces. The third tiger, as Morgan sees it, the one not caught in the words, is 'the sub-verbal tiger of the interface'. It is as though (forgive a technical translator) the Spanish and English texts were two instruction manuals for a piece of (Platonic) earth-moving equipment, the 'real thing' the words only talk about. The other poem Morgan adduces to illustrate his point is an elegy on the poet's mother by Attila József. Morgan observes, '. . . the language is simple and direct, with no punctuation, and the verse is free, but the woman in the poem has such reality that you pierce right through the words and seem to see her and her relationship to the speaker before and after death, all in one pattern of perceptions'. Here we might object that mother, and tiger, are archetypes: the non-verbal unity there is not independent of words, but outwith the poem. The notion doesn't work at all for, say, Mayakovsky's 'Fiddle-ma-Fidgin', or Morgan's own *Newspoems* — most of his work in fact, where the poem, the co-ordinates of the event, are sound, sense, rhythm, rhyme, line, local history etc and most have to be changed to suit the other observer's standpoint; these aren't ghosts waiting to be painted, but pure constructs.

What are we to make of Morgan's 'translation interface'? Is it mystic, physiological, linguistic, Platonic or archetypal? Maybe each of them by turns. For Morgan it works, and that's what matters to him. His most entertaining translations make the audience aware of it as well.

La farce de Maître Pierre Pathelin, an anonymous work of the fifteenth century, was translated for the stage by Edwin Morgan. In one scene the draper goes to Pathelin's home to collect the money he is owed. Pathelin feigns madness, uttering a tremendous tirade of flapdoodle, to the consternation of the draper and the amusement of his wife, in about seven different languages or dialects: Limousin, Picardy and Norman French, Flemish, French with a Breton accent, Breton with a French accent, Lorrainese and Latin. Five centuries on, this is probably more fun for scholars than for audiences. The edition I consulted has a footnote for every word of nonsense, which helps us compare the first two parts of Pathelin's diatribe (which I have translated from Limousin and Picardy via modern French) with Morgan's version:

PATHELIN: Crowned Mother of God, my faith, I want to go away, I renounce God, overseas. God's belly, I say flute! Don't make a racket, do your sums! Don't let him talk to me about money. Do you understand, dear cousin?

GUILLEMETTE (the wife): He had a Limousin uncle, his great-aunt's brother. I'm sure that's why he's blethering in Limousin.

THE DRAPER: Hell! He's gone off his trolley, with my cloth under his oxter!

PATHELIN: Come in, sweet lady. What do all these toads want? Back off, you heap of shite! Quick! I want to be a priest. Come on! Let the devil take his place in this nest of old priests! And should the priest really be laughing when he ought to be singing his mass?

Morgan's version:

> PATHELIN: Och, the howe-dumb-deid's ay brattlin,
> The ugsom eeries are sae ferlie,
> It's fell the fremd ma tirly-mirly,
> And fient a jouk a jaup the toaly.
> Wee chookie-burdie's melanchoaly.
> Ah cannae smoch the hough an aa.
> Forforchen auchter larder waa.
> Bawbees for kimmers, nane for you.
>
> GUILLEMETTE: You see he lived once at Tamdhu
> With his Scotch uncle, a whisky man
> At the distillery, one of the clan,
> His aunt's husband. So he speaks Scots.
>
> DRAPER: The Devil cannot change his spots
> He's spiriting my cloth to the tomb.
>
> PATHELIN: Wie eine Blume dada zum,
> Und Merz und Herz so kunterbunter,
> Kuckuckverein einander unter,
> Uber alles immer Geld.
> O, was fur ein Haifischfeld!
> Sind Sie Sie von Sinnen siechen
> Rosenkrank und Guldensieben
> Are dead und on ze Toten-pole.   (*MPP*, 39)

And so it continues to custard-pie its way through Italian, Russian and Latin. There won't be a footnote for every word of Morgan's version, because he has brought it back to the theatre: one person is talking to two others; one of them is listening earnestly and the other is enjoying the spectacle.

Is the inscrutable interface anything other than the space between two people, one speaking and the other listening? Whatever their respective languages? It is this specific phase in translation, or translation as a verbal enactment of this fraught transition, that is so central to Morgan's work.

The foreign reader sees a poem shorn of the day-to-day, the ephemeral; its outline is clearer, its context and associations less so, its register and accent might not be caught. (Maybe this helps explain why the likes of Poe and Byron could mean more at times to the French and Germans than to native English speakers.) The situation has its advantages and its drawbacks. At times the reader has the impression of going right to the heart of the poem while being unsure of the tense of a verb or the sense of a noun. Who knows? maybe the author would have left blanks at those points if he could decently have done so, but felt obliged to fill them in, thus ruining the thing for native speakers. Here is what Edwin Morgan writes on first encounters with poems to be translated:

> But again this early reading ought perhaps to be fairly impression-istic, since it is important to remain faithful to these shocks and splashes of impact, representing as they do one's first sudden glimpses of the foreign poet's world, the poet's foreign world, which one is about to enter. For example, long before one fully understands a difficult poem by Eugenio Montale, his world stirs and reveals itself: there is a shimmer, a play of light on water and on crumbling buildings, a face glancing in a mirror, an accordion being played in the twilight . . . Absorbing this atmosphere is a step in comprehension, and one grasps at this point not only the tone of the particular poem but the signature of the author's style; one begins to sense his 'hand', his way of putting things. At this stage, too, most poems yield more unmistakable pleasure than they do at any later moment of understanding . . . ('The Transla-tion of Poetry', 21)

What Morgan does with his Mayakovsky translations is to convey this 'first sudden glimpse of the foreign poet's world'; he gives us not Mayakovsky as an ideal Russian reader would understand him, but Mayakovsky as Morgan found him – full of stange invention, glinting with unfamiliar words. Morgan is not a native speaker of Scots, nor are most of his readers: he introduces the translations, in print and on stage, in English. Consider 'Ay, but can ye?', the first poem in *Wi the haill voice*, and one of Mayakovsky's earliest.

> Wi a jaup the darg-day map's owre-pentit –
> I jibbled colour fae a tea-gless;
> ashets o jellyteen presentit
> to me the great sea's camshach cheek-bleds.
> A tin fish, ilka scale a mou –
> I've read the cries of a new warld through't.
> But you
> wi denty thrapple
> can ye wheeple
> nocturnes fae a rone-pipe flute?

Early Russian audiences, too, must have found these futurist pieces very foreign. I have (or had) a recording of Mayakovsky reading this poem as late as the mid-1920s: he declaims it in the heroic mode, as though it

were the introduction to 'The Bronze Horseman' rather than a wry
riddle. He made it strange – a practice the Formalists prized – and he
kept it strange.

We can see how Morgan works towards this effect from his rough
translation into English:

> Hoof beats rang
> Apology for a song:
> Crap
> Crop
> Crape
> Croup
>
> Drunk in the bluster,
> With ice for shoe-leather,
> The street slipped along.
> The horse came a cropper
> Down on its crapper,
> and presto
> The open mouths mooched together,
> Gaper behind gaper, all in a cluster . . .
>
> (Glasgow University Library, MS Morgan 105)
>
> Horse-cluifs clantert
> giein their patter:
> crippity
> crappity
> croupity
> crunt.
>
> Bleezed in the blafferts,
> wi ice-shoggly bauchles,
> the street birled and stachert.
> The cuddy cam clunk,
> cloitit doon doup-scud,
> and wheech
> but the muckle-mou'd moochers werna lang
> in makin theirsels thrang . . .   (WHV, 30)

Pruning articles and prepositions, grafting on a verb or two, fusing
alliteration with simple sound effects so the sense has to be sought out,

all delivered in street-Scots stiffened with dictionary words, it now works more like the original:

> Bili kopyta.
> Peli budto:
> – Grib.
> Grab.
> Grob.
> Grub. –
>
> Vetrom opita,
> l'dom obuta,
> ulitsa skol'zila
> loshad' na krup
> grohnulas',
> i srazu
> za zevakoi zevaka . . .   (Mayakovsky, II, 10)

In 'The Ballad o the Rid Cadie' (*WHV*, 29), Morgan matches Mayakovsky in his sound effects, where the sounds of 'Cadet laddie', 'rid cadie', 'bluid-rid cadie' proliferate through the first half of the poem, till 'Like grumphies in claver lived the haill Cadet caboodle, / the Cadet and his cadaddy and his grampacadoodle' – then they are overtaken by the wind and the wowfs of the 'revo – wheesht though – LUTION', leaving nothing but the moral of the tale. In 'Eupatoria' (*WHV*, 70), Morgan definitely goes one better, ringing the changes on the title, from sanatorium to Eupatorianity – just as he does in 'Versailles' (*WHV*, 48), where 'Pompadour' engenders Pompadusas, Pompadoris, and Pompadorchester suite.

At the end of 'Mayakoferensky's Anectidote', immediately after a few verses of bureaucratic English (the backward elements in these translations all speak English – bureaucratic, banal or Mills & Boon) there is a send-off in neologised, legal-Latinate Scots:

> I canny sleep for waumlin thochts.
> Nicht's haurdly gane.
> Day loups. I see't aa plain:
> 'Oh for
> yin mair
> sederunt to convene
> to congree to conclude
> to comblasticastraflocate sans avizandum
> ilka sederunt and tap-table-tandem!'   (*WHV*, 44)

The message comes across straight away, but it keeps fizzing and sparking for some time afterwards. We get the delight of engaging with Mayakovsky's work — as when the man himself is praising Brooklyn Bridge:

> It's prood I am
> > o this
> > > wan mile o steel,
> > my veesions here
> > > > tak vive and forcy form—
> > a fecht
> > > for construction
> > > > > abune flims o style,
> > a strang,
> > > > trig-rivetit grid,
> > > > > > juist whit steel's for!
> > > > > > ('Brooklyn Brig', *WHV*, 61)

In the end, though, English is the chosen language of most of Morgan's translation work, and in it he pursues a different strategem, aiming for a transparency of language that distracts as little as possible from the original. It works very well, especially in the versions of Weöres and József, and other Hungarian poets: it also seems to be a good glaze to apply to Pushkin.

At times it may be felt that there is too much self-abnegation on the translator's part: I am sure that the lexis of Edwin Morgan's poems is much larger than that of his translations, and that the direct speech in his poems, which is always individual, is never so bland as in his translations. His recent work, though, has a still finer finish than, for example, the early Scève dizains. Reading Weöres or József in English I hardly think of the translater at all. And that is as it should be.

NOTES

1. *The Scottish Review*, 2:5, Winter 1976, p.23.
2. *New Hungarian Quarterly*, VIII:25, Spring 1967, p.30.
3. *Ossi di seppia* (Milan: Mondadori, 28th edn, 1983), p.116.
4. *Stihotvorenija i Poemy* (Moscow-Leningrad, 1965), p.371.
5. William Soutar, *Collected Poems*, ed. H. MacDiarmid (London, 1948), p.392.
6. Essay in A.J. Aitken, M.P. McDiarmid and D.S. Thomson eds, *Bards and Makars* (University of Glasgow Press, 1977).

Nine

The Kind of Poetry I Want:
Morgan as Critic

Jack Rillie

Confidently still, when Edwin Morgan joined his profession in University English, it was claimed to be 'The Age of Criticism', vigorous, combative, 'ardent' (in Arnold's word), certain that 'poetry will save us'. It was Kenyon, Sewanee, Chicago, Cambridge. It was Ransom, Brooks, Wimsatt, Trilling, Winters, Blackmur, Richards, Empson, Leavis. These were the apostles of Coleridge and Arnold, theologising, explicitating the implicit, setting new bearings, palpating for ambiguities, building the defence-works of Modernism. It is perhaps not surprising that Morgan should look back to the 1950s as a difficult time, sloughing off a war, learning to teach, caught in that critical millrace, and listening for the poet's voice. However uncertainly that sounded to him in those years, it was always his real vocation.

It is within that milieu that Morgan's earlier critical work was done. The essays which belong to that period, on Dunbar, Dryden, Browne and Johnson, 'Women and Poetry', Wordsworth, are all distinguishable from the mainstream of his other work in method and tone and occasion. The careful and informed elucidation of the subject has no causes to promote, no aim other than sensitively and objectively to explore the case. These essays concern themselves neither with textual emendation nor with sources; they direct themselves towards offering a fresh understanding, careful readings without being 'close-reading'. It is particularly noticeable too that, despite the conformist pressures of the critical climate, he seems in these essays almost oblivious to current orthodoxies.

Since Eliot, prolific and influential in both activities, revived the issue of the poet-critic it has made it much more problematic than it really is. To an interviewer's question about the relationship Morgan gives an affirmative but luke-warm answer, yet is characteristically grateful to the accident of a commission for an opportunity to extend or change his views (*Verse*, 36). And he denies flatly that he was at all influenced by the 'Back to Dunbar' slogan. Yet he does recognise at a more important level, an affinity: 'It was loving Dunbar because he's a kind of whittrick . . .' and '. . . the great liking I have for energy as a quality . . . attracted me . . .' (*Verse*, 30, 33).

It is 'energy' indeed which stands at the head of the Dunbar essay, making the argument. There is 'energy without order', 'order without energy'. But there is a third, 'energy as order'. 'A poet with a strong sensuous and linguistic tone to his imagination can find himself inspired within his own concern with words, with rhythm, with shape, with concatenations that are audible as well as thematic . . .' (*E*, 81–2). Here we have Hopkins as well as Dunbar – and indeed Morgan himself. He has no need to go 'back' in order to begin.

Yet, in a sense he does go back to begin, not to Dunbar, but to that mightier poet who is his great precursor, Wordsworth. 'A Prelude to *The Prelude*' (*E*, 118–29) is, on the face of it, a well-made and perceptive essay offering a reasonable and acceptable explanation of how Wordsworth gets from recollection as mere history to a *poetry* made out of the growth of a poet's mind. Opening the essay with Wordsworth's apparently naïve remark, 'I had nothing to do but describe what I had felt and thought' enables him to give to this ostensible method a doubtful prognosis and then to demonstrate the real complexity of the process by which the poem nevertheless achieves its 'victory'. But throughout the piece there is a sense of discomfort, dissatisfaction, impatience even, and it isn't, as we know from other essays and remarks, that he disapproves of Wordsworth. It is perhaps rather that Wordsworth has laid a giant's hand on his own imagination and, in order to preserve his own freedom, Morgan feels bound, partly unconsciously, to resist.

One feels, for example, that explanation would have been simplified by making more use of the Preface to *Lyrical Ballads* with all its stress on the 'permanent objects' of nature and the life of the mind in that environment. Yet, while in the end he does show the poet investing his vision in 'natural objects', he leaves open the question as to whether nature is destroyed by internalisation or still stands there as the only true source of imaginative power.

Now it is interesting that when he comes to write about Wordsworth for *Glasgow Herald* readers – 'Wordsworth in 1970' (*E*, 130–34) – the questions he puts are: '. . . what and how much, are we willing to give up?', 'A poet of nature or he is nothing'? Nature is very fine as a theme, in *The Prelude, The Excursion*, 'Tintern Abbey'. But there is something else in that last poem: the smoke rising up from the fires of those 'dwellers in the houseless woods'. A 'tiny signal', Morgan says, but 'this . . . is the real Wordsworth, unaccommodated man.'

> Despite the poet's intense advocacy of a fruitful collusion between nature and man, despite the 'gravitation and the filial bond' that connect us with the physical world . . . despite the 'auxiliar light' that like an endless servomechanism between optic nerve and sunset kept a round of glory going in the act of perception – still it was true, and Wordsworth knew it was true that the vagrant could not subsist . . . without having people to beg from . . . A labourer can look at a sunset, but if the 'auxiliar light' is fitful, unfed by the conditions of life, what good does it do to say that 'Nature never did betray / The heart that loved her'? Whose heart? What love? (*E*, 131–2)

What he directs us to are 'the smoke of man', and the 'unaccommodated' characters of *Lyrical Ballads* – Simon Lee, Harry Gill, Martha Ray and the others. A number of things can be said of all this. It is wrong. Its derision seems as unjustified as its images are inappropriate (servo-mechanisms? Wordsworth?). Setting aside the detail of the errors, however, what we are witnessing here is a creative misreading. The poet of power he admires, who promises to carry 'sensation into the midst of the objects of the science itself', is the poet of nature and natural objects, the poet for whom the city is a 'perpetual flow / Of trivial objects'. He cannot be expunged from Morgan's imagination so he has to be reinterpreted in a way which will prevent him from remaining a contrary and disruptive presence. Thus the impatience, the rather intemperate language, issues neither from dislike nor from rejection of Wordsworth but from an internal and indeed creative tension. The adherent of 'fact and science' will be the *poet* (of nature = 'the humanity of man within his whole environment', facts, science) through this very conflict with the Poet (of nature – Snowdon, the thorn, the soldier, the idiot boy, 'man and nature and human life').

The Warton Lecture of 1977 (*PP*) stunningly entitled *Provenance and Problematics of 'Sublime and Alarming Images' in Poetry* accounts in an interesting and straightforward way for the waxing and waning of the 'Sublime' from its eighteenth-century usage down to the present where, appearing only fitfully in Pound, Stevens, and MacDiarmid, its only welcoming genre would seem to be Science Fiction. The Sublime, in most of the instances provided by Burke, seems firmly anchored to real objects and situations: mountains, precipices, seas, fearful creatures, perilous situations. As such, it conforms well with Morgan's aims for poetry. But of course it is primarily an emotional effect, and it belongs not accidentally to the century of the Sentimental, the Gothic, Melodrama. And we recognise 'The intense feeling, ecstatic or terrible, without an object or exceeding its object' of which Eliot speaks. This has two effects in the subsequent development of literature: it interiorises the world, converting it into a *paysage d'ame*; it also leads to that 'literature of process' which is so distinctive a feature of this century – the *Cantos*, Stevens, Joyce, 'Happenings', the play-spaces of the avantgarde. The terms of Morgan's aesthetics welcome the latter movement with its evolutionary overtones. But that emptying, kenosis, destruction of the 'real world' which seems to have been its precondition is something he wants to reject, with symbolism and its verbal heterocosm.

One's disposition to find a snug niche for Morgan's work within a 'modernism' characterised by such preconceptions about 'process' is probably mistaken. Whittricks don't know niches from exits. Evolution, development, randomness, to say nothing of *zaum* in optophonic patterns, delight him. But then why is he 'for core thinking as opposed to flux thinking', and so wary of 'organic'?

It is, however, one of the pleasures of his *oeuvre* that he can shift gear and tone and enterprise with such competence. One goes from 'Dryden's Drudging' to 'Howlers', to 'Gorky Street'. There is an essay of 1950 – the date is important – on 'Women and Poetry'[1] which would blow the mind of Shere Hite. As I read it again I am required to blink, if only for my friend. He also edited two splendid anthologies. The *Collins Albatross Book of Longer Poems* (1963) as all anthologies must, has to face the fact that there are items which choose themselves, but within these constraints he has been characteristically independent. His Introduction discusses the history of the long poem with its narrative interests and its change and survival into the twentieth century, after Poe had decided it couldn't be 'all poetry'. The annotations are superb. The notes to 'McAndrew's Hymn' (a 'Morgan' choice) are good enough to equip an engineer for the *Jeanie Deans*. Morgan's 1980 anthology *Scottish Satirical Verse* (*SSV*) makes an equally fresh selection from the fifteenth to the twentieth century, from Anon. to Tom Leonard, drawing on this century for almost half the representation. The Introduction has a brief but sharply-focused discussion of satire in its Scottish context, the elements of narrative and comedy, and some interesting remarks on the traps set for the reader.

The critical issues germinating in the group of essays we've been discussing really only grow into more identifiable forms in what one might call, without derogation, the literary journalism. It is in these essays and reviews that I think the reader can begin to see Morgan plain. Of course the interviews by Crawford (*Verse*) and Walker (*Akros*) are immensely valuable. And Morgan is a good interviewee, frank, articulate, honest, helpful. Yet neither of these interviewers seems to have noticed that there is a yawning gap of forty years in which the victim soldiered and taught and suffered, in which the mill of the poet's mind is being stuffed with grist. But for forty years he's a Kurtz up the Congo without a Marlow.

In the 1950s and increasingly in the 1960s he comes to be engaged in the issues of Scottish letters and in the 'second wave' as he calls it, of the Scottish Renascence. His contributions to the professional journals wane. Perhaps in terms of the lines he quotes from W.C. Williams, he might say

> We go on living, we permit ourselves
> To continue – but certainly
> Not for the university . . .

and he turns his face and talent to the world.

The role he adopts, not necessarily of set purpose, is essentially that of a propagator of opinion within a specifically Scottish context. The tone changes, is more declarative, monitory, hortatory, indignant sometimes:

> The Scottish air tends to be thick with advice and assertion, much of it hectoring, strident, unconsidered . . . but the stillness out of which a personality can grow to its full stretch without spikiness and shoulder-chips (is) harder to come by . . . (*E*, 177)

Iain Crichton Smith gets a sharp 'Buck up, man!' about 'caring'. And Muir gets the short ball:

> Muir's primitivism, returning all post-atomic mankind to an Orkney farm, not without a certain austere satisfaction, seems to me more insulting than comforting to man's restless and aspiring brain. Let your survivors tame the horses of the Moon, the dragons of Mars: I would call that hope. (*E*, 193)

Tamburlaine, Faustus, and Captain Kirk are never far away when he looks for support. He tends indeed to chide less for failures in peculiarly Scottish issues, than, as with Muir or Garioch, for indifference or opposition to the challenges of science and contemporaneity.

MacDiarmid, however, occupies a quite different place in Morgan's work. Behind all the great critics there stands a paradigmatic poet: Sophocles for Aristotle, Shakespeare for Coleridge, Dante for Eliot. For Morgan, in the foreground at least, it is MacDiarmid, perfectly conscious though he is of his mentor's limitations.

In 'MacDiarmid Embattled' (*E*, 194–202), although the ostensible subject is that clumsy anti-Campbell, Spanish Civil War poem, 'The

Battle Continues', Morgan is really laying down a number of general critical markers. 'To write literature of any value one must somehow write about life.' 'To write *about* literature one must write about life.' These clear the way for our understanding of his position, though not necessarily indicating identity of views with MacDiarmid's politics in the poem. Morgan acknowledges some of the difficulties of a poetry of fact in our fear of the prosaic, but the argument is scarcely settled by appealing to Wordsworth to remind us that poetry and prose after all 'share the same human blood'. So do assassins and saints, plumbers and surgeons. Yet there is a sudden shift into a higher dimension. Beyond satire, he says, with its passion for justice and its angers, there is the passion for unity and harmony, the poet's 'labour of love' and its 'benedictive vision'; harder for the secular, or Marxist, imagination than for the Christian the task of accommodating 'the sure and blessed future to the snarl of trends in the present . . . the battle with the dying but lively forces of history and the battle with art' (*E*, 202). There is more here than a peroration for the poet of 'The Battle Continues'.

The essays, 'Poetry and Knowledge in MacDiarmid's Later Work' (*E*, 203–13) and 'MacDiarmid at Seventy-five' (*E*, 214–21) supply more detail on the issues which attend a poetry of 'fact and science'. The demands are made with a confidence in their validity which is not always earned. 'The exclusion of value/from the essence of matter of fact' has to be overcome. And the 'evolutionary credo implicit in poetry' requires that it take up the challenge, that it looks to the future. Any 'making', 'creating' is of course directed into the future, without in any but the loosest metaphorical sense being 'evolutionary'. Poetry may be 'on the side of life' in the old Leavisian sense, but it is extremely doubtful if this is what is meant. A more likely explanation offers itself in Morgan's 'James Joyce and Hugh MacDiarmid'[2] which deals with the extraordinary organic prescience found in the embryo, which grows organs with no immediate use but adaptable for some unforeseen future function. MacDiarmid borrows this from Sherrington and Morgan quotes the source in an earlier essay.[3] This is seen as a kind of analogy for the 'precognitive' gift of the artist and a reminder of his *duty* to the future. In the 'Joyce' article mentioned Morgan quotes part of the relevant passage from 'In Memorian James Joyce':

> Everywhere we find
> Prospective knowledge of needs of life
> Which are not yet but are foreknown

And he is here more explicit:

> But what of evolution, what of MacDiarmid's view of the artist as

someone creating for, and in a sense truly creating, the future . . .
(his) argument, throughout 'In Memoriam James Joyce', is that he
and Joyce were both working towards world-consciousness, and
that this was in fact the next general evolutionary step. ('Joyce and
MacDiarmid', 216)

'Precognition' seems roughly to mean that the poet creates today what
may not be understood until tomorrow, a fairly old trope invested with
strong scientific associations. It appears, however, that the 'evolutionary
credo' draws at least some of its authority from the kind of evidence of
ontogeny provided by Sherrington, but whether this is being used
simply as analogy or as supplying a kind of presumption for finding
some similar potency latent within the neurological structure of poets
is by no means clear. But the vision of the 'Prospective Poet' goes some
way beyond the 'dedicated son', though it still claims the need to be
'doctrinal and exemplary to a nation', to mankind indeed. It carries an
elevated and committed faith in the poet's mission unusual for our
century. It may have immediate reference to MacDiarmid, but the tone
he gives to his exposition does not suggest that Morgan sees himself
simply as the one who cries in the wilderness.

Morgan's Scottishness has doubtless been reinforced by MacDiarmid,
as by earlier Scottish writers. The fact that, as he tells Crawford in the
interview, he did not really become aware of the 'Scottish Renascence'
until the end of World War II was a common experience. The
intellectual climate of his generation was the poetry of the 1930s, *New
Writing, Horizon*, and behind these the greater figures of Eliot, Pound,
Yeats. And these too are part of the Scottish literary climate. Essentially
as Morgan says 'we have really had our renascence before we were ready
for it.'[4] As Arnold said of the Romantics, it 'did not know enough'. The
'second wave' he says, 'put the movement on a firmer foundation . . .
firmer in facts, firmer in scholarship'. 'Its knowledge was often scrappy,
its theorizing was often eccentric and unscientific'. Morgan therefore
takes an unillusioned look at the movement, dismissing its sloganising,
condemning the 'Scottish Heritage' label hung round our necks, and the
myths about a 'Capital centre'. He is willing even to chide gently the
ungenerous dismissal of the Kailyaird. In any case, as he says, the
movement 'will be seen to be only part of a wider twentieth-century
movement, a Peripheral Renascence of English poetry: the attempted
stabilization of an enfeebled English tradition by poets breaking into it
from its boundaries.'[4] This is the difference between timidly looking for
'international' influences on Scottish poetry and being an international
poet who is a Scotsman, a man, simply, of the twentieth-century
writing here.

His views on the language are similarly relaxed. 'Language expressing and preserving the "soul" of a people' is a very fine idea as he says. But from the mix, which language? So he suggests that it might be better to explore the 'mix' than to take up unprofitably entrenched positions which make the language problem the 'incubus' it has been. For Morgan, as we know, as it became for MacDiarmid, the choice has depended entirely on the occasion, on what the imagination itself demanded. But there is no point in asking what the minimum requirements are to be a 'Scottish' writer, or what a distinctively 'Scottish' product would be. It doesn't matter, he is saying, Write! His attempt to rid writers of their obsession with Scottishness, with language is, of course, part of his wider concern that poetry, if it is to be honest, must deal with the *world* of its time, its city streets, flight paths, science, technology, the beatnik in the kailyaird, the jingbang.

Morgan's practice as critic, as becomes apparent, is not directly to choose 'themes' to declare his positions. There is no 'Function of Criticism'. He proceeds rather by using his subject to provide openings through which he can expand and explore his own ideas. With MacDiarmid one frequently finds Morgan reinforcing the poet's ideas and so aligning himself with them, although it would be hazardous to assume that this was always the case. Yet he does share that strong *sense* of a vision which we find, sometimes raucously expressed, in MacDiarmid.

> The fact is that man must react, as man, to his whole environment. Nothing less will satisfy his hungry spirit. The future of poetry, like the future of the other arts, is bound up not only with the slowly evolving nature of man but also with the very quickly evolving relation of man to his environment. Poetry today is in process of recovering from an ambitious attempt – the attempt of Yeats, Pound, Eliot, Stevens – to separate its own artisitc evolution from the general evolution of society. . . . I am made conscious of this strange communicative gap . . . between poetry and life. Our poetry needs greater humanity; but it must be the humanity of man within his whole environment: not just the drop of dew, the lock of hair, but the orbiting rocket in Anselm Hollo, the lobotomy in Allen Ginsberg, the lunar mountains in Hugh MacDiarmid. (*E*, 14–15)

This is from the essay, 'A Glimpse of Petavius' which opens his prose collection, the prologue to the swelling act of the cosmic theme, carrying all the polemical energy and authority of a manifesto. The constitutive elements of his mission are all proclaimed or implied in these sentences: man *in* his environment, the future, evolution; orbiting rocket, lobotomy, lunar mountains; Yeats, Pound, Eliot, Stevens OUT, Ginsberg, MacDiarmid IN.

'Man' for Morgan acknowledges the interpersonal, as we have seen from his criticism of Smith for not caring *enough*, or of MacDiarmid for the lack of human warmth in his later poems. But its connotations are quite as insistently generic, moving from voyager to startrekker, to the New Man in the New Constellation. And indeed, in the features he employs as a climax to the statement, there is something of that fictionalising gloss which television gives to its headlined news items. As it turns unaccountably to what *feels* like fantasy, it begins to reflect back doubts on the content we are to give to 'man' and 'environment'. Yet he insists we dwell, and are encouraged to rejoice, in the here and now, of which the locale is the city. The city for Morgan is that street life we see in the poetry, though the architecture will be neither neo-Gothic nor the Victorian terrace but the high-rise flats. Essentially, it is the great moving toyshop of contemporaneity. But, as *From Glasgow to Saturn* is intended to remind us, Planet Earth is our home – meantime – our total environment reaches out to the cosmos.

Our understanding of the conditions under which we live and the sources of whatever power we have to control and change that environment so that we may survive, if not as individuals then as species, is vested in the sciences. It is science and its methods which deliver the only true knowledge of our condition. The basic general characteristics of the physical universe are energy, process, change, and in the biosphere evolutionary development. Within the macrocosmic laws which govern these systems there are, at microcosmic levels, random events which may or may not alter the macrosystem. Man's own evolutionary history and his increase in knowledge give grounds for assuming that the belief in human progress is justified. Optimism about our condition and our future is not only reasonable, but, since mind itself is an active agent within process, it must have confidence in that order if it is fully to co-operate.

I have no doubt simplified Morgan's beliefs, perhaps misconstrued them, but I have tried to set down as fairly as I can what I elicit from his writings, where the evidence is abundant though disseminated. Nor is there any doubt of their importance to him. He tells Marshall Walker:

> The survival instinct is important to all life but in man it takes a much greater grip of the possibilities . . . he is capable of overcoming even very great disasters. This may be in itself only partly a rational faith, just something that I feel . . . but I don't think it's entirely that. I think it would come out of an objective

reading of history . . . I don't think it's entirely irrational that one can have a hopeful or even a very hopeful long-term view of the possibilities of the human race . . . I think it goes without saying that we shall go to other environments and adapt to them perhaps even physiologically . . . (*Akros*, 22–3)

Such a position might seem unusual for a writer who grew up *entre deux guerres*, when one thinks of the intellectual climate of that time, its 'alienation', its 'wastelandism', Kafka, Musil, Greene's 'country of mortal sin', the Depression, ovens, war, Hiroshima. But in 'Hugh MacDiarmid's Later Poetry'[3] Morgan reminds us of contrary currents in the popular but reputable scientific writing of those years. He instances Sherrington, and Jeans, Huxley, Alexis Carrel, and there were of course influential writers like Wells and Stapledon. Morgan himself read widely in that same area, and it clearly left a strong impression on his thought, although for a progressivism so faith-filled and so secure one might look back to the previous century, to Comte and Spencer, but source-hunting will serve no really useful purpose here. Out of systems far less reputable – strange, ramshackle, morally dubious structures – poets such as Blake, Yeats, and Pound have made their poetry. 'Our revelations', as Stevens says, 'are not the revelations of belief, but the precious portent of our own powers.'

The set of critical principles which this infra-structure supports has something of the same resistance to classification. A 'poetry of fact and science' will manifest itself in ways which, with Whitman, Hart Crane, MacDiarmid behind us, might not startle us too much. And one can see, if a little dimly in MacDiarmid's case – and Concrete is in deep shadow – how value and fact might be said to be united, or how the science-epic simile of guinea-worm or haemolytic streptococcus might not only illustrate descriptive processes but create a new metaphor between source (outside) and text. The significance of establishing 'metaphors' of identification in this context, instead of metonymic figures needs looking into also. There is, moreover, a tendency for the science which underpins this realism to involve a kind of technological determinism, which not only expresses itself in the Pelagianism I have referred to, but extends to the materials and forms of art itself. It is not just the *exhortation* to 'meet', 'pursue' the environment (*Akros*, 9) but the fact that

> The concrete movement . . . has forced a whole series of creative confrontations on the use of language, sign, metaphor, typography, and space, *and in this there is no going back*. (E, 32)

And MacDiarmid's view of the artist as 'someone creating for and in a sense truly creating, the future', with the quite precise connotations of the 'evolution' of language, derives its authority from the sciences and ties poetry into the universal process. But we are not told how.

A number of features derive importance from the same assumptions about the future and the hope which attends it. 'Energy', as we saw, is a literary quality Morgan admires in Dunbar, Graham, Baudelaire, in 'flyting'. It moves quite naturally into his welcome for Mayakovsky's exciting revivification of language, 'mind-bending imagery' and to that 'adventurousness' of ideas and language he mentions in the Crawford interview. It is of course associated with his admiration for the heroic and that image of the Voyager which appears first in 'The Seafarer' and runs all through his poetry, to Gagarin and the sci-fi startrekkers of our future.

That same energy is of course a feature of language itself and, even within a program of Realism, justifies the linguistic experiment we see in poems Concrete (clean, dirty, ferro-), Emergent, Sound. Just reading that essay 'Into the Constellation' (*E*, 20–34) with its hi-tech vocabulary, its exotic game-players, one finds oneself asking where one has heard this wised-up, fast talk before: ' "calm down / most of what happens / happens without you" '. And here are the two de Campos, Pignatari, Gomringer, Mondrian, Arp, Vantongerloo, Max Bill, Bory, El Lissitzky, and Seiichi Niikuni. Where else is this kind of outasight, saturated reportage other than in Tom Wolfe's New Journalism? His techniques, Wolfe tells us, come from poetry, the novel, essays. But the material, the world is out there and he puts technique and scene together. Its power lies in 'the simple fact that the reader knows all this actually happened. The disclaimers have been erased. The screen is gone. The writer is one step closer to the absolute involvement of the reader that Henry James and James Joyce dreamed of and never achieved.'[5] Morgan's essay was only the clue, its style not as important as the way in which this points, with its hunger for Wolfe's own finger-licking reality, its declaration that 'the disclaimers have been erased', to 'man in his environment', 'fact and science', 'true and close to actual modern experience', in other words towards a definition of an important aspect of the kind of 'Realism' Morgan appears to be deploying.

Relevant to that project, too, are the attitudes he takes up towards 'Nature' and its associated Romantic analogy 'organic'. He tends rather to sympathise with Mayakovsky's move away from nature ('boring') towards the city, and, on more interesting grounds, with Robbe-Grillet for declaring the end of 'our love-affair with Nature'. (The idea, if not the practice, of *chosisme* must have been attractive too.) It also seems to represent for Morgan the haunts of those ecologists he inveighs against in the *Akros* interview, who reduce Scotland to 'a moor of boulders and two ospreys' (*P*, 189). More significant is the fact that the great Romantic concord between man and nature, which Wordsworth wants to define too narrowly for him through 'natural objects', carries too much transcendental freight. The nearest he gets to a Nature beyond the city is in sympathising with MacDiarmid's fondness for 'stones' and 'desert', which can be 'a challenge to man's physical exploration and endurance' – the 'journey' image again. Nature, in its strong Romantic identification with the 'rural' is, of course, set on the 'organic' side of that Organic / Mechanical dualism which persists well into the twentieth century and, for Morgan, is responsible for maintaining that disastrous gulf between city and country, Science and Art.

Organicism, to which I've already referred, was another source of resistance. With its obsessive distrust of personality, intention, belief, biography it took its autotelism to inordinate lengths, even though many of the critics kept a 'correspondence' theory in their desk drawers; with so strongly centripetal a model, the relevance or attachment of the poem to the commonsense 'real' was difficult to establish. If one wanted a poetry of 'man in his environment', one had to smash the high glazes of the urn. This is what Morgan set out to do and what his poetry in its polymorphous variety does, from the defiant jingle of his loose verbal change to the dismantling of language and the free play of the mind among the morphemes and phonemes.

There is, however, a muddle, in the mind of MacDiarmid certainly, about 'organic'. MacDiarmid likes the Coleridgean term 'coadunation'. He wants 'unity' and he favours organisation, of parts, at any rate. 'Organic' was a concept that should have suited him. And Morgan has to admit that those fine early poems are 'clear-cut completed objects', while 'The Kind of Poetry I Want' in his later work is to be 'open', unfinished even, and tolerant of a good deal of imported material. If the early poems are 'organic', and they are (but only if you choose to employ this kind of language) then one has to avoid the term. And so, though of course the word is inextricably involved with the evolutionary ideas retained and carries there no analogical force, the analogy remains to trouble the argument about the 'open' poem. For MacDiarmid, and Morgan too, want 'lucidity' as against 'ambiguity', 'Fact and science' against 'myth'. (*E*, 209–10, 214). In the 'mosaic' of *Annals*, MacDiarmid finds 'in that prodigiousness of the universe a safeguarding excellence . . .', a remark which Morgan calls 'striking and provocative'. 'What' he says, 'is being safeguarded? Multiplicity . . . from classification, mystery . . . from reason, vision . . . from theory. Can we add that nature is being safeguarded from art? It's certainly being safeguarded from any art that goes too quickly for design and order without having accepted the aleatory discipline.' There is a great deal to be unpacked in that last paragraph. One can see the shadow of the 'organic' come near, and there is perhaps too the most delicate hint of a doubt about 'art'. If only art were not just *like* life?

What we do not get from Morgan is a smoothly-sutured aesthetic. Nor is there any adherence to an identifiable critical 'school'. His mind is not naturally theoretical, nor is there that coinage of heuristic conceits which we find in Eliot. If one puts Isaiah Berlin's question, is he fox or hedgehog ('The fox knows many things, but the hedgehog knows one big thing'), like Berlin with Tolstoy, I should have to split my vote. Morgan is staggeringly well-informed, as well as being polyglot, and is meticulous in his attention to fact. Yet 'information' is also those scrapbooks, deliberately unorganised, interesting as much for their chance collocations as for the substance of individual items ('the aleatory discipline'?). He is perhaps naturally, certainly by conviction, antipathetic to the synthesising habits of the mind. Yet there *is* 'one big thing', his scientism and the strong evolutionary faith that attends it. From this come the aesthetic assumptions with which he works. But no extended discussion or defence of that 'Realism' is offered. Language is in (referential) order as it is, and there are no spectres, no 'sickness of language', no 'meaninglessness of meaning', no 'prison-house'. These are simply the minor side-effects of the real malaise of lack of trust in our own humanity.

I have been wrestling with Proteus: I knew it was Proteus all the time. And if I ask him, nevertheless, the question that buzzes between all the lines — 'is there any difference between "The Kind of Poetry I Want" and the kind of poetry I want?' he will reply,

> Bards who have shot their shout are boisterous.
> Bards have the fox's body in a box.

NOTES

1. 'Women and Poetry'. *Cambridge Journal* III:11, August 1950, pp.643–73.
2. In *James Joyce and Modern Literature*, edited by W.J. McCormack and Alistair Stead (London: Routledge & Kegan Paul, 1982), pp.202–17.
3. 'MacDiarmid's later poetry against an international background'. *Scottish Literary Journal* 5:2, December 1978, pp.20–35.
4. 'Modern Makars Scots and English'. *Saltire Review* 1:2, August 1954, pp.75–81.
5. Tom Wolfe, *The New Journalism* (London: Picador, 1975), p.49.

Ten

Edwin Morgan as Teacher

Robin Hamilton

I first encountered Edwin Morgan shortly before I matriculated at Glasgow University. In the early 1960s, Jordanhill Teacher Training College was hosting a mini-conference on modern poetry for teachers of English, and I had somehow managed to insinuate myself into the audience. At that time my poetic hero was Norman MacCaig, and I was there to hear MacCaig not so much talk about as denounce contemporary poetry. His opinion of what was happening in poetry at that time was less than favourable, though he did except Robert Graves as a valuable, if awkward and dinosaur-like, presence. From the body of the audience, a stranger to me whom MacCaig identified in his response as 'Edwin Morgan', stood up to suggest tentatively but firmly that there were some movements of interest, such as concrete poetry, of which MacCaig's denunciation should perhaps take account. Though acknowledging Edwin Morgan's own expertise in this area (and so I discovered for the first time that this member of the audience was himself a poet), neither MacCaig nor his somewhat conservative audience of school-teachers had any time for this.

My memory, of a slight, hesitant figure braving the massed establishment of Scottish teaching, stuck with me, as did the quizzical authority which MacCaig allowed the man — after all, someone whom MacCaig would treat with respect even when his own views were being challenged wasn't someone to be dismissed. In consequence, when I matriculated as a student at Glasgow University in 1965, it was with some excitement that I discovered that this same Edwin Morgan would be lecturing to the Ordinary English Class on Hugh MacDiarmid. A poet on a poet: surely this was what University English teaching was all about? Many things came across to me from that course of lectures, not least the beginnings of my love for MacDiarmid's poetry, and a continuing fascination with the protean complexities of *A Drunk Man Looks at the Thistle*. Above all, however, there was the decorum with which Edwin Morgan handled the text. He never directly alluded to the fact that he was himself a poet, but the authority which he brought to bear because of his own creative activity was patent.

At this time, Edwin Morgan wasn't widely recognised as an important poet. His work had certainly appeared in various small magazines and pamphlets, but until his first major collection, *The Second Life*, appeared from Edinburgh University Press in 1968, it was difficult to get hold of his work easily or in any great amount. Around Glasgow University there was, obviously, more of a sense than elsewhere of Edwin Morgan's range and abilities – most of all, along with Ian Hamilton Finlay, he was seen as an exponent of the Scottish-Brazilian branch of concrete poetry, but there was also the sense that the man had produced some distinguished translations from the Russian, as well as his magisterial translation of *Beowulf*.

The authority of the poet as teacher was in some ways more exciting because we had the feeling that he was *our* poet. The wider public hadn't yet discovered him, so he was still just ours. Not that he ever played on the status of his own writing: as I remember it, in none of the lectures which he gave in the four years that I was an undergraduate did he directly refer to the fact of his own writing, and even with regard to his critical studies, he was reticent. One of the highlights of the lecture course on Hugh MacDiarmid was his delighted and witty tracing of the critical brouhaha over the alleged plagiarism by MacDiarmid in the poem 'Perfect', and the convoluted debate over whether or not this relineation of the first sentence of a short story constituted an original creative intervention on MacDiarmid's part. It was only later that I found out that Morgan himself had been directly involved in the debate in the columns of the *Times Literary Supplement*. When he reached the point where, in deference to attacks on the poem, MacDiarmid had substituted another text for 'Perfect' in the American *Collected Poems*, we all felt a sense of despair at the capitulation of creative force to critical consensus. It was all the more of a relief to discover, as Edwin Morgan revealed as the crowning joke, that MacDiarmid had substituted for the plagiarised 'Perfect' an extract from yet another writer's work, this time a snatch from Hart Crane's *The Bridge*. Poetry triumphed after all over criticism, and it seems characteristic of Edwin Morgan that he chose to reveal the triumph and to avoid spoiling the joke, by retailing the climax not in the columns of the *Times Literary Supplement* but to a group of undergraduates.

The reticence, the humour, the scrupulous intelligence and the authority which Edwin Morgan brought to bear in his teaching of poetry were all there in that first course of his lectures. Looking back now, I can see that the concern with the themes which he dealt with in Hugh MacDiarmid's poetry was fuelled by an overlap with his own creative practice. Like MacDiarmid in 'Perfect' and elsewhere, Morgan was concerned – in translations, in the 'Emergent Poems', later in the *Instamatic Poems* – with the reworking and transformation into his own poetic output of other men's words. Poetry, for both MacDiarmid and Edwin Morgan, wasn't some magical Romantic inspiration, but a process of linguistic creation and transformation which could as easily digest existing verbal materials as it could the concreteness of reality itself.

This same fascination with the parallel between the practice of a past poet and his own emerged a year later when I attended Morgan's course of lectures on John Donne. In these, he anatomised the possible meanings which Donne might have concealed in the variations between the pronoun 'She' and 'Shee' which Donne used to refer to Elizabeth Drury, the young girl who was the subject of Donne's two *Anniversaries*. I'm not now, I think, absolutely convinced by the interpretations which Edwin Morgan extracted from this variation, but it certainly reflected his own delight in embedding concealed encodings in the orthographic fabric of his own verse. The best joke perhaps, is one which isn't revealed, and Edwin Morgan, in his lectures, was adept at the discretion of concealment and restricted revelation.

Writing poetry myself, having heard Edwin Morgan lecture, and developing an increasing fascination with his own work as a poet made me determined that, at some point in my undergraduate career, I'd arrange to be taught by him on a more personal level. As I was never assigned to him as a tutee, the obvious thing to do was to take his course in Scottish Literature. This took place once a week in his office, a funereal room next to the main English lecture theatre, and in the course of a year the texts which we studied moved from Henryson and Dunbar to Edwin Muir and Hugh MacDiarmid. The group of students – it was a small one, as I remember, about eight or ten of us – would have been given the text and the topic to discuss. Edwin Morgan would listen with magisterial impartiality to what must have been to him almost unbearably naive initial encounters with the central texts of Scottish literature. My most vivid memories aren't so much of the seminars themselves as of the encounters with Edwin Morgan over the essays which I wrote. This nearly always involved a greater or lesser degree of trepidation on my part – after all, there *has* to be a certain degree of diffidence in proffering an essay on Dunbar to the author of

'Dunbar and the Language of Poetry', which, when I was studying Dunbar under Edwin Morgan seemed to me the only interesting piece produced on the poet. In these individual encounters, Edwin Morgan was always more forthcoming with his own opinions than in the seminars. There, he was always concerned not to overwhelm the students with his own views. I especially remember a clash over the merits of the plays of James Bridie, which then (and indeed still) seem to me to have a moral ambiguity verging on intellectual dishonesty. I'd recently seen the premiere of John Arden's play *Armstrong's Last Goodnight* at the Citizen's Theatre, and this had struck me, in its sharp presentation of the moral issues involved, as much more to my own taste than Bridie's more complex moral explorations. Edwin Morgan was quite firm in taking the opposite stance, and he condemned my writing on Bridie as unfair to the playwright, distorted because I allowed my opinion of how I felt Bridie should have written to come between myself and the playwright.

My sense was that Edwin Morgan was happiest in the two extremes of teaching, either the lecture hall or the one-to-one encounter. This parallelled his sense of how he wanted to present his poetry. He never involved himself in writers' groups, but felt that either he should appeal to individuals for comment and criticism, or present his poetry to the proper public for poetry in the forum of the poetry reading.

Arriving at Glasgow University at this time, when so many members of the staff, not simply in the English Department but throughout the university, were poets, created certain assumptions about the place of writers in university life. It was only later, with the experience of other universities and institutions of higher education of various sorts, that I realised that it was unusual for a college to have such a range of poets on the staff as Glasgow University did in the 1960s, and that it wasn't a normal experience to find yourself being lectured on poetry by practising poets. In this period, as well as Edwin Morgan himself, Alexander Scott had been on the staff for some time, as had George Kay in the Italian Department. Kenneth White was still there when I went up in 1965, though just about to leave Glasgow for France, while Philip Hobsbaum would arrive in 1966 from Belfast where he had worked with many of the Belfast writers who were then emerging. Each of these writers had their own style of teaching and involvement with undergraduates, ranging from Kenneth White, who kept open house for disaffected undergraduate intellectuals, to Philip Hobsbaum, who set up the latest in a series of poetry groups, following on from the one he had established as a student of Leavis in Cambridge in the 1950s, and later those in London and Belfast.

As with the number of poets on the staff at Glasgow University in the 1960s, so the number of the undergraduate writers at this time was much greater than usual. What to me was the 'older' generation of writers were Colin Kirkwood, Robert Tait, and David (then D.M.) Black. The first two had been students at Glasgow University, Bob Tait in Philosophy, Colin Kirkwood in the English Department. Colin had stayed around to do graduate work on Ezra Pound, while Bob Tait had gone on to Edinburgh where he founded the magazine later to become *Scottish International*. All three were published in that journal, and when I was an undergraduate they were remote but established presences. At the same time, what can be seen with hindsight as the central group of so-called (or mis-called) Glasgow writers were going through or about to go through Glasgow University as undergraduates. Stephen Mulrine arrived one year ahead of me, in 1964. Tom Leonard I first encountered while he was working as an assistant in the University Bookshop, before he himself became a student, at about the same time that Angus Nicolson arrived at Glasgow University. Alan Spence arrived a year after me, and shortly afterwards Tom McGrath and Donald Saunders. Liz Lochhead was a student at the Glasgow School of Art. Alasdair Gray was working on *Lanark*, and Jim Kelman was still on the buses. The mix was beginning to stir. Fresh from school, it didn't occur to me that I was in the midst of a literary revival which was fairly rare. With no standards of comparison, it seemed inevitable that going up to university meant being taught by poets like Edwin Morgan and Philip Hobsbaum, and having as fellow students writers like Stephen Mulrine, Tom Leonard, and Angus Nicolson.

Within this potent mix of established and emerging writers, Edwin Morgan's work as a poet and teacher was very much at the extremes of the spectrum – either operating on an individual basis or as the 'other' Edwin Morgan, participant of a larger literary world that we aspired to when the time came and we had wiped the dust of undergraduate naïveté off our boots. Despite the wealth of magazines around the university campus between 1965 and 1969 (at one point, there were five entirely distinct literary magazines being published), when I was an undergraduate, Edwin Morgan's poems rarely appeared in them. I suspect that this was because none of the editors, then, had the temerity to approach him for material. I've since found that he's the most accommodating and generous of respondents when approached for poems for even the most obscure of magazines, but it took Tom McGrath, as editor of *GUM* but having behind him the experience of editing the *International Times*, to approach him for material, and to publish 'Stobhill' in an issue of *GUM*.

Edwin Morgan's style in dealing with undergraduate writing was on an individual basis, different, for instance, from that of Philip Hobsbaum in whose flat on Sunday evenings we used to collect to discuss each other's work. Stephen Mulrine remembers with gratitude Edwin Morgan's kindness and courtesy when being shown poems which Mulrine had written. In the same year that *The Second Life* was published, Edwin Morgan introduced the work of Mulrine, Kirkwood, Tait, and Alan Hayton in a small pamphlet published by *Akros* called *Four Glasgow University Poets*. Most of the writers who were undergraduates at this time subsequently appeared in the pages of *Akros* magazine, but then we were more prominent in the undergraduate magazines that seemed to be ubiquitous. The oldest established was the *Glasgow University Magazine*, but there was also a series of shorter-lived affairs that appeared sporadically and changed editors with almost every other issue, most notably *NiK* and *Henry Thrib*. There was also the annual undergraduate showpiece of student poetry broadcast once a year on Radio Scotland in *University Notebook*, and occasionally, student writers were included in the series of *Scottish Poetry* which first appeared in 1966, published by Edinburgh University Press. Edwin Morgan was one of the original three editors, a position which he held till the sixth issue in 1972. This publication became the most public forum for the work coming out of Glasgow University: Alan Hayton, James Aitchison, Robert Tait and Colin Kirkwood appeared in the first issue (as well as Edwin Morgan himself, Kenneth White and George Kay from among the staff). Stephen Mulrine appeared in the second issue, as did Tom McGrath at a time before he'd become a student at Glasgow. Alan Spence, myself, and Tom Leonard (with 'The Good Thief' and three other poems) all made our first appearance in the fifth issue in 1970. In this fashion, Edwin Morgan played two distinct roles in relation to us, on the one hand as a personal adviser and on the other as the impersonal editor of the anthologies in which we aspired to be printed.

Tom Leonard's 'The Good Thief' perhaps forms a paradigm of how things were at this time, in the years between 1965 and 1970. The poem began its public life read aloud to a session at Philip Hobsbaum's flat one Sunday night, passed through the student magazines (at one stage as an insert in the University Literary Society Magazine, as the printer had refused to set it up in type), and finally arrived in front of its largest audience in proper typeface, under Edwin Morgan's editorship, in *Scottish Poetry 5*.

It's never entirely easy for poets around universities, either as students or members of staff. The final rationale for a department of literature is critical rather than creative, and the creative presences always sit uneasily in this environment. Edwin Morgan managed this awkward position with tact and assurance. He could draw on his creative activities without imposing these on his teaching, and as a result developed one of the best accommodations of the writer in a university which I've come across.

I don't think I stopped being a student of Edwin Morgan's when I left Glasgow University. He gave at least one poetry reading at York while I was a student there, and at the same time I published an interview with him in the magazine *Eboracum*. The connection with Loughborough, where I now work, has been even closer. As well as the readings he's given there, Loughborough was the first university to give him an honorary degree, in 1981. The Scottish Literature course I teach is perhaps above all indebted to him, and may be the most direct reflection of his teaching that I've taken away from my years as an undergraduate. In form and content, it's very much modelled on the course which he taught me, with the exception that the chronological span embraces more of the modern period than his course did. Mine concludes, not with Hugh MacDiarmid but with a selection of contemporary Glasgow writers – Alasdair Gray, Jim Kelman, Tom Leonard – and of course, in pride of place as the climax of any contemporary study of Scottish Literature, Edwin Morgan. Thus things come full circle, with the teacher taught.

Eleven

Teaching Morgan[1]

Geddes Thomson

'Let me not be taught in the schools!' has been the cri de coeur of many a
writer, especially poets. They are remembering, of course, their own
schooldays and the weekly poetry lesson when the English teacher took
the living poem and ritually probed and dissected it until it was very
dead.

Teachers, I seem to remember from my own schooldays, liked such
lessons. There was perhaps a grim and righteous satisfaction in the
exercise of so much literary technology in the space of forty minutes:
versification, metre, rhyme schemes, figures of speech, devices of
language . . . All this was truly what teachers had been sent out to do
amongst the young. And if the young didn't like it (and they mostly
didn't) it was the young's fault. This approach to the teaching of poetry
can be traced back to the traditional college of education 'crit' lesson, in
which the student teacher taught a class for a period, observed by a
college lecturer who sat, like a bird of ill omen, at the back of the
classroom. 'Crit' lessons were feared and loathed by student teachers
because they were essentially fake pedagogical performances which
were, nevertheless, extremely important. The class, usually carefully
chosen for its submissive qualities, had been well-warned in advance of
what was expected from it − a zombie-like co-operation glossed over
with false enthusiasm.

You (and I was one such some decades ago), as aspiring dominie,
were also the prisoner of expectations. You were expected to 'perform',
to go through the whole bag of tricks, to teach what was termed 'a well-
rounded lesson' in forty minutes come hell or high water or tannoy
announcements or little boys looking for Mr Saunders, the regular class
teacher. The input was tremendous; the response from the class, apart
from a few bright sparks at the front, was pitiful.

Almost inevitably you chose some innocent poem as the vehicle for your performance. Poems were handy. They were short, but usually stuffed with technical goodies. Doing a poem to death in a period was no bother at all. Indeed, it was expected.

I recall one 'crit' lesson in which I committed the cardinal sin of moving the goal-posts slightly, of being too ambitious, of widening the scope somewhat. I decided to do *two* poems, comparing and contrasting them: Hogg's 'The Skylark' and Tennyson's 'The Eagle'. The wrath of my tutor afterwards was fearsome to behold. First of all, she didn't like Hogg's poem, considered it an unworthy companion-piece for the Tennyson. Secondly, and more importantly, I had not done the full business on 'The Eagle'. 'I would take', she said, with a fanatical gleam in her eye, 'at least two periods to do that poem. There's so much in it!'

Here is the full text of 'The Eagle':

> He clasps the crag with crooked hands:
> Close to the sun in lonely lands,
> Ringed with the azure world, he stands.
>
> The wrinkled sea beneath him crawls;
> He watches from his mountain walls,
> And like a thunderbolt he falls.

There *is* a lot in it, right enough. You could go on about alliteration, personification and contrast, but if you went on for one hour twenty minutes the average class of adolescents would be mentally climbing those mountain walls with frustration and boredom. Turning the teaching of poetry into a game of pursue the personification, identify the assonance, mug the metaphor, is not the way to teach poetry to children.

Indeed, even the phrase 'teach poetry to children' would make many teachers uneasy today, including this writer. We would prefer to create the classroom conditions under which our pupils can explore poems fruitfully through reading and discussion. Our hope – that as many of our pupils as possible obtain valid poetic experiences firmly based on the poems themselves. This, of course, is much more difficult than the ritual dissection described above. It requires a sensitive flexibility from the teacher; the adoption of a range of strategies in the classroom; an open-ness to pupil response and to the poem itself that the old regime excluded.

This is an essay about the study of Edwin Morgan's poems in secondary schools and the flexible approach outlined above will be implicit throughout the discussion, but even given this approach, difficulties remain. Granted that we explore poems, rather than teach poetry, we must also recognise that no poem exists in isolation. Every poem has a context — literary, historical, sociological, biographical. How much of this to present to a class? Only as much as is absolutely necessary is the short and not always very helpful answer.

Teachers in the last two decades have complicated matters by inventing their own contexts for poems in an attempt to make texts more relevant, accessible and attractive to pupils: for example, Morgan's 'In the Snack-bar' (*P*, 152) presented to a class as part of a thematic study on caring for others in society. There are dangers in such an approach. Poetry is not sociology, and a poem will seldom fit neatly into an invented context without neglect or distortion of some of its important features. Worse still, invented or contrived contexts often entail neglect of real and necessary contexts.

All of these considerations apply particularly to the use of Edwin Morgan's work in the classroom. His range is vast in theme, technique, language and tone. He has been exploring himself, Scotland and the universe through language for nearly forty years now and professional academics, never mind teachers, have had to work hard just to keep him in sight. It should be obvious that he cannot be adequately presented to pupils in penny numbers, as it were. The teacher's first resolve should be to present as full a range as possible of the poetry. Only thus will the pupils experience the exciting challenge that his poetry provides. The concrete and sound poems, for example, will focus the perennial and intriguing question of what is poetry and what is not. The monologues and dialogues, the marvellous world of 'voices' which Morgan creates, will stimulate imagination and emulation. The Glasgow poems and the Instamatics will demonstrate that poetry has a vital part to play in making sense of our own daily encounters with reality.

To be fair, teachers, faced with this intimidating variety, have not neglected Morgan in favour of easier options, more tractable poets. Morgan's work is taught extensively and for one very good and central reason: its appeal to young people. Teachers seem to have recognised this appeal instinctively, right from the publication of *The Second Life* in 1968. Morgan is, first of all, a poet of the present, of the headline in today's newspaper, of things that are happening here and now. He is also a poet of the future, of man's exciting possibilities. Until fairly recently the past, particularly his own past, has not featured prominently in his work. This concentration on present and future forms the basis of his appeal to young people. It finds a ready response from the existentialists who inhabit our classrooms.

The Glasgow poems included in *The Second Life* have been the bedrock of the teaching of Morgan in schools: poems such as 'Good Friday' (*P*, 145), 'King Billy' (*P*, 148), 'Trio' (*P*, 154) and 'In the Snack-bar'

(*P*, 152). They were widely taught within a year or two of the volume's publication and they are still taught. Many teachers, it must be remarked, have fallen into the attractive trap of teaching *only* the relatively early Glasgow poems and neglecting the challenging variety of Morgan's later work. 'In the Snack-bar', for example, received the doubtful accolade in the late 1970s of being top of the poetical pops with pupils sitting the Scottish 'O' Grade English examination, displacing Owen's 'Dulce et Decorum Est Pro Patria Mori'.

But as the title of his second major collection, *From Glasgow to Saturn*, indicates, Morgan *does* start from Glasgow in his exploration of the universe and so the Glasgow poems do form an appropriate starting point for classroom work. These poems are relatively straightforward when compared with his science fiction work or his experiments with concrete poetry. They are often poems of street life, of chance encounters with Glasgow humanity. They represent a deliberate attempt by Morgan to come to some sort of terms with the varied and sometimes painful reality of his native place.

In a schools radio series on Scottish Writing in 1980[2] Morgan was forthcoming on this area of his poetry:

> I began to write a number of poems about 1960, presenting people in urban settings, especially Glasgow . . . I began to bring more and more of the human life of the city into the centre of the picture, and for the first time I found that I both wanted to and was able to write immediately and directly about people, people whose lives might be different from mine but whose problems – or joys for that matter – I wanted to enter into and bring across in terms of poetry. It's arguable how far you can ever really fully understand another person's life, or way of life, yet it has always been the poet's job or gift, to use his imagination in order to get under the skin of some other existence and then to present it convincingly in terms of art to his readers.

Here is as clear a statement as we are ever likely to get of what Morgan is about in the Glasgow poems.

In the same programme Morgan points out that 'In the Snack-bar' 'came out of something that had actually happened' and that 'chance encounters, in fact, can be as fruitful a subject in poetry as more lasting relations'. Many of the Glasgow poems are based on these sudden chance encounters which actually happened and which can be funny or strange or frightening or thought-provoking; often all of those simultaneously. Glasgow, traditionally, is such a place, where the observer in the street or on the top-deck of a bus becomes participant in unexpected ways. Thus we have the drunk man in the bus in 'Good Friday'; the blind man who must visit the toilet in 'In the Snack-bar'; the happy young people in 'Trio' and 'Linoleum Chocolate' (*P*, 145). Such poems present great opportunities for the English teacher, not least because Morgan's methods are so immediately appealing to the young reader. The poems are always firmly based on reality, on concrete human situations which are at once accessible and recognisable. The Glasgow streets and locations are palpably there and are often named: London Road in 'Linoleum Chocolate', Bath Street in 'Good Friday', Monteith Row in 'Glasgow Green' (*P*, 149). The inhabitants of these streets are as recognisable as the situations.

It is, moreover, a compelling dramatised reality that Morgan presents, which sucks the reader into the world of the poem. 'In the Snack-bar' begins with: 'A cup capsizes along the formica / slithering with a dull clatter'. The 'heads turn' in the crowded snack-bar to look at the old man, the cause of the commotion, and the reader looks too, as the poet gradually reveals, in the rest of the opening verse-paragraph, the full extent of the old man's disabilities.

In 'King Billy', the opening exhibits a film technique reminiscent of the opening shot of Welles's *Citizen Kane*. The camera pans slowly downwards from the clouds 'grey over Riddrie', to the trees, the cemetery gates which gleam in the rain and the lamplight, to the 'huddled' gravestones, and finally zooms in to pick out a wreath – 'To Our Leader of Thirty Years Ago'. Again, the reader is compelled into the world of the poem.

From this firm base of dramatised reality Morgan moves out in two ways. Firstly, there is the transmutation of reality into art, the making of poetry from the experience. Secondly, Morgan explores the experience from different angles through his own reactions. This enables him to move, unobtrusively and convincingly, into important areas of social concern such as religion, crime or sexual behaviour. In fact, the art and the exploration are one and the same in practice.

Typical of this approach is 'Trio', which describes three young people in Glasgow on a cold winter evening at Christmas time. The poem begins by stressing the reality of the encounter. The street, Buchanan Street, is named. It is decorated with Christmas lights. The three are carrying objects which are described in straightforward prosaic terms – 'a new guitar', 'a very young baby', and 'a chihuahua'. A snatch of very Glaswegian dialogue completes this base of reality – 'Wait till he sees this but!' The poet could have stopped there and left us with no more than a snap-shot of reality, but he goes on to explore his reactions to the encounter and to employ art to convey them. The only figurative phrase in the opening lines – 'a cloud of happiness' – is now developed, because it is this, the young people's happiness, which gives the encounter a significance, makes it worth a second look and a reaction. The next lines expand from the prosaic identification of the objects earlier in the poem to the loving, almost talismanic detail of:

> The chihuahua has a tiny Royal Stewart tartan coat like a teapot-
> holder
> the baby in its white shawl is all bright eyes and mouth like favours
> in a fresh sweet cake,
> the guitar swells out under its milky plastic cover, tied at the neck
> with silver tinsel tape and a brisk sprig of mistletoe.
> Orphean sprig! Melting baby! Warm chihuahua!

The young people's happiness is so vivid and powerful that it transcends mere prosaic reality and, more importantly, transcends the conventional Christian Christmas message:

> The vale of tears is powerless before you.
> Whether Christ is born, or is not born, you
> put paid to fate, it abdicates
>   under the Christmas lights.
> Monsters of the year
> go blank, are scattered back,
> can't bear this march of three.

Morgan's ability to challenge conventional reactions in unexpected ways is an outstanding feature of the Glasgow poems which makes them particularly valuable for use with school pupils. In this case, for example, the average pupil is probably well aware of the usual condemnations of the modern commercial Christmas of presents, spending and self-indulgence, as a distortion of the original Christian meaning of the event. How refreshing, then, to find a writer maintaining the opposite – that the happiness is all that matters! Further consideration of the poem will reveal that much of the art is in Morgan's gentle irony, which is realised through the use of Christian elements in what is not a conventionally Christian poem. For example, the three young people are reminiscent of the wise men, the Magi, carrying gifts; the girl with the very young baby reminds us of Mary and the baby Jesus; the Christmas lights above make us think of the starry sky above Bethlehem.

'In the Snack-bar' is the most famous and popular of the Glasgow 'encounter' poems. It is a fine example of Morgan's wide-ranging compassion. As previously explained, Morgan begins by setting the scene in dramatic and realistic terms. The old blind man is presented at first through a series of observations by an outside observer. But then, in the second verse paragraph, comes a remarkable change, in which the observer identifies with the man and his life:

> A few yards of floor are like a landscape
> to be negotiated, in the slow setting out
> time has almost stopped. I concentrate
> my life to his: crunch of spilt sugar,
> slidy puddle from the night's umbrellas,
> table edges, people's feet,
> hiss of the coffee-machine, voices and laughter,
> smell of a cigar, hamburgers, wet coats steaming,
> and the slow dangerous inches to the stairs.

This act of compassionate imagination leads the reader, in turn, to identify with the old man's situation and it is precisely this ability of great literature to widen and deepen the reader's experience and sympathies that justifies the study of literature in our schools. Typical of Morgan, the poem generates concern as well as sympathy. It is no sociological tract, of course, but the reader is left to ponder various things such as the integrity of human dignity or society's care or lack of care for the handicapped.

Morgan does not ignore the darker aspects of life in his native city. A group of powerful poems depicts the violence and squalor to be found. Once again these are poems of the streets, the real 'mean streets' of Glasgow which are named for us as if to emphasise their reality. Even the harshnesses of the Glasgow climate are precisely described – the grey clouds piling up over Riddrie in 'King Billy', the 'clammy midnight' of 'Glasgow Green', the 'sluggish winds' of 'Saturday Night' (*P*, 275). No details of degradation are spared in these poems. In 'Glasgow Green' a homosexual rape in a dark city park is vividly evoked through the words of the rapist. In 'Death in Duke Street' (*P*, 276) a derelict man dies on a city pavement – 'a huddle on the greasy street'.

Some of these poems have been sources of unease and controversy amongst teachers, the subject matter just too unpalatable for delicate stomachs. A recent school anthology included 'At Central Station' (*P*, 410), a poem which describes a woman urinating in public, 'in the middle of the day'. Stories circulated about how, in some schools, the offending page was carefully cut from each copy of the textbook. Similarly, the homosexual content in Morgan's poetry has been studiously ignored or, at best, left inexplicit. One of his greatest achievements, 'Glasgow Green', a majestic and compassionate elucidation of the loneliness of the human condition, has been neglected in schools for

this reason. It is a pity that teachers have often failed to face up to the
challenging reality of these more controversial poems, because they are
depriving their pupils of the opportunity of discovering one of Morgan's
finest achievements – that he has taken poetry out of the ivory tower and
into the streets where unregenerate humanity pullulates.

In the 1980 radio programme for schools, referred to above, Morgan
chose 'At Central Station' for special attention, perhaps a broad hint to
teachers that he considered it a neglected poem. He identified it as a
companion piece to 'In the Snack-bar' and went on to remark:

> the moment – and it was only a moment (of seeing the woman
> urinating in public) – had packed into it such an extraordinary
> variety of feelings and reactions that somehow the poem itself had
> to risk a variety of tone, to bring out a meaning that was both
> horrifying and in an awful sense horrifyingly ordinary, something
> that was, if you like, a civic disgrace, and yet at the same time on
> the verge of the comic, something evoking every kind of response
> from shame to mockery to pity to admiration – and for that reason,
> for those reasons, something that the poet, who happens by pure
> accident to be passing by at that very moment, sees as significant
> and worth writing about . . . All I would claim is that there *is* a
> poetry of the immediate reality of things, and that it can be as well
> made, and have as much to say, to us, as any other kind.

Uncompromising reality would be merely shocking, disgusting and
repulsive if Morgan contented himself with reportage or description –
hellish messages from mean streets – but Morgan's controlled compassion
for those involved redeems the material from bleak pessimism. He never
forgets that these outcasts and derelicts are entitled to at least some
shreds of human dignity.

In 'At Central Station' he first of all establishes the dramatic reality of
the incident, employing the immediacy of the present tense as he so
often does and detailing time and place precisely:

> At Central Station, in the middle of the day,
> a woman is pissing on the pavement.
> With her back to the wall and her legs spread
> she bends forward, her hair over her face,
> the drab skirt and coat not even hitched up.
> Her water hits the stone with force
> and streams across the gutter.

A companion piece, perhaps, for 'In the Snack-bar' in as much as the
same human bodily function is described, but the trickle of the old
man's water was 'thin and slow', an 'apology for living' in the relative

privacy of the snack-bar toilet. It could be ignored or evaded, like his predicament. This, by contrast, is unignorable, which is, of course, the point of the poem and the very reason it has aroused such discomfort in so many readers. To make things worse, the fourth line of this prosaic introduction, 'With her back to the wall and her legs spread' has disturbing resonances relating to female dignity.

The rest of the poem, in typical Morgan fashion, explores reactions including the poet's own and the raw event congeals into significant imagery which is related to the flood of the woman's urine across the pavement. She is 'a statue in a whirlpool' of the emotions she has stirred up, 'bleeding' into the 'waves of talk' of the passing crowd 'awful ichors of need':

> Only two men frankly stop,
> grin broadly, throw a gibe at her
> as they cross the street to the betting-shop.
> Without them the indignity,
> the dignity, would be incomplete.

Discussion of this poem with a senior class would centre on that word 'dignity' in the final line of the poem.

'Glasgow Green', which is Morgan's supreme achievement in this mode, moves from setting the sordid scene:

> Meth-men mutter on benches,
> pawed by river fog. Monteith Row
> sweats coldly

to the violence of homosexual rape: 'Christ but I'm gaun to have you Mac / if it takes all night, turn over you bastard'. But the poem doesn't end there. Morgan goes on to challenge explicitly the conventional reactions of disgust and horror to such events. For him it isn't enough to condemn; some understanding is due: 'And how shall these men live?'

The second half of the poem contrasts the happiness of ordinary family life with the agony of these outcasts who act out their squalid dramas in the darkness:

> How shall the race be served?
> It shall be served by anguish
> as well as by children at play.
> It shall be served by loneliness
> as well as by family love.

The compelling movement of the verse (teachers *do* still attempt to lead their pupils to an understanding of the rhythms of poetry) reflects both the unflinching focus on the theme and the poet's purpose of stressing that this, too, is human life and must be valued as human life. The lines, in general, are short — varying from seven to nine syllables. Each line has three major syllabic stresses. These stresses vary in position. The result is a powerful slightly irregular rhythm which seems to reflect the lonely desires of the outcasts in the darkness. Here are the majestic concluding lines of the poem with the major stresses indicated:

> Let the *wo*men *sit* in the *Gre*en
> and *rock* their *prams* as the *sheets*
> *blow* and *whip* in the *sun*light.
> But the *beds* of *ma*rried *love*
> are *is*lands in a *sea* of des*ire*
> Its *waves* break *here* in this *park*
> spl*ash*ing the *flesh* as it *trem*bles
> like *drift*wood thr*ough* the d*ark*

Further examination reveals that there is added emphasis on the first stressed syllable of each line. The effect of this is to create a rhythm of surge and ebb which suggests the waves of the 'sea of desire'; sound corresponds to image and sense.

   In fact, an intricate imagery of water and liquid is used throughout the poem. The scene is suggested with 'clammy midnight' and 'Monteith Row sweats coldly'. The protagonists in the sordid drama 'sweat' in the darkness beside the 'dirty starless river'. A contrast is then drawn between the detergent-clean washing that the women hang in the park by day and:

> the real Clyde, with a dishrag dawn
> it rinses the horrors of the night
> but cannot make them clean

The poet then makes the symbolism of the liquid imagery explicit with:

> The thorn in the flesh!
> Providence, water it!
> Do you think it is not watered?
>
> Water the wilderness, walk there, reclaim it!
> Reclaim, regain, renew! Fill the barns and the vats!

We realise that the initial references to sweat and the dirty polluted river, suggesting a horror and guilt that can never be cleansed, have been transmuted to a powerful plea for the life-giving properties of water; water as the symbol of fertility. There is even a reference to the biblical miracle of water changed into wine:

> Longing,
>> longing
>>> shall find its wine

In the last eight lines of the poem (quoted above with regard to rhythm) this water imagery is carried to its conclusion. The married women, sitting rocking their prams amidst their sanitised washing in the bright day-light, are seen as the lucky ones, complacent almost, because:

> the beds of married love
> are islands in a sea of desire.
> Its waves break here, in this park,
> splashing the flesh as it trembles
> like driftwood through the dark.

We realise that Morgan is conveying through this imagery that 'the sea of desire', however sordid, is the essential human condition; that the derelicts wrestling in the darkness beside the park benches are a part of that human condition.

The decision as to when to introduce a particular Morgan poem to a class is one for the individual teacher to make. It will be obvious that such an intricate and challenging poem as 'Glasgow Green', with its subtle and integrated imagery, is only suitable for senior pupils, while the accessible compassion of 'In the Snack-bar', for example, could be presented somewhat earlier.

Although the above discussion has concentrated, for reasons of space, on the Glasgow poems, it must be repeated that the teacher's main aim should always be to attempt to present as full a range as possible of Morgan's work to the pupils at all stages. Poems which require some placing in context such as 'King Billy', 'The Old Man and the Sea' (*P*, 125) and 'The Death of Marilyn Monroe' (*P*, 126) are better presented to senior pupils, but much of Morgan's work in all his modes is suitable for junior pupils.

There is a great deal of sheer fun in Morgan which junior classes should be given the opportunity of enjoying. One thinks particularly of the sound poems such as 'The Computer's First Christmas Card' (*P*, 159) and 'Canedolia' (*P*, 137), which help to break down pupils' conventional and constrictive ideas of what poetry should be. 'A View of Things' (*P*, 187) is a particularly delightful and useful poem for juniors because of its combination of overtly simple structure and intriguingly illogical content:

what I hate about love is its dog
what I love about Hank is his string vest
what I hate about the twins is their three gloves
what I love about Mabel is her teeter
what I hate about gooseberries is their look, feel, smell and taste
what I love about the world is its shape
what I hate about a gun is its lock, stock, and barrel
what I love about bacon-and-eggs is its predictability
what I hate about derelict buildings is their reluctance to disintegrate
what I love about a cloud is its unpredictability

Emulation is positively mandatory after a reading of this, and pupils will enthusiastically set about constructing their own love/hate poems, often with hilarous and even impressive results. Similarly, 'The First Men on Mercury' (*P*, 259), at once a space poem and one of Morgan's dialogues, can lead to pupil experiments with language.

Morgan's animal poems, inexplicably neglected by many teachers, can provide an early introduction to the wide range of his technique, tone and sympathies. His concern to give the world a voice, 'to get everything speaking, as it were', which he mentioned in his important interview with Marshall Walker in 1977 (*Akros*), is well-illustrated by 'Hyena' (*P*, 236). In the poem Morgan gives us the words of an African hyena, which addresses us directly in a series of statements and questions which create the menace of a creature which waits to feed on carrion, a creature which inspires both disgust and fear in human beings:

> I am waiting for you.
> I have been travelling all morning through the bush
> and not eaten.
> I am lying at the edge of the bush
> on a dusty path that leads from the burnt-out kraal.

The techniques in this poem are simple but effective, making it accessible to junior pupils; for example, the repetition of 'I am', which takes place throughout the poem, creating the effect of a creature totally absorbed in its own necessary being. The sense of menace is increased by another simple device – a series of insinuating questions which suggest a villainous ingratiating craftiness:

> What do you think of me? . . .
> Do you like my song? . . .
> Oh and my tongue – do you like me

> when it comes lolling over my jaw
> very long, and I am laughing?

The questions have a teasing quality also. The hyena is not really interested in human reactions, which are in any case mistaken:

> I am not laughing.
> But I am not snarling either, only
> panting in the sun, showing you
> what I grip
> carrion with.

The poem has a clear structure. The last verse returns to the first line, 'I am waiting'. The hyena functions as a memento mori, because it is waiting for dead flesh, waiting 'till you are ready for me'.

Another animal poem, 'The White Rhinoceros' (*P*, 131), combines a brilliant and humorous creation of the animal's lumbering power with a serious conservation theme:

> he shook his ears
> and went on snorting, knee-deep in pawpaws.
> trundling his hunger, shrugged off the tick-birds,
> rolled up his sleeves, kicked over an anthill,
> crunched, munched, wonderful windfall,
> empty dish.

So much exuberance conveyed by assonance, personification and a profusion of verbs, but hidden nearby: 'the safety-catches started to click in the thickets'. This is a bitter-sweet poem which encapsulates the plight of the great African animals and the need to act to save them now. Morgan dramatises the latter by including a persona who tries to warn the animal of the danger it is in:

> I came up and I shouted Oh no! No! No! —
> you'll be extinct in two years!
>
> Run — white horn, tin clown, crown of rain-woods,
> venerable shiner! Run, run, run!

'The Third Day of the Wolf' (*P*, 132) deals with the escape of a Canadian timber-wolf from a zoo and the subsequent ruthless mobilisation of human resources to hunt it down. This is one of the most effective of all Morgan's poems in the classroom, because the reader is forced to experience the hunt from the wolf's point of view and forced, also, to realise the wolf's right to existence as a wild creature. The poem begins dramatically with a re-creation of the rather synthetic and exaggerated human reaction to the animal's escape:

> Lock the gates and man the fences!
> The lone Canadian timber-wolf
> has escaped into the thickets, the ditches, the distances!
> Blow the silver whistles!

The long middle verse-paragraph is an interplay of two elements: human technology in pursuit of the wolf, contrasted with the wild creature's increasing agony. There is a 'droning helicopter' overhead, the 'smell of men and guns', 'two planes diving again and again to drive it in terror towards the guns'. A car 'catches the grey thing in its rushing headlights' and 'throws it to the verge, stunned, ruptured, living, lying, / fangs dimly scrabbling the roots of Hertfordshire'. Finally the wolf is cornered, ironically, by a 'farm's pet collie' and 'The empty belly and mad yellow eyes / waiting for man were then shot'. The poem, intentionally, has the vivid, melodramatic quality of some monster hunt in the movies, in which a crazed mob destroys a creature whose only essential crime is being different. In the final verse Morgan's comment is measured and defiant:

> How strong man is
> with his helicopters and his planes,
> his radios and rifles!
> What a god for a collie!
> O wild things, wild things
> take care, beware of him.
> Man mends his fences.
> Take care, take strength.
> Take care of the warrant
> for death. How good
> he is at that,
> with his dirty sack
> ready to lay on you:
> it is necessary.
> But I have a warrant
> to lay this too,
> a wreath for wildness,
> timber-wolf, timber-wolf.

The writer is very conscious, in an essay of this length, of a sense of inadequacy with regard to the subject. Some suggestions have been offered, but whole areas of Morgan's work have been ignored or barely mentioned in the passing. Appropriately enough, this mirrors the classroom teacher's dilemma. The exigencies of time and the curriculum mean that only a selection of Morgan's work can be introduced to pupils. The important question is this: on what principles should that selection be made? I would suggest two. First of all, there should be a conscious attempt to present poems which show the relevance of poetry to the world in which we live. I am firmly convinced that this is the area of Morgan's greatest achievement and it is also the area of greatest appeal to our young people. Secondly, any selection should attempt to reflect the glorious variety of Morgan. That leaves a lot of choice. God's plenty, in fact.

NOTES

1. Certain parts of this essay appeared in a slightly different form in Geddes Thomson, *The Poetry of Edwin Morgan* (Aberdeen: ASLS, 1986) (Scotnotes No. 2).
2. Edwin Morgan, 'Scottish Writing, Writers and their Work'. BBC Scotland schools broadcast, 1980.

Twelve

Edwin Morgan: A Checklist

Compiled by Hamish Whyte

PREFATORY NOTES

This checklist must be an interim report. The full descriptive bibliography can wait for another time. It is well-nigh impossible to keep up
with Edwin Morgan. The primary aim of the checklist is to provide a
wide range of references for those who want to pursue Morgan's
whittrick to its various bolt-holes: establishment strongholds such as
the British Academy Warton lecture, underground with *Tlaloc* and
Angel Exhaust, home coverts like *The Glasgow Magazine* and *Saltire
Review*, or the warrens of international anthologies.

Morgan has been publishing poems for fifty-five years, translations
for over fifty and reviewing books indefatigably most of that time as
well. From 1957 to 1965 he and Jack Rillie compiled a 'Summary of
Periodical Literature' for the *Review of English Studies*. There were the
usual essays for academic journals, yes, but Morgan has always made a
point of writing for more popular periodicals and reviewing genres he
does not write in himself: drama (for *Encore* and the *Times* – as 'Our
Special Correspondent' – in the 1950s and 1960s) and fiction (for the
New Statesman and the *Listener* in the 1960s and 1970s). He has been
reviewing regularly for the *TLS* (fiction, translations, Scottish books,
poetry, anything) for twenty-five years. He even once had a column in
the *Scottish Daily Express*. His output of literary journalism is prodigious.

Although the poems have appeared in established periodicals – *TLS*,
New Statesman, *Lines Review* – it is obvious from a cursory glance
through the checklist that Morgan has a commitment to the fugitive.
His poems were printed (often badly) in magazines obscure, underground, avant-garde, Scottish, Irish, Welsh, English, French, American,
alien – *Poetmeat*, *Stereo Headphones*, *Second Aeon*, *OU*, *Crab Grass* – it was

important to support them. Many of them were short-lived, but they lived, their energy admired.

The checklist is not complete, none ever is. There have had to be deliberate exclusions, for reasons of space and time: radio and television broadcasts, exhibitions, talks, anthologies containing reprinted poems, a complete listing of Morgan's poems translated into other languages, for example. What is left, though, attempts to be as comprehensive as possible, to go some way towards satisfying the keenest Morgan-seeker.

The checklist is arranged in the following sections:

A Books, pamphlets, etc. by, translated by or edited by Edwin Morgan
B Books containing contributions by or edited jointly by Edwin Morgan
C Contributions to periodicals and newspapers
D Interviews
E Ephemera
F Odds and ends
G Manuscripts
H Recordings
I Musical settings
J Critical and biographical works about Edwin Morgan

The A section is a complete chronological list of Morgan's separate poetry collections, prose books and pamphlets, as well as first independent publication in book (or other) form of individual poems (e.g. A19). Place, publisher, date and contents of each are given, with brief notes; and a list of reviews which is not meant to be exhaustive, merely indicative. In the B section as well as items contributed directly to books by Morgan are included poems and essays previously published in periodicals reprinted for the first time in anthologies and collections. As in A, place, publisher and date are given, with occasional notes. The entries are arranged chronologically by year and alphabetically within each year. In B and the following sections where a title is given without quotation marks it should be assumed to be that of a poem or translation of a poem; titles of essays, reviews (usually editors' headings), articles, etc., that is, prose, are given quotation marks. In the C section entries are arranged in order of date of publication as far as possible. The name of the periodical, volume and part number, date and page references are given where known. For the purposes of this checklist Spring = March-May, Summer = June-August, Autumn = September-October and Winter = November-February. The other sections are self-explanatory. The selection of entries in the J section indicates the growing critical

interest in Edwin Morgan's work. And it should not go without saying
that any faults are my own: corrections, omissions and comments will
be gratefully received.

I should like to thank Helen Durndell, Kevin McCarra, Michael
Schmidt, Winifred Whyte and the Inter-Library Loans Department at
Glasgow University Library for their help. My debt to Edwin Morgan
himself is greater than I can repay. As well as revealing his 'Kaa' persona
(the rock snake from *The Jungle Book*) and identifying anonymous
reviews, he allowed his shelves to be rummaged at will and patiently
answered question after question and looked out obscure items: my
thanks to him for all his help and hospitality. I am not sure how much
he will enjoy having his past laid out like this – he is more one for the
future – but his life is in his work and here, to some extent at least, it is.

A

BOOKS, PAMPHLETS, ETC. BY, TRANSLATED BY, OR EDITED BY
EDWIN MORGAN

A1

The Vision of Cathkin Braes and other Poems. Glasgow: William MacLellan, 1952.

Contents: The Vision of Cathkin Braes – A Courtly Overture – Ingram Lake or, Five Acts on the House – A Snib for the Nones – Verses for a Christmas Card – A Song of the Petrel (transl. from Maxim Gorky) (pp. 5–26).

Notes: Published late September or early October.

Note

A companion volume, *Dies Irae and Other Poems and Translations*, was to have been published by Lotus Books of Hull in their Acadine Poets series (an advertisement appeared on the back cover of James Kirkup's *The Creation*, 1951), but never appeared, owing to lack of finance. The collection was finally published in *Poems of Thirty Years*.

A2

(a) *Beowulf: A Verse Translation into Modern English.* Aldington, Kent: The Hand and Flower Press, 1952.

Contents: 'Introduction' ('The Translator's Task in *Beowulf*', pp. vii–xxvii; 'The Art of the Poem', pp. xxviii–xxxvi); text (pp. 1–87); glossary of proper names (pp. 88–93); 'Translators of *Beowulf* into Modern English Verse' (p. 94).

Notes: Published 27 October 1952 in an edition of 2,000 copies. Distributed in America by the British Book Centre, New York. Separate edition proposed, but fell through.

Reviews
TLS 7 May 1954, p. 298.
Fernand Mossé. *Études Anglaises* VII, 1954, p. 413.

(b) American edition. Berkeley, Los Angeles and London: University of California Press, 1962. Paperback.

(c) Australian edition. With illustrations by George Knowlton. Sydney: Officina Pluralo, 1980. 36.5 × 24.5cm. Colophon: 'This edition of *Beowulf* consists of a standard edition of 1000 copies set in 14pt Century Schoolbook, printed letterpress on 105gm/2 Glopaque Wove for the text and Abbey Mills Laid 100gm/2 for the illustrations. In addition 100 copies have been printed on Velin Arches 270gm/2 throughout, case bound, numbered 1–100 and signed by the translator and artist.' Possibly never appeared commercially: only one copy seen (that of standard edition). Contains text and Glossary of Proper Names. 'The Translator's Task in *Beowulf*' was supposed to accompany the translation in a smaller format: not seen. Reviewed by William McCarty in *Fine Print* VIII:1, January 1982, pp.22–4.

A3

The Cape of Good Hope. Tunbridge Wells: Peter Russell, The Pound Press, 1955.

Contents: The Cape of Good Hope: I. The Cape (pp.3–4) – II. Mid-Ocean (pp.4–6) – III. A Dream at the Mysterious Barricades (pp.6–13) – IV. The Return (pp.13–[16]).

Notes: Published in an edition of 195 copies.

Reviews
George Bruce. *Saltire Review* III:8, Autumn 1956, pp.73, 75.
Voice of Scotland VI:3, October 1955, pp.31–32.

A4

Poems from Eugenio Montale. Translated by Edwin Morgan. Reading: The School of Art, University of Reading, 1959.

Contents: 'Preface' (pp.[v–viii]); from *Ossi di Seppia* (pp.2–23) – from *Le Occasioni* (pp.24–47) – from *La Bufera e Altro* (pp.48–57); 'List of Subscribers before Publication' (p.[59]).

Notes: 'Completed' 31 December 1959. Edition of 150 copies. Italian text printed facing translations.

Reviews
G.R. Kay. *College Courant* 13:25, Martinmas 1960, pp.67–68.

A5

Sovpoems. Worcester: Migrant Press, 1961. (A Migrant Pamphlet).

Contents: 'Introduction' (pp.3–6); Pasternak (pp.7–10) – Tsvetayeva (p.11) – Mayakovsky (pp.12–16) – Tikhonov (pp.17–18) – Brecht (pp.19–22) – Neruda (pp.23–27) – Martynov (pp.28–29) – Yevtushenko (pp.30–32).

Notes: Published in an edition of 300 copies. Dedicated to Frank Mason 'who first showed me the Russky Alfarit'.

Reviews
W.A.S. Keir. *New Saltire* 4, Summer 1962, p.84.

A6

Collins Albatross Book of Longer Poems: English and American Poetry from the Fourteenth Century to the Present Day. Edited by Edwin Morgan. London and Glasgow: Collins, 1963.

Contents: 'Introduction' (pp.9–14); text (pp.15–731).

Notes: Issued in two bindings, blue cloth and leather. Reprinted 1964. Also 'Students Edition', in brown cloth.

Reviews
Christopher Wiseman. *Glasgow Review* I:1, Spring 1964, pp.42–43.
TLS 7 May 1964, p.396.

A7

Poetry of Today: A Touring Exhibition. Selected by Edwin Morgan. [Glasgow:] National Book League, Summer 1964.

Notes: Duplicated typescript catalogue; 4 quarto pages stapled.

A8

Starryveldt. Frauenfeld, Switzerland: Eugen Gomringer Press, 1965. (konkrete poesie 9).

Contents: Dogs Round a Tree – Bees' nest – Summer Haiku – Down in the Forest – Scotch Cat – Like, Little Russian Cat – Chinese Cat – French Persian Cats Having a Ball – Original Sin at the Water Hole – Two by Two – Unscrambling the Waves at Goonhilly – A Mission to the Picts – Cherrystick – Instant Theatre Go Home – The Computer's First Christmas Card – Starryveldt – To Your Shelters – Hail, Flynn! – Pompidous Besprechung in Tokio – In Praise of Surtsey – O Pioneers! – Orgy – Phantom Beaver.

Notes: Published March 1965. Stapled pamphlet of 24 unnumbered pages; orange paper covers. Distributed in Britain by the Wild Hawthorn Press.

Reviews
Christopher Wiseman. *Glasgow Review* II:1, Spring 1965, p.40.
TLS 25 March 1965, p.230.

A9

Scotch Mist. Cleveland, Ohio: Renegade Press, 1965. (Polluted Lake Series 7).

Notes: Eight double leaves, 4 × 14 cm, stapled and glued into grey card cover, 4.8 × 14.4 cm.

A10

Sealwear. Glasgow: Gold Seal Press, 1966.

Notes: Poem handwritten in different coloured inks; 12 leaves, 17.8 × 11.5 cm, stapled into gold card cover, 20.2 × 12.7 cm. Produced by EM for private distribution; edition limited to 14 copies.

A11

emergent poems. Stuttgart: Edition Hansjörg Mayer, 1967. (futura 20).

Contents: message clear – dialeck piece – plea – seven headlines – nightmare – manifesto.

Notes: Single sheet 48 × 64 cm folding to 24 × 16 cm. Lines 46 and 47 of 'message clear' have been omitted.

Reviews
George Bruce. *Lines Review* 26, Summer 1968, pp.33–4.

A12

Poems by Alan Hayton, Stephen Mulrine, Colin Kirkwood, Robert Tait: Four Glasgow University Poets. Selected by Edwin Morgan. Preston: Akros Publications, 1967.

Contents: 'Editor's Note' (p.2); text (pp.3–27).

Notes: Published May 1967.

A13

gnomes. Preston: Akros Publications, 1968.

Contents: strawberry fields forever – gnomes – archives – surfeit – waves – metaphore – O.T. – dialeck piece – astrodome – strips – russian formalism – the computer's second christmas card.

Notes: Edition limited to 300 copies, the first 25 numbered and signed. Published March 1968.

Reviews
Robin Fulton. *Lines Review* 26, Summer 1968, pp.34–5.

A14

(a) *The Second Life.* Edinburgh: Edinburgh University Press, 1968.

Contents: The old man and the sea – The Death of Marilyn Monroe – Je ne regrette rien – The domes of Saint Sophia – The white rhinoceros – The third day of the wolf – Aberdeen train – The opening of the Forth Road Bridge – To Hugh MacDiarmid – To Ian Hamilton Finlay – An addition to the family – Canedolia – Starryveldt – Message clear – Bees' nest – French Persian cats having a ball – Orgy – To Joan Eardley – Linoleum chocolate – Good Friday – The starlings in George Square – King Billy – Glasgow Green – The suspect – In the snack-bar – Trio – Pomander – Summer haiku – Siesta of a Hungarian snake – Boats and places – Seven headlines – The computer's first Christmas card – Opening the cage – The chaffinch map of Scotland – The second life – The sheaf – The unspoken – From a city balcony – When you go – Strawberries – The witness – One cigarette – The picnic – Absence – Without it – The welcome – O pioneers! – Construction for I.K. Brunel – Unscrambling the waves at Goonhilly – The Tower of Pisa – Spacepoem 1: from Laika to Gagarin – Chinese cat – Islands – In Sobieski's Shield – From the domain of Arnheim – For the International Poetry Incarnation – What is 'Paradise Lost' *really* about? – The ages – A view of things (pp.1–88).

Notes: Published January 1968. Computer typeset.

Reviews
George Bruce. *Lines Review* 26, Summer 1968, pp.33–4.
Tom Buchan. *New Edinburgh Review* 1, February 1969, p.36.
Martin Dodsworth. *Listener* LXXIX:2035, 28 March 1968, p.414.
Thomas E. Luddy. *Library Journal* 93:14, August 1968, p.2882.
A.M. Rigg. *Mercat* (Cumnock Academy magazine) 1968, p.34.

Iain Crichton Smith. *Akros* 3:7, March 1968, pp.61–6.
Julian Symons. *New Statesman* 75:1926, 9 February 1968, p.179.
TLS 15 February 1968, p.155.

(b) Paperback edition: as (a) but with card cover. Issued February 1981. There are two states: the first has the last line of 'Strawberries' omitted on p.60; the second has a cancel leaf (pp.59–60) with the last line of 'Strawberries' restored. Both have the full stop at the end of 'Canedolia' omitted on p.21.

A15

Proverbfolder. Corsham, Wiltshire: Openings Press, 1969.

Contents: 1. bis dat qui cito dat – 2. more haste less speed – 3. every cloud has a silver lining – 4. a rolling stone gathers no moss – 5. time and tide wait for no man – 6. an army marches on its stomach – 7. necessity is the mother of invention – 8. cant see the wood for the trees – 9. where theres smoke theres fire – 10. make hay while the sun shines – 12. every dog has its day.

Notes: Each proverb printed on a separate sheet, 48.2 cm square, and contained in heavy card folder 48.5 × 49 cm. Published September 1969 in an edition of 25 copies. A collaboration between EM and students of Bath Academy of Art: Caroline Robinson, Pete Jeurges, Debora Fulford, Simon Farrell, Bruce Brown, David Shilbeck, Paul Brown, Audrey Owen, Kit Gregory, Peter Warner, Mike Goater, Malcom McGregor.

A16

The Horseman's Word: A Sequence of Concrete Poems. Preston: Akros Publications, 1970. (Parklands Poets No. 5).

Contents: Arabian Nights Magic Horse – Clydesdale – Newmarket – Centaur – Eohippus – Kelpie – Hrimfaxi – Zane's – Hortobágy – Elegy (pp.3–12).

Notes: The first 50 copies numbered and signed.

Reviews
Patrick MacCrimmon. *The Chapman* 1, September 1970, [back page].

A17

Interferences. Glasgow: Midnight Press, [1970]. (Poetry Glasgow 3).

Contents: 'not to be deflected' – 1. 'brigantine tacking' – 2. ' "your filthy altars – " ' – 3. ' "it was a Roman soldier" ' – 4. 'they put me in this bed, and said' – 5. 'bringing you live' – ' "you want river Ob go backwards can do" '.

Notes: Single sheet 38 × 25.5 cm folding to 19.5 × 12.7 cm. Renumbered, the poems were included in 'Interferences: a sequence of 9 poems' in *From Glasgow to Saturn*.

A18

Twelve Songs. West Linton: The Castlelaw Press, 1970.

Contents: In Glasgow – Oban Girl – The Apple's Song – Columba's Song – Kierkegaard's Song – Shantyman – Tropic – Fado – Blackbird Marigolds – The Loch Ness Monster's Song – Flakes – Off Course (pp.3–14).

Notes: 500 copies printed of which 100 were printed on Hodgkinson's hand-made paper and issued in card covers and signed by EM, and 400 printed on Guard Bridge Trident paper and issued in paper wrappers. Published August 1970. Printed by Alex Frizell.

Reviews

John Fuller. *Listener* 24 December 1970, p.888.

Robert Garioch. *Lines Review* 36, March 1971, pp.45–7.

A19

The Dolphin's Song. Leeds: School of English Press, 1971. (NPA Broadsheets No. 2).

Notes: Signed limited edition of 50 copies. Each sheet measures 29 × 22.5 cm.

A20

Song of the Child. West Linton: The Castlelaw Press, 1971.

Notes: Privately printed for EM as Christmas greetings 1971. Folded sheet in green paper wrappers.

A21

(a) *Glasgow Sonnets*. West Linton: The Castlelaw Press, 1972.

Contents: I ('A mean wind wanders through the backcourt trash.') – II ('A shilpit dog fucks grimly by the close.') – III ('See a tenement due for demolition?') – IV ('Down by the brickworks you get warm at least.') – V ('"Let them eat cake" made no bones about it.') – VI ('The North Sea oil-strike tilts east Scotland up,') – VII ('Environmentalists, ecologists') – VIII ('Meanwhile the flyovers breed loops of light') – IX ('It groans and shakes, contracts and grows again.') – X ('From thirtieth-floor windows at Red Road') (pp. 5–14).

Notes: 125 copies numbered and signed. All copies contain errata slip. Issued in red paper wrappers.

Reviews

Anne Cluysenaar. *Stand* 14:3, 1973, pp.70–71.

Douglas Dunn. *Ostrich* 7, January 1973, pp.[25–7].

Robert Garioch. *Lines Review* 45, June 1973, pp.54–5. Reprinted in *A Garioch Miscellany*, ed. Robin Fulton (Edinburgh: Macdonald, 1986), pp.186–8.

E. Jennings. *Weekend Scotsman* 7 July 1973, p.3.

TLS 19 January 1973, p.69.

(b) *Glasgow Sonnets: poems*. [Glasgow: Glasgow School of Art, 1984].

Notes: A5 stapled booklet, printed on pale grey paper. Designed and illustrated by Gerry Rafferty as a project at GSA.

A22

Instamatic Poems. London: Ian McKelvie, 1972.

Contents: Glasgow 5 March 1971 – Glasgow 5 March 1971 – Nice 5 March 1971 – Belfast 5 March 1971 – Bedfordshire 5 March 1971 – Renfrewshire 5 March 1971 – Chicago May 1971 – Germany December 1970 – Manchester Undated Reported September 1971 – Nigeria Undated Reported October 1971 –

Leatherhead Surrey September 1971 – Aviemore Invernessshire August 1971 –
Bangkok February 1971 – Hamburg December 1971 – Mougins Provence
September 1971 – Madrid November 1971 – Naples February 1972 – Venice
April 1971 – Kishinev USSR November 1970 – London June 1971 – London
June 1971 – Shrewsbury February 1971 – London June 1970 – Burma June
1971 – Fallin Stirlingshire October 1970 – Rockall Invernessshire June 1972 –
Ellingham Suffolk January 1972 – Lancashire November 1971 – Vienna
December 1971 – San Pedro Bay Los Angeles July 1971 – Washington
September 1971 – London March 1971 – Innsbruck July 1971 – Translunar
Space March 1972 – Bangaon India July 1971 – Glasgow October 1971 –
Bradford June 1972 – Addlestone Surrey October 1971 – Budapest Undated
Reported April 1971 – Mid-Atlantic July 1971 – Nullarbor Plain South
Australia January 1972 – Campobasso Italy Undated Reported March 1971 –
Edinburgh March 1971 – Fort Benning Georgia April 1971 – Seend Wiltshire
April 1972 – London November 1971 – London November 1971 – Truk
Lagoon Undated Reported February 1972 – Glasgow November 1971 – Milan
Undated Reported October 1971 – Glasgow November 1971 – Milan Undated
Reported October 1971 – Glasgow November 1971 – Heaven September 1971
AD (pp.7–41).

Notes: Printed by the Vineyard Press in an edition of 750 copies of which 25
copies were printed on laid paper, specially bound, numbered and signed. All
copies should contain an errata slip.

Reviews
D. Campbell. *Scottish International* 6:3, March 1972, pp.32–33.
Tom McGrath. *Glasgow Review* V:1, Summer 1974, pp.42–43.
A. Maclean. *Listener* 16 August 1972, pp.223–4.
Clive Steele. *Aquarius* 6, September 1973, pp.119a–20.
TLS 9 March 1972, p.270.

A23

Wi the Haill Voice: 25 poems by Vladimir Mayakovsky. Translated into Scots with a
glossary by Edwin Morgan. South Hinksey, Oxford: Carcanet Press, 1972.

Contents: 'Introduction' (pp. 7–17); Ay, but can ye? – Forcryinoutloud! –
Fiddle-ma-fidgin – War declarit – Hymn to a jeddart-justicer – To the
bourgeoisie – The ballad o the rid cadie – A richt respeck for cuddies –
Vladimir's ferlie – Respeck for a lassie – Mandment No. 2 to the army o the arts
– Mayakonferensky's Anectidote – I'm aff – Versailles – A fareweel – The
Atlantic – Brooklyn Brig – Whit mair? – Goavy-dick! – Eupatoria – May Day –
Anent the deeference o tastes – Awa wi it! – Comrade teenager – Wi the haill
voice (pp.19–87); 'Glossary' (pp.89–93).

Notes: Published in cloth and paperback editions. 1500 copies.

Reviews
George Bruce. *ASLS Occasional Papers* No. 1, September 1972, pp.7–9.
Anne Cluysenaar. *Stand* 14:1, 1973, p.73.
Robin Fulton. *Scottish International* 5:6, August 1972, pp.32–3.
Hugh MacDiarmid. *Cambridge Review* 94:2210, 17 November 1972, pp.37–41.
P. Morgan. *Stand* 14:2, 1973, p.61.
Roderick Watson. *Library Review* 23:6, Summer 1972, p.258.

A24

(a) *From Glasgow to Saturn*. Cheadle: Carcanet Press, 1973.

Contents: Columba's Song – Floating off to Timor – In Glasgow – Kierkegaard's Song – Tropic – Shantyman – Oban Girl – The Woman – The Apple's Song – Drift – Fado – After the Party – At the Television Set – From the North – The Milk-cart – Estranged – For Bonfires i–iii – Blue Toboggans – Song of the Child – Lord Jim's Ghost's Tiger Poem – Flakes – Hyena – The Loch Ness Monster's Song – The Mill – London – Interferences: a sequence of 9 poems – Che – The Fifth Gospel – Afterwards – The Gourds – Last Message – Frontier Story – The Barrow: a dialogue – Thoughts of a Module – The First Men on Mercury – Spacepoem 3: Off Course – A Too Hot Summer – Itinerary – Boxers – Letters of Mr Lonelyhearts i–iii – A Jar Revisited – Pleasures of a Technological University – The Computer's First Dialect Poems – The Computer's First Code Poem – Not Playing the Game – Rider i–v – Guy Fawkes Moon – Saturday Night – Death in Duke Street – Christmas Eve – Stobhill – Glasgow Sonnets i–x (pp.9–96).

Notes: Published March 1973. Issued bound in black cloth, with yellow dust jacket. 2000 copies.

Reviews
D. Black. *Lines Review* 49, June 1974, pp.28–33.
Alan Brownjohn. *New Statesman* 86:2209, 20 July 1973, p.94.
E. Jennings. *Weekend Scotsman* 28 July 1973, p.3.
Alasdair Maclean. *Listener* 25 October 1973, p.566.
John Matthias. *Poetry* CXXIV:1, April 1974, pp.51–2.
M. Relich. *Scottish International* 6:6, August 1973, pp.34–5.
Dabney Stuart. *Library Journal* 98:20, 15 November 1973, p.3381.
TLS 20 July 1973, p.827.

(b) American edition. Chester Springs, Pennsylvania: Dufour, 1973.

(c) 2nd impression, 1974. As (a) ('printed by photolithography from the original printing') but issued in paperback with cream dust jacket. 1500 copies.

A25

The Whittrick: A Poem in Eight Dialogues 1955–1961. Preston: Akros Publications, 1973.

Contents: Dialogue I: James Joyce and Hugh MacDiarmid – Dialogue II: Hieronymus Bosch and Johann Faust – Dialogue III: Queen Shahrazad and King Shahriyar – Dialogue IV: Charlotte and Emily Brontë – Dialogue V: Marilyn Monroe and Galina Ulanova – Dialogue VI: The Brahan Seer and Lady Seaforth – Dialogue VII: Hakuin and Chikamatsu – Dialogue VIII: Grey Walter and Jean Cocteau (Assisted by Roddy and Eck – and the Whittrick) (pp.5–42).

Notes: First 25 copies numbered and signed. Stapled pamphlet. Published April 1973.

Reviews
TLS 18 May 1973, p.548. See also letter from Stewart Conn, *TLS* 1 June 1973, p.617, referring to broadcast of the Bosch-Faust dialogue on the Scottish Home Service in January 1966.

A26

¦ ? *Nuspeak 8, being a visual poem*. Glasgow: Scottish Arts Council, December 1973.

Notes: Stapled card folder containing 4 sheets each 29.5 × 21 cm; one sheet for each punctuation point. *Nuspeak*: SAC newspaper.

Reviews
Kontexts 6&7, 1975.

A27

Essays. Cheadle Hulme: Carcanet New Press, 1974.

Contents: 'Preface' (p.vii); Part One: 'A Glimpse of Petavius'; 'The Poet and the Particle'; 'Into the Constellation: Some Thoughts on the Origin and Nature of Concrete Poetry'; 'The Walls of Gormenghast: An Introduction to the Novels of Mervyn Peake'; 'Three Views of Brooklyn Bridge'; 'Introduction to *Wi the Haill Voice: 25 Poems by Vladimir Mayakovsky Translated into Scots*'; 'Zbigniew Herbert'; 'Heraclitus in Gorky Street: The Theme of Metamorphosis in the Poetry of Andrei Voznesensky' (pp.3–78); Part Two: 'Dunbar and the Language of Poetry'; 'Dryden's Drudging'; 'A Prelude to *The Prelude*'; 'Wordsworth in 1970'; 'The Poetry of Robert Louis Stevenson' (pp.82–149); Part Three: 'Registering the Reality of Scotland'; 'The Resources of Scotland'; 'The Beatnik in the Kailyard'; 'Scottish Poetry in the 1960s'; 'Edwin Muir'; 'MacDiarmid Embattled'; 'Poetry and Knowledge in MacDiarmid's Later Work'; 'MacDiarmid at Seventy-five'; 'The Raging and the Grace: Some Notes on the Poetry of Iain Crichton Smith'; 'James Bridie'; 'The Novels of Robin Jenkins' (pp. 153–245); Part Four: 'The Bicentenary'; 'A Hantle of Howlers'; 'The Compleat Writer's Guide, USA-USSR' (pp.249–94).

Notes: Published October 1974. 1000 copies.

Reviews
Robin Fulton. *Books Abroad* 49:4, Autumn 1975, p.774.
Hugh Nelson. *Chapman* III:5, 1975, p.23.
Robert Nye. *Weekend Scotsman* 7 December 1974, p.4.
Jack Rillie. *Lines Review* 57, March 1976, pp.14–21.

A28

Fifty Renascence Love-Poems translated by Edwin Morgan. Reading: Whiteknights Press, 1975.

Contents: Francesco Petrarca (pp.15–25) – Maurice Scève (pp.27–57) – Garcilaso de la Vega (pp.59–65) – Torquato Tasso (pp.67–75) – Giambattista Marino (pp.77–9).

Notes: Colophon: 'This book of poems is the fourth to be issued by Whiteknights Press. The texts of the series are selected by Ian Fletcher, of the Department of English in the University of Reading, and each volume is designed by a student of typography under the general direction of Michael Twyman in the Department of Typography & Graphic Communication. This volume was designed by Robin Kinross. It was set in "Monotype" Times New Roman series 327 and printed on Grosvenor Chater Chariot (creamy) Cartridge 100 g/m^2 . . . .' Edition of 200. Printed with parallel Italian, French and Spanish texts.

Reviews
T.E. May. *Scottish Literary Journal Supplement* 5, Winter 1977, pp.58–60.

A29

Grierson. Ashington, Northumberland: MidNAG Publications, [1975]. (Poetry Poster no. 26).

Notes: Poster, 58 × 41 cm, printed in grey, white, yellow and black; edition of 400. Designed by Birtley Aris.

A30

Rites of Passage: translations. Manchester: Carcanet New Press, 1976.

Contents: Andrei Voznesensky (pp. 13–28) – Yevgeny Yevtushenko (pp. 29–31) – Boris Pasternak (pp. 32–43) – Yevgeny Vinokurov (p.44) – Salvatore Quasimodo (pp.45–53) – Guillevic (pp.54–56) – Eugenio Montale (pp.57–81) – William Shakespeare (pp.82–3) – Giacomo Leopardi (pp.84–99) – August, Graf Von Platen (p.100) – Anglo-Saxon Poems (pp.101–11) – Friedrich Hölderlin (pp.112–17) – Federico García Lorca (pp.118–23) – Luis Cernuda (p.124) – Leonid Martynov (pp.125–9) – Jacques Prévert (p.130) – Henri Michaux (pp.131–7) – Robert Rozhdestvensky (pp.138–40) – Bertolt Brecht (pp.141–4) – Marina Tsvetayeva (p.145) – Hans Magnus Enzensberger (pp.146–8) – Haroldo de Campos (pp.149–55) – Eugen Gomringer (pp.156–63) – Yury Pankratov (p.164) – Edgard Braga (pp.165–8) – Nanni Balestrini (pp.169–70) – Vladimir Mayakovsky (pp.171–87); 'Glossary of Scots Words' (pp.188–90).

Notes: Published August 1976. Cover title: *Rites of Passage: selected translations*. Issued in cloth and paperback editions. 1500 copies.

Reviews
D. Campbell. *Q* 19, January 1977, pp.10–11.
Douglas Dunn, *Encounter* 49:4, October 1977, p.93.
Robin Fulton. *World Literature Today* 51:2, Spring 1977, pp.339–40.
W. Pickard. *University of Edinburgh Journal* 27:4, December 1977, pp.308–9.
Charles Tomlinson. *TLS* 18 March 1977, p.294.

A31

Hugh MacDiarmid. Edited by Ian Scott-Kilvert. London: Longman Group for the British Council, 1976. (Writers and Their Work 252).

Contents: 'Hugh MacDiarmid' (pp.3–33); 'Hugh MacDiarmid: A Select Bibliography' (pp.34–9).

Notes: Stapled pamphlet. Actually published in March 1977.

Reviews
C. Milton. *Scottish Literary Journal Supplement* 5, Winter 1977, p.55.

A32

The New Divan. Manchester: Carcanet New Press, 1977.

Contents: The New Divan – Memories of Earth – Space Sonnet & Polyfilla – Pictures Floating from the World – The Reversals – Twilight of a Tyranny –

The World – A Girl – Three Trees – On John Maclean – Vico's Song – Sir
Henry Morgan's Song – Shaker Shaken – Lévi-Strauss at the Lie-detector –
Wittgenstein on Egdon Heath – Ten Theatre Poems – Five Poems on Film
Directors – School's out – Adventures of the Anti-sage – The Divide – Smoke –
The Beginning – The Planets – The Question – Resurrections – Unfinished
Poems (pp.7–118).

Notes: Published April 1977. Issued in cloth and paperback editions, 1000 of
each.

Reviews
G.M. Brown. *Weekend Scotsman* 28 May 1977, p.3.
Douglas Dunn. *Encounter* 49:4, October 1977, p.93.
Robin Fulton. *World Literature Today* 52:4, Autumn 1978, p.629.
Desmond Graham. *Stand* 19:1, 1977, pp.74–9.
A. Massie. *Scottish Review* 9, 1978, pp.42–4.
B. Morrison. *TLS* 14 October 1977, p.1192.
Carol Rumens. *Pick* 2:7/8, Summer 1978, pp.38–41.

A33

Particle Poem ('Three particles . . .'). Durham: North Gate Press, 1977.
(Colpitts Poetry Cards, no. 1).

Notes: White card, 15 × 10.5 cm; printed in black.

A34

Colour Poems. Glasgow: Third Eye Centre, 1978.

Contents: Dapple – Flicker – Mutation – Pink Peace-Red War – Figures.

Notes: Published May 1978. A suite of 5 silkscreen prints 58.5 × 40.5 cm on
Esparto paper, printed by John Taylor at the Glasgow Print Studio. Edition of
100 copies, of which 50 have each print numbered and signed by EM. 6 leaves
including contents leaf, contained in clear plastic envelope printed with title.

A35

Platen: Selected Poems (August Graf von Platen-Hallermunde, 1796–1835)
translated by Edwin Morgan. West Linton: The Castlelaw Press, 1978.

Contents: The Pilgrim at St. Yuste – Vesuvius in December 1830 – 'Love is my
betrayer' – A Sigh in Winter – 'And I started up sharp in the night' – 'Fain
would I live in safest freedom' – Tristan – 'Whitely the lily wavers' – To a
Woodbine Tendril – 'The new shoots scatter their scent far away' – 'Truest of
sages are you to me' – 'Forfairn's my hert' – 'Time and space, torment' – 'Who
has ever held life in his hand' – 'At least to be at peace' – Venetian Sonnets
(pp.5–31).

Notes: Edition of 150 copies numbered and signed, 50 of which for private
distribution. Bound in marbled paper-covered boards and issued in clear plastic
wrapper.

A36

Provenance and Problematics of 'Sublime and Alarming Images' in Poetry. London: The
British Academy, [1979]. (Warton Lecture in English Poetry 1977).

Notes: Published March 1979. Stapled paper-covered pamphlet offprinted from the Proceedings of The British Academy, Volume LXIII (1977). Printed by Oxford University Press.

A37

Star Gate: Science Fiction Poems. Glasgow: Third Eye Centre, 1979.

Contents: Instamatic The Moon February 1973 (1973) – The Worlds (1976) – Particle Poems (1977) – Era (1978) – Foundation (1978) – A Home in Space (1979) – The Mouth (1979) – The Clone Poem (1979) – The Moons of Jupiter (1979) (pp.5–20).

Notes: Edition of 600 ordinary copies and 50 copies numbered and signed. Stapled pamphlet, card covers. Published in connection with 'High Frontier 1970–1980' exhibition and events at Third Eye Centre, 15 September until 14 October 1979.

Reviews
Ian Campbell. *Lines Review* 73, June 1980, p.11.
James McGonigal. *Words Review* (Supplement to *Words* 10) [July] 1980, pp.2–3.

A38

Scottish Satirical Verse: an anthology. Manchester: Carcanet New Press, 1980.

Contents: 'Introduction' (pp.xi–xix); text (pp.1–186); 'Notes' (pp.187–213); 'Glossary' (pp.215–36).

Notes: Issued in cloth and paperback editions, 1000 of each. Published June 1980.

Reviews
Alan Bold. *Weekend Scotsman* 28 June 1980, p.3.
Robert Calder. *New Edinburgh Review* 52, November 1980, pp.31–2.
Russell Davies. *Sunday Times* 7 September 1980, p.42.
Douglas Dunn. *London Review of Books* 5–19 March 1981, p.23.
Gavin Ewart. *TLS* 19 September 1980, p.1019.
Sheila Hearn. *Cencrastus* 4, Winter 1980–81, p.49.
Ruth McQuillan. *Scottish Literary Journal Supplement* 16, Spring 1982, pp.28–9.
William Reid. *Books in Scotland* 9, Winter 1981–82, p.16.

A39

9 1 word poems. Glasgow: Mariscat Press, 1982.

Contents: A Far Cool Beautiful Thing, Vanishing – The Dear Green Plaice – Homage to Zukofsky – The Dilemmas of a Horn – Ada Nada Paradada – Lattice, Lettuce, Ladders – Wet Dry Wet Dry Wet Asdic – Dangerous Glory – O Vapour-trails! O Water-melons!

Notes: Hand-produced, typed, stapled pamphlet with card cover, 11.8 × 9.2 cm; edition of 3 copies for private circulation, May 1982. Cover title: *nine one word poems*.

A40

The Apple-Tree: A medieval Dutch play in a version by Edwin Morgan. Glasgow: Third Eye Centre, 1982.

Contents: 'Preface' (p.4); 'Introduction' by Jan Karel Kouwenhoven (pp.5–7); text (pp.8–24).

Notes: Note on p.1: 'Published August 1982 in an edition of 25 numbered clothbound copies signed by the authors, and 750 ordinary paperback copies, on the occasion of the world premiere performance of the translation by the Medieval Players at Third Eye Centre on Friday 13th August, 1982.' J.K. Kouwenhoven supplied EM with a literal translation of the Dutch text. An article on EM and the play, 'In a medieval world they are going Dutch' by Mary Brennan, appeared in the *Glasgow Herald* 3 August 1982, p.4, with a photograph of EM and the Producer Dick McCaw.

Reviews
Mary Brennan. *Glasgow Herald* 16 August 1982, p.5 (of the performance).

A41

Poems of Thirty Years. Manchester: Carcanet New Press, 1982.

Contents: 'Preface' (p.v.); *Dies Irae* (1952): Dies Irae – Stanzas of the Jeopardy – 'What waves have beaten . . .' – A Warning of Waters at Evening – The Sleights of Darkness – The Sleights of Time – Sleight-of-Morals – Harrowing Heaven, 1924 – From the Anglo-Saxon: The Ruin – The Seafarer – The Wanderer – Riddles: Swallows – Swan – Bookworm – Storm – From the Middle English: The Grave – *The Vision of Cathkin Braes* (1952) – *The Cape of Good Hope* (1955) – *The Whittrick: A Poem in Eight Dialogues* (1961) – from *Emergent Poems* (1967): Plea – Dialeck Piece – Nightmare – Manifesto – from *Gnomes* (1968): Strawberry Fields Forever – Archives – Astrodome – The Computer's Second Christmas Card – *The Second Life* (1968) – from *Penguin Modern Poets 15* (1969): The Flowers of Scotland – *The Horseman's Word* (1970) – from *Instamatic Poems* (1972): Glasgow 5 March 1971 ('With a ragged diamond') – Glasgow 5 March 1971 ('Quickly the magistrate') – Nice 5 March 1971 – Chicago May 1971 – Germany December 1970 – Nigeria Undated Reported October 1971 – Leatherhead Surrey September 1971 – Aviemore Invernessshire August 1971 – Mougins Provence September 1971 – Venice April 1971 – London June 1970 – Rockall Invernessshire June 1972 – Ellingham Suffolk January 1972 – Lancashire November 1971 – Washington September 1971 – Translunar Space March 1972 – Bangaon India July 1971 – Glasgow October 1971 – Bradford June 1972 – Campobasso Italy Undated Reported March 1971 – London November 1971 ('At the Festival of Islam') – Glasgow November 1971 ('It is a fine thronged . . .') – Glasgow November 1971 ('The "speckled pipe" of the MacCrimmons') – Milan Undated Reported October 1971 – *From Glasgow to Saturn* (1973) – *The New Divan* (1977) – *Star Gate: Science Fiction Poems* (1979) – Uncollected Poems (1976–1981): The Rock – The Mummy – Five Waiting Poems – Instructions to an Actor – The Archaeopteryx's Song – A Good Year for Death – Migraine Attack – At Central Station – Winter – New Year Sonnets i–x – Surrealism Revisited – Interview – Ore – Stele – Gorgon – Fountain – Book – Mt. Caucasus – On the Water – Moving House – Home on the Range – On the Needle's Point – In the Bottle – Jordanstone Sonnets i–iii – Caliban Falls Asleep in the Isle Full of Noises – Iran – The Coals – On the Train i–iii – A Riddle – A Pair of Cats – Little Blue Blue – Eve and Adam – Grendel – Tarkovsky in Glasgow – Jack London in Heaven – Cinquevalli (pp.3–442).

Notes: Published August 1982.

Reviews

Alan Bold. *Weekend Scotsman* 21 August 1982, p.5.

Alan Bold, *Sunday Standard* 12 December 1982, p.8 ('Reviewers' Choice for Christmas').

Dick Davis. *Listener* 108:2791, 16 December 1982, p.23.

Martin Dodsworth. *Guardian* 30 September 1982, p.16.

Robin Fulton. *World Literature Today* 57:3, Summer 1983, p.460.

Robert Greenwood. *Charterhouse Times* (St Bartholomew's Hospital) 2:2, Late Summer [October], 1983, pp.1–2.

Robin Hamilton. *Lines Review* 85, June [July] 1983, pp.41–4.

John Lucas. *New Statesman* 104:2700 & 2701, 17–24 December 1982, p.45.

David McDuff. *Stand* 24:3, [1983], pp.70–71.

Tom McGrath. *Glasgow Herald* 21 August 1982, p.11 (Weekender p.5).

Alasdair Macrae. *British Book News* January 1983, pp.51–2.

Stephen Mulrine. *Akros* 17:51, October 1983, pp.105–10.

Walter Perrie. *Chapman* VIII:1 (No.37), Autumn 1983, pp.19–27.

Peter Porter. *Observer* 23 January 1983, p.47.

Stephen Regan. *Poetry Review* 73:1, March 1983, pp.65–6.

Jack Rillie. *College Courant* 70, March 1983, pp.18–20.

Peter Robinson. *Argo* (incorporating *Delta*) 4:3 (no.66), 1983, pp.37–9, 41–2.

Carol Rumens. *TLS* 10 December 1982, p.1376.

Alexander Scott. *Scottish Review* 28, November 1982, pp.22–6.

Peter Scott. *Gay News* 247, 19 August – 1 September 1982, p.48.

Paul Strang. *Sunday Standard* 22 August 1982, p.10.

George Szirtes. *Literary Review* 57, March 1983, pp.42–3.

John Wain. *London Magazine* 23:4, July 1983, pp.75–78.

Roderick Watson. *Studies in Scottish Literature* XXI, 1986, pp.227–9.

Kenneth White. *Cencrastus* 12, Spring 1983, pp.32–5.

Alan Young. *PN Review* 38, [Spring] 1984, pp.53–4.

A42

A Celebration: For the opening of the Studio Theatre, Third Eye Centre, Glasgow, 30 April 1983. Glasgow: Third Eye Centre, 1983.

Contents: [Photograph of children at Third Eye Centre] [p.1]; A Celebration [p.2]; 'With Best Wishes from Third Eye Centre' [p.3]; [description of Third Eye Centre and Acknowledgements] [p.4].

Notes: Card 23 × 31.5 cm folded to 23 × 15.75 cm. Published in an edition of 75 copies numbered and signed by EM and 150 ordinary copies. Poem in rhyming couplets ('Good people from the theatre of life, / Although I have no tape to cut with knife,') read at opening of Studio Theatre in Third Eye Centre.

A43

Noise and Smoky Breath: Glasgow Poems and Visual Images 1900–1983. Glasgow: Third Eye Centre and Glasgow District Libraries Publications Board, 1983.

Contents: [Address] [pp. 1–3]; [photograph of EM reading at Third Eye Centre, 1978] [p.4].

Notes: Stapled pamphlet. Edition of 150 copies. Text of the address given by EM to launch the anthology *Noise and Smoky Breath: An Illustrated Anthology of Glasgow Poems*, edited by Hamish Whyte, and open the accompanying exhibition, 'Noise and Smoky Breath: Visual Images of Glasgow 1900–1983', selected by George and Cordelia Oliver, at The Mitchell Library, Glasgow, 5 May 1983. P.[1] includes photograph of EM giving the address.

A44

Grafts/Takes. Glasgow: The Mariscat Press, 1983.

Contents: *Grafts*: Resistance – Midwinter – Casts – Albion – Fall – Heaven – Island – Story – Poetry – Beginnings – Encounter – Quest – Geode – Skins – Snorkelling – Trap – Starlings – Remora – Trench – Testament (pp.9–28) – *Takes*: Palo Alto California Undated Reported July 1971 – London July 1972 – Calne Wiltshire March 1971 – Venice September 1972 – Glasgow October 1972 – Brisbane November 1972 – Darmstadt September 1972 – Dona Ema Brazil April 1972 – Italy Undated Reported November 1972 – London November 1972 – London August 1972 – Walt Disney World Florida October 1972 – Andes Mountains December 1972 – Reykjavik July 1972 – Udal North Uist 1972 – Stoke-on-Trent January 1973 – New York 1971 – London January 1973 – Sydney Australia September 1973 – London October 1973 (pp.9–28).

Notes: Edition of 300 copies: 26 clothbound copies lettered and signed by EM and 274 ordinary paperback copies; all with dust jacket by Alasdair Gray. Two collections bound back to back. The poems in *Grafts* 'are based on fragments from abandoned poems by Michael Schmidt . . . There was no collaboration: I merely used the alien material as if the lines (as often happens) had suddenly floated into my head.' (Note by EM on p.[7]) The poems in *Takes* 'were written after the publication of *Instamatic Poems* . . . and may be taken as a supplement to that collection.' (Note on p.[7]) Published June 1983.

Reviews
Jim Burns. *Tribune* 18 November 1983, p.9.
Andrew Dorward. *New Edinburgh Review* 63, Autumn 1983, pp.37–8.
Douglas Dunn. *TLS* 20 January 1984, p.54.
[J.C.R. Green]. *Printers Pie* 3, [October] 1983, p.34.
Colin Milton. *Scottish Literary Journal Supplement* 23, Winter 1985, p.61.
Hayden Murphy. *Chapman* VIII:2 (No.39), Autumn 1984, p.64.
Robert Sheppard. *PN Review* 37 (10:5), February 1984, p.52.
Iain Crichton Smith. *Scottish Review* 32, November 1983, pp.40–41.
Paul Strang. *Sunday Standard* 24 July 1983, p.16.

A45

Master Peter Pathelin. Glasgow: Third Eye Centre, 1983.

Contents: 'Introduction' by Carl Heap (pp.[4–6]); 'Translator's Note' by EM (pp.[6–7]); text (pp.8–63).

Notes: Published November 1983 in an edition of 1100 paperback copies. Cover title: *Master Peter Pathelin: An Anonymous 15th Century French Farce* Translated by Edwin Morgan. The world première performance by The Medieval Players took place at The Crawford Centre for the Arts, St Andrews University, 11 October 1983. The book is illustrated with drawings by Helen Wilks.

A46

Glasgow Poster Poems. Glasgow: National Book League (Scotland), 1983.

Contents: 1 The Subway Giraffe – 2 The Subway Cat – 3 The Subway Piranhas – 4 The Subway Budgie.

Notes: 4 posters, each 30 × 20 cm, each a different colour (tan, violet, pink, green) with text in white. The posters were part of a series commissioned by the Scottish Arts Council for display in the Glasgow Underground but rejected by Strathclyde Passenger Transport Executive as unsuitable ('there are no piranhas in the Underground'). See articles and correspondence in the *Glasgow Herald* 23 June 1982, p.1; 29 June 1982, p.6; 7 July 1982, p.6; and *Glasgow Chamber of Commerce Journal* August 1982, p.249.

A47

(a) *Sonnets from Scotland*. Glasgow: The Mariscat Press, 1984.

Contents: Slate – Carboniferous – Post-Glacial – In Argyll – The Ring of Brodgar – Silva Caledonia – Pilate at Fortingall – The Mirror – The Picts – Colloquy in Glaschu – Memento – Matthew Paris – At Stirling Castle, 1507 – Thomas Young, M.A. (St Andrews) – Lady Grange on St Kilda – Theory of the Earth – Poe in Glasgow – De Quincey in Glasgow – Peter Guthrie Tait, Topologist – G.M. Hopkins in Glasgow – 1893 – The Ticket – North Africa – Caledonian Antisyzygy – Travellers (1) – Travellers (2) – Seferis on Eigg – Matt McGinn – Post-Referendum – Gangs – After a Death – Not the Burrell Collection – 1983 – A Place of Many Waters – The Poet in the City – The Norn (1) – The Norn (2) – The Target – After Fallout – The Age of Heracleum – Computer Error: Neutron Strike – Inward Bound – The Desert – The Coin – The Solway Canal – A Scottish Japanese Print – Outward Bound – On Jupiter – Clydegrad – A Golden Age – The Summons (pp.9–59) – Hors Série [back cover].

Notes: Published 30 November 1984 in an edition of 1000 copies: 250 hardback and 750 paperback; with cover design by Alasdair Gray.

Reviews

James Aitchison. *Glasgow Herald* 5 January 1985, p.10.
James Aitchison. *Scottish Review* 37/38, May 1985, pp.105–6
John Barnie. *Planet* 52, August/September 1985, pp.120–22.
Alan Bold. *Weekend Scotsman* 15 December 1984, p.5.
D. Bolton. *University of Edinburgh Journal* XXXII:1, June 1985, p.53.
S.J. Boyd. *Poetry Review* 75:1, April 1985, p.58.
Jim Burns. *Tribune* 12 April 1985.
Douglas Dunn. *TLS* 26 April 1985, p.470.
[Robin Hamilton]. *Edinburgh Review* 67/8, [January 1985], pp.144–7.
Elin Haugen [R. Crawford and D. Kinloch]. *Verse* 2, 1985, p.47.
Nicholas Jacobs. *Balliol College Annual Record* 1985, p.80.

Angus MacPhee. *Teaching English* 19:2, Spring 1986, p.49.
Ken Edward Smith. *Anglo-Welsh Review* 80, 1985, pp.102–3.
Roderick Watson. *Studies in Scottish Literature* XXI, 1986, pp.251–2.

(b) 2nd impression, published September 1986; 1000 paperback copies. As (a) but with press comments substituted for the poem on the back cover.

A48

Selected Poems. Manchester: Carcanet Press, 1985.

Contents: from *Dies Irae* (1952): Stanzas of the Jeopardy – from *The Vision of Cathkin Braes* (1952): Verses for a Christmas Card – *Concrete Poems* (1963–1969): Message Clear – Dialeck Piece – Strawberry Fields Forever – Archives – Astrodome – Starryveldt – Siesta of a Hungarian Snake – The Computer's First Christmas Card – Opening the Cage – Chinese Cat – Clydesdale – Centaur – from *The Second Life* (1968): The Death of Marilyn Monroe – The White Rhinoceros – Aberdeen Train – Canedolia – To Joan Eardley – The Starlings in George Square – King Billy – Glasgow Green – In the Snack-bar – Trio – The Second Life – From a City Balcony – Strawberries – One Cigarette – Absence – In Sobieski's Shield – From the Domain of Arnheim – What is 'Paradise Lost' *Really* About? – A View of Things – from *Penguin Modern Poets 15* (1969): Phoning – *Instamatic Poems* (1971–1973): Glasgow 5 March 1971 ('With a ragged') – Venice April 1971 – London June 1970 ('It is opening night') – Glasgow November 1971 ('The "speckled pipe" ') – Glasgow October 1972 ('At the Old Ship Bank') – Darmstadt September 1972 – Dona Ema Brazil April 1972 – Andes Mountains December 1972 – London January 1973 ('It is not a pile') – from *From Glasgow to Saturn* (1973): Columba's Song – Floating off to Timor – In Glasgow – The Apple's Song – At the Television Set – Blue Toboggans – Lord Jim's Ghost's Tiger Poem – Hyena – The Loch Ness Monster's Song – Afterwards – Thoughts of a Module – The First Men on Mercury – Spacepoem 3: Off Course – Itinerary – Not Playing the Game – Rider – Stobhill – Glasgow Sonnets – from *The New Divan* (1977): The World – Shaker Shaken – Vico's Song – Resurrections – from *Star Gate* (1979): Particle Poems – A Home in Space – The Mouth – The Moons of Jupiter – from *Poems of Thirty Years* (1982): The Mummy – Instructions to an Actor – Migraine Attack – Winter – Surrealism Revisited – On the Water – On the Needle's Point – The Coals – Little Blue Blue – Grendel – Jack London in Heaven – Cinquevalli – from *Grafts/Takes* (1983): Resistance – Heaven – Story – Remora – French – Testament – *Uncollected Poems*: Night Pillion (1956) – from the *Dictionary of Tea* (1966) – Cook in Hawaii (1974) – The Break-In (1982) – An Alphabet of Goddesses (1982) (pp.9–139).

Notes: Published 23 April 1985. Paperback edition only.

Reviews
Alan Bold. *Poetry Review* 75:3, October 1985, p.60.
Denis Donoghue. *London Review of Books* 7:19, 7 November 1985, p.21.
Douglas Dunn. *Glasgow Herald* 28 December 1985, p.11 (Weekender 4).
Kevin McCarra. *Scottish Literary Journal Supplement* 23, Winter 1985, pp.65–6.
Mark Ravenhall. *Darts* (Sheffield University), 26 June 1985.

Roger D. Webster. *The Green Book* 2:4, [Autumn 1986], p.53.
Hamish Whyte [and Kevin McCarra]. *The Glasgow Magazine* 6, Summer
1985, p.39.
Hamish Whyte. *Prospice* 18, [July] 1986, pp.147–51.

A49

From the Video Box. Glasgow: The Mariscat Press, 1986.

Contents: 1 ('I saw that Burning of the Books in China') – 2 ('I have just watched
that fearful programme') – 3 ('This is the first time I have ever recorded') – 4
('I never believed in legendary heroes') – 5 ('I am not here to talk about a
scratch') – 6 ('my friend and I watched that scratch that scratch video') – 7 ('It is
hard to know what it is I saw.') – 8 ('This is the most ridiculous thing I ever
experienced') – 9 ('At last, a programme for the colour-blind!') – 10 ('I never
really took to Shakespeare') – 11 ('Poor Barbary! I must tell you') – 12 ('Oh the
sheer power of that witch, that bitch, that') – 13 ('I don't watch television,') –
14 ('Wait noo, wait a minute. Right.') – 15 ('I know you won't mind if I use
your box') – 16 ('There may be a case for subliminal images') – 17 ('That was so
strange last night –') – 18 ('There is one word') – 19 ('I was galloping down
through Patagonia') – 20 (' "Video wall, video wall," ') – 21 ('Against my will,
and I emphasise that,') – 22 ('I put up the biggest dish in Perthshire') – 23 ('It is
grand and fine to think') – 24 ('Hullo there. That's my hamster, by the way,') –
25 ('If you ask what my favourite programme is') – 26 ('What was the best
programme?') – 27 ('The programme that stays most in my mind').

Notes: Published May 1986 in an edition of 300 copies. Stapled pamphlet, with
cover design by David Neilson.

Reviews
Robin Bell. *Books in Scotland* 21, Summer 1986, p.16.

A50

Newspoems. London: wacy!, [1987]. (wacy! 007).

Contents: Found Concrete Poem: The Enactment – Ballad 13 – An Unpublished
Poem by Zukofsky – Caedmon's Second Hymn – New English Riddles: 2 –
Scrumwear – Möbius's Bed – Car Goes Ape – Hooked – Forgetful Duck –
Notice in Hell – Advice to a Corkscrew; [list of wacy! publications];
Unpublished Poems by Creeley: 5 – Ball – The Computer's First Translation –
Pigeons: Elizabethan – Hex – Revolt of the Objects – Hair-raising –
Unpublished Poems by Creeley: 2 – Visual Soundpoem – Epitaph –
Hypermarine – Unpublished Poems by Creeley: 1 – Apple Girl – Idyll –
Cooked – Charon's Song – Legend – Sick Man – Notice in Heaven – Joe's Bar –
Revolt of the Elements – Early Days for Dr Moreau – Scotland Enters the
Common Market – The Commonest Kind – Said the Pigeon; [title page]; 'Note
on "Newspoems" '; [letter from EM to Steve Pereira of wacy!]; Cain Said – Holy
Flying Saucer Satori – In Mid-Trepan – Talk About Camp – Come in Old Cock
– Unpublished Poems by Creeley: 3 – New English Riddles: 1 – Beckford
Heard a Voice Saying – Unpublished Poems by Creeley: 4 – Unpublished
Poems by Creeley: 6 – Concrete Ballad of Reading Gaol.

Notes: Published March 1987. Stapled pamphlet, published in an edition of 58.

The contents of each copy are in a different order. The contents listed above are those of copy No. XXI, printed on pink and white paper. For EM's preferred order see *Themes on a Variation*.

A51

Roadworks: Song Lyrics for Wildcat by David Anderson and David MacLennan. Selected by Edwin Morgan. Glasgow: Third Eye Centre, 1987.

Contents: 'Preface' by David Anderson and David MacLennan (p.[ii]); 'Introduction' by Liz Lochhead (pp.1–2); 'The Wildcat's Play and Prey' by Edwin Morgan (pp.3–5); text (pp.6–83); 'Index of Songs' (p.84).

Notes: Published May 1987 in an edition of 2000 paperback copies.

A52

Twentieth Century Scottish Classics. Glasgow: Book Trust Scotland, 1987.

Contents: [Introduction] (p.[iii]); [EM's annotated list of 54 'Scottish Classics' of fiction] (pp.1–19).

Notes: Published October 1987. Stapled pamphlet.

Reviews
Simon Berry. *Scotsman* 22 May 1987, p.4 (review of talk at Book Trust Scotland by EM on Choosing the 'Scottish Classics').
Ian Campbell. *Books in Scotland* 28, Summer 1988, p.14.
PN Review 61 (14:5), [March] 1988, p.10.

A53

Themes on a Variation. Manchester: Carcanet Press, 1988.

Contents: The Dowser (1986) – Variations on Omar Khayyám (1984) – Stanzas (1986) – The Room (1985) – Dear man, my love goes out in waves (1987) – Waking on a Dark Morning (1986) – The Gurney (1986) – The Bench (1985) – Nineteen Kinds of Barley (1984) – A Trace of Wings (1985) – The Hanging Gardens of Babylon (1982) – A Bobbed Sonnet for Code Cobber (1986) – The Computer's First Birthday Card (1966) – Byron at Sixty-Five (1985) – Shakespeare: a Reconstruction (1986) – To the Queen: a Reconstruction (1987) – Chillon: a Reconstruction (1987) – True Ease in Writing: a Reconstruction (1987) – On Time: a Reconstruction (1987) – Not Marble: a Reconstruction (1987) – Halley's Comet (1985) – The Gorbals Mosque (1984) – Rules for Dwarf-Throwing (1986) – The Bear (1987) – Save the Whale Ball (1981) – Dom Raja (1986) – The Change (1987) – Vereshchagin's Barrow (1982) – *Newspoems* (1965–1971): Holy Flying Saucer Satori – The Computer's First Translation – Cain Said – Notice in Hell – Notice in Heaven – The Commonest Kind – Sick Man – Joe's Bar – Early Days for Dr Moreau – Hex – In Mid-Trepan – Hooked – Charon's Song – Epitaph – Legend – Revolt of the Elements – Revolt of the Objects – Hair-raising – Apple Girl – O for a Life of Sensations – Cooked – Beckford Heard a Voice Saying – Forgetful Duck – Said the Pigeon – Pigeons: Elizabethan – Car Goes Ape – Möbius's Bed – Come in Old Cock – Idyll – Caedmon's Second Hymn – New English Riddles: 1 – New English Riddles: 2 – Ballad 13 – Scrumwear – Talk About Camp – Hypermarine – Ball

– Scotland Enters the Common Market – Advice to a Corkscrew – An
Unpublished Poem by Zukofsky – Unpublished Poems by Creeley: 1 –
Unpublished Poems by Creeley: 2 – Unpublished Poems by Creeley: 3 –
Unpublished Poems by Creeley: 4 – Unpublished Poems by Creeley: 5 –
Unpublished Poems by Creeley: 6 – Concrete Ballad of Reading Gaol – Visual
Soundpoem – Found Concrete Poem: The Enactment – In Silhouette – *From the
Video Box* (1986) – *Sonnets from Scotland* (1984) (pp. 11–166).

Notes: Published May 1988. Paperback edition only.

Reviews
James Aitchison. *Glasgow Herald* 28 May 1988, p. 10 (Weekender p. 3).
Colin Bell. *Books in Scotland* 28, Summer 1988, p. 24.
Douglas Dunn. *Punch* 24 June 1988, p.[45].
Douglas Dunn. *Glasgow Herald* 3 December 1988, p. 22 (Weekender p. 2)
    (chosen as one of his 'Books of the Year').
Edinburgh Review 82, Winter [May] 1989, pp. 142–4.
Mark Ford. *London Review of Books* 11:2, 19 January 1989, p. 14.
Ian Gregson. *New Welsh Review* 4, Spring 1989, pp. 71–2.
Alan Jenkins. *Observer* 10 July 1988, p. 42.
Kevin McCarra. *Scotsman* 14 May 1988, Weekend p. X.
Stephen Mulrine. *Chapman* 55–6, Spring 1989, pp. 176–7.
Hayden Murphy. *Lines Review* 107, December 1988, pp. 35–6.
Thom Nairn. *Scottish Literary Journal Supplement* 29, Winter 1988 [March
    1989], pp. 46–9.
Peter Reading, *TLS* 10–16 June 1988, p. 650 (note: last 2 lines of 'Pilate at
    Fortingall' wrongly quoted; letter from PR, *TLS* 17–23 June 1988, p. 677,
    purports to correct them but still gets them wrong; letter from EM, TLS 1–7
    July 1988, p. 733, corrects them).
William Scammell. *Guardian* 10 June 1988, p. 10.
Iain Crichton Smith. *Cencrastus* 32, New Year [February] 1989, p. 13.
Marshall Walker. *Landfall* (NZ) 170(43:2), June 1989, pp. 242–8.
Alan Young. *PN Review* 66 [15:4], [? Spring] 1989, pp. 53–4.
Catherine Lockerbie, 'Scottish poet well versed in art of surprise', *Scotsman* 14
    May 1988, p. 7 (review of reading at People's Palace to launch *Themes on a
    Variation*).

A54

Tales from Limerick Zoo. Illustrations by David Neilson. Glasgow: The Mariscat
Press, 1988.

Contents: The Amoeba – The Anaconda – The Bonxie – The Borzoi – The Carp –
The Cat – The Dog – The Dolphin – The Elk – The Emu – The Flounder – The
Fox – The Griffin – The Hare – The Ibis – The Impala – The Jerboa – The Krill
– The Lamprey – The Macaw – The Muskellunge – The Natterjack – The Otter
– The Owl – The Porker – The Potto – The Quahog – The Quail – The Rat –
The Sewellel – The Starfish – The Tick – The Unicorn – The Viper – The Vole –
The Vulture – The Warthog – The Whale – The Whippet – The Wombat –
The Xanthura – The Yak – The Zebra – The Zebu.

Notes: Published November 1988. Stapled pamphlet; edition of 350 copies.

Reviews
Robin Bell. *Books in Scotland* 30, Spring 1989, p.21.
Robert Nye. *Scotsman* 3 December 1988, Weekender p.VI.

B

BOOKS CONTAINING CONTRIBUTIONS BY OR EDITED JOINTLY BY
EDWIN MORGAN

1953
B1   *The Golden Horizon*. Edited by Cyril Connolly. London: Weidenfeld,
     1953.
     Envoi ('The Ruin' transl. from Anglo-Saxon). (p.596)

B2   *Springtime: An Anthology of Young Poets and Writers*. Edited by G.S.
     Fraser and Iain Fletcher. London: Peter Owen, 1953.
     An Extract from The Wanderer (transl. from Anglo-Saxon) – Délie,
     Obiect de Plvs Havlte Vertu XXIV (transl. from Maurice Scève).
     (pp.123–4)

1954

B3   *Lyric Poetry of the Italian Renaissance: An anthology with verse translations*.
     Collected by L.R. Lind. With an introduction by Thomas G. Bergin.
     New Haven: Yale University Press / London: Oxford University Press,
     1954.
     [13] Tuscan Folk Songs. (pp.45–51)
     Transl. into Scots.

B4   *New Poems 1954*. Edited by Rex Warner, Christopher Hassall and
     Laurie Lee. London: Michael Joseph, 1954. (A P.E.N. Anthology)
     Harrowing Heaven, 1924. (pp.165–6)

1955

B5   *New Poems 1955*. Edited by Patric Dickinson, J.C. Hall and Erica Marx.
     London: Michael Joseph, 1955. (A P.E.N. Anthology)
     Northern Nocturnal. (pp.103–4)

1958

B6   *The International Who's Who in Poetry*. Edited by Geoffrey Handley-
     Taylor. London: Cranbrook Tower Press, 1958. 2 vols.
     'Poetry in Scotland'. (Vol.2, pp.158–63)

1959

B7   *Honour'd Shade: An Anthology of New Scottish Poetry to Mark the Bicentenary
     of the Birth of Robert Burns*. Edited by Norman MacCaig. Edinburgh:
     Chambers, 1959.
     Mayakonferensky's Anectidote – The Window ('What waves have
     beaten . . .') – What is 'Paradise Lost' *really* about? (pp.79–82)

B8   *Encyclopaedia Britannica: A New Survey of Universal Knowledge.* Vol. 20
(Sarsaparilla to Sorcery). Chicago, London and Toronto: Encyclopaedia
Britannica Ltd, 1959.
'[Scottish Literature:] In Scots and English'. (pp. 182–5)
Signed 'E.G.M.'

1960

B9   *An Anthology of German Poetry from Hölderlin to Rilke in English Translation.*
Edited by Angel Flores. Garden City, New York: Anchor Books,
Doubleday & Co., Inc., 1960. (Anchor A 197)
Evening (transl. from Joseph von Eichendorff) – The Pilgrim at St
Yuste – Love is my Betrayer – A Sigh in Winter – Fain Would I Live
in Safest Freedom – Whitely the Lily Wavers . . . – The New Shoots
Scatter their Scent Far Away – Truest of Sages are You to Me –
Forfairn's my Hert – Time and Space, Torment . . . – Venetian
Sonnets – Who has Ever Held Life in his Hand – At Least to be in
Peace . . . (transl. from August, Graf von Platen) – 'Yonder's a
lanely fir-tree' – The Lorelei – 'I see ye like a flooer' – Whaur? – The
Stane wi its Runes Rises Frae the Sea – Hoo the Warld Wags (transl.
from Heinrich Heine) – From a Church Tower (transl. from Eduard
Mörike). (pp. 111; 129, 132, 134, 135–6, 137, 138–45, 149, 150;
175, 178–9, 182, 185, 189, 200; 271)

1961

B10 *New Poems 1961: A P.E.N. Anthology of Contemporary Poetry.* Edited by
William Plomer, Anthony Thwaite and Hilary Corke. London: Hutch-
inson, 1961.
Dialogue VII: Hakuin and Chikamatsu. (pp. 73–8)
From *The Whittrick.*

1962

B11 *Afmæliskveðjur heiman og handan: Til Halldórs Kiljans Laxness sextugs.*
[Edited by Jakob Benediktsson, Sigurður Pórarinsson, Kristján
Karlsson and Tómas Guðmundsson]. Reykjavík: Helgafell-Ragnar
Jónsson, 1962.
'*The Atom Station* and the Degrees of Realism'. (pp. 89–93)

B12 *An Anthology of Medieval Lyrics.* Edited by Angel Flores. New York: The
Modern Library, Random House, 1962.
'Pale beauty! and a smile the pallor there' – 'The woods are wild and
were not made for man' – 'The eyes that drew from me such fervent
praise' – 'Great is my envy of you, earth, in your greed' (all transl.
from Petrarch) – Stanzas on the Death of his Father (transl. from
Jorge Manrique). (pp. 259–60, 264, 266, 266–7; 344–52)

B13 *Hugh MacDiarmid: A Festschrift.* Edited by K.D. Duval and Sydney
Goodsir Smith. Edinburgh: K.D. Duval, 1962.
'Poetry and Knowledge in MacDiarmid's Later Work'. (pp. 129–39)
Reprinted in *Hugh MacDiarmid: A Critical Survey*, ed. Duncan
Glen (Edinburgh: Scottish Academic Press, 1972), pp. 192–202;
and in *Essays*, pp. 203–13.

B14   *The Novel Today.* Edited by Andrew Hook. Edinburgh: Edinburgh
      International Festival, 1962.
          'The Young Writer in Scotland'. (pp.35–8).
          Programme and notes for International Writers' Conference,
          McEwan Hall, Edinburgh, 20–24 August, 1962.

B15   *Poetry Supplement.* Edited by John Fuller. London: Poetry Book Society,
      Christmas, 1962.
          The Old Man and the Sea. (p.[4])

                                    1963

B16   *The Concise Encyclopaedia of English and American Poets and Poetry.* Edited
      by Stephen Spender and Donald Hall. London: Hutchinson, 1963.
          'Anglo-Saxon Poetry'. (pp.30–32, 49)
          New edition 1970. (pp.8–12)

B17   *The Concise Encyclopedia of Modern World Literature.* Edited by Geoffrey
      Grigson. London: Hutchinson, 1963.
          'Blok'. (pp.74–5)
          'Esenin'. (pp.134, 153)
          'Genet'. (pp.166–7)
          'Golding'. (pp.189–90)
          'Mayakovsky'. (pp.284–5)
          'Montale'. (pp.290, 309)
          'Neruda'. (p.318)
          'Pasternak'. (pp.347–9)
          'Prishvin'. (pp.361–2)
          'Sholokhov'. (pp.407–8)
          'Tikhonov'. (p.443)
          'Traven'. (p.450)
          Unsigned. EM also contributed articles on Lewis Grassic Gibbon,
          Christopher Logue, Robert Lowell, Hugh MacDiarmid, Laura
          Riding, and Dylan Thomas: the Gibbon piece (p.168) was
          rewritten by Grigson, Lowell (pp.263–4) was 'much edited',
          MacDiarmid (p.267) 'much cut and rearranged', Logue and Riding
          omitted and in the Thomas piece (pp.439–40) only a few of EM's
          phrases remain. The first paragraph of Traven was rewritten,
          Prishvin lacks examples and quotation omitted from Tikhonov.
          Corrections: Esenin, p.153b1 – for 'joujik' read 'moujick'; 20–21
                        – for 'Pis-mok' read 'Pis'-mok'; 37 – for 'Slonin'
                        read 'Slonim'.
                       Gibbon, p.168b2 – for 'thought' read 'thoughts'.
                       Lowell, p.264a11 – for 'has' read 'had'.
                       Mayakovsky, p.285b36 – for 'T. Lindsay' read 'J.
                        Lindsay'.
                       Montale – unattributed quotation from EM's transla-
                        tion of 'Mediterraneo VII' from *Ossi di seppia*.
                       Neruda, p.318b16 – for '*Espana*' read 'España'; 24 –
                        for 'Machu' read 'Macchu'; 36 – for 'Sitten' read
                        'Sillen'.

Pasternak, p.348b26 – for '1923' read '1924'; 40 –
for 'social' read 'socialist'; p.349a18 – for 'Borger'
read 'Berger'.
Sholokhov, p.408a17 – for 'from Tikhi' read 'from
end of Bk II of Tikhi'.
Traven – add dates: (c.1895–).

A second, revised, edition in a new format was published in 1970.
The only correction taken into account was the Gibbon correction.
'Blok'. (pp.59–60)
'Esenin'. (pp.116–17) [bibliography omitted]
'Genet'. (pp.135–6)
'Gibbon'. (p.137)
'Golding'. (pp.142–3)
'Lowell'. (pp.214–5)
'MacDiarmid'. (p.219)
'Mayakovsky'. (pp.239–41)
'Montale'. (pp.247–8)
'Neruda'. (pp.260–61)
'Pasternak'. (pp.276–8) [bibliography reduced]
'Prishvin'. (pp.291–2) [bibliography omitted]
'Sholokhov'. (p.330)
'Thomas'. (pp.349–50)
'Tikhonov'. (pp.353–4)
'Traven'. (pp.360–1)

B18 *Medieval Age*. Edited, with an Introduction, by Angel Flores. New
York: Dell Publishing Co., Inc., 1963. (Laurel Masterpieces of World
Literature)
The Wanderer – The Seafarer (both transl. from Anglo-Saxon) –
Count Arnaldos (transl. from Spanish) – Inferno, Canto V, 11.73–142
(transl. from Dante). (pp.129–32, 132–6, 412, 501–3)

1965

B19 *The Encore Reader*. Edited by Charles Marowitz, Tom Milne and Owen
Hale. With a Foreword by Richard Findlater. London: Methuen, 1965.
'That Uncertain Feeling'. (pp.52–6)
B20 *Between Poetry and Painting*. London: Institute of Contemporary Arts,
1965.
[Statement on concrete poetry]. (pp.69–71)
Exhibition catalogue.
B21 *konkrete poesie international*. Stuttgart: Max Bense and Elisabeth Walther,
[May 1965]. (rot 21)
bees' nest. (p.[4])

1966

B22 *Astronauts of Inner-Space: An International Collection of Avant-Garde
Activity*. General editor Jeff Berner. San Francisco/London: Stolen Paper
Review Editions/*The Times* Publishing Company, 1966.
The Computer's First Christmas Card – Letter to a French Novelist.
(pp.62, 65)

B23 *Best Poems of 1965: Borestone Mountain Poetry Awards 1966: A Compilation*
of Original Poetry published in Magazines of the English-speaking World in
1965. Eighteenth Annual Issue. Edited by Lionel Stevenson, Howard
Sergeant, Waddell Austin, Hildegarde Flanner, Gertrude Claytor,
Frances Minturn Howard, Gemma D'Auria. Palo Alto, California:
Pacific Books, 1966.
In Sobieski's Shield. (pp.62–4)

B24 *Modern Scottish Poetry: An Anthology of the Scottish Renaissance.* Edited by
Maurice Lindsay. 2nd edition, revised. London: Faber and Faber, 1966.
To Joan Eardley – King Billy – Aberdeen Train – Good Friday.
(pp.157–61)

B25 *The Oxford Book of Scottish Verse.* Chosen by John MacQueen and Tom
Scott. Oxford: The Clarendon Press, 1966.
The Second Life. (pp.604–5)

B26 *Scottish Poetry Number One.* Edited by George Bruce, Maurice Lindsay
and Edwin Morgan. Edinburgh: Edinburgh University Press, 1966.
Strawberries – The Death of Marilyn Monroe – In the Snack-bar.
(pp.22–7)
Reviews: N. MacCaig, *New Statesman* 22 April 1966, pp.583–4;
Albert D. Mackie, *English* XVI:96, 1967, pp.237–8 (also of *SP 2*);
TLS 7 July 1966, p.596.

1967

B27 *An Anthology of concrete poetry.* Edited by Emmett Williams. New York:
Something Else Press, 1967. (Clothbound and paperback editions)
[The Computer's First Christmas Card] – Starryveldt – [Pomander] –
From an Old Scottish Chapbook – The Chaffinch Map of Scotland –
Off Course – Seven Headlines. (7 unnumbered pages)
Each poem is followed by a note by EM.

B28 *Arran Children Writing: A selection of the entries to the Arran Children's*
Creative Writing Competition sponsored by the Isle of Arran Film Society Season
1966–67. [Brodick]: Isle of Arran Film Society, [1967].
[Comment on winner]. (p.1)
EM was judge of the competition.

B29 *artypo: art, made with the help of graphic techniques.* Eindhoven: Grafische
School, 1967.
The Chaffinch Map of Scotland. (item 62)
Catalogue of exhibition for the opening of the Eindhoven Graphic
School. Text in Dutch, English, French and German.

B30 *A Book of Scottish Verse.* Selected by R.L. Mackie. Second edition. The
Selection revised with a new Introduction by Maurice Lindsay. London:
Oxford University Press, 1967. (The World's Classics 417)
Aberdeen Train – King Billy – Absence – From the Domain of
Arnheim. (pp.433–7)
The book was partly reset with corrections in 1968.

B31 *Concrete Poetry: An International Anthology.* Edited by Stephen Bann.
London: London Magazine Editions, 1967.

The Chaffinch Map of Scotland – Bees' Nest – Summer Haiku –
French Persian Cats Having a Ball – Unscrambling the Waves at
Goonhilly – The Computer's First Christmas Card – Starryveldt.
(pp. 169–75)

B32   *experimentální poezie*. Prague: Odeon, 1967.
      Chinese Cat – French Persian Cats Having a Ball. (pp. 151–2)

B33   *Gyémánttengely: A Költészet Napjai Budapesten 1966*. Budapest:
      Szépirodalmi Könyvkiadó, 1967.
      Ó, ÚTTÖRŐK! [O, Pioneers!] – MARYLIN [sic] MONROE
      HALÁLA (transl. by Zsuzsanna Takács). (pp. 280–2)
      Diamond-axle: Poetry Days in Budapest, 1966 celebrates an interna-
      tional poetry festival that EM and George MacBeth attended. The
      book also includes a photograph of EM and GM between pp. 16
      and 17, a photograph of EM between pp. 160 and 161 and a
      caricature of EM by György Rózsabegyi opp. p. 272.

B34   *Poems Addressed to Hugh MacDiarmid and Presented to him on his Seventy-
      fifth Birthday* . . . Edited by Duncan Glen. Preston: Akros Publica-
      tions, 1967. Printed by Thomas Rae, Greenock.
      To Hugh MacDiarmid. (pp. 40–41)
      350 numbered copies signed by editor and artist. The first 50
      copies also signed by the poets and the printer.

B35   *Scottish Poetry Number Two*. Edited by George Bruce, Maurice Lindsay
      and Edwin Morgan. Edinburgh: Edinburgh University Press, 1967.
      From the Domain of Arnheim – An Addition to the Family – From a
      City Balcony – Pomander. (pp. 94–9)
      SP 1 & 2 were reviewed by Albert Mackie in *English* XVI:96,
      Autumn 1967, pp. 237–8.

B36   *Segni nello spazio*. Trieste: L'azienda autonoma di soggiurno, 1967.
      Message Clear. (p. 68)
      Catalogue of exhibition of experimental poetry.

1968

B37   *Best Poems of 1967: Borestone Mountain Poetry Awards 1968: A Compilation
      of Original Poetry published in Magazines of the English-speaking World in
      1967*. Twentieth Annual Issue. Edited by Lionel Stevenson, Howard
      Sergeant, Waddell Austin, Hildegarde Franner, Frances Minturn
      Howard, Gemma D'Auria. Palo Alto, California: Pacific Books, 1968.
      After the Party. (p. 84)

B38   *Innovations: Essays on Art & Ideas*. Edited by Bernard Bergonzi. London:
      Macmillan, 1968.
      'Concrete Poetry'. (pp. 213–25)

B39   *Quadlog*. Bibury (Glos.): Arlington Mill, 1968.
      [Newspoems:] Unpublished Poems by Creeley: 1 – Triumph.
      Catalogue for Arlington Quadro, an exhibition held 3 August to
      mid-September 1968 at Arlington Mill of British and Portuguese
      concrete poetry and related work. Includes photograph of the
      Newspoems.

B40   *publications by edition and works by hansjörg mayer.* [Stuttgart: Hansjörg
       Mayer, 1968].
           dialeck piece. (p.26)
           Published as part of exhibition at Haags gemeentemuseum, 5
           October – 24 November 1968.

B41   *Scottish Poetry Number Three.* Edited by George Bruce, Maurice Lindsay
       and Edwin Morgan. Edinburgh: Edinburgh University Press, 1968.
           Blackbirds – The Furies – For Bonfires. (pp.82–6)

                                   1969

B42   *4.* Stuttgart: Jurgen Brenner, 1969. (150 numbered copies signed by
       contributors)
           [Untitled poem]. (pp.48–51)
           Visual poem based on the word for 4 in twelve languages. Printed
           in blue, red, black and green.

B43   *Penguin Modern Poets 15.* Alan Bold, Edward Brathwaite, Edwin
       Morgan. Harmondsworth: Penguin Books, 1969.
           After the Party – To Joan Eardley – King Billy – The Suspect – Trio
           – Good Friday – In the Snack-Bar – Glasgow Green – Phoning –
           Drift – An Addition to the Family – Aberdeen Train – The Flowers
           of Scotland – Archives – Che – The Old Man and the Sea – The Death
           of Marilyn Monroe – Astrodome – Not Playing the Game – A Snib
           for the Nones – A Courtly Overture – The White Rhinoceros –
           Frontier Story – The Computer's First Christmas Card – A View of
           Things – In Sobieski's Shield – From the Domain of Arnheim –
           Floating off to Timor – Strawberry Fields Forever – For Bonfires.
           (pp.125–75)

B44   *Scottish Poetry Number Four.* Edited by George Bruce, Maurice Lindsay
       and Edwin Morgan. Edinburgh: Edinburgh University Press, 1969.
           Floating off to Timor – London (1: St James's Park – 2: Soho – 3: The
           Post Office Tower). (pp.90–98)
           Reviewed by Douglas Gifford, *Lines Review* 31, January 1970,
           pp.44–6.

                                   1970

B45   *The Akros Anthology of Scottish Poetry 1965–1970.* Edited with an
       introduction by Duncan Glen. Preston: Akros Publications, 1970.
           Glasgow Green – Itinerary – Strawberry Fields Forever – Friendly
           Village. (pp.41–4)

B46   *Catalogue: Visual Poetry.* [Sunderland:] Ceolfrith Bookshop Gallery,
       [1970]. (Ceolfrith 1)
           News from Budapest.
           The Catalogue consists of loose sheets (some stapled) – an essay,
           'Concrete Poetry' by Stuart Mills, 'Poem Cards', Biographical
           Notes and a list of works in the exhibition – all contained in a clear
           plastic bag with printed card wrapper stapled over the opening.
           EM's contribution, described in the catalogue as a 'poem card', is
           in fact a duplicated sheet of cream Recorder paper, 204 ×

254 mm. The exhibition ran from 10–30 June 1970 and EM exhibited 'French Persian Cats Having a Ball' and 'The Chaffinch Map of Scotland'.

B47   *Contemporary Poets of the English Language.* Edited by Rosalie Murphy. Deputy editor James Vinson. With a preface by C. Day Lewis. Chicago and London: St James Press, 1970.
EM's contribution consists of articles on D.M. Black (pp. 100–101), Ian Hamilton Finlay (pp. 369–70), Robert Garioch (p. 401), W.S. Graham (pp. 436–7), W. Price Turner (p. 1108) and a statement on his own poetry (p. 775).

B48   *Creatures Moving.* Edited by Geoffrey Summerfield. Harmondsworth: Penguin Books, 1970. (Penguin English Project Stage One)
Orgy – Heron – The Chaffinch Map of Scotland – French Persian Cats Having a Ball – Hyena – The Third day of the Wolf. (pp. 31–7, 41, 66, 95–6, 97–8)

B49   *New English Dramatists 14.* Introduced by Edwin Morgan. (David Storey, *The Restoration of Arnold Middleton*; Peter Terson, *The Mighty Reservoy*; Stewart Conn, *The King*; Ian Hamilton Finlay, *Walking through Seaweed* and *The Estate Hunters*; B.S. Johnson, *You're Human like the Rest of Them*; George MacBeth and J.S. Bingham, *The Doomsday Show*). Harmondsworth: Penguin Books, 1970 (Penguin Plays)
'Introduction'. (pp. 7–18)

B50   *The Penguin Book of Scottish Verse.* Edited by Tom Scott. Harmondsworth: Penguin Books, 1970.
The Sheaf. (p. 501)

B51   *Scottish Poetry 5.* Edited by George Bruce, Maurice Lindsay and Edwin Morgan. Edinburgh: Edinburgh University Press, [1970].
Afterwards – The Milk-Cart – At the Television Set – Thoughts of a Module. (pp. 65–8)

B52   *The Theater of Jean Genet: A Casebook.* Edited by Richard N. Coe. New York: Grove Press, 1970.
'Thief into Poet . . . into Dramatist'. (pp. 36–9)
This essay on Genet's poetry also includes an extract from EM's translation of Genet's 'The Condemned Man'.

B53   *Things Working.* Edited by Penny Blackie. Harmondsworth: Penguin Books, 1970. (Penguin Education, Penguin English Project Stage One)
A View of Things – How to Find Heath Robinson – Construction for I.K. Brunel – O Pioneers! – The Computer's Second Christmas Card – Spacepoem 1: from Laika to Gagarin – Off Course. (pp. 13, 31, 66–7, 71, 108, 110, 118)

B54   *Selected Poems: Sándor Weöres* Translated with an Introduction by Edwin Morgan [and] *Ferenc Juhász* Translated with an Introduction by David Wevill. Harmondsworth: Penguin Books, 1970.
'Introduction'; Eternal Moment – The First Couple – The Underwater City – To Die – Wedding Choir – The Colonnade of Teeth – Whisper in the Dark – The Scarlet Pall – Clouds – The Lost Parasol – Moon and Farmstead – Orpheus Killed – Queen Tatavane – In the

Window-Square – Rayflower – Terra Sigillata – In Memoriam Gula
Juhász – Signs – Internus – Mountain Landscape – The Secret
Country – Difficult Hour – Coolie – Monkeyland (pp.9–13; 15–71)
EM's translations are noticed in an article, 'Penguin's European
Poets', in the *TLS* 6 August 1971, p.938.

1971

B55 *Mindplay: An Anthology of British Concrete Poetry.* Edited by John J.
Sharkey. London: Lorimer Publishing, 1971. (Cloth and paper editions)
Instant Theatre Go Home – Orgy – The Little White Rows of
Scotland – The Chaste Town – The Computer's First Code Poem –
Archives – Red. (pp.65–71)

B56 *This Book is a Movie: An Exhibition of Language Art and Visual Poetry.*
Edited by Jerry G. Bowles and Tony Russell. New York: Dell
Publishing Co., 1971. (A Delta Original)
Blues and Peal: Concrete 1969 – The Fleas – The Day the Sea Spoke –
Assassin – A Child's Coat of Many Colours – The Computer's First
Code Poem – Rainbow. (pp.230–7)

B57 *Twelve Modern Scottish Poets.* Edited by Charles King. London: University of London Press for the English Association, 1971. ('Paper' and
'limp' editions)
Aberdeen Train – Trio – One Cigarette – In the Snack-Bar –
Shantyman – Che – Canedolia – King Billy – From the Domain of
Arnheim. (pp.130–40)
2nd impression 1973.

B58 *Ventures.* Edited by Elwyn Rowlands. Harmondsworth: Penguin Books,
1971. (Penguin Education, Penguin English Project Stage One)
Goal! – Strips. (pp.56–7, 73)
'Goal!' is overprinted on photograph by John Walmsley and
although the text of 'Strips' is the same as in *gnomes* this is a pop art
version, illustrated with 'Zing', 'Eek', etc.

1972

B59 *British Poetry Since 1960: A Critical Survey.* Edited by Michael Schmidt
and Grevel Lindop. South Hinksey, Oxford: Carcanet Press, 1972.
'Scottish Poetry in the 1960s'. (pp.132–9)
Reprinted in *Essays*, pp.177–85.

B60 *found poems.* Edited by Malcolm Parr. Cardiff: Second Aeon Publications, 1972.
my uncle. (p.14)
From William Cowper's letters.

B61 *New Poems 1971–72: A P.E.N. Anthology of Contemporary Poetry.* Edited
by Peter Porter. London: Hutchinson, 1972.
The First Men on Mercury. (pp.117–18)
The biographical note on EM on p.180 credits him as translator of
'The Cape of Good Hope by Jean Cocteau' and misprints *Sovpoems* as
Fovpoems.

B62 *Scottish Poetry 6.* Edited by George Bruce, Maurice Lindsay, and Edwin
     Morgan. Edinburgh: Edinburgh University Press, [1972].
          Stobhill. (pp.97–102)

B63 *Text-Bilder Visuelle Poesie International.* Edited by Klaus Peter Dencker.
     Koln: Verlag M. DuMont Schanberg, 1972.
          Jigsaw 1: Skaters – Jigsaw 2: Moonshot – Jigsaw 3: Rough Diamond.
          The poems are printed on the inside of the book's cover which is of
          thick card folded over as if deliberately to conceal the poems.
          There is no mention of them in the index. The poems are
          represented as uncut-out jigsaw pieces.

B64 *Typewriter Poems.* Edited by Peter Finch. Cardiff: Second Aeon Publica-
     tions, 1972.
          A Child's Coat of Many Colours. (26)

                                    1973

B65 *Beyond this Horizon: An Anthology of Science Fiction and Science Fact.* Edited
     by Christopher Carrell. Sunderland: Ceolfrith Press, 1973.
          Twilight of a Tyranny – Space Sonnet & Polyfilla. (pp.58–58)

B66 *Breaththrough Fictioneers: an anthology.* Edited and with an introduction
     by Richard Kostelanetz. West Glover, Vermont: Something Else Press,
     1973. (Cloth and paper editions)
          From the Archives of F.L.U.F.F. (Federation of Lovers of Undiscov-
          ered Forces and Frontiers). (pp.80–81)

B67 *The Greek Anthology and Other Ancient Epigrams: A Selection in Modern Verse
     Translations.* Edited with an introduction by Peter Jay. London: Allen
     Lane, 1973.
          Nos 22, 23 (Aischylos), 162 (Herakleitos), 165 (Hegisippos), 233
          (Philip V of Macedon), 438 (Statilius Flaccus), 451 (Thallos), 453
          (Honestus), 455, 457–8 (Antiphanes), 459–70, 472–5 (Philip), 479–
          80 (Alpheios), 499 (Isidoros), 625–32 (Lucian). (pp.42, 96, 97, 121,
          207, 212, 213, 214, 215–19, 220, 224, 233, 279–81)
              Published in Penguin Books (Penguin Classics) in 1981; revised
              Penguin edition, 1981.

B68 *Homage to John MacLean.* Edited by T.S. Law and Thurso Berwick.
     Larkhall: The John MacLean Society, 1973. Second edition published in
     1979 by Edinburgh University Students Publications Board, with a
     foreword by Owen Dudley Edwards.
          On John MacLean. (pp.36–7)
          Notes on the poem on p.45.

B69 *The House That Jack Built: Poems for Shelter.* Edited by Brian Patten and
     Pat Krett. London: George Allen & Unwin, 1973. (Hardback and
     paperback editions)
          Two Glasgow Sonnets: I – II. (pp.32–3)
              II here is actually III of the final sequence and the sonnets here are
              broken into stanzas, two of four lines and two of three in each
              sonnet.

B70   *New Poems 1972–73: A P.E.N. Anthology of Contemporary Poems.* Edited
       by Douglas Dunn. London: Hutchinson, 1973.
       From Glasgow Sonnets (i – x). (p. 117)

B71   *Open Poetry: Four Anthologies of Expanded Poems.* Edited by Ronald Gross
       and George Quasha, with Emmett Williams, John Colombo and
       Walter Lowenfels. New York: Simon and Schuster, 1973.
       Newspoems: Cain Said – Möbius's Bed – Hooked – New English
       Riddles: 1 – New English Riddles: 2 – Holy Flying Saucer Satori –
       Visual Soundpoem. (pp. 493–6)

B72   *Petőfi Sándor (1823–1849).* Budapest: Ifjúsági Lapkiadó Vállalat,
       [1973].
       Fate, give me space . . . – Respublica – Europe is silent . . . – The
       Wind – Homer and Ossian (all transl. from Petőfi). (pp. 7, 9, 10–12,
       14, 16–23)

B73   *Poetry of the Committed Individual: A 'Stand' Anthology of Poetry.* Edited by
       Jon Silkin. Harmondsworth: Penguin Books in association with Victor
       Gollancz, 1973.
       Goya – The first ice – Earth – Parabolic ballad (all transl. from
       Andrei Voznesensky) – Stalin's heirs (transl. from Yevtushenko).
       (pp. 223–6, 227–9)
       Hardback edition published by Gollancz.

B74   *Summer Coming: Collected Poems from St Albans School of Art by Students,
       Staff and Visitors Summer 1973.* Compiled by Peter McGuffog, John
       Fuller, Robert Hepworth, Philip Pacey, Oliver Dowlen. St Albans:
       School of Art, 1973.
       Instamatics: Udal North Uist 1972 – Reykjavik July 1972 – Stoke-
       on-Trent January 1973. (pp. 8–9)

                                    1974

B75   *British Literature Volume 1: Old English to 1800.* Edited by H. Spencer,
       B.J. Layman and D. Ferry. Lexington (Mass.): Heath, 1974.
       Beowulf. (complete translation)

B76   *New Poems 1973–74: A P.E.N. Anthology of Contemporary Poetry.* Edited
       by Stewart Conn. London: Hutchinson, 1974.
       School's Out. (pp. 109–12)

B77   *Scottish Poetry 7.* Edited by Maurice Lindsay, Alexander Scott, Roderick
       Watson. Glasgow: University of Glasgow Press, 1974. (Paperback and
       hardback editions)
       School's Out – Vico's Song. (pp. 56–9)

B78   *Poetry Dimension 2: A Record of the Poetry Year.* Edited by Dannie Abse.
       London: Abacus / Robson Books, 1974. (Paperback and hardback
       editions)
       Hyena; 'Notes on one Poet's Working Day'. (pp. 121–2; 219–23)

B79   *Worlds: Seven Modern Poets: Charles Causley, Thom Gunn, Seamus Heaney,
       Ted Hughes, Norman MacCaig, Adrian Mitchell, Edwin Morgan.* Edited by
       Geoffrey Summerfield. Photographs by Fay Godwin, Larry Herman and
       Peter Abramowitsch. Harmondsworth: Penguin Education, 1974.

Reprinted 1976, 1979. Reissued 1986 with new cover and new ISBN
in Penguin Poets series.

'There is a poetry before poetry . . .'; Trio – The Suspect – Glasgow
Green – In the Snack-Bar – One Cigarette – The Death of Marilyn
Monroe – Glasgow Sonnets (v – vi) – Glasgow 5 March 1971 – For
Bonfires – *from* London (The Post Office Tower) – Spacepoem 3: Off
Course – The First Men on Mercury – The Moon February 1973 –
Translunar Space March 1972 – Message Clear – Newmarket –
Bradford June 1972 – Aviemore Invernessshire August 1971 –
Germany December 1970 – Chicago May 1971 – *from* Interferences
(1 – 4 – 5 – 9). (pp.228–9; 240–61)

Photographs of EM by Larry Herman on pp.230, 237.

1975

B80   *Contemporary Poets*. Second Edition. With a Preface by C. Day Lewis.
Edited by James Vinson with Associate Editor, D.L. Kirkpatrick.
London & New York: St James Press, 1975.
Essays on: D.M. Black (p.127); Ian Hamilton Finlay (pp.492–3);
Robert Garioch (p.531); W.S. Graham (pp.575–6); Dom Sylvester
Houédard (pp.729–30); Tom Leonard (p.893); Liz Lochhead (p.926);
W. Price Turner (p.1575); Douglas Young (p.1731).

B81   *Glasgow Handbook 1975*. Glasgow: Glasgow University Students Repre-
sentative Council, 1975.
Pleasures of a Technological University – Glasgow Sonnet i. (pp.4,
78)
On p.5 is a photograph of modern sculpture in a quadrangle of
Glasgow University.

B82   *New Poems 1975: A P.E.N. Anthology of Contemporary Poetry*. Edited by
Patricia Beer. London: Hutchinson, 1975.
Three Poems from *The New Divan* (1 – 7 – 8). (pp.140–41)

B83   *New Poetry 1: An Anthology*. Edited by Peter Porter and Charles
Osborne. London: The Arts Council of Great Britain, 1975. (Paperback
and hardback editions)
The skomorokh – The spirit of theatre. (pp.177–8)

B84   *Poetry Dimension Annual 3: The Best of the Poetry Year*. Edited by Dannie
Abse. London: Robson Books, 1975. (Paperback and hardback editions)
The Chorus. (p.164)

B85   *Scottish Poetry 8: An Anthology*. Edited by Maurice Lindsay, Alexander
Scott, Roderick Watson. Cheadle: Carcanet Press, 1975. (Cloth and
paper editions)
from Five Film Directors (Grierson – Kurosawa) – *from* Ten Theatre
Poems (The Chorus – The Mask – The Fan – The Spirit of Theatre).
(pp.56–60)

B86   *Trees: An Anthology*. Devised by Angus Ogilvy. Stirling: Stirling
Gallery, 1975.
Three Trees: Lightning Tree – Water-Skiers Tree – Impacted
Windscreen Tree. (nos.9–11)

1976

B87   Ronald Butlin, *Stretto*. Edinburgh, 1976.
       [Blurb on back cover].

B88   *East European Poets* Prepared for the Course Team by Professor Edwin
       Morgan, University of Glasgow [and] *Poetry in Public* Prepared for the
       Course Team by Alasdair Clayre. Milton Keynes: The Open University
       Press, 1976. (The Open University, Arts: A Third Level Course:
       Twentieth Century Poetry, Unit 32)
              East European Poets: 'Introduction' (p.7); 'Zbigniew Herbert' (pp.8–
       11); 'Miroslav Holub' (pp.12–16); 'Vasko Popa' (pp. 16–20); 'Sugges-
       tions for Further Study' (p.34); 'References and Further Reading'
       (p.34).

B89   *Scottish Poetry Nine*. Edited by Maurice Lindsay, Alexander Scott,
       Roderick Watson. Manchester: Carcanet Press / Scottish Arts Council,
       1976.
              Resurrections – Three Trees – The World. (pp.52–6)

B90   *Scottish Short Stories 1976*. Edited by Edwin Morgan, Philip Zeigler and
       Trevor Royle. London: Collins, 1976.
              'Preface', (pp.7–8)
              Signed 'E.M.'.

B91   *Tom Macdonald*. Glasgow: Third Eye Centre, 1976.
              'Introduction'. (pp.1–3)
              Catalogue of exhibition 19 May–6 June 1976.

1977

B92   *Bards and Makars: Scottish Language and Literature: Medieval and
       Renaissance*. Edited by Adam J. Aitken, Matthew P. MacDiarmid,
       Derick S. Thomson. Glasgow: University of Glasgow Press, 1977.
       'Gavin Douglas and William Drummond as Translators'.
       (pp.194–200)
              Paper read at the First International Conference on Scottish
              Language and Literature, Medieval and Renaissance, held in
              Edinburgh from September 10–16, 1975.

B93   *Birds: An Anthology of New Poems*. Edited by Angus Ogilvy, George
       Sutherland, Roderick Watson. Illustrations by children from Central
       Region Schools. Stirling: Stirling Gallery, [1977].
              The Archaeopteryx's Song. (p.11)

B94   *Madeira & Toasts for Basil Bunting's 75th Birthday*. Edited by Jonathan
       Williams. Dentdale: Jargon Society, March 1, 1975 [1977]. (Jargon
       66)
              An Ode Recoded (Re-assembled from the words in BB's 'Empty vast
              days . . .', First Book of Odes, no.5).
              1250 copies printed.

B95   *Modern Hungarian Poetry*. Edited, and with an Introduction, by Miklós
       Vajda. Foreward by William Jay Smith. New York / Guilford:
       Columbia University Press, 1977. Pubished in Hungary by Corvina
       Press, Budapest.

Translations from: Lajos Kassák: Craftsmen – Baffling Picture –
Young Horseman – Like This – Snapshot – I am with you (pp. 1–4);
Milán Füst: 'If my Bones Must be Handed Over' – Old Age (pp. 5–7);
Lőrinc Szabó: Prisons – The Dreams of the One – All for Nothing –
From Cricket Music (Farewell – . . . on the outlook tower . . . – . . .
in the big blue meadow . . .) (pp. 8–13); Anna Hajnal: Separate
Time (p. 48); Amy Károlyi: *From* The Third House (1 – 3 – 4 – 9)
(pp. 52–5); István Vas: Budapest Elegy – It Doesn't Count (pp. 62–3,
72–5); Lászlo Kálnoky: De Profundis – Despair – Instead of an
Autobiography (pp. 84–6); Sándor Weöres: The Lost Parasol – Le
Journal – Monkeyland – Queen Tatavane – Internus (Growing Old –
Self-Portrait with Dog – Dissolving Presence – Double-Faced – Out
of the Inner Infinity – The Muddy Drink is Going Down and the
Bottom of the Glass Shows Through – Nocturne) (pp. 88–109, 110–
14); Zoltán Jékely: The Elegy of a Bronze Age Man (pp. 118–21);
László Benjámin: Poem by an Unknown Poet from the Mid-
Twentieth Century – Cave Drawings (pp. 122–5); Imre Csanádi:
Silent Prayer of Peasants – Holiday-Afternoon Rhapsody – Confession of Faith – Small Craftsman (pp. 130–35); János Pilinsky:
Postscript (pp. 148–9); István Kormos: I am being dragged by red
dolphins – The Lament of Orpheus – Voyage – After Us – Deep Sea
(pp. 161–4); Mihály Váci: The Most-Age (pp. 166–7); László Nagy:
The Bliss of Sunday (pp. 169–76); István Simon: Rhapsody on Time
(pp. 188–91); Gábor Garai: A Man is Beaten Up – In Hungarian
(pp. 229–30, 232); Sándor Csoóri: Barbarian Prayer – Ague (pp. 234–
5); Istvan Eörsi: When Things Fall Upwards (p. 238); Ágnes Gergely:
Crazed Man in Concentration Camp (p. 240); Mihály Ladányi: We
Just Sit About Quietly – Lenin – Inventory – About the Hero – For
the Record (pp. 246–8, 249–50); Ottó Orbán: Gaiety and Good
Heart – To be Poor – Report on the Poem – The Apparition – The
Ladies of Bygone Days (pp. 251–2, 253–7).

B96   *Poems for Shakespeare 6.* Edited and with an Introduction by Roger
       Pringle. London: Globe Playhouse Publications, 1977.
       Instructions to an Actor. (pp. 39–40)
          Edition limited to 1000 numbered copies. A limited, numbered
          edition of 120 copies, of which 100 were for sale, signed by the
          poets and specially bound, was printed.

B97   *A Sense of Belonging: Six Scottish Poets of the Seventies.* Compiled by Brian
       Murray and Sydney Smith. Bishopbriggs, Glasgow: Blackie, 1977.
       ('Educational' and 'General' editions)
          A Child's Coat of Many Colours – Glasgow 5 March 1971 – Fallin
          Stirlingshire October 1970 – Germany December 1970 – The
          Woman – Clydesdale – For Bonfires – Ellingham Suffolk January
          1972 – Death in Duke Street – Grierson – Glasgow October 1972 –
          Glasgow Sonnets (i – iii). (pp. 49–57)

1978

B98   *Alphabetical & Letter Poems: A Chrestomathy.* Edited & Introduced by

Peter Mayer. Foreword by Edwin Morgan. London: The Menard Press, 1978.

'Foreword'; Soviet Alphabet (transl. from Mayakovsky) — Alphabet (transl. from Brecht) — Alpha. (pp.7–9; 55–6; 57–9; 96)

A version of 'Alpha' titled 'All the Secrets' was published in the magazine *Pick* 2:7/8, Summer 1977, p.4, with an extra 8 lines at the beginning and slight changes in the last 2 lines.

B99　*Night Ride and Sunrise: An Anthology of New Poems.* Edited and introduced by Edward Lowbury. Aberystwyth: Celtion Publishing Company, 1978. (Hardbound and paperbound editions)

Into the Interior. (p.32)

Includes prize-winning entries in a national poetry competition organized by the British Migraine Association. EM's poem was published in *Akros* 13:38, August 1978, p.84, as 'Migraine Attack'.

B100　*Our Duncan, who art in Trent . . . .: A festschrift for Duncan Glen.* Edited by Philip Pacey. Preston: The Harris Press, Preston Polytechnic, Spring 1978.

Target. (p.9)

B101　*Poets and Peasants: An Anthology for Oxfam's Move Against Poverty Campaign.* Edited by W.A. Smith. Edinburgh: W.A. Smith, 1978.

In that room . . . (p.23)

1979

B102　Ronald Butlin, *Creatures Tamed by Cruelty: Poems in English and Scots and Translations.* Edinburgh: Edinburgh University Students Publications Board, 1979.

'Introduction'. (pp.7–8)

Reviewed by Carl MacDougall, *Akros* 16:46, April 1981, pp.45–52, with mention of EM's introduction on p.47 and comparison of EM's translation of Luis Cernuda's 'The City Cemetery' with RB's.

B103　*The Elek Book of Oriental Verse.* General Editor Keith Bosley. London: Paul Elek, 1979.

from the Reamker (*c. 17th century*) — *from* The Code of Behaviour for the Young (*c. 1700*) (edited and transl. from the Khmer by Judith Jacob and EM). (pp.95–6)

B104　*JW/50* [cover title]: *A 50th Birthday Celebration for Jonathan Williams.* Gathered by Thomas A. Clark, David Wilk, & Jonathan Greene. Edited by Jonathan Greene. New York: *Truck* / Frankfort: Gnomon, 1979. (*Truck* 21)

Postal.

Issued as a special edition of *Truck* magazine (in a limited edition of 750 copies) and as a book by Gnomon.

1980

B105　*The Age of MacDiarmid: Essays on Hugh MacDiarmid and his Influence on Contemporary Scotland.* Edited by P.H. Scott and A.C. Davis. Edinburgh: Mainstream Publishing, 1980.

'MacDiarmid and Scotland'. (pp.193–201)
Reviewed by Alexander Scott, *Scottish Review* 21, February 1981,
p.62, and Geddes Thomson, *Akros* 16:47, August 1981,
pp.96–7.

B106   Thomas A. Clark, *Ways Through the Bracken*. [Dentdale:] Jargon
Society, 1980.
5-line quotation from letter to Jonathan Williams on back flap of
dust jacket.

B107   *Contemporary Poets*. Third Edition. Preface to the first edition by C. Day
Lewis. Preface to the third edition by Marjorie Perloff. Editor James
Vinson. Associate editor D.L. Kirkpatrick. London: Macmillan, 1980.
Essays on: D.M. Black (pp.126–7); Ian Hamilton Finlay (pp.492–3);
Robert Garioch (pp.532–3); W.S. Graham (pp.582–3); Dom
Sylvester Houédard (p.746); Tom Leonard (p.898); Liz Lochhead
(p.929); W. Price Turner (pp.1563–4).

B108   *List of ublications*. Glasgow: Third Eye Centre, [1980]
'Edwin Morgan writes [on his *Colour Poems*]'. (p.[2])
This comment was not published with the *Colour Poems* (1978).

B109   *Ocean at the Window: Hungarian Prose and Poetry since 1945*. Edited by
Albert Tezla. Minneapolis: University of Minnesota Press, 1980.
The Bliss of Sunday (transl. from László Nagy). (pp.188–94)

B110   *Performing Arts: An Illustrated Guide*. Consultant Editor Michael
Billington. Foreword by Sir John Gielgud. London: Macdonald Educa-
tional, 1980.
'Poetry Reading'. (pp.204–5)
EM listed as a consultant editor. His (edited) article is unsigned.

1981

B111   *Columba: [An] Opera in three Acts Opus 77* by Kenneth Leighton to a
libretto by Edwin Morgan. Glasgow: Royal Scottish Academy of Music
and Drama, 1981.
'Columba: The Libretto'. (p.[18])
Programme for the first performances of *Columba* in the Theatre
Royal, Glasgow, 16, 18 and 19 June 1981, by the Opera Class of
the RSAMD.

B112   *A Companion to Scottish Culture*. Edited by David Daiches. London:
Edward Arnold, 1981.
'Literature in the Twentieth Century'. (pp.220–2)

B113   *Comparative Criticism: A Year Book*. Volume 3. Edited by E.S. Shaffer.
Cambridge: Cambridge University Press, 1981.
'On Hugh MacDiarmid's *Complete Poems 1920–1976*'. (pp.303–9)
Review-essay on the *Complete Poems* and *The Socialist Poems of Hugh
MacDiarmid*, ed. T.S. Law and Thurso Berwick. Also issued as an
offprint.

B114   *Identities: An Anthology of West of Scotland Poetry, Prose and Drama*. Edited
by Geddes Thomson. Introduction by Edwin Morgan. London and
Edinburgh: Heinemann Educational Books, 1981.

'Introduction'; Trio – In the Snack-Bar – Glasgow Sonnet i – Glasgow 5 March 1971 – King Billy. (pp.ix–xi; 66–7, 79–80, 88, 176, 190–1)

B115 *Let Wives Tak Tent*. Stirling: Scottish Theatre Company, 1981.
Prologue ['Let more than wives tak tent, let all tak tent!'].
Programme for STC's first production, Robert Kemp's Scots version of Molière's *L'Ecole Des Femmes*, at MacRobert Centre, Stirling University, 16 March 1981.

B116 *Seven Poets: Hugh MacDiarmid, Norman MacCaig, Iain Crichton Smith, George Mackay Brown, Robert Garioch, Sorley MacLean, Edwin Morgan.*
Edited by Christopher Carrell. Glasgow: Third Eye Centre, 1981.
(Clothbound and card cover editions)
'Edwin Morgan' [interview with Marshall Walker]; Glasgow 5 March 1971 – The Death of Marilyn Monroe – From a City Balcony – The New Divan 81 – Trio – Eve and Adam – Jack London in Heaven – 'In a Convex Mirror,' Etc. – The Coals. (pp.78–83; 79–86)

1982

B117 *Glasgow University S.R.C. Students' Handbook*. Glasgow: Glasgow University Students Representative Council, 1982.
'First Impressions'. (p.33)
First impressions of Glasgow University 1937–38.

B118 *James Joyce and Modern Literature*. Edited by W.J. McCormack and Alistair Stead. London, Boston, Melbourne and Henley: Routledge & Kegan Paul, 1982.
'James Joyce and Hugh MacDiarmid'. (pp.202–17)
Paper given at a conference held in April 1982 in Leeds under the auspices of the School of English of the University of Leeds, to commemorate the centenary of James Joyce. Reviewed by A.M. McCleery, *Scottish Literary Journal Supplement* 23, Winter 1985, p.41.

B119 *Not Just Another Pile of Bricks*. Edited by J.C. Allard and M.S. Prochak. Colchester: Ampersand Press, 1982.
The Solway Canal – Vereshchagin's Barrow. (pp.73–5)
Limited to 300 copies. Anthology of poets represented at the Essex Festival of Contemporary Arts.

B120 Craig Pollard and Steve Davies, *The Long Path*. Lampeter: Outcrop Publications, 1981 [April 1982].
. EM's contribution is the blurb on the back cover of this collection of poems.

B121 *Vladimir Mayakovsky: Three Views*. London: Scorpion Press, 1982.
'Mayakovsky: The Poet and His Language'. (pp.10–11)
Three essays (by Susan P. Compton, EM and Edward Braun) and a biography (by Milena Kalinovska) written to coincide with the British showings of the 'Vladimir Mayakovsky: Twenty Years of Work' exhibition.

1983

B122   *Byron: Wrath and Rhyme.* Edited by Alan Bold. London and Totowa
       (New Jersey): Vision Press and Barnes & Noble, 1983.
       'Voice, Tone, and Transition in *Don Juan*'. (pp.57–77)
       Reviewed by Richard Cronin, *Glasgow Herald* 6 August 1983, p.8
       (Weekender 2).

B123   *A History of Hungarian Literature.* Edited by Tibor Klaniczay. Budapest:
       Corvina Press, 1983.
       Excerpts from: The Puszta, in Winter – One Thought Keeps
       Tormenting Me . . . – September's End (transl. from Sándor Petőfi)
       – All for Nothing (transl. from Lőrinc Szabó) – The Lost Parasol
       (transl. from Sándor Weöres). (pp.226, 227, 228, 435, 438)
       Reviewed by George Gömöri, *TLS* 6 July 1984, p.766.

B124   *Noise and Smoky Breath: An Illustrated Anthology of Glasgow Poems 1900–*
       1983. Edited by Hamish Whyte. Glasgow: Third Eye Centre and
       Glasgow District Libraries Publications Board, 1983. (Paperback and
       clothbound editions)
       Night Pillion – To Joan Eardley – The Starlings in George Square –
       King Billy – Glasgow Green – Trio – Rider – In Glasgow – Glasgow
       Sonnets – On John Maclean – By the Preaching of the Word – At
       Central Station – G.M. Hopkins in Glasgow. (pp.41–2, 50, 51–3,
       54–5, 55–7, 58, 79–83, 84, 91–5, 115–6, 117, 144, 155)
       Reprinted August 1983, November 1984, February 1986, April
       1988 (paperback edition).

B125   *Scotland and the Lowland Tongue: Studies in the Language and Literature of*
       Lowland Scotland in Honour of David D. Murison. Edited by J. Derrick
       McClure, with a Foreword by A.J. Aitken. Aberdeen: Aberdeen
       University Press, 1983.
       'Glasgow Speech in Recent Scottish Literature'. (pp.195–208)

B126   *Whales: A Celebration.* Edited by Greg Gatenby. Boston and Toronto:
       Little Brown, 1983.
       The Dolphin's Song. (p.99)

B127   *Writers' Choice: A Library of Rediscoveries.* Edited by Linda Sternberg Katz
       and Bill Katz; with an introduction by Doris Grumbach. Reston,
       Virginia: Reston Publishing Company, 1983.
       EM recommends: Edward Bellamy, *Looking Backward*, 1888; George
       Douglas Brown, *The House with the Green Shutters*, 1901; Alexander
       Trocchi, *Cain's Book*, 1960. (pp.9; 17–18; 120)

1984

B128   *Glasgow: A Celebration.* Edited by Cliff Hanley. With photographs by
       Oscar Marzaroli. Edinburgh: Mainstream Publishing, 1984.
       [Four Glasgow Subway Poems:] The Subway Budgie – The Subway
       Giraffe – The Subway Cat – The Subway Piranhas. (pp.130–2)

B129   Liz Lochhead, *Dreaming Frankenstein & Collected Poems.* Edinburgh:
       Polygon Books, 1984.
       'Foreword'. (p.[5])

B130   Oscar Marzaroli, *One Man's World: Photographs 1955–84.* Glasgow:

Third Eye Centre and Glasgow District Libraries Publications Board, 1984.

'Glasgow: The Changing Face, 1958–68'. (pp. 15–18)

B131 *New Writing Scotland 2*. Edited by Alexander Scott and James Aitchison. Aberdeen: Association for Scottish Literary Studies, 1984.

Three Poems from *Sonnets from Scotland*: Theory of the Earth – Post-Glacial – Pilate at Fortingall. (pp. 27–8)

Reviewed by Trevor Royle, *Scottish Review* 37/8, May 1985, p. 104.

B132 *Poems for Poetry 84*. London: The Poetry Society, 1984.

The Poet in the City. (p. 10)

Correction: 1. 12 – for 'sterm' read 'stern'.

B133 *Poetry Supplement Winter 1984*. Edited by Gavin Ewart. London: Poetry Book Society, 1984.

from Sonnets from Scotland: At Stirling Castle, 1507 – Computer Error: Neutron Strike. (pp. 26–7)

B134 *Words 3*. Edited by Geoffrey Summerfield and Richard Andrews. London: Cassell, 1984.

The Suspect – The First Men on Mercury – For Bonfires ii – Glasgow Sonnet i; 'Edwin Morgan says'. (pp. 13, 67, 97–98)

EM's comment is on 'For Bonfires ii' and 'Glasgow Sonnet i'.

1985

B135 Angela Catlin, *Natural Light: Portraits of Scottish Writers*. Introduction by Trevor Royle. Leith: Paul Harris Publishing / Waterfront, 1985.

North Africa. (p. 80)

Photograph of EM on p. [81].

B136 *Contemporary Poets*. Fourth Edition. Edited by James Vinson and D.L. Kirkpatrick. Preface to the first edition by C. Day Lewis. Preface to the third edition by Marjorie Perloff. London and Chicago: St James Press, 1985.

Articles on: David Black (pp. 62–63); Ian Hamilton Finlay (p. 264); W.S. Graham (pp. 316–7); Dom Sylvester Houédard (p. 408); Tom Leonard (pp. 488–9); Liz Lochhead (p. 508).

B137 *Poems from Italy*. Edited by William Jay Smith and Dana Gioia. St Paul, Minnesota: New Rivers Press, 1985. (A New Rivers Abroad Book) Edition of 200 clothbound and 2,000 paperback copies.

On Poets (transl. from Lodovico Ariosto, *Orlando Furioso*, Canto XXXV) – With Heart and Breast of Brimstone, Flesh of Flax (transl. from Michelangelo) – Silent the Forests (transl. from Torquato Tasso). (pp. 197, 201, 235)

Enlarged edition of book first published in 1972.

1986

B138 Christopher Barker, *Portraits of Poets*. Edited by Sebastian Barker. Manchester: Carcanet Press, 1986.

The Poet. (p. 68)

Photograph of EM on p. 69.

B 139   Moira Burgess, *The Glasgow Novel: A Survey and Bibliography*. Preface by
         Edwin Morgan. Motherwell / Glasgow: Scottish Library Association /
         Glasgow District Libraries, 1986.
             'Preface'. (pp. 5–10)

B 140   *Dream*. Edited by Keith Murray. Aberdeen: Keith Murray Publications,
         1986. (KMP 1)
             The Gorbals Mosque. (p. [11])

B 141   *A Garioch Miscellany*. Selected and edited by Robin Fulton. Edinburgh:
         Macdonald, 1986.
             'Two comments'. (pp. 22–6)
                 Texts taken from two Scotsoun cassettes: *Robert Garioch: Poems
                 Selected by Edwin Morgan* and *In Mind o a Makar*.

B 142   *Hardy to Heaney: Twentieth Century Poets: Introductions and Explanations*.
         Edited by John Blackburn. Edinburgh: Oliver & Boyd, 1986.
             'William Carlos Williams'. (pp. 59–65)

B 143   *With a Poet's Eye: A Tate Gallery Anthology*. Edited by Pat Adams.
         London: The Tate Gallery, 1986.
             The Bench. (pp. 138, 140)
                 Reproduction of 'Benches', painting by Tom Phillips on p. 139.

                                          1987

B 144   *Leopardi: A Scottis Quair*. [Translations by] Douglas Dunn, Alastair
         Fowler, Valerie Gillies, Alastair Mackie, Edwin Morgan, Iain Crichton
         Smith, Derick Thomson, Christopher Whyte. Edited by R.D.S. Jack,
         M.L. McLaughlin and C. Whyte. Edinburgh: Edinburgh University
         Press for the Italian Institute, Edinburgh, 1987.
             Flinder (Odi, Melisso) – The Aesome Blackie (Il passero solitario) –
             Tae his Sel (A se stesso). (pp. 25, 40–41, 57)
                 A volume of poems presented to Francesco Cossiga, president of
                 the Italian Republic in commemoration of his admission to the
                 Honorary Degree of Doctor *honoris causa* of the University of
                 Edinburgh 21 November 1987. Reviewed by Thom Nairn,
                 Cencrastus 32, New Year [February] 1989, p. 50, and by
                 P. McCarey, *Verse* 5:2, July 1988, p. 67.

B 145   *Meet and Write: A teaching anthology of contemporary poetry*. Book two.
         Edited by Sandy and Alan Brownjohn. London: Hodder and Stoughton,
         1987.
             'I was born in Scotland . . .'; The First Men on Mercury – The Loch
             Ness Monster's Song – Spacepoem 3: Off Course – Flakes. (pp. 36–8;
             39–43)
                 EM's prose contribution is part autobiography, part comment on
                 the poems.

B 146   *New Writing Scotland 5*. Edited by Carl MacDougall and Edwin Morgan.
         Managing Editor, Hamish Whyte. Aberdeen: Association for Scottish
         Literary Studies, 1987.

B 147   *Poems for Shakespeare 10*. Edited with an Introduction by Charles
         Osborne. London: Bishopsgate Press, 1987.
             The Bear. (p. 55)

B148 *The Poetry Book Society Anthology 1987/88.* Edited with an Introduction by Gillian Clarke. London: Hutchinson and The Poetry Book Society, 1987.
Poem ['Dear man, my love goes out in waves']. (p.74)
Correction: 1.17 – delete comma.

B149 *A Selection of the Prizewinners from The Scottish National Open Poetry Competitions 1972–1986.* Compiled and edited by Samuel W. Gilliland and Henry Mair. With forewords by S.W. Gilliland, Norman MacCaig, Henry Mair and Edwin Morgan. Paisley: Wilfion Books, 1987. (The Scotland Alive Series Vol.4)
'Labourers in the vineyard'. (p.v)

B150 *The Yearbook of English Studies.* Volume 17. London: Modern Humanities Research Association, 1987.
'The Sea, the Desert, the City: Environment and Language in W.S. Graham, Hamish Henderson, and Tom Leonard'. (pp.31–45)
Also issued as an offprint.

1988

B151 *First and Always: Poems for The Great Ormond Street Children's Hospital.* Compiled and edited by Lawrence Sail. Introduction by Ted Hughes. London: Faber and Faber, 1988.
The Revolution. (p.41)

B152 *Images for Africa.* Compiled and edited by Jane Glencross. Brecon: Water Aid, 1988.
The Dowser. (pp.128–9)

B153 *New Writing Scotland 6.* Edited by Carl MacDougall and Edwin Morgan. Managing Editor, Hamish Whyte. Aberdeen: Association for Scottish Literary Studies, 1988.

B154 *Our Lives: Poems by Strathclyde Young People.* Edited by Chris Carrell and Katya Young. Glasgow: Third Eye Centre and Strathclyde Community Relations Council, 1988. (A Multi-Racial Action Year Publication)
'The Judges' Verdict' (with Gurmeet Mattu and Katya Young). (pp.14–15)
Publication of winners of poetry competition. EM was one of the judges.

B155 Roberto Sanesi, *Four Poems.* Translated into Scots and English [by Alexander Hutchison, Tessa Ransford, Edwin Morgan and Rosalind Brackenbury]. With an original colour etching by the author. Milan: Grafica Uno, October 1988.
As if it was a Life, Living.
Sheet folded into five sections. In brown card folder. To commemorate the reading by RS in Edinburgh, September 1988. Colophon: 'The booklet was printed by Ruggero Olivieri in Garamond on handmade paper BFK Rives. The etching was pulled by Giorgio Upiglio in 50 copies numbered and signed by the author for the Scottish Poetry Library on the occasion of the Edinburgh International Festival.'

B156 Sándor Weöres, *Eternal Moment: Selected Poems.* Edited, and with an

introduction, by Miklos Vajda. Foreword by William Jay Smith.
Afterword by Edwin Morgan. Drawings by Sándor Weöres, Translated
from the Hungarian by Alan Dixon, Daniel Hoffman, Hugh Maxton,
Edwin Morgan, William Jay Smith, George Szirtes. London: Anvil
Press Poetry, 1988, in association with Corvina Press, Budapest.
(Paperback and hardback editions)
  The Old Ones (pp.21–2) – Eternal Moment (p.25) – Homeward
  Bound (pp.26–8) – For my Mother (pp.29–30) – To the Moon (p.32)
  – Self-Portrait (p.36) – The First Couple (pp.37–38) – De Profundis
  (pp.39–40) – The Underwater City (p.42) – Wedding Choir (p.43) –
  To Die (p.44) – 'Eternal darkness clings . . .' (p.45) – Whisper in
  the Dark (p.46) – The Colonnade of Teeth (pp.47–8) – from the Fifth
  Symphony: The Scarlet Pall (pp.51–2) – Signs (p.53) – Clouds (p.56)
  – The Lost Parasol (pp.69–78) – Le Journal (pp.79–84) – Moon and
  Farmstead (p.85) – Monkeyland (pp.86–7) – from Orpheus: Orpheus
  Killed (pp.88–9) – Queen Tatavane (pp.90–93) – Ars Poetica (p.94)
  – In Memoriam Gyula Juhász (p.95) – Terra Sigillata (pp.96–7) –
  Mountain Landscape (p.98) – Wallpaper and Shadows (p.99) –
  Rayflower (p.100) – A Session of the World Congress (p.103) –
  Difficult Hour (pp.104–5) – In the Window-Square (p.106) –
  Internus (pp.109–12) – The Secret Country (pp.113–14) – Coolie
  (p.115) – Toccata (pp.120–22); 'AFTERWORD: The Challenge of
  Weöres' (p.147).
     Reviewed by George Gömöri, *TLS* 24 February-2 March 1989,
     p.200 and by Robert Calder, *Chapman* 55–6, Spring 1989,
     pp.180–81.

B157   *Zwei Sprachen – zwei Städte / Two Tongues – Two Towns: Dichter aus
       Glasgow und Nürnberg schreiben / Poetry from Glasgow and Nürnberg.* Edited
       by Reinhardt Knodt and Jack Withers. Translated by Donal
       McLaughlin and Ulrike Seeberger. Frankfort: Dağyeli Verlag, 1988.
          The Dowser. (pp.26–7; German translation, pp.28–9)

1989

B158   *Catgut and Blossom: Jonathan Williams in England.* From an idea of David
       Annwn, with assistance from Harry Gilonis and Simon Cutts. London:
       Coracle Press, 1989.
          For Jonathan Williams at 60. (p.31)
          A tribute for JW's 60th birthday.

B159   *The History of Scottish Literature, Volume 3: Nineteenth Century.* Edited by
       Douglas Gifford. General editor, Cairns Craig. Aberdeen: Aberdeen
       University Press, 1989.
          'Scottish Poetry in the Nineteenth Century'. (pp.337–51)

B160   Nancy Brysson Morrison, *The Gowk Storm.* Introduced by Edwin
       Morgan. Edinburgh: Canongate Publishing, 1989. (Canongate Classics
       20)
          'Introduction'. (pp.vii–xii)

B161   *National Poetry Competition 1988 Prizewinners.* London: The Poetry
       Society, 1989.

'I found that reading some 5000 poems . . .' (pp.[4–5])
The judges were Jonathan Barker, EM and George Szirtes.

B162 Mario Papa and Alison Silver, *Concepts and Meaning: An integrated course for upper – intermediate students*. Bologna: Zanichelli, 1989.
The Apple's Song; 'To the Students'. (pp.86; 87)
EM comments on the kind of poetry that he writes and likes.

B163 *First Impressions*. [Edited by] Jim Sweetman, Programme Director. London: Collins Educational, 1989. (Collins English Programme 1)
'Meet a Poet'. (pp.19–20)
Texts of 'The Computer's First Christmas Card' and 'Off Course' with background notes by EM. In section called 'List Poems'. Photograph of EM on p.19.

B164 *The Best of Scottish Poetry*. Edited by Robin Bell. Edinburgh: Chambers, 1989.
[Comment on 'Glasgow Green' and 'The Coals']; Glasgow Green – The Coals. (pp.138–41)

B165 *And Thus Will I Freely Sing: An Anthology of Lesbian and Gay Writing from Scotland*. Edited by Toni Davidson. Introduced by Edwin Morgan. Edinburgh: Polygon, 1989.
'Introduction'; Floating off to Timor – From a City Balcony. (pp.11–13; 127–30)

B166 J. Leslie Mitchell (Lewis Grassic Gibbon), *Gay Hunter*. With an introduction 'Lewis Grassic Gibbon and Science Fiction' by Edwin Morgan. Edinburgh: Polygon, 1989. (Cosmos 3)
'Lewis Grassic Gibbon and Science Fiction'. (pp.i–viii)
Correction: p.i – for 'Wells' ' read 'Wells's'.

B167 Sándor Csoóri, *Barbarian Prayer: Selected Poems*. Selection by Mátyás Domokos. Foreword by Len Roberts. Budapest: Corvina, 1989.
Barbarian Prayer – Ague (trans. from Csoóri). (pp.16, 18)

B168 *New Writing Scotland 7*. Edited by Edwin Morgan and Hamish Whyte. Aberdeen: Association for Scottish Literary Studies, 1989.
'Introduction'. (p.ix)

C

CONTRIBUTIONS TO PERIODICALS AND NEWSPAPERS

Note: EM, Bob Tait and Robert Garioch edited the journal *Scottish International* from No.1, January 1968 until No.9, February 1970; from then until the last issue, Vol.7 No.2, March 1974, EM and Robert Garioch acted as Editorial Advisers.

1936

C1 Song of the Flood. *High School of Glasgow Magazine* XXXV:2, April 1936, p.135.
Signed 'KAA, IVC'.

C2 'The Island'; The Pond: Two Moods. *High School of Glasgow Magazine* XXXV:3, June 1936, pp.219; 224.

Signed KAA. EM shared the Form IV Prize for English Composition
Presented by the High School Latin Class 1867–72. (p.254)

C3   'Kyriof: a mystery' (story); 'View from the Art Room' (drawing); 'Art
      Club' (notes on term's activities). *High School of Glasgow Magazine*
      XXXVI: 1, December 1936, pp.36–7; 64; 85.
      'Kyriof' signed KAA. EM was secretary of the Art Club. On p.100
      EM is noted as Sub-Editor of the magazine.

1937

C4   'Art Club' (notes). *High School of Glasgow Magazine* XXXVI: 2, March
      1937, p.179.

C5   [Coronation] II; The Opium Smoker; 'A Votary of Bast' (story); 'Hypno-
      phantas' (story); 'Art Club' (notes). *High School of Glasgow Magazine*
      XXXVI: 3, June 1937, pp.217; 230–31; 243–4; 260–61; 289.
      Coronation I by A.H.G. appeared on p.216; EM's poem is signed
      'E.G.M., VB'. The other poem and the two stories are signed Kaa.
      Prizes won by EM: Tom Andrew Prize in English (p.270); Prize for
      English Composition and London Club Gold Medal for Excellence in
      French (p.271); Prize for excellence of contributions in prose and
      verse to School Magazine (p.272). On p.296 EM noted as Sub-
      Editor.

C6   Nocturne: Ruins and Music. *GUM* (*Glasgow University Magazine*)
      15 December 1937, p.148.
      Signed KAA.

1938

C7   When the Blind Dream – Twilight – From the French of Paul Verlaine
      (Autumn – Night – Strains of Forgetfulness I & II). *GUM* 2 February
      1938, pp.189, 190, 203.
      Signed KAA.

C8   Think! – Evening Light. *GUM* 16 March 1938, pp.239, 243.
      Signed KAA.

C9   [Two poems:] Fulfilment / Today: strife / Tomorrow: ennui / Lastly:
      fulfilment – From a Silk-painting by Ma Yüan. *GUM* 20 April 1938,
      pp.269, 283.
      Signed KAA. P.283 carries a note from the editor to KAA: 'Many
      thanks for your continued prolixity, high standard of work and
      excellence of caligraphy [sic]. The one about music was not up to
      your usual mark; there are far too many adjectives and a few cliches
      among them. Could you be just a trifle less grandiose? I trust that
      you will ignore the misbegotten wit of a sub-editorial zany
      exemplified elsewhere on this page.' On p.283 'From a Silk-painting
      by Ma Yüan' appears under the heading 'Two Studies in Solitude' as
      the first, with a note: '(The composer of this poem suggested that its
      effect would be enhanced if it were printed in capitals.)'; the second,
      'From a Tweed-carving by Ma Gosh' by BAA has a note: '(So the
      composer of this one put his in wee letters – just to be different.)'

C10   [Three poems:] The Chinese Girl's Regret – Ephemera – Maya: Dream-

Reality / Reality-Dream. *GUM* 4 May 1938, pp.293, 300 ('Maya').
Signed KAA. In 'The Chinese Girl's Regret', 1.4, for 'sum' read 'sun'.

C11 [Two poems:] To Grock: Sans Adjectives – The Golden Age: Palaces. *GUM* 18 May 1938, pp.315, 319.
Signed KAA. 'To Grock' is a reply to the editor (see *GUM* 20 April 1938, p.283).

C12 Doubt. *GUM* 16 November 1938, p.71.
Signed KAA.

1939

C13 The Mockingbird – The Chinese Girl's Regret – Forgetfulness – Moonlove. *Poetry of Today* (1)–1939–(51), pp.11–12, 45, 83.
Poetry of Today was a quarterly supplement of *The Poetry Review*.

C14 Dusty Flower – Plainsong for a Lovely Lady – 'One with the Sun . . . .'. *GUM* 15 March 1939, pp.311 ('Dusty Flower'), 320.
Signed KAA.

C15 To Sandra. *GUM* 3 May 1939, p.342.
Signed KAA. First line: 'I am that city, granite of your tears'. See *GUM* 15 March 1939, p.320: 'This Sombre Evening' by 'SANDRA' ('Over the city pallid night is drawn').

C16 The Soldier, 1939. *GUM* LI:1, 18 October 1939, p.7.
Signed KAA.

C17 'The Phoenix of the Cinderheap'. *GUM* LI:4, 29 November 1939, p.5.
Reply to article 'The Jaded Cinderheap' in *GUM* LI:3, 15 November 1939, p.4 which attacked modern poetry. EM praises 'the fine work' of Clifford Dyment and Dylan Thomas. Signed KAA.

1946

C18 'Plastic Scots' (letter). *Glasgow Herald* 15 November 1946, p.4.

1947

C19 'Russian Transliteration' (letter). *Times Literary Supplement* 2 August 1947, p.391.
Discussing S.S. Morrison's letter, *TLS* 12 July 1947, p.351, which refers to letter from Denis Binyon, *TLS* 5 July 1947, p.337.

1949

C20 The Ruin (transl. from Anglo-Saxon). *Horizon* XIX: 109, January 1949, p.3.

C21 'A Hopkins Phrase' (letter). *Times Literary Supplement* 27 May 1949, p.347.
On the reading of 'vermilion' in G.M. Hopkins's 'The Windhover', with reference to letter from B. de Vere Nicol, *TLS* 13 May 1949, p.313.

C22 The Mystery. *College Courant* (Glasgow University) 1:2, Whitsun 1949, pp.118–19.

C23 'The Good Land of Lebanon' (article). *Glasgow Herald* 17 September 1949, p.3.
Originally titled 'The Glory of Lebanon'.

C24 A Warning of Waters at Evening. *Accent* (Urbana, Illinois) IX:2, Winter 1949, pp.117–18.
Also in *The Month* (N.S.) 3:5, May 1950, pp.339–40.

1950

C25 'Giacomo Manzù' by Italo Faldi (transl. by EM). *The Month* (N.S.) 3:1, January 1950, pp.48–54.

C26 'Graham's Threshold' (review of W.S. Graham, *The White Threshold*). *Nine* II:II [No.3], May 1950, pp.100–103.

C27 The Sleights of Darkness. *Poetry London* 5:18, May 1950, p.17.

C28 [Review of J.W.R. Purser, *The Soliloquists*]. *College Courant* II:4, Whitsun 1950, pp.154–5.

C29 'Women and Poetry' (essay). *Cambridge Journal* III:11, August 1950, pp.643–73.

C30 [Review of L. and E.M. Hanson, *The Four Brontës*]: *Cambridge Journal* IV:1, October 1950, pp.62, 64.

C31 'Forfairn's my hert, ye loe me nane!' (transl. from August Graf Von Platen, 'Mein Herz ist Zerrissen') – Three Anglo-Saxon Riddles (Bookworm – Swan – Swallows). *Nine* III:I (6), December 1950, pp.22; 46–7.

1951

C32 ' "Strong Lines" and Strong Minds: reflections on the prose of Browne and Johnson'. *Cambridge Journal* IV:8, May 1951, pp.481–91.

C33 four dizains from *Délie, Obiect de Plvs Havlte Vertv* (XVIII – CXLVIII – CCXXVIII – CCCCXLVI) (transl. from Maurice Scève). *Nine* III:II (7), Autumn 1951, pp.157–9.

1952

C34 'Dunbar and the Language of Poetry' (essay). *Essays in Criticism* II:2, April 1952, pp.138–58.
Reprinted in *Essays*, pp.81–99. Referred to by David Craig in *Lines Review* 13, Summer 1957, p.26, in the course of a letter re R.L.C. Lorimer and James Kinsley's articles on Scottish Literary Studies in *LR* 10, 11 and 12; answered by letters from Kinsley and EM in *LR* 14, Spring 1958, pp.26–8.

C35 'Different Approaches' (review of Elizabeth Sewell, *The Structure of Poetry* and Augustus Ralli, *Poetry and Faith*). *Nine* III:3 (8), Spring (April) 1952, pp.278–80.

C36 DÉLIE CXCII (transl. from Maurice Scève). *Colonnade* 1:2, Winter 1952, p.49.

1953

C37 Délie, Obiect de Plus Haulte Vertv CXXVI (transl. from Scève). (*Colonnade* 1:3, Spring 1953 in) *Adam* XXI:234, 1953, p.33.

C38 'Dryden's Drudging'. *Cambridge Journal* VI:7, April 1953, p.414–29.
Reprinted in *Dryden: a collection of critical essays* edited by B.N.
Schilling (New Jersey: Prentice-Hall, 1963) and in *Essays*,
pp.100–117.

C39 [Review of Jean H. Hagstrum, *Samuel Johnson's Literary Criticism*].
Cambridge Journal VII:2, November 1953, pp.124, 126.

C40 [Review of *L'Allelujah: Poesie di Ennio Contini, e la Prima Decade dei
Cantos di Ezra Pound* tradotti da Mary de Rachewiltz]. *Nine* IV:1 (10),
Winter 1953–4, pp.65–6.

1954

C41 Mayakonferensky's Anectidote (transl. from Mayakovsky). *Lines Review*
4, January 1954, pp.8–10.

C42 The Seafarer (transl. from Anglo-Saxon). *The European* 14, April 1954,
pp.51–3.

C43 Harrowing Heaven, 1924. *Saltire Review* I:1, April 1954, p.57.

C44 Night (transl. from Michelangelo) – Silent the Forests (transl. from
Tasso). *College Courant* 6:12, Whitsun 1954, p.89.

C45 Sleight-of-Morals. *Listen* 1:2, Summer 1954, p.6.

C46 Anent the Deeference o Tastes (transl. from Mayakovsky). *Lines Review*
5, June 1954, p.21.

C47 'Modern Makars Scots and English'. *Saltire Review* I:2, August 1954,
pp.75–81.
Text of talk to Saltire Society given 2 March 1954 under the title,
'The Auld Leid and the New Makars'.

C48 Cheiromantia. *Lines Review* 6, September 1954, p.26.

C49 'Society Choices' (review of V. Watkins, *The Death Bell*; N. Nicholson,
The Pot Geranium; Alexander Buist, *The Gleam and the Dark*). *Saltire
Review* I:3, Winter 1954, pp.88–9.

1955

C50 The Sleights of Time. *The Poet* 12, [1955], p.[5].

C51 Dialogue 1: James Joyce and Hugh MacDiarmid. *Saltire Review* II:4,
Spring 1955, pp.56–9.

C52 Four Poems: Two Russian Poems ('I loed ye but. Aiblins intil my briest'
by Pushkin – 'O had I but known that it ends like this,' by Pasternak) –
Casida of the Bright Death (transl. from García Lorca) – What Waves
Have Beaten on the Glass. *The Voice of Scotland* VI:1, April 1955,
pp.9–11.

C53 The Cat – The Carp – The Dromedary (transl. from Apollinaire).
Glasgow Herald 30 April 1955, p.3.

C54 'Enigma and Paradox: Reading the Face of Russia' (article). *Glasgow
Herald* 18 June 1955, p.4.

C55 'The Pleasures of Clarity [in poetry]' (essay); [letter on the spelling of
Scots]. *Lines Review* 9, August 1955, pp.11–16; 32.
The original title of the essay was 'From Clarity to Clarty'.

C56   'A Prelude to *The Prelude*' (essay). *Essays in Criticism* V:4, October 1955,
       pp.341–53.
           Reprinted in *British Romantic Poets* edited by S.K. Kamar (New York:
           New York University Press, 1966 and London: U.L.P., 1967) and in
           Essays, pp.118–29.

C57   Two Cranes (transl. from Yekaterina Shevelyova) – Anent the
       Deeference o Tastes (transl. from Mayakovsky); [comments on recent
       visit to Russia]. *Soviet Weekly* 13 October 1955, p.9.
           All critical remarks were cut out from EM's comments.

C58   'Communicators' (article on Yekaterina Shevelyova); [review of J.
       Kinsley, *Scottish Poetry*]. *Saltire Review* II:6, Winter 1955, pp.66–9; 75,
       77.

C59   [Review of B. Ifor Evans, *W.P. Ker as a Critic of Literature* (the W.P.
       Ker Lecture)]. *College Courant* 8:15, Martinmas 1955, pp.73–5.

1956

C60   What is 'Paradise Lost' *Really* About? *The Poet* 13, [1956], p.[7].

C61   Dunce (transl. from Jacques Prévert). *Saltire Review* III:7, Spring 1956,
       p.28.

C62   [Review of George Gordon, *The Lives of Authors*]. *College Courant* 3:6,
       Whitsun 1956, pp.146–7.

C63   The Skerry (frae the French o Guillevic) – Three Translations: Winter
       and War (from 'The Pulkovo Meridian' by Vera Inber) – Contra Spem
       Spero (from the Ukrainian of Lesya Ukrainka) – The Antiar, or Upas-
       Tree (transl. from Pushkin). *The Voice of Scotland* VII:2, July 1956,
       pp.16–20.

C64   On the Beach (transl. from Henri de Régnier). *Glasgow Herald* 14 July
       1956, p.3.

C65   'Scots and English' (review of E.A. Robertson, *Voices frae the City of
       Trees*; S.G. Smith, *Omens*; R.C. Saunders, *XXI Poems*). *Saltire Review*
       III:8, Autumn 1956, pp.64–5.

C66   'Jujitsu for the Educated: Reflections on Hugh MacDiarmid's poem *In
       Memoriam James Joyce*'. *The Twentieth Century* 160:955, September 1956,
       pp.223–31.
           On p.228, 1.22, 'the' should read 'that'.

C67   Hoo the Warld Wags (transl. from Heine). *Saltire Review* III:9, Winter
       1956, p.16.

C68   Dialogue II: Hieronymus Bosch and Johann Faust – From Cathkin
       Braes: a view of Korea. *The Voice of Scotland* VII:3 & 4, October 1956 –
       January 1957, pp.7–10, 11–12.
           A note on 'Dialogue II' on p.10 states 'The first of this series of
           poems, entitled "Joyce and MacDiarmid" appeared in a previous issue
           of *The Voice of Scotland*.' In fact, it appeared in *Saltire Review* II:4,
           Spring 1955, pp.56–9.

C69   [Letter on Colin Wilson's article, 'A Writer's Prospect']. *London
       Magazine* 3:11, November 1956, pp.65–6.

Wilson's article appeared in *London Magazine* 3:8, August 1956. EM advocates interest in Russian authors.

C70 'A Hantle of Howlers' (article). *The Twentieth Century* 160:958, December 1956, pp.518–30.

Reviewed in Miscellany, *Manchester Guardian* 7 December 1956 ('New Critics'); Editorial Diary, *Glasgow Herald* 10 December 1956 ('A Whish to Bring Joy' and see *Errata, Glasgow Herald* 11 December 1956); and *Life* 28 January 1957 ('Double, Double, Vorpal Burbles').

1957

C71 'A Hantle of Howlers (continued)'. *The Twentieth Century* 161:959, January 1957, pp.30–38.

Corrections: p.30, item 101 – for 'temperament' read 'temperment'; p.30, item 122 – for 'writing' read 'writting'; p.32, 1.21 – for 'attention' read 'attension'.

On p.79 there is a letter from Donald MacRae commenting on first part of 'A Hantle of Howlers'. In *TTC* 161:960, February 1957, pp.178–9 there is a letter from John Wain on both parts of article; in *TTC* 161:965, July 1957, p.76 a letter from Denis Donoghue refers to EM as spotting a howler by DD in the previous issue and salutes EM as 'the Inspector Maigret of the academic world'; and the article is referred to by W.S. Keir in *TTC* 162:975, May 1958, pp.466–7. The two parts were reprinted in *Essays*, pp.255–76.

C72 'Summary of Periodical Literature' (with John A.M. Rillie). *Review of English Studies* (N.S.) VIII:29, February 1957, pp.109–12.

Unsigned.

C73 [Letter on howler in letter from D. MacRae, 'What is a Howler?', in *TTC* 161:959, January 1957, p.79]. *The Twentieth Century* 161:960, February 1957, p.179.

C74 Imaginary Conversation: Marilyn Monroe and Galina Ulanova; [review of E. Pound, *Section: Rock Drill* and J. Holloway, *The Minute*]. *Saltire Review* IV:10, Spring 1957, pp.34–7; 75–7.

A footnote to 'Imaginary Conversation' states that it 'is the fifth of a series of entirely imaginary dialogues entitled *The Whittrick*.'

C75 [Letter on letters from John Wain and Donald MacRae on howlers in *TTC* 161:960, February, pp.178–9 and *TTC* 161:959, January 1957, p.79]. *The Twentieth Century* 161:961, March 1957, pp.303–4.

Correction: p.304, 1.4 – insert full stop.

C76 [Review of Donald Davie, *Articulate Energy*]; 'Summary of Periodical Literature' (with J.A.M. Rillie). *Review of English Studies* (N.S.) VIII:30, May 1957, pp.212–14; 219–21.

'Summary' unsigned.

C77 The Woman (transl. from Herman Florov) – At Night (transl. from Bella Akhmadulina) – In the Electric Train (transl. from Lina Kostenko). *Soviet Literature* 12, [December] 1957, p.162.

Under heading, 'Englishman Translates Soviet Poetry'.

C78 [Review of Elio Chinol, *P.B. Shelley*]; 'Summary of Periodical Litera-

ture' (with J.A.M. Rillie). *Review of English Studies* (N.S.) VIII:31,
August 1957, pp.323–4; 351–3.
   'Summary' unsigned.

C79   [Review of *Wordsworth in Scotland* (Signet Press)]; Night Pillion. *Saltire Review* IV:12, Autumn 1957, pp.54–5; 73.

C80   'Mr Eliot's Knots' (review of T.S. Eliot, *On Poetry and Poets*). *Glasgow Herald* 26 September 1957, p.3.

C81   [Review of John Speirs, *Medieval English Poetry*]. *Saltire Review* IV:13, Winter 1957, pp.75, 77.

C82   'Summary of Periodical Literature' (with J.A.M. Rillie). *Review of English Studies* (N.S.) VIII:32, November 1957, pp.458–61.
   Unsigned.

C83   'The Giant Albion: Blake after 200 years' (article). *Glasgow Herald* 28 November 1957, p.3.
   Mention of Blake, *The Complete Writings*, ed. G. Keynes and V. de Sola Pinto, *The Divine Vision*.

1958

C84   [Review of W.H. Auden, *Making, Knowing and Judging* and Sir George Rostrevor Hamilton, ed., *Essays and Studies*]; 'Summary of Periodical Literature' (with J.A.M. Rillie). *Review of English Studies* (N.S.) IX:33, February 1957, pp.123, 125; 126–8.
   'Summary' unsigned.

C85   [Letter on Scottish literary criticism]. *Lines Review* 14, Spring 1958, pp.27–8.
   In answer to letter from David Craig in *LR* 13, Summer 1957, pp.26–8.

C86   Peeweet (transl. from 'Ossi di Seppia' by Eugenio Montale). *Partisan Review* 25:2, Spring 1958, p.273.

C87   [Review of Douglas Young, *The Puddocks*]. *Saltire Review* V:14, Spring 1958, pp.67, 69.

C88   'The Compleat Writers' Guide USA – USSR'. *The Twentieth Century* 163: 973, March 1958, pp.202–19.
   Corrections: p.202, 1.12 – for 'Alvarez in' read 'Alvarez on'; p. 206, 1.32 – for 'television' read 'tollvision'.
   Originally a talk given to the Glasgow University Literary Society, February 1953. Reprinted in *Essays*, pp.277–94.

C89   A Glasgow Cemetery (transl. from Luis Cernuda) – Letter to a Young Dramatist, Labouring Under the Spell of Fry. *The Voice of Scotland* VIII: 3&4, [?March 1958], pp.7, 20–22.

C90   'That Uncertain Feeling' (article on current drama). *Encore* 5:1 (14), May–June 1958, pp.18–21.

C91   'Summary of Periodical Literature' (with J.A.M. Rillie). *Review of English Studies* (N.S.) IX:34, May 1958, pp.235–7.

C92   'Byron: Poet or Hero?' (review of L. Marchand, *Byron: A Biography*). *Glasgow Herald* 10 May, 1958, p.3.
   Includes part of transl. of Pushkin, 'To the Sea'.

C93   'Yesterday and Today' (review of N. Virta, *Alone* and L. Obukhova, *A Tale of Polesie*). *Anglo-Soviet Journal* XIX:2, Summer 1958, p.31.

C94   Motet (transl. from *Le Occasioni* by Montale). *Partisan Review* 25:3, Summer 1958.

C95   The Creator and the Computer. *Saltire Review* V:15, Summer 1958, pp.51–4.

C96   'Chekhov '58'. *Encore* 5:2 (15), July-August 1958, pp.6–10.

C97   [Review of Bernard Groom, *The Diction of Poetry from Spenser to Bridges*]; 'Summary of Periodical Literature' (with J.A.M. Rillie). *Review of English Studies* (N.S.) IX:35, August 1958, pp.346–7; 349–52. 'Summary' unsigned.

C98   McGonagall at the Festival. *Glasgow Herald* 6 September 1958, p.3. Originally the last couplet referred to the recent British Association deliberations, but as these had finished by the time the *Herald* received the poem EM was asked, by Anne Donaldson, to change the ending. He obliged immediately, accepting her suggestion of referring to the Mod.

C99   'At Embro Tae The Ploy'. *Encore* 5:4 (17), November-December 1958, pp.6–9.

C100   'Summary of Periodical Literature' (with J.A.M. Rillie). *Review of English Studies* (N.S.) IX:36, November 1958, pp.455–7. Unsigned.

C101   At Night (transl. from Bella Akhmadulina). *Glasgow Herald* 27 December 1958, p.3.

1959

C102   Sleight-of-Morals. *Chicago Review* 13:1, Winter-Spring 1959, p.36.

C103   'Forgotten Men (1): Vladimir Mayakovsky'. *Encore* 6:1 (18), January–February 1959, pp.6–8. Original title: 'Neglected Playwrights: Mayakovsky'.

C104   [Letter deploring absence of Mervyn Peake from consideration in symposium on New Novelists in *London Magazine* 5:11, November 1958]. *London Magazine* 6:1, January 1959, p.64.

C105   'Summary of Periodical Literature' (with J.A.M. Rillie). *Review of English Studies* (N.S.) X:37, February 1959, pp.109–12. Unsigned.

C106   'Off the Main Line' (review of Olga Forsh, *Palace and Prison* and Konstantin Feding, *Sanatorium Arktur*). *Anglo-Soviet Journal* XX:1, Spring 1959, p.40.

C107   March (transl. from Pasternak's *Dr Zhivago*). *Glasgow Herald* 7 March 1959, p.3.

C108   '299'. *Encore* 6:3 (20), May–June 1959, pp.31–2. On 299 Experimental Theatre, Glasgow.

C109   'Summary of Periodical Literature' (with J.A.M. Rillie). *Review of English Studies* (N.S.) X:38, May 1959, pp.218–20. Unsigned.

C110   'The Variety of Short Story Writing' (review of Mikhail Prishvin,
        Nature's Diary; Boris Lavrenyov, *The Forty-First*; Mikhail Kotsynbinsky,
        Chrysalis; and *25 Stories from the Soviet Republics*). *Anglo-Soviet Journal*
        XX:2, Summer 1959, pp.35–6.

C111   'MacDiarmid Embattled' (essay). *Lines Review* 15, Summer 1959,
        pp.17–25.
            Reprinted in *Essays*, pp.194–202.

C112   The Whittrick: Dialogue III: Queen Shahrazad and King Shahriyar;
        ['Affirmation' in response to questionnaire on 'the don as poet, or the
        poet as don']. *Universities Quarterly* 13:4, August–October 1959,
        pp.355–8; 359–60.

C113   'Summary of Periodical Literature' (with J.A.M. Rillie). *Review of
        English Studies* (N.S.) X:39, August 1959, pp.333–6.

C114   ' "Pincher Martin" ' (letter). *Times Literary Supplement* 28 August 1959,
        p.495.
            Refers to letter from J.C. Maxwell, *TLS* 21 August 1959, p.483, on
            similarity between *Pincher Martin* and Ambrose Bierce's 'An Occur-
            rence at Owl Creek Bridge'.

C115   [Review of C. Logue, *Songs*]. *Saltire Review* VI:19, Autumn 1959,
        pp.72–3.

C116   Song (transl. from André Salmon). *Glasgow Herald* 26 September 1959,
        p.5.

C117   The Wedding Party (transl. from Pasternak). *Tomorrow* 2, October–
        November 1959, p.21.

C118   [Review of Kurt Wittig, *The Scottish Tradition in Literature*]. *Scottish
        Historical Review* XXXVIII:2 (126), October 1959, pp.159–60.

C119   The Plum-Tree (transl. from Brecht). *Critical Quarterly* 1:4, Winter
        1959, p.350.

C120   'Chicken on the Fringe' (review of John McGrath, *Why the Chicken*).
        Encore 6:5 (22), November–December 1959, pp.44, 46.

C121   'Summary of Periodical Literature' (with J.A.M. Rillie). *Review of
        English Studies* (N.S.) X:40, November 1959, pp.439–41.

1960

C122   [Review of William Dunbar, *Poems*, ed. J. Kinsley and R.A. Foakes,
        The Romantic Assertion]; 'Summary of Periodical Literature' (with J.A.M.
        Rillie). *Review of English Studies* (N.S.) XI:41, February 1960, pp.71–3,
        105–7; 122–5.

C123   'Translations and Approximations' (review of Molière, *The Misanthrope*,
        transl. Richard Wilbur; Schiller, *Mary Stuart*, transl. Stephen Spender;
        Perse, *Anabasis*, transl. T.S. Eliot; John Cairncross, *By a Lonely Sea*).
        Listen 3:3&4, Spring 1960, pp.28–31.

C124   'Very like a whale' (dialogue on abstract art). *Saltire Review* VI:20,
        Spring 1960, pp.25–33.

C125   Four translations from Vladimir Mayakovsky: Ay, but can ye? – The
        Ballad o the Rid Cadie (1917) – A Richt Respeck fur Cuddies –

Eupatoria (Health resort on the Black Sea). *Migrant* 5, March 1960, pp.5–9.

> Corrections: 'A Richt Respeck fur Cuddies' 1.43 – for 'haw' read 'hae'; 1.45 – for 'Oneywey' read 'Onywey'; in Glossary for 'clanjam-fry' read 'clamjamfry'. 'Eupatoria' 1.10 – for 'Eupatotaptoos' read 'Eupataptoos'; in Glossary for 'Kilquhanty' read 'Kilquhanity'. Offprint issued.

C126 '*Pincher Martin* and *The Coral Island*'. *Notes and Queries* N.S. 7:4, April 1960, p.150.

C127 [Review of Masood-ul-Hasan, *Donne's Imagery*]; 'Summary of Periodical Literature' (with J.A.M. Rillie). *Review of English Studies* (N.S.) XI:42, May 1960, pp.233–4; 236–40.

C128 'Jean Genet: a life and its Legend' (article). *Sidewalk* 1:1, [May 1960], pp.63–6.

C129 'Russian Anthology' (review of Stephen Graham, ed., *Great Russian Short Stories*). *Anglo-Soviet Journal* XXI:2, Summer 1960, p.38.

C130 [Two poems:] The Bridge (Written for an amateur film, *The Bridge*, made by Crawford Robb) – Eupatoria (transl. from Mayakovsky). *College Courant* 12:24, Whitsun 1960, pp.93, 109.

> Correction: 'Eupatoria' 1.8 – for 'Eupajallocks' read 'Eupajollocks'.

C131 Night (transl. from Pasternak). *Glasgow Herald* 11 June 1960, p.8.

C132 [Review of Christine Brooke-Rose, *A Grammar of Metaphor* and Francis Berry, *Poets' Grammar: Person, Time and Mood in Poetry*]; 'Summary of Periodical Literature' (with J.A.M. Rillie). *Review of English Studies* (N.S.) XI:43, August 1960, pp.340–43; 345–9.

C133 [3-line comment on Francis Pollini's *Night*, as from review]; Sebastopol 1905 (transl. from Pasternak, *Lieutenant Schmidt*, Part I, Section 4) – You Though (transl. from Henri Michaux) – Four Poems by Salvatore Quasimodo (And Soon the Sun Goes Down – Bygone Winter – The Rain is with us Again – Instead of a Madrigal) – Well, What Then? (transl. from Mayakovsky). *Sidewalk* 1:2, [August 1960], pp.8; 18, 22, 23–4, 29.

> EM's review of *Night* appeared in *Gambit* Spring 1961.

C134 'The Walls of Gormenghast: An Introduction to the Novels of Mervyn Peake'. *Chicago Review* 14:3, Autumn-Winter 1960, pp.74–81.

> Corrections: p.74, 1.2 – for 'air' read 'flair'; p.76, 1.1 – for 'pschology' read 'psychology'; p.77, 1.5 – for 'stratced' read 'stracted'.
>
> Reprinted in *Essays,* pp.34–42.

C135 'Soviet Short Stories' (review of *Such a Simple Thing and Other Soviet Stories*; Andrejs Upits, *Outside Paradise and Other Stories*; Victor Kin, *Across the Lines*; Sergei Antonov, *It Happened in Penkovo*). *Anglo-Soviet Journal* XXI:3, Autumn 1960, pp.34–5.

C136 Desire for Fame (transl. from Pushkin) – Versailles (transl. from Mayakovsky). *Saltire Review* VI:22, Autumn 1960, pp.40–42.

C137 *from* The Waves (transl. from Pasternak). *Migrant* 8, September 1960, p.1.

C138   Letter to a Young Rhetor, Studying at Oxford. *Essays in Criticism* X:4,
        October 1960, pp.434–5.
        Printed under the heading *The Critical Muse*. Originally sent as a
        private letter to George Hunter, 6 February 1948.
        Offprint issued.

C139   'Heroes at Edinburgh'. *Encore* 7:6 (28), November–December 1960,
        pp.38–40.

C140   'Summary of Periodical Literature' (with J.A.M. Rillie). *Review of
        English Studies* (N.S.) XI:44, November 1960, pp.455–9.

C141   'Poets and Polemics' (Review of Renato Poggioli, *The Poets of Russia
        1890–1930*). *Anglo-Soviet Journal* XXI:4, Winter 1960, pp.42–3.

                                      1961

C142   'Summary of Periodical Literature' (with J.A.M. Rillie). *Review of
        English Studies* (N.S.) XII:45, February 1961, pp.109–12.

C143   'Davidson, the Odd Poet Out' (review of *John Davidson: A Selection of his
        Poems*, ed. M. Lindsay). *Glasgow Herald* 23 March 1961, p.7.

C144   [Review of Sir Cecil Kisch, *Alexander Blok, Prophet of Revolution* and
        Charles Tomlinson, *Versions from Fyodor Tyutchev 1803–1873*]. *Anglo-
        Soviet Journal* XXII:1, Spring 1961, pp.37–8.

C145   [Review of Francis Pollini, *Night*; Philip O'Connor, *Steiner's Tour*;
        Akbar del Piombo, *The Hero Maker*]. *Gambit* Spring 1961, pp.32–3.
        Originally written for *Sidewalk*.

C146   'Poetry in rock 'n roll sends me, says Edwin Morgan' (article). *Scottish
        Daily Express* 29 April 1961, p.8.
        Under the heading: '*Viewpoint*: where guest critics have their say'.

C147   'Summary of Periodical Literature' (with J.A.M. Rillie). *Review of
        English Studies* (N.S.) XII:46, May 1961, pp.225–8.

C148   'An Egg-Head – but he rode and fought with the wild Cossacks' (review
        of I. Babel, *Collected Short Stories*). *Scottish Daily Express* 6 May 1961,
        p.11.

C149   'Unsuspecting, you take to culture' (article on paperbacks). *Scottish
        Daily Express* 20 May 1961, p.8.

C150   'Mayakovsky's "Bedbug" ' (review of Mayakovsky, *The Bedbug and
        Selected Poetry*). *Anglo-Soviet Journal* XXII:2, Summer 1961, p.37.

C151   Whit Mair (transl. from Mayakovsky). *Lines Review* 17, Summer 1961,
        p.13.

C152   'The Camera's fascinating forerunner . . .' (review of *Gibbon's Journey
        from Geneva to Rome*, ed. G. Bonnard). *Scottish Daily Express* 17 June
        1961, p.11.
        Unsigned – the review was cut.

C153   'Summary of Periodical Literature' (with J.A.M. Rillie). *Review of
        English Studies* (N.S.) XII:47, August 1961, pp.331–7.

C154   'Who will Publish Scottish Poetry?' (review of Margaret Tait, *Origins
        and Elements*; Alan Jackson, *Underwater Wedding*; Tom Scott, *An Ode Til*

New Jerusalem; Alan Riddell, *Majorcan Interlude*; I.H. Finlay, *Glasgow Beasts, an a Burd*). *New Saltire* 2, November 1961, pp.51–6.

Pp.53–6 consists of a short essay on the publishing of modern Scottish poetry. Scottish publishers replied in *New Saltire* 3, Spring 1962, pp.40–42. Answered by EM in *Scotsman* 12 May 1962, Weekend Magazine, p.4.

C155 'Leigh Hunt and Bacon'. *Notes and Queries* N.S. 8:11, November 1961, p.346.

Under *Replies* in answer to query in *N&Q* 8:8, August 1961, p.308, concerning source of quotation by Bacon in an unpublished MS by Hunt.

C156 'The Edinburgh Festival'. *Encore* 8:6 (34), November–December 1961, p.37–9.

C157 'Summary of Periodical Literature' (with J.A.M. Rillie). *Review of English Studies* (N.S.) XII:48, November 1961, pp.444–8.

1962

C158 [Review of G.S. Fraser, *Ezra Pound*; D.W. Jefferson, *Henry James*; J.M. Cohen, *Robert Graves*; F. Kermode, *Wallace Stevens*; S.C. Sen Gupta, *Towards a Theory of the Imagination*]; 'Summary of Periodical Literature' (with J.A.M. Rillie). *Review of English Studies* (N.S.) XIII:49, February 1962, pp.103–4; 105–8.

C159 'Ehrenburg Memoirs' (review of Ilya Ehrenburg, *People and Life*). *Anglo-Soviet Journal* XXIII:1, Spring 1962, pp.34–5.

A letter concerning the review from Dr L. Crome appeared in *A-SJ* XXIII:2, Summer 1962, pp.47–8; answered by EM on p.48.

C160 'The Drama Critic' (letter); 'The Beatnik in the Kailyard' (essay). *New Saltire* 3, Spring 1962, pp.48; 65–74.

The letter was in reply to Warrington Minge on critics of Edinburgh Festival Fringe productions in *New Saltire* 2, November 1961, pp.71–2. 'The Beatnik in the Kailyard' was answered in verse by MacDiarmid ('Question to Edwin Morgan') in *New Saltire* 4, Summer 1962, p.50 (See also Hamish Whyte, 'MacDiarmid and the Beatniks', *Scottish Literary Journal* 13:2, November 1986, pp.87–90) and was reprinted in *Essays*, pp.166–76.

C161 Fiddle-ma-Fidgin (transl. from Mayakovsky); 'Translator's note'. *The Review* 1, April/May 1962, pp.26–8.

C162 The night sky hung . . . (transl. from Tyutchev). *Poor.Old.Tired.Horse.* 1, [April 1962], p.[1].

C163 Forcryinoutloud – Hymn to a Jeddart-Justicer (both transl. from Mayakovsky) – That tear on your face (translation from József). *Poor.Old.Tired.Horse.* 2, May 1962, pp.[2], [4].

C164 [Review of *John Davidson: A Selection of his Poems*, ed. M. Lindsay; *Poems and Ballads by John Davidson*, selected by R.D. Macleod; R.D. Macleod, *John Davidson: a study in personality*; *Studies in Romanticism* 1:1, 1961; *Osmania Journal of English Studies* 1, 1961; *Modern Drama* IV:2, 1961 (the last three with J.A.M. Rillie)]; 'Summary of Periodical Literature' (with J.A.M. Rillie). *Review of English Studies* (N.S.) XIII:50, May 1962, pp.210–11; 222–8.

C165   'Poet and Public' (article). *Scotsman* 12 May 1962, Weekend Magazine, p.4.

On difficulties of younger poets getting published; also in answer to publishers who replied to EM's article in *New Saltire* 2 (see *New Saltire* 3, Spring 1962, pp.40–42). Answered by Hugh MacDiarmid in *Scotsman* 18 May 1962, p.15 (under heading ' "Teddyboy Poetasters" ').

C166   Instead of a Madrigal – To the New Moon (both transl. from Salvatore Quasimodo). *Critical Quarterly* 4:2, Summer 1962, pp.174–5.

P.175 also has a note on Quasimodo.

C167   The Avalanche – Winter Morning (both transl. from Pushkin). *New Saltire* 4, Summer 1962, pp.43–4.

P.50 carries a letter in verse from Hugh MacDiarmid on 'The Beatnik in the Kailyard' in *New Saltire* 3, Spring 1962, pp.65–74.

C168   'jean genet: "a legend to be legible" ' (article). *The Outsider* (New Orleans) 2, Summer 1962, pp.35–40.

C169   Meeloneys Reply to McBnuigrr – Holiday Evening (latter transl. from Leopardi). *Poor.Old.Tired.Horse.* 3, [June 1962], p.[4].

C170   'The Case of Hugh MacDiarmid' (review of Hugh MacDiarmid, *Collected Poems*). *The Review* 3, August/September 1962, pp.25–30.

C171   Linoleum Chocolate – To Joan Eardley – Good Friday. *Lines Review* 18, [August] 1962, pp.35–6.

C172   Heart-Innocent – Mother – Elegy (all transl. from A. József). *Mainstream* (New York) 15:8, August 1962, pp.41–3.

C173   'The Beat Vigilantes' (article). *New Saltire* 5, August 1962, pp.75–80.

C174   'Summary of Periodical Literature' (with J.A.M. Rillie). *Review of English Studies* (N.S.) XIII:51, August 1962, pp.328–32.

C175   'Hugh MacDiarmid: The Poet at 70: An Appreciation'. *Glasgow Herald* 11 August 1962, p.9.

C176   'The Fold-In Conference'. *Gambit* (Edinburgh University), Autumn 1962, pp.14–16, 21–3.

'This account of the first Writers' Conference at the Edinburgh International Festival of 1962 is dedicated to William Burroughs. The general theme of the Conference was The Novel.' (p.14)

C177   I'm Aff (transl. from Mayakovsky). *Breakthru* 1:6, September-October 1962.

C178   The Death of Marilyn Monroe. *New Statesman* LXIV:1650, 26 October 1962, p.572.

C179   The Old Man and the Sea; [Review of H. MacDiarmid, *Collected Poems*]. *Critical Quarterly* 4:4, Winter 1962; pp.321; 374–5.

C180   The Star'ings in George Square. *Lines Review* 19, Winter 1962, pp.25–6.

C181   'Edinburgh Festival'. *Encore* 9:6 (40), November–December 1962,
       pp.47–50.

C182   'Summary of Periodical Literature' (with J.A.M. Rillie). *Review of
       English Studies* (N.S.) XIII:52, November 1962, pp.440–44.

C183   The First Ice (transl. from Voznesensky). *Poor.Old.Tired.Horse.* 5,
       [December 1962], p.[1].

                                     1963

C184   Dogs Round a Tree – Original Sin at the Water-Hole. *Fish-Sheet* 1,
       [1963], p.[3].
       Folded sheet printed on pp.[2 & 3].

C185   The Death of Marilyn Monroe. *Life* 25 January 1963, p.93.
       Printed in article 'The Growing Cult of Marilyn' under the heading
       'The Laments of Angry Poets' (poets are 'indignantly parceling out
       the blame for her suicide . . . Edwin Morgan . . . puts the finger on
       all of society . . . punctuating his blast with highly un-English
       outcries of "Strasberg!" and "DiMaggio!" ').

C186   'Edwin Muir' (essay). *The Review* 5, February 1963, pp.3–10.
       Reprinted in *The Modern Poet: Essays from 'The Review'*, ed. Ian
       Hamilton (London: Macdonald, 1968), pp.42–9; and in *Essays*,
       pp.186–193.

C187   [Review of Geoffrey Dutton, *Walt Whitman*]; 'Summary of Periodical
       Literature' (with J.A.M. Rillie). *Review of English Studies* (N.S.)
       XIV:53, February 1963, pp.102–3; 103–8.

C188   '*Foreign Literature*' (review of D.J. Mossop, *Baudelaire's Tragic Hero: A
       Study of the Architecture of 'Les Fleurs du Mal'* and *Flowers of Evil*, rendered
       into English by Florence L. Friedman). *Durham University Journal* March
       1963, pp.83–4.

C189   Unemployed (transl. from József). *Poor.Old.Tired.Horse.* 6, [March
       1963], p.[2].

C190   New York Airport at Night (transl. from Voznesensky). *Poor.Old.
       Tired.Horse.* 7, [May 1963], pp.[2–3].

C191   'Summary of Periodical Literature' (with J.A.M. Rillie). *Review of
       English Studies* (N.S.) XIV:54, May 1963, pp.222–4.

C192   'The Young Russian' (review of Yevtushenko, *Selected Poems* and Anselm
       Hollo, *Red Cats*). *The Nation* 25 May 1963, pp.446–7.

C193   Foggy Street – Wings – Goya (all transl. from Voznesensky).
       Cleft 1:1, June 1963, pp.22–3.
       Corrections: 'Foggy Street' 1.5 – for 'everything' read 'everything's';
       'Wings' – put last line first.

C194   'A Glimpse of Petavius' ('abbreviated' essay on poetry and science).
       Gambit Summer 1963, pp.12–18.
       Reprinted in *Essays*, pp.3–15.

C195   Letter to My Mother (transl. from Quasimodo) – The White
       Rhinoceros. *Lines Review* 20, Summer 1963, pp.25–7.

C196   Make Do – The Lake – Empty Sea – My Story, Nautically (all transl.
       from Renzo Laurano); 'The Poet and the Particle' (essay on R. Garioch's
       'The Muir'). *New Saltire* 8, June 1963, pp.43; 59–61.
       'The Poet and the Particle' was reprinted in *Essays*, pp.16–19.

C197   Slow Song (transl. from Y. Pankratov) – Parabolic Ballad (transl. from
       Voznesensky) – Poem (transl. from Khlebnikov). *Poor.Old.Tired.Horse.*
       8, [August 1963], pp.[1], [2], [4].

C198   'Three Scottish Poets' (review of N. MacCaig, *A Round of Applause*;
       George MacBeth, *The Broken Places*; Tom Scott, *The Ship and Ither
       Poems*). *The Review* 8, August 1963, pp.41–5.

C199   'Summary of Periodical Literature' (with J.A.M. Rillie). *Review of
       English Studies* (N.S.) XIV:55, August 1963, pp.327–32.

C200   'Careful Portraits' (review of Ilya Ehrenburg, *First Years of Revolution,
       1918–[21]*). *Anglo-Soviet Journal* XXIV:3&4, Autumn 1963, pp.46–7.

C201   'Miscellany' (review of R. Nye, *Juvenilia 2*; K. White, *Wild Coal*; Crae
       Ritchie, *Come In World*; D.M. Black, *From the Mountain*; H.R. Bramley,
       Verse One); 'Reporter in Verse' (review of M. Lindsay, *Snow Warning*).
       New Saltire 9, September 1963, pp.52–3; 53–4.

C202   'MacDiarmid and Sherrington'. *Notes and Queries* N.S. 10:10, October
       1963, pp.382–4.
       On MacDiarmid's use, on p.143 of *In Memoriam James Joyce*, of
       quotation from Sir Charles Sherrington, *Man on his Nature*, 1940.

C203   'Summary of Periodical Literature' (with J.A.M. Rillie). *Review of
       English Studies* (N.S.) XIV:56, November 1963, pp.440–43.

C204   The Domes of Saint Sophia; 'Six Best Sixty-Three' (EM's six 'books of
       the year': James Baldwin, *The Fire Next Time*; W.H. Auden, *The Dyer's
       Hand*; Alexander Trocchi, *Cain's Book*; D. Storey, *Radcliffe*;
       G. Maxwell, *The Rocks Remain*; *Jazz Poems*. Also ran: C. Mackenzie, *My
       Life and Times* Octaves 1 and 2; Yevtushenko, *A Precocious Autobiography*;
       H. Miller, *Tropic of Cancer*; M. Spark, *The Girls of Slender Means*; I.
       Murdoch, *The Unicorn*; J. Kennaway, *The Bells of Shoreditch*; R. Jenkins,
       A Love of Innocence; J. Prebble, *The Highland Clearances*; S. O'Casey,
       Autobiography; *The Letters of Van Gogh*). *New Saltire* 10, December
       1963, pp.14–15; 51–4.

1964

C205   In Praise of Surtsey – French Persian Cats Having a Ball. *Die Sonde*
       (Frankfurt) 64, 1964, p.98.
       Includes German translation of 'In Praise of Surtsey'.

C206   French Persian Cats Having a Ball. *OU* 22, [?1964].
       Correction: 1.29 – for 'chat' read 'cha'.
       French magazine edited by Henri Chopin; folder containing folded
       sheets.

C207   o pioneers! *labris* (Lierre, Belgium) 2, January 1963 [1964], p.13.
       Corrections: 1.3 – for 'begun' read 'begum'; 1.10 – for 'Willubugan'
       read 'Willubugmn'.

C208 [Review of *Victorian Poetry* 1:1 (with J.A.M. Rillie)]; 'Summary of Periodical Literature' (with J.A.M. Rillie). *Review of English Studies* (N.S.) XV:57, February 1964, pp.119; 120–23.

C209 'Close reading and closed poems: II – the poets'; King Billy – The Unspoken – Trio; [review of Pushkin, *Selected Verse*, ed. J. Fennell]. *Glasgow Review* I:1, Spring 1964, pp.9–11; 35–7; 47.

C210 Islands. *New Statesman* LXVII:1721, 6 March 1964, p.368.

C211 Two by Two – Scotch Cat – Down in the Forest – Bees' Nest – Like, Little Russian Cat. *labris* 3, April 1964, pp.33–4.
   Corrections: p.34: 'Bees' Nest' 11.5 & 11 – for 'obysy' read 'obusy'; 'Russian' misprinted 'Tussian'.

C212 Breath of Corruption – Chinese Cat – Siesta of a Hungarian Snake – Earth (transl. from Voznesensky). *Cleft* 1:2, May 1964, pp.16, 19.

C213 [Review of Elizabeth Sewell, *The Orphic Voice*]; 'Summary of Periodical Literature' (with J.A.M. Rillie). *Review of English Studies* (N.S.) XV:58, May 1964, pp.226–8; 236–40.

C214 [Review of *The Penguin Book of Japanese Verse*]. *The Glasgow Review* I:2, Summer 1964, pp.46–8.

C215 Brazilian 'Football' – Instant Theatre Go Home. *Poor.Old.Tired.Horse.* 10, [June 1964], p.[4].
   Correction: 'Brazilian "Football" ' 1.3 – for 'Goal! Goal! Goal!' read 'Gaol! Gaol! Gaol!'.

C216 'Armstrong's last Goodnight' (review of John Arden play, Citizens' Theatre, Glasgow). *Encore* 11:4 (50), July-August 1964, pp.47–8, 50–51.
   Originally titled 'Johnny Arden, Tak Tent!'. Letter from John Arden in reply, *Encore* 11:5 (51), September–October 1964, pp.50–52.

C217 'Summary of Periodical Literature' (with J.A.M. Rillie). *Review of English Studies* (N.S.) XV:59, August 1964, pp.342–7.

C218 Letter to a French Novelist – O Pioneers! – Instant Theatre Go Home – 'SIMPLE MYTH LITERATURE PEN SET' – The Computer's First Christmas Card – Canedolia. *Times Literary Supplement* 6 August 1964, pp.682, 686, 687, 691, 702.
   Corrections: 'O Pioneers' 1.7 – for 'begbugn' read 'bengug'; 'Instant Theatre Go Home' 1.2 – for 'HA! If' read 'HA!lf'.
   Special number of *TLS*, 'The Changing Guard', on avant-garde writing.

C219 The Open Pomander. *Link* (Gloucester College of Art) September/ October 1964.

C220 Pavloviana (transl. from José Paulo Paes) – 'bloody sand' – Bhite & Wlack (both transl. from Augusto de Campo) – The Suicide, or Descartes à Rebours (transl. from José Paulo Paes) – Two Poems: 'from deep' – 'untracked' (both transl. from Eugen Gomringer); [review, included in 'Little Magazines' section, of Portuguese publications: *Poesia Experimental* No.1; Herberto Helder, *Electrònicolírica*; E.M. de Melo e Castro, *Ideogramas, Poligonia do Soneto* and *objecto poemático de efeito progressivo*]. *Times Literary Supplement* 3 September 1964, pp.790, 802; 828.

> The review on p.828 is unsigned.
> 2nd special number on the avant-garde: 'Any Advance? The Changing Guard – 2'.

C221   Bestiary (transl. from Apollinaire) – Make Do (transl. from Renzo Laurano). *Poor. Old.Tired.Horse.* 11, [October 1964], pp.[3], [4].

C222   [Review of *The Esdaile Notebook*]. *The Glasgow Review* I:4, Winter 1964/65, pp.16–17.

C223   [Construction for I.K. Brunel]. *Link* November/December 1964, p.[10].

C224   'Summary of Periodical Literature' (with J.A.M. Rillie). *Review of English Studies* (N.S.) XV:60, November 1960, pp.456–9.

C225   'The Poet Cultivating Thistles' (review of Duncan Glen, *Hugh MacDiarmid and the Scottish Renaissance*). *Glasgow Herald* 28 November 1964, p.13.

1965

C226   Bring me the sunflower – A vague cicada (both transl. from Montale). *Adam* 300, 1965.

C227   In Sobieski's Shield. *Ambit* 23, 1965.

C228   One Cigarette – From the Domain of Arnheim. [*Epos*] 1, [1965], pp.[1–2].

> Titled *16 Poems*. Glasgow University Literary Society Magazine.

C229   Aberdeen Train. *Extra Verse* 16, 1965, p.18.

C230   Three Cats (French Rocket Cat October 1963 – Gone Cat – Royal Prerogative Cat). *Poor.Old.Tired.Horse.* 12, [1965], p.[4].

C231   Boats and Places. *Poor.Old.Tired.Horse.* 15, [1965], p.[4].

C232   'A Traverse Year', *Encore* 12:1 (No.53) January–February 1965, pp.31–9.

C233   The Second Life. *Peace News* 8 January 1965.

C234   'Mr. MacDiarmid and Dr. Grieve' (letter). *Times Literary Supplement* 28 January 1965, p.67.

> Part of correspondence on MacDiarmid's poem, 'Perfect'.

C235   'Summary of Periodical Literature' (with J.A.M. Rillie). *Review of English Studies* (N.S.) XVI:61, February 1965, pp.110–14.

C236   'Organs and Lemans' (review of S.G. Smith, *Carotid Cornucopius*). *New Statesman* LXIX:1769, 5 February 1965, p.208.

C237   The Old Man and the Sea – The White Rhinoceros – [translations:] The American Nightingale (transl. from Yevtushenko) – History (transl. from Robert Rozhdestvensky) – Poets – Spring (both transl. from Svetlana Yevseyeva) – The 'City of Science' at Novosibirsk (transl. from Bella Akhmadulina). *el corno emplumado* 14, April 1965, pp.73–4; 77–82.

> Text of 'The White Rhinoceros' badly treated.

C238 'West Coast Scottish' (review of Alan Sharp, *A Green Tree in Gedde*; Wallace Hildick, *Lunch with Ashurbanipal*; Frank Sargeson, *Collected Stories*; *German Short Stories*, ed. R. Newnham; Alan Burns, *Europe After the Rain*). *New Statesman* LXIX:1777, 2 April 1965, pp.538–9.

C239 'Summary of Periodical Literature' (with J.A.M. Rillie). *Review of English Studies* (N.S.) XVI:62, May 1965, pp.228–31.

C240 [Review of plays by Saul Bellow, *The Wen* and *Orange Souffle* at the Traverse Theatre, Edinburgh]. *Times* 11 May 1965, p.15.

C241 'A Russian Elite' (review of Valeriy Tarsis, *Ward 7*; Chukwemeka Ike, *Toads for Supper*; Robert Heinlein, *Tunnel in the Sky*; *Spectrum IV*, ed. K. Amis and R. Conquest; *New Writings in SF 4*, ed. John Carnell; Edgar Mittelholzer, *The Aloneness of Mrs Chatham*). *New Statesman* LXIX:1783, 14 May 1965, p.772.

C242 An Addition to the Family. *The Glasgow Review* II:2, Summer 1965, p.17.

C243 'Poets of the Sixties I: Iain Crichton Smith'; Je ne regrette rien (In memory of Edith Piaf). *Lines Review* 21, Summer 1965, pp.9–17; 41–2. The article on I.C. Smith was reprinted in *Essays*, pp.222–31, as 'The Raging and the Grace: Some Notes on the Poetry of Iain Crichton Smith'.

C244 [Review of Bob Cobbing, *Sound Poems*; Augusto de Campo and Jeffrey Steele, *Opening Number 2*; d.a. levy, *Farewell the Floating Cunt*]. *Poetmeat* 9/10, Summer 1965, p.9.

C245 'Recent Russian Poetry' (article); Translations: Goya – The First Ice – Earth – New York Airport at Night (from The Three-Cornered Pear): The Façade – The Airfield – The Interior – Structures (Andrei Voznesensky) – History (Robert Rozhdestvensky) – 'The whole earth's like a sleeping garden,' (Ivan Kharabarov) – Slow Song (Yury Pankratov) – Stalin's Heirs (Yevgeny Yevtushenko) – Heart-Innocent – Keep Going! – They'd Love Me (Attila József). *Stand* 7:2, [Summer 1965], pp.5–9; 10–19, 46–9. Biographical note on József by EM on p.46: 'The present translations . . . have been made through the medium of existing translations in other European languages.'

C246 The Third Day of the Wolf. *Peace News* 11 June 1965.

C247 'Theatre of Cruelty: Peter Weiss's Fairy-tale' (review of Peter Weiss, *A Night with Guests* and Peter Barnes, *Sclerosis* at Traverse Theatre, Edinburgh). *Times* 21 June 1965, p.6. Unsigned.

C248 'Sleeping Birds' (review of John Hersey, *White Lotus*; Heinrich Boll, *The Clown*; Godfrey Smith, *The Network*). *New Statesman* LXIX:1789, 25 June 1965, p.1018.

C249 'Summary of Periodical Literature' (with J.A.M. Rillie). *Review of English Studies* (N.S.) XVI:63, August 1965, pp.338–42.

C250 'Shambling Man' (review of M. Bradbury, *Stepping Westward*; Elizabeth Bowen, *A Day in the Dark*; David Thomson, *Break in the Sun*; John Broderick, *The Waking of Willie Ryan*; C.H. Sisson, *Christopher Homm*;

Jean Lartéguy, *Yellow Fever*; R. Chandler, *The Smell of Fear*). *New Statesman* LXX:1795, 6 August 1965, pp.191–2.

C251 'Signs and Wonders' (article). *New Statesman* LXX:1796, 13 August 1965, pp.226–7.
   On Glasgow under heading 'Arts & Entertainment Out of London'. Partly reprinted in *Glasgow Observed*, ed. S. Berry and H. Whyte (Edinburgh: John Donald, 1987), pp. 249–51.

C252 'Concrete Poetry' (essay). *Peace News* 20 August 1965, pp.6–7.
   Includes 'Sharpeville' and 'Pomander'.

C253 'Pushing Forty' (review of P.H. Newby, *One of the Founders*; David Pryce-Jones, *Quondam*; James Merrill, *The (Diblos) Notebook*; A.C.H. Smith, *The Crowd*; Hunter Davies, *Here We Go Round the Mulberry Bush*; Montague Haltrecht, *A Secondary Character*). *New Statesman* LXX:1801, 17 September 1965, p.406.

C254 'Concrete, Theory and Praxis' (review of *Invenção* no.4, 1964; Mário Chamie, *Lavra Lavra*; Yone Giannetti Fonseca, *A fala e a forma*); Selling Watermelons (transl. from Voznesensky). *Times Literary Supplement* 30 September 1965, pp.866; 870.
   Review unsigned.

C255 'Edinburgh's New Civic Theatre Draws on Italy and Poland' (review of Goldoni, *The Servant o Twa Maisters* and Slawomir Mrozek, *Out at Sea* and *Police* at Royal Lyceum, Edinburgh). *Times* 8 October 1965, p.16.
   Unsigned.

C256 'Eventful Verse Play by a Canadian Author' (review of James Reaney, *The Killdeer* at Citizens' Theatre, Glasgow). *Times* 12 October 1965, p.14.
   Unsigned: 'From Our Special Correspondent in Glasgow'.

C257 'Love Lessons' (review of K. Vonnegut Jr, *God Bless You, Mr Rosewater*; W. Saroyan, *One Day in the Afternoon of the World*; Wilfrid Sheed, *Square's Progress*; Compton Mackenzie, *Coral*; James Michener, *The Source*; John Christopher, *A Wrinkle in the Skin*; *A Century of Great Short Science Fiction Novels*, ed. Damon Knight; *New Writings in SF* 6, ed. John Carnell; *Analog Anthology*). *New Statesman* LXX:1807, 29 October 1965, p.658.

C258 O Pioneers! *Evergreen Review* 38, November 1965, p.26.
   In feature, 'New Sounds in British Poetry' compiled by Anselm Hollo, including Pete Brown, Michael Horovitz, Jim Burns, Andrew Crozier, Dave Cunliffe, Anselm Hollo, Jeff Nuttall, Tom Raworth.

C259 'Summary of Periodical Literature' (with J.A.M. Rillie). *Review of English Studies* (N.S.) XVI:64, November 1965, pp.454–7.

C260 'The Man Who Wouldn't Grow Up' (review of Günter Grass, *Onkel, Onkel* at Traverse Theatre, Edinburgh). *Times* 11 November 1965, p.18.

C261 'Mighty Wind' (review of Nikos Kazantzakis, *Report to Greco* and Mervyn Jones, *A Set of Wives*). *New Statesman* LXX:1813, 10 December 1965, p.941.

C262 [Review of Marlowe, *Dr Faustus* at Close Theatre, Glasgow]. *Times* 15
December 1965, p.7.
Unsigned.

1966

C263 Ode – March – Unemployed – The Woodcutter – Night in the Suburbs
– Elegy – 'What reader would I most want to have' – 'Fifteen years now
I've been writing' (all transl. from A. József). *Arion* (Budapest) 1, 1966,
pp.127, 129, 131, 133, 135, 137, 142–4.

C264 From an Old Scottish Chapbook – Off Course – The Chaffinch Map of
Scotland. *Joglars* (Providence, R.I.) 3, 1966, pp.[36–8].

C265 Roman Holiday – Rublyov Road (both transl. from Voznesensky).
Modern Poetry in Translation 1, [?1966], p.11.
Correction: 'Rublyov Road' l.1 – for 'scooter' read 'scooters'.

C266 'THE POET SALUTES THE DIVINE/EJACULATOR' (transl. from
Pierre Albert-Birot, from 'Poèmes à la chair' in *Grabinoulor*). *Tlaloc* 12 /
How 6, [?1966], [back cover].
Issue 6 of 2nd series of *Tlaloc*.

C267 siesta di un serpente ungherese – gatto cinese. *modulo* (Genoa) 1,
[January 1966]. pp.80–81.

C268 Autumn in Sigulda (transl. from Voznesensky). *Times Literary Supplement* 6 January 1966, p.5.

C269 'Nice Brown Trout' (review of Moray McLaren, *The Shell Guide to
Scotland*; *Glasgow at a Glance*, ed. A. McLaren Young and A.M. Doak;
Jack House, *The Heart of Glasgow*; Cliff Hanley, *A Skinful of Scotch*;
Douglas Young, *Edinburgh in the Age of Sir Walter Scott*). *New Statesman*
71:1817, 7 January 1966, pp.20–21.

C270 Message Clear. *Times Literary Supplement* 13 January 1966, p.22.
Correspondence: *TLS* 20 January 1966, p.43 (Arnold Hyde, Jack
Bevan)
TLS 3 February 1966, p.83 (Heather Bremer who
sets out the 'message')
TLS 10 February 1966, p.103 (EM who corrects 2
of H. Bremer's phrases).

C271 'Lost Millionaire' (review of N. Freeling, *The King of the Rainy Country*;
Jean Potts, *The Only Good Secretary*; Alexander Baron, *Strip Jack Naked*;
Wendy Owen, *There Goes Davy Cohen*; Peter Cowan, *The Empty Streets*;
Junichiro Tanizaki, *Diary of a Mad Old Man*). *New Statesman* 71:1819,
21 January 1966, p.96.

C272 The Computor's [sic] Second Birthday Card. *ICA Bulletin* 155,
February 1966, p.14.

C273 Strawberries – The Opening of the Forth Road Bridge 4 September
1964 – The Suspect. *Scottish Field* February 1966, p.53.
Corrections: 'Strawberries' – delete final full stop; 'The Suspect' –
delete final full stop. The lineation of 'The Suspect' differs markedly
from the version in *TSL* and *POTY*.

C274   'Message Clear' (letter). *Times Literary Supplement* 10 February 1966,
       p.103.
       Corrects Heather Bremer's interpretation of 'Message Clear' in *TLS* 3
       February 1966, p.83.

C275   'Realistic Mob Effects' (review of Shakespeare, *Julius Caesar* at Citizens'
       Theatre, Glasgow). *Times* 14 February 1966, p.14.

C276   [Review of E.C. Mason, *Rilke*]. *Critical Quarterly* 8:1, Spring 1966,
       p.89.

C277   Parabolic Ballad (transl. from Voznesensky). *Stand* 8:1, [Spring] 1966,
       pp.6–7.

C278   [Review of *A First-Draft Version of 'Finnegans Wake'*, ed. David
       Hayman]. *Notes & Queries* N.S. 13:3, March 1966, pp.107–9.

C279   'Conrad Commanding' (review of Harry Kressing, *The Cook*; A. Hind,
       The Dear Green Place; William Eastlake, *Castle Keep*; Andre Pieyre, *The
       Girl on the Motorcycle*, transl. by Alexander Trocchi; William Sansom,
       The Ulcerated Milkman; Dino Buzzatti, *Catastrophe*). *New Statesman*
       71:1825, 4 March 1966, p.303.

C280   Pleasures of a Technological University. *New Statesman* 71:1828, 25
       March 1966, p.433.

C281   Message Clear. *Feuilleton* (Germany) 71, 26/27 March 1966.

C282   Message Clear. *Chicago Daily News* 9 April 1966, 'panorama' section,
       [front cover].
       Subheaded 'A Poem for Easter'.

C283   'Unconcerned' (review of John O'Hara, *The Lockwood Concern*; Hortense
       Calisher, *Journal from Ellipsia*; J.G. Ballard, *The Crystal World*; Jane
       Smith, *The Green Wind*; E.V. Cunningham, *Penelope*; Fernando Arrabal,
       The Burial of the Sardine). *New Statesman* 71:1831, 15 April 1966,
       pp.545–6.

C284   'Passing Through' (review of J. Kerouac, *Desolation Angels*; Ann Quin,
       Three; William McIlvanney, *Remedy Is None*; Edward Hulton, *Conflicts*;
       Ivor Cutler, *Cock-a-Doodle-Don't!*). *New Statesman* 71:1837, 27 May
       1966, p.784.

C285   'Modern Scottish Poetry' (review of *Modern Scottish Poetry*, ed. Maurice
       Lindsay). *Poetry Wales* 2:2, Summer 1966, pp.38–40.

C286   OPENING THE CAGE: 14 Variations on 14 Words – 'The Middle
       High German Kiss'. *labris* 3–4, July 1966, pp.104–5.
       Corrections: p.104, 1.8 – for 'ans' read 'and'; p.105, 1.4 – for
       'middle-high!' read 'middle – high!'

C287   'Miss Gaskell' (review of Jane Gaskell, *The City* and *All Neat in Black
       Stockings*; Robin Cook, *The Legacy of the Stiff Upper Lip*; Angela Carter,
       Shadow Dance; Celia Dale, *A Helping Hand*; James T. Farrell, *Lonely for
       the Future*; F. Dürrenmatt, *Once a Greek*; Hal Clement, *Close to Critical*;
       D.F. Jones, *Colossus*). *New Statesman* 72:1843, 8 July 1966, p.61.

C288   'Granite Man' (review of L.G. Gibbon, *A Scots Quair*; Ian Munro, *Leslie
       Mitchell: Lewis Grassic Gibbon*). *New Statesman* 72:1848, 12 August
       1966, p.234.

C289 'Rough Justice' (review of M. Spillane, *The Twisted Thing*; Thomas Boileau and Pierre Narcejac, *Choice Cuts*; Robert Sheckley, *Mindswap*; André Norton, *Lord of Thunder*; M. Villa-Gilbert, *Mrs Cantello*; Dacia Maraini, *The Holiday*). *New Statesman* 72:1849, 19 August 1966, p.266.

C290 The computer's first birthday card – 'isle' – 'ballad' – 'white swallow' – 'one' – 'living deadman living' (5 poems transl. from Edgard Braga, *Soma*). *Beloit Poetry Journal* 17:1, Fall 1966, pp.28–33.

C291 No Gold and Laurel (transl. from Lajos Kassák) – Postscript (transl. from János Pilinszky). *New Hungarian Quarterly* VII:23, Autumn 1966, pp.117–18, 130–31.
　　'Postscript' reprinted in *NHQ* XXI:77, Spring 1980, pp.119–20.

C292 'Blue in the Head' (review of Yevtushenko, *Poems*, transl. by P. Levi and R. Milner-Gulland). *Times Literary Supplement* 22 September 1966, p.880.
　　Unsigned.

C293 'Predestination' (review of C. Pavese, *Summer Storm*; Leonardo Sciascia, *The Council of Egypt*; Halldor Laxness, *The Fish Can Sing*; Sean Hignett, *A Picture to Hang on the Wall*; Jerzy Peterkiewicz, *Inner Circle*; J.B. Priestley, *Salt Is Leaving* and *The Moments*). *New Statesman* 72:1855, 30 September 1966, pp.485–6.

C294 From a City Balcony – Phoning. *Lines Review* 22, Winter 1966, pp.21–2.

C295 'Two Russian Poets' (review of Voznesensky, *Selected Poems*, transl. by H. Marshall; *The Poetry of Yevgeny Yevtushenko*, transl. by G. Reavey; Y. Yevtuskenko, *Poems*, transl. by P. Levi and R. Milner-Gulland). *Glasgow Herald* 5 November 1966, p.9.

C296 'German study of betrayal staged' (review of Wolfgang Borchert, *The Man Outside* at Traverse Theatre, Edinburgh). *Times* 8 November 1966, p.14.
　　Unsigned.

C297 'Russian Solo' (review of *The Poetry of Yevgeny Yevtushenko*, transl. by George Reavey); 'Wrapping it Up' (review of Hugh MacDiarmid, *The Company I've Kept*). *Times Literary Supplement* 17 November 1966, p.1047.
　　Unsigned.

C298 'Caveman' (review of Jack London, *The Sea Wolf, White Fang, The Iron Heel* and *The Klondike Dream*, ed. by A. Calder-Marshall; Franklin Walker, *Jack London and the Klondike*; Sean O'Faolain, *The Heart of the Sun*; David Garnett, *Ulterior Motives*). *New Statesman* 72:1863, 25 November 1966, pp.797–8.

1967

C299 Glasgow Green. *Akros* 2:4, January 1967, pp.18–20.

C300 Transient Servitude – Alea I – Semantic Variations (all transl. from Haroldo de Campos). *El Corno Emplumado* 21, January 1967, pp.71–7.

C301 'Original play by Lawrence revived' (review of D.H. Lawrence, *The*

Daughter-in-Law at Traverse Theatre, Edinburgh). *Times* 28 January 1967, p. 13.
> Unsigned. Title printed as *The Mother-in-law*.

C302   For Bonfires. *Epos* (Glasgow University Literary Society) 3, February 1967, pp. 9–10.

C303   'Steak Tartare' (review of R. Queneau, *Between Blue and Blue*; Mary Lavin, *In the Middle of the Fields*; Clifford Simak, *Why Call Them Back from Heaven?*; George Lanning, *The Pedestal*; Charles Wright, *The Wig*; Isaac Rosenfield, *Alpha and Omega*). *New Statesman* 73:1873, 3 February 1967, pp. 156–7.

C304   'Four plays that justify the subliminal theatre' (review of Paul Foster, *Dead and Buried* at Traverse Theatre, Edinburgh). *Times* 28 February 1967, p.8.
> Unsigned. The four plays are: *The Recluse*; *Hurrah for the Bridge*; *Balls*; *The Hessian Corporal*.

C305   Metaphore – 16 Yearth (latter transl. from Ernst Jandl) – 'sandman' (transl. from Friedrich Achleitner). *Lines Review* 23, Spring 1967, pp. 40–41.

C306   'Poetry and Translation' (essay); I am being dragged by red dolphins – The Lament of Orpheus (both transl. from István Kormos). *New Hungarian Quarterly* VIII:25, Spring 1967, pp. 27–30; 31.

C307   'Brechtian rarity at Glasgow' (review of Brecht, *The Visions of Simone Machard* at Citizens' Theatre, Glasgow). *Times* 1 March 1967, p. 10.

C308   'Student Verse Competition'. *Radio Times* 174:262, 16 March [18–24 March] 1967, p. 19.
> Note on Scottish Home Service programme *University Notebook*, 19 March 1967.

C309   'God's Pickings' (review of Syed Waliullah, *Tree Without Roots*; John Barry, *The Bridge of Abydos*; Axel Jensen, *Epp*). *New Statesman* 73:1879, 17 March 1967, pp. 372–3.

C310   'Scalped by a Bourbon' (review of *Selected Letters of Dylan Thomas*, ed. Constantine Fitzgibbon). *The Review* 17, April 1967, pp. 41–4.

C311   Not Playing the Game. *New Statesman* 73:1883, 14 April 1967, p. 510.

C312   [Comment on Festive Permutational Poem for Festival of Concrete Poetry, Brighton]. *Form* 4, 15 April 1967, p. 17.

C313   'Joy Called Grief' (review of Nell Dunn, *Poor Cow*; Simon Gray, *Little Portia*; Michael Ayrton, *The Maze Maker*). *New Statesman* 73:1885, 28 April 1967, pp. 584–6.

C314   'Scottish play about two women' (review of Stewart Conn, *I Didn't Always Live Here* at Citizens' Theatre, Glasgow). *Times* 1 May 1967, p. 6.
> Initialled.

C315   'A play worth seeing' (review of Peter Nichols, *A Day in the Death of Joe Egg* at Citizens' Theatre, Glasgow). *Times* 23 May 1967, p. 6.
> Initialled.

C316   A man is beaten up (transl. from Gábor Garai) – The Elegy of a Bronze
        Age Man (transl. from Zoltán Jékely). *New Hungarian Quarterly*
        VIII:26, Summer 1967, pp.92–3, 172–5.

C317   After the Party. *New Statesman* 73:1890, 2 June 1967, p.769.

C318   A view of things. *Listener* LXXVII:1994, 15 June 1967, p.793.

C319   From *The Dictionary of Tea. teapoth* [i.e. *Poor.Old.Tired.Horse.*] 23, [July
        1967], p.[11].

C320   'Good Man, Good Poet?' (review of P.H. Butter, *Edwin Muir: Man and
        Poet*; D. Hoffman, *Barbarous Knowledge*). *Times Literary Supplement* 6 July
        1967, p.601.
        Unsigned.

C321   'Work-Shy Element' (review of Joseph Brodsky, *Elegy to John Donne*).
        Times Literary Supplement 20 July 1967, p.637.
        Unsigned.

C322   'MacDiarmid at 75' (essay). *Listener* 78:2002, 10 August 1967,
        pp.176–7.
        Shortened version of broadcast on BBC Third Programme, 10 August
        1967. Reprinted in *Essays*, pp.211–21, as 'MacDiarmid at Seventy-
        five'.

C323   'Poems by and for MacDiarmid' (review of Hugh MacDiarmid, *A Lap of
        Honour* and *Poems Addressed to Hugh MacDiarmid*). *Glasgow Herald* 12
        August 1967, p.9.

C324   '[Scottish Writing Today:] II. The Novel and the Drama'. *English*
        XVI:96, Autumn 1967, pp.[227]–9.
        Scottish number.

C325   Barbarian Prayer – Ague (both transl. from Sándor Csoóri). *New
        Hungarian Quarterly* VIII:27, Autumn 1967, pp.84–5.

C326   [2 photographs of] Festive permutational poem (1. poster; 2. bus
        window with section of poem). *Poor.Old.Tired.Horse.* 24, [?Autumn
        1967], pp.[6–7].
        Made for the Festival of Concrete Poetry, Brighton.

C327   astrodome – original sin at the water hole – archives. *Chicago Review*
        19:4, September 1967, pp.101–3.
        Published separately as *The Chicago Review Anthology of Concretism*,
        edited by Eugene Wildman (Chicago: Swallow Press, 1967); EM's
        poems on pp.105–7.

C328   'Bitter play on abortion' (review of Stanely Eveling, *Come and be Killed* at
        Traverse Theatre, Edinburgh). *Times* 13 September 1967, p.6.

C329   [Review of Brecht, *The Resistible Rise of Arturo Ui* at Citizens' Theatre,
        Glasgow]. *Times* 4 October 1967, p.8.

C330   A Jar Revisited – Saturday Night. *Lines Review* 25, Winter 1967/68,
        pp.6–7.

C331   Seven from The Greek Anthology (transl. from Meleager [A.P.5.25 –
        A.P.5.144 – A.P.5.190 – A.P.7.476] and Paul the Silentiary

(A.P.5.258 – A.P.5.266 – A.P.5.279]). *Arion* (Austin, Texas) 6:4, Winter 1967, pp.492–3.
Also issued as an offprint.

C332   Postscript (transl. from János Pilinszky). *Stand* 8:4, [?Winter] 1967, pp.60–61.
Biographical note on Pilinszky on p.60.

C333   [9 One Word Poems:] A Far Cool Beautiful Thing, Vanishing – The Dear Green Plaice – Homage to Zukofsky – The Dilemmas of a Horn – Ada Nada Paradada – Lattice, Lettuce, Ladders – Wet Dry Wet Dry Wet Asdic – Dangerous Glory – O Vapour-trails! O Water-melons! *Poor.Old.Tired.Horse.* 25, November 1967, p.[2].
One Word Poem issue. Design and calligraphy by Jim Nicholson.

C334   'Siberian Dam and Achilles Heart' (review of Yevtushenko, *Poems*, transl. by H. Marshall, and *The Bratsk Station and other poems*; Andrei Voznesensky, *Antiworlds* and *Akhilesovo serdtse*). *Times Literary Supplement* 2 November 1967, p.1039.
Unsigned.

C335   'New Patterns in British Poetry' (article). *National Herald* (Lucknow, India) 26 November 1967.

C336   The Little White Rows of Scotland. *Broadsheet* 3, December 1967.

C337   Frontier Story. *Listener* 78:2019, 7 December 1967, p.764.

C338   'Diabolical Experiment' (review of Mikhail Bulgakov, *The Master and Margarita*). *Times Literary Supplement* 7 December 1967, p.1181.
Unsigned.

1968

C339   Abandoned Objects (transl. from Lajos Kassák). *Arion* (Budapest) 2, 1968.

C340   3 Newspoems (Advice to a Corkscrew – The Chaste Town – Visual Soundpoem). *Exit* 5–6, [1968].
British Visual Poetry issue. Poems printed as broadsides and issued in clear polythene bag.

C341   'Heraclitus in Gorky Street: The Theme of Metamorphosis in the Poetry of Andrei Voznesensky' (essay). *Scottish International* 1, January 1968, pp.21–37.
Reprinted in *Essays*, pp.71–8.

C342   'The Show Goes On' (review of M. Bulgakov, *Black Snow*). *Times Literary Supplement* 25 January 1968, p.77.
Unsigned.

C343   Boxers. *Scotsman* 3 February 1968, *weekend scotsman*, p.2.

C344   The Woman. *Sunday Times* 4 February 1968, p.4.

C345   'Guthrie among the bodysnatchers' (review of James Bridie, *The Anatomist* at Citizens' Theatre, Glasgow). *Times* 15 February 1968, p.6.

C346   Two from Homer (*Iliad* 14.1–108 – 17.626–761). *Arion* (Austin, Texas) 7:1, Spring 1968, pp.102–9.
Also issued as an offprint.

C347   *from* Cricket Music (Farewell – . . . on the outlook tower . . . – . . . in the big blue meadow . . .) – The Dreams of the One – Prisons – All for Nothing (all transl. from Lőrinc Szabó). *New Hungarian Quarterly* IX:29, Spring 1968, pp.52–7.

C348   The Flowers of Scotland. *Scottish International* 2, April 1968, p.3.

C349   Shantyman. *Scotsman* 20 April 1968, *weekend scotsman*, p.5.

C350   'On a Slow River' (review of Willa Muir, *Belonging*); 'Life Without Father' (review of Vitaly Syomin, *Seven in One House*). *Times Literary Supplement* 25 April 1965, pp.412; 441.
        Unsigned.

C351   The Computer's First Code Poem, With Rhyme. *Broadsheet* 4, May 1968.

C352   A Too Hot Summer. *'Listener* 79:2042, 16 May 1968, p.631.

C353   'Iain Crichton Smith' (article). *Oban High School Magazine* 13, June 1968, p.31.

C354   '*Poor.Old.Tired.Horse.'* (article on magazine). *Lines Review* 26, Summer 1968, pp.41–2.

C355   What is 'Paradise Lost' *really* about? *College Courant* 20:40, Whitsun [June] 1968, p.13. Printed as advertisement for *The Second Life*.

C356   Tape Mark I (transl. from Nanni Balestrini); 'Note on simulated computer poems'; The Computer's First Christmas Card – The Computer's Second Christmas Card – The Computer's First Code Poem, with Rhyme. *Studio International* [August] 1968, pp.55–6; 57.
        Special issue of *SI*: 'Cybernetic Serendipity: the computer and the arts'; published for exhibition at ICA, 2 August–20 October 1968. 'Code Poem' 1.6 – for 'Z' read 'V'.

C357   Itinerary. *Akros* 3:8, August 1968, p.15.

C358   Huge Voice – Landscapes – The Future – Voices (all transl. from Henri Michaux). *Scottish International* 3, August 1968, pp.6–9.

C359   'If my bones must be handed over' – Old Age (both transl. from Milán Füst). *New Hungarian Quarterly* IX:31, Autumn 1968, pp.167–9.

C360   'Almost Human' (review of M. Bulgakov, *The Heart of a Dog*). *Times Literary Supplement* 5 September 1968, p.937.
        Unsigned.

C361   Drowsing (transl. from Hans Magnus Enzensberger). *Times Literary Supplement* 12 September 1968, p.1020.

C362   'Another point of departure' (review of David Mowat, *Anna-Luse* and Ellen Dryden, *Natural Causes* at Traverse Theatre, Edinburgh). *Times* 7 October 1968, p.6.

C363   Tale about These and Those – Tale about the Morning and the Evening (both transl. from György Somlyó). *New Hungarian Quarterly* IX:32, Winter 1968, pp.157–8.

C364   'Zbigniew Herbert' (essay); [review of Blok's *Twelve*, transl. by Robin Fulton]. *Lines Review* 27, November 1968, pp.4–7; 36–7.
        'Zbigniew Herbert' was reprinted in *Essays*, pp.67–70.

C365   Economic Miracle (transl. from H.M. Enzensberger). *Times Literary Supplement* 7 November 1968, p.1254.

C366   'Plot against words' (review of Jean-Claude van Itallie, *War* and John Guare, *Muzeeka* at Traverse Theatre). *Times* 28 November 1968, p.7.

C367   Message Clear. *South African Outlook* 98:1171, December 1968, p.[183].

C368   A Child's Coat of Many Colours – The Moment of Death. *Unit* (University of Keele) 12, December 1968, p.23.

C369   Floating off to Timor. *Phoenix* (Glasgow University) [?1968/1969], pp.[5–6].
        Poem written March 1968.

                                         1969

C370   Che. *BO HEEM E UM* 4, [?1969], p.[4].

C371   'Three Views of Brooklyn Bridge' (essay on Hart Crane, Mayakovsky and Lorca); Brooklyn Brig (transl. from Mayakovsky) – Sleepless City (transl. from Lorca). *Akros* 3:9, January 1969, pp.38–45; 50–55.
        'Three Views of Brooklyn Bridge' reprinted in *Essays*, pp.43–57.

C372   'Not much beneath the Skin' (review of Rosalyn Drexler, *The Line of Least Existence* at Traverse Theatre, Edinburgh). *Times* 13 January 1969, p.5.

C373   Flag in the Snow (transl. from Magda Gutai) – Gaiety and Good Heart (transl. from Ottó Orbán). *New Hungarian Quarterly* X:33, Spring 1969, pp.63, 140.

C374   Strawberry Fields Forever. *Stereo Headphones* 1:1, Spring 1969, p.[9].

C375   Lord Jim's Ghost's Tiger Poem – At the Television Set – Making a Poem. *Scotsman* 29 March 1969, *weekend scotsman*, p.3.
        Corrections: 'LJGTP' 1.3 – for 'he' read 'we'; 1.18 – for 'out' read 'our'; 'Making a Poem' 1.2 – for 'frosts' read 'frost'; 1.17 – delete 'on'; 1.35 – for 'It comes' read 'It comes,'.

C376   'Mailer Speaking for Himself' (review of *Armies of the Night* and *Miami and the Siege of Chicago*); London. *Scottish International* 6, April 1969, pp.24–8; 45–8.

C377   A Child's Coat of Many Colours – Silver Bird. *neue texte* (Linz) 2, May 1969, pp.[3], [15].
        Correction: p.[3], 1.1 – for 'fest' read 'feet'.

C378   The Quarrel. *Form* 1, Summer 1969, pp.24–5.

C379   Song on the Plain – Separate Time (both transl. from Anna Hajnal) – The Pretty Lass of Komárom (transl. from Anon.). *New Hungarian Quarterly* X:34, Summer 1969, pp.64, 171.

C380   A Stroll in the Country – A Graceful Message of Dismissal (both transl. from Endre Ady). *New Hungarian Quarterly* X:35, Autumn 1969, pp.46–8.

C381   The Computer's First Birthday Card. *Private Library* (2nd Series) 2:3, Autumn 1969, p.99.
As illustration in article by Stuart Mills on Concrete Poetry.

C382   The Loch Ness Monster – The Computer's First Translation. *Second Aeon* 10, [September 1969], pp.23; [inside back cover].
'The Computer's First Translation' was issued as one of six concrete poem cards contained in a clear plastic bag stapled to the inside back cover, as supplement to *SA* 10: yellow card printed in black, 9.8 cms × 15.3 cms. Described as 'one of a series of newspaper found poems'.

C383   [Review of Iain Crichton Smith, *The Last Summer*]. *Scottish International* 7, September 1969, p.61.

C384   'Jealous Energy' (review of J. Kennaway, *The Cost of Living Like This*; Rosemary Tonks, *Businessmen as Lovers*; Joseph Martindale, *Dry Mass*; V.S. Pritchett, *Blind Love and Other Stories*). *Listener* 82:2111, 11 September 1969, pp.352–3.

C385   The Mill. *Listener* 82:2112, 18 September 1969, p.381.

C386   'Imperfect Communication' (review of W. Trevor, *Mrs Eckdorf in O'Neill's Hotel*; Calder Willingham, *Providence Island*; G. Tindall, *Someone Else*; J.C. Oates, *Expensive People*). *Listener* 82:2115, 9 October 1969, p.493.

C387   The Milk-Cart. *Sunday Times* 26 October 1969.

C388   Letter to my Wife – Forced March (both transl. from Miklós Radnóti) – When things fall upwards (transl. from István Eörsi) – Crazed Man in Concentration-Camp (transl. from Ágnes Gergely). *New Hungarian Quarterly* X:36, Winter 1969, pp.42–4, 107, 110.

C389   Rider; [review of I.C. Smith, *From Bourgeois Land*]. *Scottish International* 8, November 1969, pp.15–19; 61.

C390   'Molecules of the Turmoil' (review of P.P. Read, *Monk Dawson*; E.J. Howard, *Something in Disguise*; R. Jones, *A Way Out*; A. Field, *Fractions*). *Listener* 82:2119, 6 November 1969, p.636.

C391   Black and Gold: Olympic Games, 17 October 1968. *Mandate* (University of East Anglia) December 1969, p.2.

C392   'The Crummles at Christmas' (review of *The Melodrama of Nicholas Nickleby as performed by the Vincent Crummles Company*, adapted from Dickens by Caryl Brahms and Ned Sherrin, at the Citizens' Theatre, Glasgow). *Times* 31 December 1969, p.11.

C393   'Making the world tense' (review of T. McGuane, *The Sporting Club*; C. Winton, *Painting for the Show*; R. Dahl, *29 Kisses*). *Listener* 82:2123, 4 December 1969, pp.799–800.

1970

C394   Kierkegaard's Song. *Aquarius* 3, 1970.

C395   Interview (transl. from Gábor Görgey). *Arion* (Budapest) 3, 1970, pp.53–8.

C396   The Apple's Song. *Second Aeon* 11, [1970], p.82.

C397   Afterwards – Friendly Village; [review of Alan Jackson, *The Grim
        Wayfarer* and D. Black, *The Educators*]. *Akros* 4:12, January 1970,
        pp.74; 88–92.

C398   Whisper in the Dark – Moon and Farmstead – Orpheus Killed – In the
        Window-Square – In Memoriam Gyula Juhász – Monkeyland – The
        Lost Parasol (all transl. from Sándor Weöres). *Lines Review* 31, January
        1970, pp.3–17.

C399   'Violent Fruit' (review of Hortense Calisher, *The New Yorkers*; Rudolf
        Wurlitzer, *The Octopus*; Alistair Mair, *The Ripening Time*). *Listener*
        83:2129, 15 January 1970, p.93.

C400   Guy Fawkes Moon. *Mandate* January 1970, p.9.

C401   Thoughts of a Module. *Phoenix* (Glasgow University) January 1970,
        p.[13].

C402   'Vanbrugh restored' (review of *The Provok'd Husband*, Arts Theatre
        Group, Glasgow University). *Times* 23 January 1970, p.9.

C403   'Translator's Tightrope: Review Article' (review of [*Delos:*] *A Journal on
        and of Translation*, ed. D.S. Carne-Ross; and Theodore Savory, *The Art
        of Translation*). *New Edinburgh Review* 5, February 1970, pp.33–4.
        Contents title: 'The Translator's Tightrope'.

C404   By the Fire. *Onyx* 3, February 1970.
        Poster poem on yellow paper printed in black, orange and blue.
        40.75 cms × 30.6 cms.
        Onyx 3 was issued in the form of a folder containing duplicated
        sheets.

C405   Visual Soundpoem – Newspoem: Sick Man. *Scottish International* 9,
        February 1970, pp.46, 52.

C406   'Dystopias and Eutopias' (review of Yevgeny Zamyatin, *We* and Barry
        Cole, *The Search for Rita*). *Listener* 83:2132, 5 February 1970, p.190.
        Letter from Robin Milner-Gulland commenting on review, *Listener*
        83:2133, 12 February 1970, p.218.

C407   The Bliss of Sunday (transl. from László Nagy) – To be Poor (transl.
        from Ottó Orbán). *New Hungarian Quarterly* XI:37, Spring 1970,
        pp.106–13, 113.

C408   Blues and Peal: Concrete 1969. *Stereo Headphones* 1:2–3, Spring 1970,
        [inside back cover]. Also De Luxe edition of *SH*, with handwritten
        colour poem, 'Dapple' inserted.

C409   The Curtain. *Broadsheet* 10, [March 1970].

C410   'Speeding' (review of A. Kavan, *Julie and the Bazooka*; J. Elliott, *Another
        Example of Indulgence*; C. Kersh, *The Aggravations of Minnie Ashe*; V.
        Frolov, *What it's all about*). *Listener* 83:2137, 12 March 1970, p.351.

C411   'Don't Damn Him with Daffodils' (essay). *Glasgow Herald* 4 April
        1970, p.6.
        Reprinted in *Essays*, pp.130–34, as 'Wordsworth in 1970'.

C412 'Was he mad?' (review of Campbell Black, *The Puctual Rape*; I.C. Smith, *Survival Without Error*; Giles Gordon, *Pictures from an Exhibition*; Leonard Cohen, *Beautiful Losers*). *Listener* 83:2141, 9 April 1970, p.488.

C413 Pest Elegy – It Doesn't Count (both transl. from István Vas). *New Hungarian Quarterly* XI:38, Summer 1970.

C414 Letters of Mr Lonelyhearts: 1. *Transatlantic Review* 36, Summer [July] 1970, pp.69–70.

C415 'New England Baroque' (review of F. Bluecher, *The Entrance to Porlock*; M. Haltrecht, *The Edgware Road*; D. Cilento, *Hybrid*; J. Woolf, *Emma with Objects*; P. Chaplin, *A Lonely Diet*). *Listener* 84:2153, 2 July 1970, p.24.

C416 'Brooklyn Boys' (review of J. Neugeborn, *Corky's Brother*; A. Huth, *Nowhere Girl*; R. Cook, *A State of Denmark*; W. Sheed, *The Critic*; L.G. Gibbon, *Spartacus*). *Listener* 84:2157, 30 July 1970, p.157.

C417 'Can the thistle change its spots?' (article on Scotland). *Planet* 1, August/September 1970, pp.9–13.

C418 '1980' (review of A. Mitchell, *The Bodyguard*; B. Rees, *Diminishing Circles*; H. Tracy, *The Butterflies of Province*). *Listener* 84:2161, 27 August 1970, p.284.

C419 The Nameless – Legacy – Another Law (all transl. from Sándor Rákos). *New Hungarian Quarterly* XI:39, Autumn 1970, pp.74–5.

C420 The Computer's First Dialect Poems: The Furze Kidder's Bating (Northamptonshire) – The Birkie and the Howdie (Lowland Scots). *Wave* 1, Autumn 1970, pp.20–21.

C421 The D.I.Y. Scottishness Test Kit Poem. *Infringe* September 1970.

C422 'Private Flashpoints' (review of R. Fuller, *The Carnal Island*; M. Hastings, *Tansy is me*; T. de V. White, *The March Hare*; M. Orsler, *The Big Dig*). *Listener* 84:2165, 24 September 1970, p.428.

C423 De Profundis – Despair – Instead of an Autobiography (all transl. from László Kálnoky). *New Hungarian Quarterly* XI:40, Winter 1970, pp.54–6.

C424 'The Cenci' (review of Artaud, *The Cenci* at Close Theatre, Glasgow). *Gambit* 5:17, November 1970, pp.75–6.

C425 The Moment of Death. *neue texte* 5 & 6, November 1970, p.[56].

C426 'Ravine of horror' (review of A. Anatoli [Kuznetsov], *Babi Yar*); 'From Blok to Yevtushenko' (review of A. Blok, *The Twelve*, transl. by J. Stallworthy and P. France; *The New Russian Poets 1953–1968*, ed. and transl. by George Reavey; *The Poetry of Yevgeny Yevtushenko*, ed. and transl. by G. Reavey; Yevtushenko, *Idut belye snegi*; A. Voznesensky, *Antiworlds and the Fifth Ace*; Leonid Martynov, *Lyudskiye imena*; Yevgeni Vinokurov, *Zrelishcha*; Rimma Kazakova, *Yelki zelyonye*; Rasul Gamzatov, *Chotki let*). *Times Literary Supplement* 27 November 1970, pp.1377; 1389–90.
    Unsigned.

C427   'The Bicentenary' (article on Glasgow University in 2070). *College Courant* 22:45, Martinmas [December] 1970, pp.36–8.
       Reprinted in *Essays*, pp.249–54.

C428   The Fleas. *Crab Grass* (Belfast) 3, December 1970, p.[3].

C429   Found Poem: White Quartz. *Son of Phoenix* [December 1970].
       Contents of magazine printed on separate sheets in stapled envelope.

C430   'Favourite Islands' (review of K. Williamson, *The Atlantic Islands*; D. Cooper, *Skye*; P.A. Macnab, *The Isle of Mull*; R. MacLellan, *The Isle of Arran*). *Listener* 84:2179, 31 December 1970, p.918.

                                    1971

C431   'Towards a Literary History of Scotland' (article). *Scottish Literary News* 1:2, January 1971, pp.37–40.

C432   'Registering the Reality of Scotland' (essay). *Planet* 4, February/March 1971, pp.43–7.
       Reprinted in *Essays*, pp.153–7.

C433   'At the eleventh hour' (review of M. Bulgakov, *The White Guard*). *Times Literary Supplement* 5 February 1971, p.144.
       Unsigned.

C434   The First Men on Mercury. *Listener* 85:2186, 18 February 1971, p.206.

C435   Le Journal (transl. from Sándor Weöres). *New Hungarian Quarterly* XII:41, Spring 1971, pp.67–72.

C436   Zoo – Rainbow. *Stereo Headphones* 4, Spring 1971, pp.[32–3].

C437   Death in Duke Street. *Phoenix* (Glasgow University) [March 1971], p.[1].

C438   'Up the allegorical river' (review of Robert Jones, *Ratnose*). *Times Literary Supplement* 7 March 1971, p.241.
       Unsigned.

C439   Estranged. *Folio* (Glasgow School of Art) 4, April 1971, p.[32].

C440   'Critic as poet' (review of A.D. Hope, *A Midsummer Eve's Dream* and *Dunciad Minor*). *Times Literary Supplement* 9 April 1971, p.418.
       Unsigned.

C441   'Friends in Flux' (review of P. Callow, *Flesh of the Morning*; S. Brata, *Confessions of an Indian Woman Eater*; D. Stivens, *A Horse of Air*; J. Mossman, *Lifelines*). *Listener* 85:2196, 29 April 1971, p.559.

C442   [Instamatics:] Glasgow 5 March 1971 ('With a ragged') – Glasgow 5 March 1971 ('Quickly the magistrate') – Nice 5 March 1971 – Belfast 5 March 1971 – Bedfordshire 5 March 1971 – Renfrewshire 5 March 1971. *Lon Chaney* [1, May 1971, three unnumbered pages].

C443   The Fifth Gospel. *Scottish International* 14, May 1971, pp.22–3.

C444   newspaper poems (found concrete poem: the enactment – an unpublished poem by zukofsky). *Second Aeon* 13 [May 1971], p.29.

C445   FROM THE ARCHIVES OF F.L.U.F.F. (Federation of Lovers of

Undiscovered Forces and Frontiers). *Second Aeon* 14, [?Summer 1971], p.104.

> Corrections: 1.9 – add ' after 'place.'; 1.11 – add ' after 'fluff.'; 1.23 – for 'Well's' read 'Wells's'.

C446　Death in Duke Street – Heron – The Dolphin's Song – Hyena – The Gourds – Last Message – Zoo. *Spirit* (Seton Hall University, South Orange, N.J.) XXXVIII:2, Summer 1971, pp.20–26.

> 'Ten Scottish Poets' issue.
> Correction: 'Death in Duke Street' 1.7 – for 'Wrang' read 'wrang'.

C447　'Creative Writing and the University' (article). *College Courant* 23:46, Whitsun [June] 1971, pp.17–18.

C448　'President Chance' (review of J. Kosinski, *Being There*; J. Fortune and J. Wells, *A Melon for Ecstasy*; M. Jones, *Mr Armitage isn't back yet*; P. Theroux, *Jungle Lovers*; J. Hone, *The Private Sector*). *Listener* 85:2202, 10 June 1971, p.760.

C449　Last Message. *Ariel* (University of Calgary) 2:3, July 1971, p.59.

C450　'North London Christmas' (review of S. Mackay, *An Advent Calendar*; A. Bloomfield, *Life for a Life*; C. Glyn, *The Tower and the Rising Tide*; S. Lauder, *Camp Commander*; A. Wesker, *Six Sundays in January*). *Listener* 85:2206, 8 July 1971, p.56.

C451　Quatrains (transl. from Rasul Gamzatov). *Broadsheet* 12, [August 1971].

C452　'Dublin Pride' (review of T. de V. White, *Mr Stephen*; E. Davie, *Creating a Scene*; A.L. Barker, *Femina Real*). *Listener* 86:2210, 5 August 1971, p.185.

C453　'A Courageous Gesture' (review of *Primer of experimental poetry 1, 1870–1922*, ed. E. Lucie-Smith). *Library Review* 23:3, Autumn 1971, pp.118–19.

C454　The Nightingale (transl. from Yevgeny Vinokurov) – You Must Live! – The Sheepskin Coat (both transl. from Leonid Martynov). *Stand* 12:3, [Autumn] 1971, pp.56–7.

C455　[Letter on the possibility of a writers' union]. *Scottish International* September 1971, p.18.

C456　'Young too late' (review of M. Richler, *St Urbain's Horseman*; E. Taylor, *Mrs Palfrey at the Claremont*). *Listener* 86:2214, 2 September 1971, p.312.

C457　'Dicey' (review of L. Rhinehart, *Dice Man*; B. Rubens, *Sunday Best*; M. Bragg, *The Nerve*; P.P. Read, *The Professor's Daughter*; I. Litvinov, *She Knew She was Right*). *Listener* 86:2218, 30 September 1971, p.453.

C458　'Hi-Fi in Vietnam' (review of Len Deighton, *Declarations of War*; S. Raven, *Sound the Retreat*; S. Hill, *Strange Meeting*). *Listener* 86:2222, 28 October 1971, p.593.

C459　'New Poetry' (review of *Caribbean Voices*, comp. John Figueroa; Alice V. Stuart, *The Unquiet Tide*; P.A. Stalker, *The Elephant, the Tiger and the Gentle Kangaroo*). *Library Review* 23:4, Winter 1971, p.164.

C460   Voyage – After Us – Deep Sea (all transl. from István Kormos). *New Hungarian Quarterly* XII:44, Winter 1971, pp.35–7.

C461   'James Bridie'. *Scottish International* November 1971, pp.22–6.
        Text of talk given to the English Association, November 1967.
        Reprinted in *Essays*, pp.232–41.

C462   On Arran. *Scottish Literary News* 2:1, November 1971, p.26.

C463   'War without action' (review of H. Wouk, *The Winds of War*; J.
        Gillespie, *A Disappointment in Love*; E. Cooper, *The Overman Culture*;
        J.T. Story, *The Wind in the Snottygobble Tree*). *Listener* 86:2226, 25
        November 1971, p.738.

1972

C464   Stobhill. *Glasgow University Magazine* 83:1, [January 1972], pp.21–5.

C465   'Bereavements' (review of D. Cook, *Albert's Memorial*; J. Johnston, *The
        Captains and the Kings*; S. Selvon, *Those who eat the Cascadura*). *Listener*
        87:2235, 27 January 1972, p.120.

C466   Instamatic London July 1971 – Instamatic Budapest Undated
        (Reported April 1971) – Instamatic Germany December 1970. *Scottish
        International* 5:1, January 1972, p.84.

C467   'Glimpses of a cloud in trousers' (review of Wiktor Woroszylski, *The
        Life of Mayakovsky* and Y. Yevtushenko, *Stolen Apples*). *Glasgow Herald* 5
        February 1972, Saturday Extra, p.II.

C468   'World's End' (review of B. Hines, *First Signs*; A. Waugh, *A Bed of
        Flowers*; B. Killick, *The Nannies*). *Listener* 87:2239, 24 February 1972,
        pp.252–3.

C469   [Participating in 'The State of Poetry – A Symposium']. *The Review* 29–
        30, Spring-Summer 1972, pp.53–5.
            Answering questions: '1. What, in your view, have been the most (a)
            encouraging, (b) discouraging features of the poetry scene during the
            past decade? 2. What developments do you hope to see during the
            next decade?'

C470   'Into the Constellation: Some Thoughts on the Origin and Nature of
        Concrete Poetry'; Two Newspoems: A Definite Article – The Com-
        puter's First Translation. *Akros* 6:18, March 1972, pp.3–18; 19–20.
        'Into the Constellation' was reprinted in *Essays*, pp.20–34.

C471   The Gourds. *Scottish Literary News* 2:2 & 3, March 1972, p.52.

C472   'Empty-Hearted Labyrinths' (review of E. Figes, *B*; H. Fleetwood, *A
        Painter of Flowers*; A. Grey, *A Man Alone*; V. Bykov, *The Ordeal*). *Listener*
        87:2243, 23 March 1972, p.393.

C473   [Review of Pete Brown, *Old Pals Act*]. *Scottish International* 5:4, April
        1972, pp.36–7.

C474   'Psophie' (review of R. Tonks, *The Halt during the Chase*; S. Clayton,
        Sabbatical; C. Storr, *Black God, White God*; E. Jenkins, *Dr Gully*; J.
        Blish, *The Day after Judgment*; F. MacColla, *The Albannach*). *Listener*
        87:2247, 20 April 1972, p.524.

C475   I (First Section) – Grief (both transl. from Mayakovsky) – Christmas Eve. *Broadsheet* 14, [May 1972].

C476   strangeler *(from* Interferences). *Crab Grass* 5, [May 1972].

C477   'Brownstone study' (review of L.J. Davis, *A Meaningful Life*; P. Kitchen, *Paradise*; Amos Oz, *My Michael*). *Listener* 87:2251, 18 May 1972, p.660.

C478   Glasgow Sonnets (i – ii – vi – v). *Stand* 13:2, [Summer] 1972, p.15.

C479   [Answer to questionnaire on 'typographical problems in concrete poetry]; The Computer's First Christmas Card – instamatic london june 1970. *Second Aeon* 15 [June] 1972, pp.40; 41, 93.

C480   Instamatic: Aviemore, Invernessshire, August 1971 – Instamatic: Mougins, Provence, September 1971 – Instamatic: Heaven, September 1971 AD – Instamatic: Nigeria, Undated (reported October 1971). *Decal* 1, [July 1972], pp.51–4.

C481   'The Resources of Scotland' (essay); Glasgow Sonnets (iii – iv – vii – ix – x). *Times Literary Supplement* 28 July 1972, pp.885–6; 886.
    'The Resources of Scotland' was 4th in a series, 'The Sense of Place' and was reprinted in *Essays*, pp.158–65, with the correction indicated in *TLS* 4 August 1972, p.919.

C482   'Olsen and Olson' (letter). *Times Literary Supplement* 4 August 1972, p.919.
    On misspelling of Olson in article 'The Resources of Scotland', *TLS* 28 July 1972, p.885.

C483   instamatic vienna december 1971 – instamatic london november 1971 – instamatic san pedro bay los angeles july 1971. *Second Aeon* 16/17, [?Autumn] 1972, pp.135–6.

C484   17 Instamatic Poems: Fallin Stirlingshire October 1970 – Kishinev USSR November 1970 – Shrewsbury February 1971 – London March 1971 – Edinburgh March 1971 – Campobasso Italy Undated (Reported March 1971) – Fort Benning Georgia April 1971 – Venice April 1971 – Chicago May 1971 – Burma June 1971 – London June 1971 – Innsbruck July 1971 – Mid-Atlantic July 1971 – Bangaon India July 1971 – Leatherhead Surrey September 1971 – Manchester Undated (Reported September 1971) – Washington September 1971 – The Barrow: a dialogue. *Lines Review* 42 & 43, September 1972 – February 1973, pp.15–26.

C485   Two Instamatic Poems: Glasgow October 1971 – Naples February 1972. *Broadsheet* 15, September 1972.

C486   [Quotation in] 'Commentary'. *Times Literary Supplement* 15 September 1972, p.1059.
    The article (on poetry) quotes EM as anxious to see even more 'poems in three dimensions in public places . . .'.

C487   Instamatic: Ellingham Suffolk January 1972 – Bangkok [February 1972] – Rockall Invernessshire [June 1972]. *Samphire* 2:1, October 1972, pp.2–3.

C488   Antonioni – Grierson. *Phoenix* [November 1972], pp.8–9.

C489   Six Instamatic Poems: Milan Undated Reported October 1971 – Seend
        Wiltshire April 1972 – Glasgow November 1971 – Nullarbor Plain
        South Australia January 1972 – Truk Lagoon Undated Reported
        February 1972 – Bradford June 1972. *Akros* 7:20, December 1972,
        pp.11–13.

                                    1973

C490   'Notes on the Poet's Working Day'; Instamatics (London August 1972
        – Italy Undated Reported November 1972 – Darmstadt September
        1972 – Brisbane November 1972 – Dona Ema Brazil April 1972 –
        Glasgow October 1972). *Ambit* 54, 1973, pp.29–31; 52–3.
        'Edwin Morgan and Jim Burns participated in a symposium organ-
        ised by Ambit for the London Borough of Camden . . . on The Poet's
        Life – 1972 Style' (note on p.29). EM's notes were written on 11
        November 1972.

C491   Le Journal (transl. from Sándor Weöres). *Chapman* II:4, 1973,
        pp.[24–8].

C492   [Review of D.K.C. Todd, *Nuns on the Beach*]. *Durham University
        Journal* 1973.

C493   instamatic vienna december 1971 – instamatic london november 1971
        – instamatic san pedro bay los angeles july 1971. *Second Aeon* 16 & 17,
        1973, pp.135–6.

C494   Godard. *Ostrich* (Whitley Bay) 7, January 1973, p.[24].

C495   Instamatic Andes Mountains December 1972. *Machars '73* [February]
        1973, p.19.

C496   Wallpaper and Shadows (transl. from Sándor Weöres). *Lines Review* 44,
        March 1973, p.4.

C497   [Review of *Vladimir Mayakovsky: Poems*, transl. by Dorian Rottenberg].
        Ostrich 8, April 1973, pp.[44–5].

C498   Kurosawa – Godard. *Phoenix* (G.U. Lit. Soc.) April 1973, pp.6–7.

C499   Instamatic: Walt Disney World Florida October 1972 – London
        November 1972 – Venice September 1972 – Calne Wiltshire March
        1971. *Scottish Literary News* 3:1, April 1973, pp.29–31.

C500   'What I like about "Wirraw" '. *Wirraw* (St Mungo's Academy) [2], May
        1973, [inside back cover].

C501   the flowers of scotland – instamatic [London January 1973]. *Iron* 2,
        Summer 1973, pp.4–5.

C502   The Madman – This speculation . . . . – 'Every flower . . . .' – The Poets
        of the 19th Century – The Puszta, in Winter – Among the Hills – A
        Bush to the Storm – 'Ruined garden there . . . .' – At the End of the
        Year (all transl. from Sándor Petőfi). *New Hungarian Quarterly* XIV:50,
        Summer 1973, pp.108–19.

C503 'Edwin Morgan writes . . . .'. *Poetry Book Society Bulletin* 77, Summer
1973, p.[1].
On *From Glasgow to Saturn*, a PBS choice. Reprinted in *Poetry Book
Society: the first twenty-five years*, edited by Eric W. White (London:
Poetry Book Society, 1979), p.51.

C504 [Letter on Anne Cluysenaar's review of *Wi the Haill Voice* in *Stand* 14:1,
1973]. *Stand* 14:2, [?Summer] 1973, p.61.

C505 The Han Princess. *Wave* 7, Summer 1973, p.17.

C506 Bella Akhmadulina – Violets – Italian Garage (all transl. from
Voznesensky). *Aegis* (Cambridge) 1, June 1973, pp.3–6.

C507 School's Out. *High School of Glasgow Magazine* LXXII, June 1973,
pp.28–30.
'We are indebted to Mr Edwin G. Morgan . . . who was once an
Editor of this Magazine, for a group of four poems . . . that were
specially written for our readers' (editorial, p.13).

C508 [Review of Paul Celan, *Selected Poems* and C.P. Cavafy, *Passions and
Ancient Days*]. *Lines Review* 45, June 1973, pp.59–61.

C509 'The novels of Robin Jenkins examined' (review-article on *A Far Cry
from Bowmore*). *Listener* 90:2311, 12 July 1973, pp.58–9.
Reprinted in *Essays*, pp.242–5, as 'The Novels of Robin Jenkins'.

C510 School's Out. *Aquarius* 6 (Scottish number), September 1973, pp.63–6.
The poem 'fathoms deep my love' on p.55 is erroneously attributed to
EM. A note in *Aquarius* 7, 1974, p.109, reads: 'APOLOGIES: To
Edwin Morgan. The poem . . . was linked by our error to his name.
Will the real author please step forward and we can apologise to him,
also.'

C511 'Bob Tait: an appreciation'. *Scottish International* 6:7, September 1973,
p.28.
On Tait's giving up editorship of *SI*.

C512 Dialogue of Hamlet and his Conscience – August: asters (both transl.
from Marina Tsvetayeva). *Broadsheet* 19 [October 1973].

C513 Red War / Pink Peace. *Pink Peace* (Folkestone) 9, Winter 1973–74,
p.27.
Title transposed.

C514 'A Scots Quartette' (review of Tom Leonard, *Poems*; Robin Hamilton,
Poems; James Kelman, *An Old Pub near the Angel*; John Herdman, *A
Truth Lover*). *Eboracum* (York) 17, Winter 1973, pp.14–15.

C515 The Round – INSTAMATIC London October 1973 – INSTAMATIC
Sydney Australia September 1973 – INSTAMATIC Palo Alto California Undated Reported July 1971 – Reversals. *Fuse* 4, November 1973,
pp.46–8.

C516 Memories of Earth. *Akros* 8:23, December 1973, pp.15–23.

1974

C517 from The New Divan: 54–61. *Ambit* 60, 1974, pp.13–15.

C518   Fragment from *The New Divan* [37]. *Aquarius* 7, 1974, p.26.

C519   lévi-strauss at the lie-detector – wittgenstein on egdon heath. *Second Aeon* 19–21, [1974], pp.103–4.

C520   The Return of the Chief (transl. from Tsvetayeva). *Broadsheet* 20, [March 1974].

C521   The Blue Seesaw – Instamatic New York 1971 – Sir Henry Morgan's Song. *The Little Word Machine* 4/5, April 1974, pp.52–3.

C522   Craftsmen – Baffling Picture – Young Horseman – Like This – Snapshot – I am with you (transl. from Kassák). *New Hungarian Quarterly* XV:54, Summer 1974, pp.93–6.

C523   'Comments Flying Southwards'; Treated Found Poem: The Awakening (from David Gray's poem 'My Epitaph') – Three Found Poems from Cowper's Letters (My Uncle – My Dog – My Greenhouse) – Three Found Poems from 'Tramps across Watersheds' by A.S. Alexander (Glasgow, 1925) (Dunbar Highway at Night – 'Jock Tamson's Bairns' at Dawn – Gowrie in the Gloamin') – Ten Newspoems (Charon's Song – Aere Perennius – Said the Pigeon – Pigeons: Elizabethan – Lunar Module – Revolt of the Elements – Notice in Heaven – Unpublished Poems by Creeley: 6 – Epitaph – Hair-Raising). *Stereo Headphones* 6, Summer 1974, pp.38; 39–41.
        Reviewed in *Kontexts* 6 & 7, 1975.

C524   Scene – Vico's Song – By the Preaching of the Word. *Broadsheet* 21, June 1974.

C525   The Drum. *Limestone* June 1974, p.9.
        Earlier 'uncorrected' version.

C526   10 Poems from The New Divan (21–30). *The New Review* 1:3, June 1974, pp.34–6.

C527   Poems from The New Divan (62–4). *The Honest Ulsterman* 44/45, August/October 1974, pp.40–41.

C528   10 Theatre Poems: The Drum – The Chorus – The Mask – The Fan – The Skomorokh – The Shadow – The Soliloquy – The Codpiece – The Hanamichi – The Spirit of Theatre. *Akros* 9:25, August 1974, pp.3–9.

C529   'Homeward bound' (review of *Selected Letters of Edwin Muir*, ed. P.H. Butter). *New Review* 1:5, August 1974, pp.74–76.

C530   Poems from The New Divan: 43–6. *Weighbauk* 2, August 1974, pp.[4–5].

C531   Seven poems from The New Divan (47–53). *Lines Review* 50, September 1974, pp.5–7.

C532   'Political theory and poetic licence' (review of E.J. Brown, *Mayakovsky: A Poet in the Revolution*; Marina Tsvetayeva, *Selected Poems*; Bella Akhmadulina, *Fever and other new poems*; Viktor Bokov, *Izbrannoye*; Boris Slutsky, *Godovaya strelka*; Y. Yevtushenko, *Stolen Apples*; Andrei Voznesensky, *Ten' zvuka*; *The Living Mirror: five young poets from Leningrad*, ed. Suzanne Massie). *Times Literary Supplement* 11 October 1974, pp.1132–3.

C533　The Blue Tenniel. *The Blue Tunnel* [December 1974].
　　　　Single A4 sheet. Signed 'Edwin Morgan' but not EM's signature.

C534　'The Poetry of Robert Louis Stevenson'. *Scottish Literary Journal* 1:2,
　　　　December 1974, pp.29–44.
　　　　The Edinburgh Stevenson Lecture 1970. Reprinted in *Essays*,
　　　　pp.135–49.

C535　'The dark side of Fairyland' (review of I. and P. Opie, *The Classic Fairy
　　　　Tales*). *Times Literary Supplement* 6 December 1974, p.1371.

C536　Poems from The New Divan (37–40). *Poetry Book Society Poetry
　　　　Supplement* Christmas 1974.

1975

C537　'Newspoems' (on their composition); [Newspoems:] Aere Perennius – O
　　　　For a Life of Sensations – Mosaicist with a Book – Wach Auf, Du Christ
　　　　– Holy Flying Saucer Satori – A Levitation of the Trinity – Unpublished
　　　　Poem by Creeley – Idyll. *Graphic Lines* (Preston Polytechnic School of
　　　　Art and Design) 1, 1975, pp.47–8; 49–54.

C538　[Contribution to] 'The lasting impact of Goodsir Smith' (obituary of
　　　　Sydney Goodsir Smith). *Glasgow Herald* 17 January 1975, p.2.

C539　'Psychopathology of literary life' (review of Iain Crichton Smith,
　　　　Goodbye, Mr Dixon). *Times Literary Supplement* 17 January 1975, p.48.

C540　The Barrow: A Dialogue – Six Instamatics (Glasgow 'With a ragged
　　　　diamond' – Glasgow 'Quickly the magistrate' – Nice 'White curtains' –
　　　　Belfast 'A boy burns' – Bedfordshire 'A Pakistani' – Renfrewshire 'Some
　　　　men stand round') – Stobhill – The Fifth Gospel. *The Literary Review*
　　　　(Fairleigh Dickinson University, New Jersey) 18:3, Spring 1975,
　　　　pp.265–79.

C541　Poems from THE NEW DIVAN (73–8). *Meridian* 6, Spring 1975,
　　　　pp.16–18.

C542　Glasgow Sonnets i, x. *Phoenix* 13 (incorporating 14/15, Poets' Work-
　　　　sheets Section), Spring 1975, pp.61–2.
　　　　Includes reproduction of MS. draft of each poem.

C543　The New Divan 81–2. *Broadsheet* 23, March 1975.

C544　20 poems from The New Divan (1–20). *Poetry Review* 65:2 & 3, [March]
　　　　1975, pp.142–51.

C545　'Up the allegorical river' (review of Robert Jones, *Ratnose*). *Times
　　　　Literary Supplement* 7 March 1975, p.241.

C546　6 poems from The New Divan (65–70). *Akros* 9:27, April 1975,
　　　　pp.75–6.

C547　Poems from The New Divan (73–80). *Oasis* (Glasgow University) [1,
　　　　April 1975], pp.32–4.

C548　'At fever pitch' (review of Yevgeny Zamyatin, *The Dragon and other
　　　　stories*). *Times Literary Supplement* 18 April 1975, p.422.

C549　The New Divan 71–2. *Sphinx* (Liverpool University) [May 1975].

C550 'Sorting out the aliens' (review of Arkadi and Boris Strugatski, *Hard to be a God*). *Times Literary Supplement* 23 May 1975, p.555.

C551 'The healer's art' (review of M. Bulgakov, *The Country Doctor's Notebook*). *Times Literary Supplement* 30 May 1975, p.584.

C552 Afterwards. *Calgacus* 1:2, Summer 1975, p.48.

C553 Chile – The Apparition – Report on the Poem – The Ladies of Bygone Days (all transl. from Ottó Orbán) – Silent Prayer of Peasants – Holiday-Afternoon Rhapsody – Confession of Faith – Small Craftsman (all transl. from Imre Csánadi). *New Hungarian Quarterly* XVI:58, Summer 1975, pp.85–9, 109–13.

C554 Poems from The New Divan (38–42). *Iron* 9, June/August 1975, pp.12–13.
      Corrections: 38 – put last 7 lines after 1.3; 42, 1.7 – for 'my' read 'the' and insert 'God / I'm glad my phone's booked' before 'This'; delete comma in last line.

C555 'Party man's progress' (review of Vladimir Maximov, *The Seven Days of Creation*). *Times Literary Supplement* 13 June 1975, p.643.

C556 We just sit about quietly – For the Record – Lenin – About the Hero-Equation – Inventory (all transl. from Mihály Ladányi). *New Hungarian Quarterly* XVI:59, Autumn 1975, pp.69–73.

C557 Ode: To My Socks – Ode: Boy with Hare (transl. from Neruda). *Chapman* 3:3, [September] 1975, pp.14–17.

C558 'Between language and science' (review of *The Admirable Urquhart: Selected Writings*, ed. Richard Boston). *Times Literary Supplement* 24 October 1975, p.1254.

C559 Rhapsody on Time (transl. from István Simon). *New Hungarian Quarterly* XVI:60, Winter 1975, pp.60–3.

C560 'Belli in translation' (letter). *Times Literary Supplement* 7 November 1975, p.1332.
      Answering Anthony Burgess who had claimed (*TLS* 31 October 1975, p.1296) that Belli's sonnets had never been translated.

C561 Warhol. *Asphalt Garden* 3, [December 1975], p.10.

C562 'Extensive horizons' (review of C. Sansom, *An English Year*; B. Jones, *The Spitfire on the Northern Line*; T. Blackburn, *The Devil's Kitchen*; J. Heath-Stubbs, *A Parliament of Birds*). *Times Literary Supplement* 5 December 1975, p.1452.

1976

C563 The girls are loved – Balance – Oh life (transl. from Kassák). *The Hungarian P.E.N.* 17, 1976.

C564 Chicago North Side – Cook in Hawaii. *Words Broadsheet* 25, 1976.

C565 Song of Opposites – Swallow Song. *Words Broadsheet* 30, [1976].

C566 A Girl. *Oasis* 1:3, [February 1976], p.2.

C567 'A Russian in New York' (review of Arthur A. Cohen, *A Hero in his Time*). *Times Literary Supplement* 27 February 1976, p.213.

C568 In Hungarian (transl. from Gábor Garai). *New Hungarian Quarterly* XVII:61, Spring 1976, p.182.

C569 The World. *The Scottish Review* 1:2, Spring 1976, pp.10–11.

C570 [Review of *For Sydney Goodsir Smith*; S.G. Smith, *Collected Poems*; A. Fowler, *Catacomb Suburb*]. *Lines Review* 57, March 1976, pp.40–43.

C571 'Growing up alien' (review of David Markish, *The Beginning*). *Times Literary Supplement* 23 April 1976, p.481.

C572 Stobhill – The Old Man and the Sea – From the Domain of Arnheim. *Nagyvilág* (Budapest) 21:5, May 1976.
Translated into Hungarian.

C573 Wind in the Crescent (transl. from Montale) – In Me Is Daith (transl. from Michelangelo). *Lallans* 6, Whitsunday 1976, p.19.

C574 'End of the affair' (review of Philip Callow, *The Story of My Desire*). *Times Literary Supplement* 21 May 1976, p.601.

C575 The Third House (I – III – IV – VII – IX) (transl. from Amy Károlyi). *New Hungarian Quarterly* XVII:62, Summer 1976, pp.27–30.

C576 The Divide – Smoke – The Beginning – The Planets – The Question – Resurrections. *Perfect Bound* [1], Summer 1976, pp.50–55.

C577 'Fieldfares and fox-reek' (review of Ted Hughes, *Season Songs*). *Times Literary Supplement* 16 July 1976, pp.882–3.

C578 'Siege mentalities' (review of Victor Serge, *Conquered City*). *Times Literary Supplement* 30 July 1976, p.951.

C579 'The Poetry of T.S. Law' (review of *Abbey Craig tae Stirlin Castle*; *Aftentymes a Tinkler*; *Whyles a Targe*). *Akros* 11:31, August 1976, pp.93–6.

C580 Warning Poem – Shaker Shaken. *Words* 1, Autumn 1976, pp.48–9.

C581 'Forgotten?' (letter). *Times Literary Supplement* 17 September 1976, p.1168.
In answer to letter from Frank Taylor in *TLS* 10 September 1976, p.1117 on names from Thomas Urquhart's *Trissotetras* listed in Alastair Fowler's poem 'Forgotten' in *TLS* 20 August 1976, p.1034.

C582 The Horse Dies The Birds Fly Away (transl. from Lajos Kassák) – Pest Elegy – It doesn't count (both transl. from István Vas). *Lines Review* 59, September 1976, pp.7–22, 33–6.

C583 'One: two: three:' (review of Robert Creeley, *Mabel: A Story and Other Prose*). *Times Literary Supplement* 15 October 1976, p.1307.

C584 Adventures of the Anti-Sage (In the Country – Subsea – Electronic – Imprisoned). *Perfect Bound* [2], Winter 1976–7, pp.20–23.

C585 from THE NEW DIVAN (91–100). *Singe* 5, Winter 1976–77, ff.[16–20].

C586 'The Translation of Poetry' (essay). *Scottish Review* 2:5, Winter 1976, pp.18–23.

C587   Poems from the New Divan: 83–90. *Palantir* 4, November 1976,
        pp.3–6.

C588   'Nivols' (review of Miguel de Unamuno, *Novela/Nivola* and *Ficciones:
        Four Stories and a Play*). *Listener* 96:2487, 9 December 1976,
        pp.750–51.

C589   'A fresh look at James Hogg' (review of Douglas Gifford, *James Hogg* and
        James Hogg, *The Brownie of Bodsbeck*, ed. D.A. Mack). *Q* 19 November
        1976, pp.9–10.

C590   'Edwin Morgan: An Interview by Marshall Walker'; Unfinished Poems:
        A Sequence for Veronica Forrest-Thomson. *Akros* 11:32, December
        1976, pp.3–23; 25–35.
            The interview includes the texts of 'French Persian Cats Having a
        Ball', 'Centaur', 'Siesta of a Hungarian Snake', 'Instamatic Shrews-
        bury February 1971', 'Instamatic Heaven September 1971 AD' and
        'Oban Girl'. The interview was published separately by Akros
        Publications in 1977. On p.25 there is a note on Veronica Forrest-
        Thomson by EM.

C591   'The louring Highlands' (review of Neil Gunn, *The Grey Coast*; *Morning
        Tide*; *Young Art and Old Hector*; *The Green Isle of the Great Deep*). *Times
        Literary Supplement* 3 December 1976, p.1504.

1977

C592   The Rock. *Aquarius* 9, 1977, p.47.

C593   'I am a Siberian' – Incantation (both transl. from Yevtushenko). *Poetry
        and Audience* 23, 1977, pp.10–12.

C594   Six Waiting Poems: The Men – The Women – The Children – The Dog
        – The Worlds – The Poet. *Lines Review* 60, January 1977, pp.32–5.

C595   [Contribution to] 'What they read in '77'. *7 Days* 13 January 1977,
        p.6.

C596   'Neither here nor there' (review of S. Beckett and others, *New Writing
        and Writers*). *Times Literary Supplement* 21 January 1977, p.49.

C597   'Political Pound' (review of C. David Heymann, *Ezra Pound: The Last
        Rower*; Eugene P. Nassar, *The Cantos of Ezra Pound*; *Understand the
        Weapon, Understand the Wound: Selected writings of John Cornford with some
        letters of Frances Cornford*, ed. J. Galassi). *Times Higher Education
        Supplement* 25 February 1977, p.20.

C598   Particle Poems. *Clunch* (Polytechnic of North London) 1, March 1977,
        pp.3–5.

C599   'Joyce: portrait of the artist as a radical' (review of R. Ellmann, *The
        Consciousness of Joyce*). *Sunday Times* 13 March 1977, p.39.

C600   'Unique unity' (review of Elisabeth W. Schneider, *T.S. Eliot: The
        Pattern in the Carpet*). *Times Higher Education Supplement* 18 March 1977,
        p.24.

C601   'The world of Baba Yaga' (review of *Russian Fairy Tales*, collected by

Aleksandr Afanas'ev, translated by Norbert Guterman, illustrated by Alexander Alexeieff). *Times Literary Supplement* 25 March 1977, p.357.

C602 The Mummy. *Open Space* (Aberdeen University) 7, April 1977, p.32.

C603 'Preview' (of radio and television programmes). *Radio Times* 9–15 April 1977, p.19.

C604 'A literary history' (review of Maurice Lindsay, *History of Scottish Literature*). *Q* 15 April 1977, p.10.

C605 'The road ahead' (review of Ilya Ehrenburg, *The Life of the Automobile*). *Times Literary Supplement* 15 April 1977, p.450.

C606 'An eye on everything' (review of H.M. Enzensberger, *Raids and Reconstructions* and *Mausoleum*). *Listener* 97:2506, 28 April 1977, p.546.

C607 'Amang the Buiks' (review of *Nuova Poesia Scozzese*, ed. Nat Scammacca and Duncan Glen). *Lallans* 8, Whitsunday 1977, pp.32–4.

C608 'Preview'. *Radio Times* 21–7 May 1977, p.17.

C609 All the Secrets. *Pick* 2:7/8, Summer 1977, p.4.
Published as 'Alpha' in *Alphabetical and Letter Poems* (Menard Press, 1978), p.96, without first 8 lines and last two lines changed: for 'into' read 'in', for 'that is' read 'that's all'.

C610 'The thing's the thing' (review of A. Burgess, *Abba Abba*). *Times Literary Supplement* 3 June 1977, p.669.

C611 'Preview'. *Radio Times* 9–15 July 1977, p.13.

C612 'Coming to terms with trash' (review of John Gardner, *October Light*). *Times Literary Supplement* 12 August 1977, p.977.

C613 'Preview'. *Radio Times* 20–26 August 1977, p.13.

C614 'Situations for snooving' (review of Robert Garioch, *Collected Poems*). *Times Literary Supplement* 9 September 1977, p.1077.

C615 'Robert Garioch' (letter). *Times Literary Supplement* 30 September 1977, p.1108.
Correcting 'meaningless gloss' added by sub-editor to review of RG's *Collected Poems*.

C616 'Preview'. *Radio Times* 22–28 October 1977, p.17.

C617 [Review of Gordon Wright, *MacDiarmid: An Illustrated Biography*]. *Library Review* vol. 26, Winter 1977, pp.364–6.

C618 [Review of Alan Spence, *Its Colours They Are Fine*]. *Words* 4, Winter 1977, pp.56–7.

C619 'Silent provocation' (review of I.C. Smith, *The Hermit and other stories*). *Times Literary Supplement* 25 November 1977, p.1373.

C620 A Good Year for Death. *Lines Review* 63, December 1977, pp.6–7.

C621 The Archaeopteryx's Song – A Good Year for Death. *Thoth* 1, December 1977, p.11.

Note on p. 1: '*Thoth*'s editorial policy is to publish work read at
Morden Tower or written since the reading.'
Photograph of EM by Alan C. Brown on p.3.

C622   'Preview'. *Radio Times* 10–16 December 1977, p.19.

1978

C623   from The New Divan (86–87) – Particle Poems (1–6). *Lettera* 15,
February 1978, pp.62–65.
Special edition of the Italian language magazine edited from Cardiff
by John Freeman. Published separately by Blackweir Press, Cardiff
1978, as *Poetry in English Now*.

C624   'Preview'. *Radio Times* 11–17 February 1978, p.19.

C625   'Preview'. *Radio Times* 1–7 April 1978, p.17.

C626   'Struggle and surrender' (review of John Berryman, *Henry's Fate and
other poems*). *Listener* 99:2557, 27 April 1978, pp.552–3.

C627   [Review of Andrew Greig, *Men on Ice*]. *Scottish Review* 10, [May] 1978,
pp.37–8.

C628   'Preview'. *Radio Times* 20–26 May, p.17.

C629   New Year Sonnets (1–10). *Perfect Bound* 5, Summer 1978, pp.60–64.

C630   The Mummy. *Broadsheet* 30, June 1978.

C631   'Preview'. *Radio Times* 15–21 July 1978, p.15.

C632   'Devil's work' (review of Emma Tennant, *The Bad Sister*). *Times Literary
Supplement* 21 July 1978, p.817.

C633   At Central Station – Migraine Attack – Winter – Instructions to an
Actor. *Akros* 13;38, August 1978, pp.83–6.
'Migraine Attack' published in *Night Ride and Sunrise* (Celtion
Publishing Company, 1978), p.32, under the title 'Into the
Interior'.

C634   To a Woodbine Tendril – Vesuvius in December 1830 (both transl.
from Platen) – 'Poetry smoulders . . .' (transl. from Yevtushenko) –
from Vestiges of Creation: Stele – Gorgon – Foundation. *Perfect Bound*
6, [Autumn] 1978, pp.36–7, 44–5, 69–71.
Two lines from EM's poem 'Surrealism Revisited' printed on back
cover.

C635   Surrealism Revisited – Happiness. *Palantir* 9, September 1978,
pp.30–31.

C636   'Preview'. *Radio Times* 2–8 September 1978, p.17.

C637   'Gods of mud' (review of Ted Hughes, *Cave Birds*). *Listener* 100:2576, 7
September 1978, p.318.

C638   'MacDiarmid the poet dies at 86' (obituary). *Sunday Times* 10 September
1978, p.2.

C639   'Preview'. *Radio Times* 7–13 October 1978, p.23.

C640   'The pursuit of Peter Pan' (article). *Times Literary Supplement* 13 October
1978, p.1160.

On BBC productions of *The House with the Green Shutters* (radio) and *The Lost Boys* (BBC2 TV) and the kailyard writers.

C641 'Scottish Poetry in English' (article). *Books in Scotland* 3, Winter 1978/79, pp.8–9.

C642 [Review of *Modern Scots Verse 1922–1977*, ed. Alexander Scott and *North-East Muse Anthology*, ed. Cuthbert Graham]. *Scottish Review* 12, [November] 1978, pp.38–40.

C643 [Review of John Herdman, *Pagan's Pilgrimage*]. *Words* 6, [?November] 1978, p.54.

C644 'The Thirties connection' (review of S. Spender, *The Thirties and After*). *Listener* 100:2584, 2 November 1978, pp.588–9.

C645 'Preview'. *Radio Times* 18–24 November 1978, p.21.

C646 'MacDiarmid's Later Poetry Against an International Background' (essay). *Scottish Literary Journal* 5:2, December 1978, pp.20–35.
Originally as part of paper, 'Plagiarism: the writer as cannibal', given to Glasgow University Literary Society 26 October 1978.

1979

C647 The Grey Man – Interview; [Contribution to symposium] 'What it Feels Like to be a Scottish Poet'. *Aquarius* 11 (in Honour of Hugh MacDiarmid), 1979, pp.52–4; 71–3.

C648 On the Needle's Point – In the Bottle. *Divan* (Liverpool) 1, 1979, pp.[4–5].

C649 Three Poems from a sequence (Ore – Era – Fountain). *Maxy's Journal* 3, 1979, pp.40–42.

C650 Book (from 'Vestiges of Creation' sequence). *AMF* 2, [March 1979], p.9.

C651 On the Water. *Kudos* 1, [March] 1979, p.20.
Illustrated by photograph by Graham Sykes of stretch of water on p.21.

C652 'Preview'. *Radio Times* 24–30 March 1979, p.23.

C653 'Provenance and Problematics of "Sublime and Alarming Images" in Poetry' (Warton Lecture on English Poetry British Academy 1977: read 14 December 1977). *Proceedings of the British Academy* vol.LXIII, 1977, pp.293–313. (London: Published for the British Academy by the Oxford University Press)
Copyright date is 1978 but not issued until March 1979. Also published separately.

C654 'Their Noble Rage' (review of Douglas Dunn, *Barbarians* and Yevtushenko, *The Face behind the Face*). *New Edinburgh Review* 46, May 1979, pp.29–30.

C655 'Preview'. *Radio Times* 19–25 May 1979, p.27.

C656 6 Found Poems (Glasgow – By the Banks of Molendinar – Rough Neuk Quarry and Pond – Sta' o' Stable – Small Holdings – Evandale Glow-

worms at Night). *South East Arts Review* Summer 1979, pp.23–6.
The second poem is mistitled 'By the Banks of the Molendinar'.

C657   The Mouth. *Blueprint* 5, June 1979, pp.40–41.

C658   'Vigorous tears' (review of G. Hill, *Tenebrae*). *Listener* 101:2614, 7 June 1979, pp.790–91.

C659   On the Water. *Third Eye Centre Programme* 8 June–31 July 1979, p.7.

C660   A Home in Space. *Third Eye Centre Programme* August–September 1979, p.9.

C661   'Preview'. *Radio Times* 14–20 August 1979, p.21.

C662   'Fringe Peake' (review of Mervyn Peake, *The Wit to Woo* by Nottingham Theatre group at Edinburgh). *Mervyn Peake Review* 9, Autumn 1979, pp.31–2.

C663   Ancient Forest – Once More: In the intermissions of dream – And: like a white leaf – Field: height of Winter – Once More: Places in the Forest (5 poems transl. from Gennady Aigi). *Cencrastus* 1, Autumn 1979, p.23.
Includes a brief introduction by EM.

C664   'Preview'. *Radio Times* 1–7 September 1979, p.19.

C665   Caliban Falls Asleep in the Isle Full of Noises. *Hibernia* 43:37, 20 September 1979, p.20.

C666   'Poets in Schools' (article). *Bookmark* (Moray House College of Education) 3, Winter 1979, pp.2, 4–11.

C667   'Texts and Contexts' (review of Kenneth Quinn, *Texts and Contexts: The Roman Writers and their Audience*). *Literary Review* 3, 2–15 November 1979, p.13.

C668   'Preview'. *Radio Times* 24–30 November 1979, p.27.

C669   'The love-story of a cloud in trousers' (review of Ann and Samuel Charters, *I Love: The Story of Vladimir Mayakovsky and Lili Brik*). *Glasgow Herald* 6 December 1979, p.12.

1980

C670   Moving House – Hotel Registration. *New Poetry* 48, Spring 1980, pp.16–17.

C671   Iran. *Open Space* (Aberdeen) Spring 1980, p.28.

C672   Three poems from *Vestiges of Creation* sequence (Tomb – Mt. Caucasus – Trilobites). *Thames Poetry* 1:8, March 1980, pp.5–7.
Correction: 'Trilobites' 1.18 – for 'of' read 'or'.

C673   'Preview: Edwin Morgan on BBCtv and Radio from Scotland'. *Radio Times* 5–11 April 1980, p.27.

C674   'Chronicles of chaos' (review of M.E. Saltykov-Shchedrin, *The History of a Town*). *Times Literary Supplement* 23 May 1980, p.572

C675   Home on the Range – Fountain. *Samphire* 3:7, Summer 1980, pp.36–7.

C676   Jack London in Heaven – The Blackbird – Little Blue Blue. *Lines Review* 73, June 1980, pp.5–9.

C677 Jordanstone Sonnets 1–3. *Seer* 3, June 1980.

C678 'Saltykov-Shchedrin' (letter). *Times Literary Supplement* 13 June 1980, p.672.
Correcting misprint in EM's review, *TLS* 23 May 1980, p.572.

C679 Cinquevalli – Newspoems (Unpublished poems by Creeley: 2 – Unpublished poems by Creeley: 3 – Unpublished poems by Creeley: 4 – Joe's Bar). *Words* 10, [July] 1980, pp.2, 35, 48, 54.

C680 'Dancing the reel' (review of Thomas Crawford, *Society and the Lyric: A Study of the Song Culture of 18th-Century Scotland*). *Listener* 104:2670, 17 July 1980, pp.86–7.

C681 The Coals. *Listener* 104:2672, 31 July 1980, p.153.

C682 'Preview'. *Radio Times* 9–15 August 1980, p.15.

C683 'The Future of the Antisyzygy' (essay). *Bulletin of Scottish Politics* I:1, Autumn 1980, pp.7–20.
Text of paper delivered at conference on periodical publishing in smaller nations, organized by the Scottish International Institute, June 1978.

C684 What am I? – The Possible Variations – Flame and Darkness (all transl. from László Kálnoky). *New Hungarian Quarterly* XXI:79, Autumn 1980.

C685 'Poetry – the Place of the Will' (review of *Poetry Book Society: the first 25 years 1954–1978*, ed. Eric W. White). *Literary Review* 25, 19 September – 2 October 1980, p.18.

C686 'Armenian Poetry' (review of *Anthology of Armenian Poetry*, transl. and ed. Diana Der Hovanessian and Marzbed Margossian). *Cencrastus* 4, Winter 1980–81, p.42.

1981

C687 Grendel – Eve and Adam. *Angel Exhaust* 4, [1981], pp.[37–8].

C688 'Poems and persons' (review of William H. Pritchard, *Lives of the Modern Poets*). *Listener* 105:2695, 8 January 1981, pp.55–6.

C689 'Forever Amber' (review of Roger Zelazny, *The Courts of Chaos*). *Times Literary Supplement* 13 February 1981, p.158.

C690 Casts – Midwinter – Encounter – Albion – Fall. *Lines Review* 76, March 1981, pp.8–10.
Note on p.8: 'Examples from a collection of joint poems [by EM and Michael Schmidt], quantitatively about 10% MS and 90% EM. MS sent EM batches of what he called his gallstones or chips and shavings from the workshop floor – short fragments of a line or two from abandoned poems. EM then used these fragments as starting-points – oyster-grit – for new poems of his own, the original material being kept intact, though it might appear in any part of the poem.'

C691 'Empire of the stars' (review of Doris Lessing, *The Sirian Experiments*). *Times Literary Supplement* 17 April 1981, p.431.

C692   'The poetry of W.S. Graham' (review-essay). *Cencrastus* 5, Summer [May] 1981, pp.8–10.

      Graham's work assessed on the basis of his *Collected Poems*.

C693   'Academy to premiere opera at Theatre Royal'. *Scottish Opera News* 56, May 1981, p.3.

      Includes portion of programme note by EM on the opera *Columba* by Kenneth Leighton and EM.

      Also photograph of EM and Leighton.

C694   Newspoems: Hex – Talk about Camp – Caedmon's Second Hymn – Naw Hen, Ah Flogged Ma Unicycle – In Silhouette – Ballad 13 – The Commonest Kind. *Words* 11–12, [May] 1981, pp.16, 25, 27, 38, 51, 58.

      'The Commonest Kind' not listed in Contents.

C695   'An opera on St Columba: A note from the composer, Kenneth Leighton . . . and from the librettist, Edwin Morgan'. *Musical Times* cxxii:1660, June 1981, pp.371, 373.

      Text of programme note. Advertisement for opera on p.372.

C696   'Crises in the life of a restless poet' (review of H. Carpenter, *W.H. Auden: A Biography*). *Glasgow Herald* 7 July 1981, p.12.

C697   'Robert Garioch 1909–1981'; On the Train (Glasgow-Nottingham 10–3–1981) – Grendel. *Lines Review* 77, June [August] 1981, pp.13–15; 44–6.

      'On the Train' was written on the way to receive an Hon. D.Litt. at Loughborough University.

C698   'The reproductive system' (review of *Seeing Is Not Believing*, exhibition at National Gallery of Scotland). *Times Literary Supplement* 21 August 1981, p.957.

C699   Tropic – Oban Girl. *Olusum* (Turkey) 46/47, August–September 1981, p.58.

      Translated into Turkish by C. Ayral and A. Isfendiyar.

C700   [Address to the Congregation at Loughborough University, 10 July 1981, on receiving the degree of Doctor of Letters, *honoris causa*]. *Gazette* (Loughborough University) 65, September 1981, pp.16–17.

C701   A Pair of Cats – A Riddle. *Palantir* 18, September 1981, pp.30–31.

C702   'Poet with personal commitment' (article on W.S. Graham). *Glasgow Herald* 4 September 1981, p.4.

      Graham had recently given readings in Scotland.

C703   'The diagnostic disease' (review of *The Brothers Karamazov* performed by the Brighton Theatre at the Edinburgh Festival). *Times Literary Supplement* 11 September 1981, p.1035.

C704   'Images in illustration' (review of *Landscape Poets: Thomas Hardy*, selected and edited by Peter Porter; *Landscape Poets: Robert Burns*, selected and edited by Karl Miller). *Times Literary Supplement* 25 September 1981, pp.1095–6.

      Also includes comment on T. & A. Gunn, *Positives*; F. Godwin & T. Hughes, *Remains of Elmet*; A. Ginsberg, *Ankor Wat*.

C705 'Born of frustration' (review of E. Montale, *Altri versi e poesie disperse*). *Times Literary Supplement* 16 October 1981, p.1191.

C706 Tarkovsky in Glasgow. *Quarto* 23, November 1981.

C707 'The poet and his camera' (review of Y. Yevtushenko, *Invisible Threads*). *Times Literary Supplement* 6 November 1981, p.1288.

C708 [Last 6 lines of poem for opening of play *Let Wives Tak Tent*]. *Cencrastus* 7, Winter [December] 1981–82, p.10.

C709 [Review of Roy Fisher, *Poems 1955–1980* and *Talks for Words*]. *Lines Review* 79, December 1981, pp.23–6.

C710 'MSS in a Bottle' (article). *Poetry Review* 71:4, December 1981, pp.26–8.
On the judging of the 1981 National Poetry Competition.

C711 'A travelling poet who has reached the Golan heights: Edwin Morgan writes about his recent poetry reading tour in Israel'. *Glasgow Herald* 1 December 1981, p.4.

C712 'Fuori di casa: Eugenio Montale'. *Hellas* 2/3, 31 December 1981, pp.55–56.
Translation into Italian by P.N. Rossi of part of EM's review of Montale in *TLS* 16 October 1981, p.1191 (here misprinted 16 November). Also issued as an offprint.

1982

C713 'Some classical ephemera' (review of Mayakovsky exhibition, 'Twenty Years of Work' at Fruitmarket Gallery, Edinburgh). *Times Literary Supplement* 5 February 1982, p.133.

C714 'Protective Gestures: The Poetry of Peter Porter' (essay). *New Edinburgh Review* 56, Winter 1981–82 [February 1982], pp.25–7.

C715 'Forays into fiction' (review of F.R. Hart and J.B. Pick, *Neil M. Gunn: A Highland Life*). *Times Literary Supplement* 19 February 1982, p.192.

C716 A Woman Visiting – Joviana – 'The semiologist is the sorcerer' – Motives – Dislodged – 'Making the best of a bad job' – 'For me / you are the needle of the scales' – The Bard – Disciple of the Muses (all transl. from E. Montale). *Outcrop* (Lampeter) 3, Spring 1982, pp.49–51.
'Translator's note' on p.49: 'Eugenio Montale, the leading Italian poet, died a few months after the publication of his last book, *Altri Versi* (Milan: Mondadori, 1981). The following translations of nine of his poems from that collection are offered as a tribute to his memory.'

C717 'Recent Scottish Writing'. *English Ayr* 7, [March 1982], p.63. List of a 'personal selection of contemporary Scottish writing'.

C718 Save the Whale Ball (heading in *The Times*, 2 June 1981). *Dalhousie Review* 61:2, Summer 1981 [May 1981], pp.251–2.

C719 Save the Whale Ball. *Logos* 7/8, [June 1982], p.11.

C720 The Subway Cat. *Glasgow Herald* 23 June 1982, p.1.
One of a series of poster poems commissioned by the Scottish Arts Council for the Glasgow Underground but rejected by Strathclyde

Passenger Transport Executive. Printed in article, 'Subway animal poems rejected by PTE' by Tom Shields, with comment by EM.

C721   The Subway Piranhas. *Glasgow Herald* 29 June 1982, p.6.
        One of Underground poster poems. Printed in Tom Shields's column, 'Tom Shields on Tuesday'. Correspondence about the affair appeared in the *Glasgow Herald* 7 July 1982, p.6.

C722   Ten Poems [by EM and Michael Schmidt]: Resistance – Island – Story – Poetry – Beginnings – Quest – Geode – Starlings – French – Testament. *Lines Review* 81, June 1982, pp.5–11.
        Note on p.5 is the same as that prefacing five poems by EM and MS in *LR* 76, March 1981, p.8.

C723   The Subway Giraffe. *Glasgow Chamber of Commerce Journal* August 1982, p.249
        One of Underground poster poems. In short article, 'Literature of the underground'.

C724   [Review of Tom Leonard, *Ghostie Men*]. *Aquarius* 13/14, 1981/1982 [September 1982], pp.149–51.

C725   The Solway Canal. *Akros* 17:50, October 1982, p.44.
        The first of what became the *Sonnets from Scotland*.

C726   James Joyce and Hugh MacDiarmid. *James Joyce Broadsheet* 9, October 1982, p.3.

C727   Bradford, Czerwiec 1972 (Bradford June 1972) – Podejrzany (The Suspect) – RFN, Grudzień 1970 (Germany December 1970) – Pociąg do Aberdeen (Aberdeen Train) – Aviemore, Invernessshire, Sierpeń 1971 (Aviemore Invernessshire August 1971) – Glasgow, 5 Marca 1971 – Trio. *Literatura na Świecie* 10 (135), October 1982, pp.9–13.
        Translated into Polish by Andrzej Szuba. The first appearance of EM's poems in Poland.

C728   Amsterdam Revisited. *Quarryman* (University College, Cork) [1], August [October] 1982, p.6.

C729   'Finding a place' (review of George MacBeth, *Poems from Oby*). *Times Literary Supplement* 19 November 1982, p.1282.

C730   from AN ALPHABET OF GODDESSES for Pat Douthwaite (Lethe – Medea – Nemesis – Eileithyia). *New Edinburgh Review* 60, Winter [December] 1982, p.24.
        Under heading: MYTHOLOGICAL POEMS.

C731   A *mot* and its range. *Stereo Headphones* 8–9–10, [?December] 1982, p.78.
        Printed under the heading 'Edwin Morgan (Glasgow) 8.4.80' in answer to questions on ' "Advances", and the Contemporary Avant-Garde'.

C732   Sonnets from Scotland (The Age of Heracleum – Carboniferous – 1893 – The Picts – The Desert – The Coin). *The Glasgow Magazine* 1, Winter [December] 1982, pp.19–22.
        'The Age of Heracleum' was printed as 'The Age of Herculaneum' and the dedication to 'Carboniferous' appeared as 'For I.C.' instead of

'For I.R.' Errata slips were issued which still managed to get 'Heracleum' wrong.

1983

C733 From 'Sonnets from Scotland' (Matt McGinn – Outward Bound – The Norn (1) – The Norn (2) – The Target – Gangs). *Cencrastus* 11, New Year [January] 1983, p.15.
Corrections: 'The Norn (1)' 1.5 – for 'Schielhallion' read 'Schiehallion'; 'The Norn (2)' 1.2 – for '*le*' read '*les*'; 1.7 – for 'lead,' read 'lead.'; 'Gangs' 1.11 – for 'ye bams' read 'ya bams'.

C734 'The Dancing Dervish revolution in Scottish way of life' (article). *Glasgow Herald* 24 January 1983, p.9.
Illustrated by Roy Petrie.
'The Next 200 – 2183. The Glasgow Herald has been reporting the news for the past 200 years, but what will be making the headlines in 200 years' time. Beginning today, a series of guest writers report back from the year 2183.'

C735 [Review of I.C. Smith, *Murdo and other stories*]. *Scottish Literary Journal Supplement* 17, Winter 1982 [February 1983], pp.94–6.

C736 Four poems from AN ALPHABET OF GODDESSES for Pat Douthwaite (Aphrodite – Bacche – Circe – Demeter). *Literary Review* 56, February 1983, p.42.
Correction: 'Demeter' 1.6 – for 'burns' read 'burrs'.

C737 'Turning Back' (review of L.G. Gibbon, *The Speak of the Mearns*). *The Glasgow Magazine* 2, Spring 1983, pp.21–3.

C738 TWO POEMS from An Alphabet of Goddesses *for Pat Douthwaite* (Hecate – Fortuna). *Poetry Review* 73:1, March 1983, p.41.

C739 'The Politics of Poetry' (review of Cairns Craig, *Yeats, Eliot, Pound and the Politics of Poetry*). *Cencrastus* 12, Spring [April] 1983, p.44.

C740 Thirteen Poems (Mozart: Cassation 1 – A Note: Apophatic – Lake and Bird – Suburban House – M.K. – The Birches Rustle – Hills: Pines: Midday – Pines-with-Birch – Dream: Birches – View with Trees – KRCh – 80 – Play-Poem – Lament-and-I) (all transl. from Gennady Aygi). *Scottish Slavonic Review* 1, [April] 1983, pp.58–71.
There is 'a note on the poet' on pp.58–9. Original Russian on pages facing the translations.
Corrections: p.59, 1.5 – for 'Creely's' read 'Creeley's;
p.61, 'Mozart: Cassation 1' 1.3 – insert 'mozart' after 'divine'; 'A Note: Apophatic' – 11.1 & 2 should not be justified;
p.63, 'Suburban House' 1.3 – insert dash after 'secretive';
p.65, 'The Birches Rustle' – insert dedication 'To V. Korsunsky' after title and dashes after 11.4, 6, 8, 11;
p.69, 'Play-Poem' 1.6 – substitute '(' for the first '–'.

C741   from AN ALPHABET OF GODDESSES for Pat Douthwaite (Gaea –
       Kore). *Strata* 1, Easter 1983, pp.5–6.
       Note on p.5: 'Pat Douthwaite, the Glasgow artist to whom the
       sequence is dedicated, had an exhibition of drawings at the
       Edinburgh Festival.' PD is actually from Paisley.

C742   The Break-In. *Broadsheet* [April 1983].

C743   Memento (from 'Sonnets from Scotland'). *Grampian English Views* 6:2,
       Spring 1983, p.43.

C744   *from* AN ALPHABET OF GODDESSES (Oreithyia – Urania). *The Poet's
       Voice* 3, [July 1983], p.3.
       Corrections: 'Oreithyia' 1.12 – for 'wilderness' read 'wildness';
       'Urania' 1.10 – insert 'streaming' between 'her' and 'robes'.

C745   'A charmed life' (review of Ronald Kingley, *Pasternak: A Biography*).
       Observer Review 7 August 1983, p.24.

C746   [Review of Matthew P. McDiarmid, *Robert Henryson*; David Daiches,
       Robert Fergusson; Thomas Crawford, *Walter Scott*; Kenneth Buthlay,
       Hugh MacDiarmid (Scottish Writers Series)]. *Scottish Review* 31, August
       1983, pp.53–6.

C747   'Novy Mir and the Stalinist Whirlwind' (review of E. Ginzburg, *Within
       the Whirlwind*; *'Novy Mir': A Case Study in the Politics of Literature 1952–
       1958*, ed. E.R. Frankel). *Cencrastus* 14, Autumn 1983, p.54.

C748   Vereshchagin's Barrow. *The Third Eye* August–September 1983,
       pp.[9–10].
       'Special primitive issue'.

C749   from *Sonnets from Scotland* (The Ticket – Thomas Young, M.A. (St
       Andrews) – Silva Caledonia – After a Death – The Ring of Brodgar –
       Caledonian Antisyzygy). *New Edinburgh Review* 63, Autumn 1983,
       p.15.

C750   [Review of *The Images Swim Free: A Bi-Lingual Selection of Poetry* by
       Maksim Bahdanovič, Aleś Harun and Żmitrok Biadula]. *Scottish
       Slavonic Review* 2, [?Autumn] 1983, pp.177–8.

C751   from An Alphabet of Goddesses (Xenaea – Youth – Zeuxippe). *Labrys*
       9, November 1983, pp.171–2.
       Corrections: 'Xenaea' 1.4 – for 'in' read 'into'; 'Youth' 1.8 – for
       'memory' read 'memory.'; 1.9 – for 'be memory' read 'be the
       memory'.

C752   The Hanamichi – The Spirit of Theatre – Kurosawa (transl. into
       Japanese by Osaka Osamu). *Tree(s)* 10, December 1983, pp.12–17.
       Also article on EM by OO.

1984

C753   [from] AN ALPHABET OF GODDESSES (For Pat Douthwaite):
       Ismene – Jocasta – Terpsichore – Vixen. *Literary Review* 67, January
       1984, p.47.

C754   Homeward Bound – For My Mother – De Profundis – Self-Portrait –

'Eternal Darkness Clings . . .' – Ars Poetica (all transl. from S. Weöres). *New Hungarian Quarterly* XXV:93, Spring 1984, pp.54–62.

C755   Inward Bound – Poe in Glasgow (from *Sonnets from Scotland*). *Scratchings* (Aberdeen University) 4, April 1984, pp.[4, 28].

C756   'Musing on the buses' (review of James Kelman, *The Busconductor Hines*). *Times Literary Supplement* 13 April 1984, p.397.

C757   On Jupiter (from *Sonnets from Scotland*). *Blind Serpent* (Dundee) 3, July 1984, p.[1],

C758   [Review of J.F. Hendry, *The Sacred Threshold: A Life of Rilke*]. *Scottish Review* 34, May [July] 1984, pp.47–8.

C759   'GARIOCH' (review of R. Garioch, *Complete Poetical Works*). *Cencrastus* 17, Summer 1984, pp.45–6.

C760   'Glasgow Writing'. *Books in Scotland* 15, Summer 1984, pp.4–6.
       Condensed version of talk given during the Strathclyde Writers Festival in May 1984 at the University of Strathclyde.

C761   'The poet as letter-writer: Edwin Morgan finds a fuller picture of the age – and the man' (review of *The Letters of Hugh MacDiarmid*, ed. Alan Bold and *The Thistle Rises: An Anthology of Poetry and Prose* by Hugh MacDiarmid, ed. Alan Bold). *Guardian* 23 August 1984, p.8.

C762   from AN ALPHABET OF GODDESSES (Gaea – Kore – Wisdom). *The Poet's Voice* 2:2 (5th issue), [?August 1984], pp.4–5.
       Corrections: 'Gaea' 1.21 – for 'not beauty then, not goodness yet,' read 'not beauty then, / not goodness yet,'; 'Kore' 1.16 – for 'She would make love to the very trees' read 'She would make love / to the very trees'.

C763   'Translating Poetry for the *NHQ*'. *New Hungarian Quarterly* XXV:95, Autumn 1984, pp.86–7.

C764   Nineteen Kinds of Barley – from Sonnets from Scotland (The Mirror – Matthew Paris); 'Matieres D'Angleterre' (review of *Matières d'Angleterre: Anthologie bilingue de la Nouvelle Poésie Anglaise*). *Verse* 1, [October 1984], pp.4–6; 46–7.
       Reviewed by Anne Varty, *College Courant* 74, March 1985, p.41 and by Nicolas Jacobs, *Balliol College Annual Record* 1985, p.80.

C765   'The Poetry of Norman MacCaig'. *Books in Scotland* 16, Autumn [December] 1984, pp.4–6.
       Shortened version of talk given at conference on Scottish literature organized by the ASLS at University of Strathclyde, 6 October 1984.

C766   [from Sonnets from Scotland:] Carboniferous – Pilate at Fortingall – Theory of the Earth – G.M. Hopkins in Glasgow – North Africa – Caledonian Antisyzygy – Matt McGinn – Gangs – Not the Burrell Collection – A Place of Many Waters – Computer Error: Neutron Strike – A Golden Age. *Glasgow Herald* 1 December 1984, p.7 (Weekender, p.1).
       Includes 'Poet's place for looking out at the universe', article on *Sonnets from Scotland* by Lesley Duncan, based on interview with EM.

C767   [Review of I.C. Smith, *The Exiles*]. *The Glasgow Magazine* 5, Winter
       1984/85 [December 1984], pp.20–22.

1985

C768   [Review of Roland Mathias, *Burning Brambles: Selected Poems 1944–
       1979*]. *Powys Review* 4:3 (No.15), 1984–1985 [?May 1985], pp.70–72.

C769   [Review of Robert Crawford and W.N. Herbert, *Sterts & Stobies*]. *The
       Glasgow Magazine* 6, Summer [June] 1985, pp.33–4.

C770   'Alexander Trocchi: A Survey' (essay). *Edinburgh Review* 70, August
       1985, pp.48–58.

C771   Variations on Omar Khayyam. *Ethos* (Toronto) 1:4, Summer 1985,
       pp.57–8.

C772   [Review of Boris Pasternak, *Selected Poems*, transl. by J. Stallworthy and
       P. France and *Poems of Boris Pasternak*, transl. by Lydia Pasternak
       Slater]. *Scottish Slavonic Review* 5, Autumn 1985, pp.149–50.

C773   Halley's Comet. *Strawberry Fare* (St Mary's College, Twickenham),
       Autumn 1985, p.36.

C774   Without Hope – Elegy – Mother (all transl. from Attila József) – Ideal
       Hangman (transl. from Győző Határ) – Crazed Man in Concentration
       Camp (transl. from Ágnes Gergely). *Translation* vol. XV, Fall 1985,
       pp.33–7, 76–7, 128.
       Not on p.326 states that EM was awarded the Soros Translation
       Award for 'Selection of Poems' by Attila József.

C775   Cantus Interruptus (A poem which would have been written in
       November 1972 if the writer had not had to take a seminar). *College
       Courant* 75, September 1985, p.25.
       See *Ambit* 54, 1973, pp.29–31, 'Notes on the Poet's Working Day'.

C776   'Country's turbulent past portrayed in verse' (article). *Glasgow Herald* 1
       October 1985, p.4.
       On Hungarian poetry featured in Hungarian Festival, Glasgow.

C777   Five Poems from *Sonnets from Scotland*: Slate – Matthew Paris – A Place
       of Many Waters – A Scottish Japanese Print – A Golden Age. *Ninth
       Decade* 5, [October] 1985, pp.4–6.

C778   FROM THE VIDEO BOX (1–3). *Orbis* 58/59, Autumn/Winter 1985,
       pp.58–9.
       Scottish issue.

C779   A Trace of Wings. *Conjunctions* 8 [?Winter] 1985, p.152.
       Tribute to Basil Bunting.

C780   Arran Potatoes – From the Video Box 5. *The Glasgow Magazine* 7,
       Winter 1985/86, pp.37, 47.

C781   [Contribution to] 'Pageant of Worthies'. *Lantern* (Lanark Teachers
       Magazine) 3:1, Winter 1985, p.6.
       'Celebrities' were asked which worthies in Shakespeare (or literature
       in general) reminded them in some way of themselves.

1986

C782   The Room. *Word & Image* 2:1, January–March 1986, p.86.
On Magritte's *Souvenir de voyage III*; there is a black and white
reproduction on p.87.

C783   Attila József – Culture – In the End – Sorrow – It is a Fine Summer
Evening – A True Man (all transl. from Attila József). *Verse* 5, [January]
1986, pp.50–54.
Note on p.54: 'The above poems were translated with the aid of
rough versions supplied by George Cushing, Professor of Hungarian
at London University, and were read at the Hungarian Festival held
in Glasgow in 1985'.

C784   'Early Finlay' (essay). *Cencrastus* 22, Winter [February] 1986, pp.21–3.
Included in Ian Hamilton Finlay Retrospective.

C785   Autumn (fragment) (transl. from Pushkin). *Scottish Slavonic Review* 6,
Spring 1986, pp.63, 65, 67.
Russian text on pp.62, 64, 66.

C786   'On Sydney Goodsir Smith's *Perpetual Opposition* and *Deviation Tactics*'
(essay). *Radical Scotland* 20, April/May 1986, pp.38–9.

C787   From the Video Box 6. *Images* (Paisley) 2, [May 1986], p.67.
Correction: 1.4 – for 'it' read 'that'.

C788   'Settling the quisquous' (review of *The Concise Scots Dictionary*). *Times
Literary Supplement* 9 May 1986, p.491.
See letter from J.P. Kenyon commenting on remark by EM on phrase
'to get aff at Paisley', *TLS* 30 May 1986, p.591; further correspondence, *TLS* 6 June 1986, p.619.

C789   The Fatties at the Baths – The Translator's Death – Meeting – Findings
– Further Findings – One Leader, Two Busts (all transl. from László
Kálnoky). *New Hungarian Quarterly* 27:102, Summer 1986, pp.79–86.

C790   [Review of Roderick Watson, *MacDiarmid*]. *Powys Review* VII:18,
[July] 1986, pp.90–92.

C791   From the Video Box 7, 8, 9, 13, 15, 16, 17. *Edinburgh Review* 73,
August 1986, pp.26–31.

C792   Dom Raja. *The Green Book* 2:4, [Autumn 1986], pp.28–9.

C793   Autumn – XXX – September Morning Nocturne – Lichtenstein –
Magic – Spring (all transl. from Ivan Blatný). *Scottish Slavonic Review* 7,
Autumn 1986, pp.91, 93, 95.
Czech text on pp.90, 92, 94 and note on Blatný by Jan Čulík on
pp.94–5.

C794   'The Italian Influence' (review of R.D.S. Jack, *Scottish Literature's Debt to
Italy*). *Books in Scotland* 22, Autumn 1986, p.6.

C795   Six Poems: My Mother Washing Clothes a Wreath – 'Freight Trains
Shunt . . .' – Dead Landscape – Profit – In Light, White Clothes –
'Well, in the end I have found my home . . .' (all transl. from Attila
József). *Numbers* 1, Autumn 1986, pp.39–46.

Correction: p.42, 1.12 ('Dead Landscape') – for 'cracking' read 'crackling'.

C796   'A Note on William Montgomerie'. *Chapman* 46 (IX:3), Winter 1986–87 [December 1986], pp.1–3.
Corrections: p.1, 1.21 – delete comma after 'ulfire'; p.2, 1.9 – for 'Johnson' read 'Jonson'; p.3, 1.28 – for 'underlying' read 'undying'.

1987

C797   The Dowser. *Fox* (Edinburgh University) 3, 1987, p.4.

C798   Quiet Evening Psalm (transl. from A. József) – The Dowser – The Gurney. *Stride* 27, 1987, pp.39–41.

C799   Byron at Sixty-Five. *London Review of Books* 9:1, 8 January 1987, p.9.

C800   'W.S. Graham: A Poet's Letters'. *Edinburgh Review* 75, November 1986 [February 1987], pp.[39]–48.
On EM's correspondence with W.S.G. Contribution to special issue on Graham.

C801   [Review of N. Ya. Dyakonova, *Stivenson i angliyskaya literatura XIX veka*; V. Mayakovsky, *Love is the Heart of Everything*; S. Weöres, *If All the World Were a Blackbird*, transl. by A. Fenton]. *Scottish Slavonic Review* 8, Spring 1987, pp.132–3, 143–4, 146–7.

C802   Stanzas. *Lines Review* 100, March 1987, pp.34–9.

C803   Waking on a Dark Morning. *The News* 1, April 1987, pp.[8–9].

C804   The Seamy Garment. *Glasgow Herald* 25 April 1987, p.9.
Correction: 1.16 – for 'tae' read 'taen'.

C805   Reconstructions (Shakespeare: A Reconstruction – To the Queen: A Reconstruction – Chillon: A Reconstruction – True Ease in Writing: A Reconstruction – On Time: A Reconstruction – Not Marble: A Reconstruction). *Verse* 4:2, June 1987, pp.10–16.
Note on p.10: 'In December 1986 Edwin Morgan and Peter McCarey began "re-constructing" some fairly well-known poems. The series was initiated by Peter McCarey, who worked first on each poem, Edwin Morgan countering with his own contribution. In the sequence as it appears here, McCarey's rehab is in each case followed by Morgan's reconstruction.' The series is titled 'Rehabs and Reconstructions'.

C806   Rules for Dwarf-Throwing. *The North* (Huddersfield), [July] 1987, p.38.
Correction: 1.17 – for 'straightjacket' read 'straitjacket'.

C807   [The Vanished Mandate]. *Listener* 30 July 1987, p.13.
Under the heading 'Poetical polemic'. The poem was read on Channel 4's *Comment* programme.
Corrections: 1.6 – delete 'for'; 1.16 – for 'has' read 'had'; 1.33 – delete 'a'; 11.39–40 should divide: 'The Scottish Secretary chose a / N anorexia nervosa'.

C808   'The Outer Limits' (article). *Festival Field* [Supplement to *Scottish Field*] August 1987, p.15.
On the Edinburgh Festival Fringe.

C809 The Horse Dies the Birds Fly Away (transl. from Lajos Kassák). *New Hungarian Quarterly* XXVIII:106, Summer 1987, pp.87–100.
Correction: p.99, 2nd last line – for 'cysters' read 'oysters'.

C810 Three Poems: The Aesome Blackie – Flinder – Tae his Sel (transl. from Giacomo Leopardi). *Numbers* 3 (II:2), Autumn 1987, pp.39–43.
Glossary on p.44.

C811 'Oblique Thrusts' (review of Miroslav Holub, *The Fly*). *Poetry Review* 77:3, Autumn 1987, pp.16–17.

C812 'Salute to a local hero' (review of Matt McGinn, *McGinn of the Calton*). *Scotsman* 24 October 1987, Weekend p.IV.

1988

C813 Glasgow Green – Trio – Siesta of a Hungarian Snake – The Computer's First Christmas Card – Instamatic Shrewsbury February 1971 – The First Men on Mercury – From the Domain of Arnheim (transl. into Macedonian by Violeta Khristovka). *Delo 74* XV:1–2, January–April 1988, pp.78–88.
In article, 'A Scottish Bard: Edwin Morgan and his Poetry', pp.74–88.

C814 'High Malady' (review of M. Tsvetaeva, *Selected Poems*, transl. by D. McDuff; A. Wearne, *Out Here*; G. Bruce, *Perspectives*; A. Mackie, *Ingaitherins*; N. Kreitman, *Touching Rock*; D. Gordon, *The Low Road Hame*; W.S. Milne, *Twa-Three Lines*). *Cencrastus* 28, Winter 1987/88 [February 1988], pp.17–19.

C815 [Remarks on 'British poetry']. *Glasgow University Magazine* 2, March 1988, p.18.
In article by Allan Brown, 'Muse at Ten', on contemporary British poetry (also quoting Philip Hobsbaum, Seamus Heaney and Tony Harrison).

C816 Dido. *Verse* 5:1, February [March] 1988, pp.43–[45].
Interview: 'Edwin Morgan talking with Robert Crawford' on pp.27–42.

C817 'The Way we Write Now: Edwin Morgan surveys recent collections by Scottish poets' (review of N. MacCaig, *Voice-over*; Stewart Conn, *In the Kibble Palace*; Brian McCabe, *One Atom to Another*; Kathleen Jamie and Andrew Greig, *A Flame in Your Heart*; Kathleen Jamie, *The Way We Live*; Freddy Anderson, *At Glasgow Cross*). *Poetry Review* 78:1, Spring [May] 1988, pp.42–4.

C818 'Centuries of culture and turbulence' (review of *Longer Scottish Poems, Vol. 1: 1375–1650*, ed. Priscilla Bawcutt and Felicity Riddy and *Longer Scottish Poems, Vol. 2: 1650–1830*, ed. Thomas Crawford, David Hewitt and Alexander Law). *Times Literary Supplement* 6–12 May 1988, p.499.

C819 'How Good a Poet is Drummond?' (essay). *Scottish Literary Journal* 15:1, May 1988, pp.14–24.
Paper read at Quatercentenary Conference on William Drummond, 11 December 1985.
Correction: p.22, 1.30 – for 'might' read 'night'.

C820   'An island boy's bout among the boors' (review of David Profumo, *Sea
        Music*). *Times Literary Supplement* 20–26 May 1988, p.553.

C821   [Contribution to] 'The Power of Speech'. *Independent* 10 June 1988, p. 12.
        'Six writers on why they choose to read their work aloud': Douglas
        Dunn, Michael Horowitz, EM, Amelia Rosselli, Roy Fisher, Valerie
        Bloom.

C822   'Themes on a variation' (letter). *Times Literary Supplement* 1–7 July 1988,
        p.733.
        Correction of Peter Reading's correction (*TLS* 17–23 June, p.677) of
        misquotation of last two lines of 'Pilate at Fortingall' in PR's review
        of *Themes on a Variation* in *TLS* 10–16 June 1988, p.650. Reprinted
        in 'Pseuds Corner', *Private Eye* 696, 19 August 1988, p.8.

C823   Five Poems: 'Fly, poem . . .' – I Open the Door – My Mother –
        Meditative – Everything's Old (transl. from A. József). *Edinburgh
        Review* 80–81, May [August] 1988, pp.126–9.

C824   'TREES ARCH' (transl. from Lajos Kassák). *Illuminations* VII,
        Summer / Autumn [August] 1988, pp.15–18.
        Reproduction of EM's handwritten translation. Note by EM on p. 15.

C825   Scots Sang (transl. from Pushkin). *Scottish Slavonic Review* 10, Spring
        [August] 1988, p.259.
        Russian text on p.258.

C826   'From the personal outwards' (review of Y. Yevtushenko, *Almost at the
        End*; A. Voznesensky, *An Arrow in the Wall*; Irina Ratushinskaya, *Grey
        is the Colour of Hope* and *Pencil Letter*; Nika Turbina, *First Draft*). *Times
        Literary Supplement* 26 August – 1 September 1988, p.940.

C827   Xenia I – Mediterranean: 'What do we know . . .' (both transl. from
        Montale). *Clanjamfrie* 3, Summer / Autumn [September] 1988.
        Corrections: 'Xenia I' 1.14 – insert full stop after 'bandages';
        'Mediterranean' 1.1 – for 'of tomorrow' read 'of our tomorrow'; 1.11
        – for 'sum' read 'sun'.

C828   'Doing justice to man and poet' (review of Alan Bold, *MacDiarmid*).
        Glasgow Herald 10 September 1988, p. 18 (Weekender 2).
        Correction: col.b, 1.8 – after 'reversal of' insert 'his former distrust of
        it, his absorption of a range of'.

C829   [Statement on use of lower case in concrete poetry]. *octavo* 88.5
        [?October 1988], p.16.

C830   'The seeds of optimism' (review of E.P. Thompson, *The Sykaos Papers*).
        Times Literary Supplement 4–10 November 1988, p.1237.

C831   What Sort of World do they Want Anyway (The Burn – The Blue
        Rings – The Revolution – The Thesis – The Antithesis – The
        Synthesis). *Glasgow Herald* 12 November 1988, (Weekender 7).
        Corrections: 'The Revolution' 1.10 – for 'bursting sonic' read
        'drunken sonic'; 'The Thesis' 1.8 – insert comma after 'snored'.

C832   'A New Tradition' (review of Les A. Murray, *The Daylight Moon* and
        Chris Wallace-Crabbe, *I'm Deadly Serious*). *Cencrastus* 31, Autumn
        [December] 1988, pp.49–50.

C833   [EM chooses his] 'Books of the Year'. *Glasgow Herald* 3 December 1988,
       p.23 (Weekender 3).

C834   [Contribution to] 'Cultured views of Berlin'. *Scotland on Sunday* 18
       December 1988, p.38.
       Reports on visit to Berlin by Stephen Mulrine, Jack Withers, Liz
       Lochhead and EM.

1989

C835   'Unfinished Business' (review of Primo Levi, *Collected Poems*). *Poetry
       Review* 78:4, Winter 1988–89 [January 1989], pp.16–18.

C836   A Chapter. *Gown* (Queens University Belfast) Literary Supplement
       January 1989, p.4.
       From work-in-progress, 'social' poems with different settings but
       same metre.

C837   'Sándor Weöres' (obituary). *Independent* 1 February 1989, p.15.

C838   A Decadence. *Owl* Vol. 1, March 1989, p.2.
       Corrections: 1.4 – for 'Of' read 'of'; 1.9 – for 'Spelt out' read 'spelt-
       out'; 1.10 – for 'clock-work' read 'clockwork'.

C839   An Island – A Ceremony. *The Rialto* (Norwich) 13, Spring [March]
       1989, pp.16–17.
       Illustration by Roy Trower on p.16.

C840   The Eternal Way – Two Untitled Poems (all transl. from Leonid
       Martynov) – Dolphins (transl. from Viktor Sosnora) – Untitled Poem –
       Untitled Poem from Sequence 'The Ditch' (both transl. from
       Voznesensky). *Chapman* 55–6, Spring [April] 1989, pp.37–9.
       Note on the poets on p.39.

C841   An Abandoned Culvert – The Last Intifada; [review of R.S. Thomas,
       Welsh Airs and Oliver Reynolds, *The Player Queen's Wife*]. *New Welsh
       Review* 4, Spring 1989, pp.56; 73–5.
       'Intifada' wrongly printed in italics.

C842   Of Melancholy More than of Fear – As if it was a Life, Living (transl.
       from Roberto Sanesi). *Lines Review* 109, June 1989, pp.27–8.
       Note on p.27: 'Roberto Sanesi . . . read and discussed the art of
       translation with Edwin Morgan at the Edinburgh International
       Festival in 1988. The . . . poems were translated especially for that
       event.'

C843   'Bohemian rhapsodies' (review of Harry Mathews, *Collected Longer Prose*
       and Kenneth White, *Travels in the Drifting Dawn*). *Sunday Times* 25
       June 1989, Books p.G5.
       Corrections: col.b, 1.14 – for 'constructive' read 'constrictive'; col.c,
       1.3 – for 'natively' read 'nately'.

C844   Three Poems: An Offer – A Statue – An Elegy; 'be-Imaged Languages'
       (review of *Poems of Paul Celan*, translated by Michael Hamburger). *Poetry
       Review* 79:2, Summer 1989, pp.8–9; 24–5.

C845   'Poetry and Science' (article). *Scottish Poetry Library Newsletter* 13,
       Summer 1989, p.[1].

Corrections: Col.a, 1.5 – for 'sufficienty' read 'sufficiently'; col.b, 1.4 – for 'enviromentalists' read 'environmentalists'; col.b, 1.30 – for 'no' read 'so'.

C846   Cook in Hawaii – An Island. *Landfall* (New Zealand) 170 (43:2), June 1989, pp. 191–2.

C847   October in Albania. *The SCOT-FREE Magazine* 1, [August 1989], p.4. Corrections: 1.3 – for 'crypto Scots' read 'crypto-Scots'; 1.4 – insert comma after 'Byron'; 1.17 – for 'SHQIPERIA' read 'SHQIPËRIA'; 1.18 – for 'Shqiperia' read 'Shqipëria'; 1.32 – for 'martyrs' read 'Martyrs'; 1.43 – insert comma after 'down'.

C848   'Kenneth White: A Scottish Transnationalist' (article). *Books in Scotland* 31, Summer 1989, pp. 1–2.

C849   'Dedication to cause of Scots literature' (obituary of Alexander Scott). *Glasgow Herald* 15 September 1989, p. 17.

C850   'Continental search' (review of Hans Magnus Enzensberger, *Europe, Europe: Forays into a Continent*). *Glasgow Herald* 30 September 1989, p.22.

C851   Persuasion. *Poetry Review* 79:3, Autumn 1989, p.37.

C852   'Caring about continuity' (review of R.F. Mackenzie, *A Search for Scotland*). *Times Literary Supplement* 20–26 October 1989, p.1163.

C853   [Review of Anna Akhmatova, *Selected Poems*. transl. by Richard McKane, and *Poems*]. *Scottish Slavonic Review* 12/13, Spring/Autumn 1989, pp.202–3.

C854   A Cabal. *Poetry Review* 79:4, Winter 1989/90, p.51.

C855   A Vanguard – A Pastoral – Days – A Needle – Difference. *Bête Noir* 7, Spring [December] 1989, pp. 1–5.

C856   [Contribution to] 'Books of the Year'. *Glasgow Herald* 1989, p.21 (Weekender 3).

C857   'Working one's passage on the ship of death, with an anarchist at the wheel'. *Glasgow Herald* 30 December 1989, p.21 (Weekender 3). EM writes about a favourite book, B. Traven, *The Death Ship*.

D

INTERVIEWS

D1   EM and Thomas Wilson interviewed on their opera, *The Charcoal Burner*. *Scottish International* 6, April 1969, pp. 15–17.

D2   With D.E. Caricature by Coia. *Scottish Field* June 1969, p.25. Includes 'The Flowers of Scotland'.

D3   With David Smith. *Glasgow University Magazine* 82:2, February 1971, pp.24–6.

D4   With John Schofield. *New Edinburgh Review* 19, 1972, pp. 12–14.

D5   With Raymond Gardner. 'No mean citizen'. *Guardian* 9 May 1972.
     Article based on interview. Photograph.

D6   With Robin Hamilton. *Eboracum* (York) 11½ [sic], [1972], pp.[5,7,8].
     Only part of the interview was published. A copy of the complete
     transcript is in the Edwin Morgan Collection, Mitchell Library,
     Glasgow.

D7   With Marshall Walker. *Akros* 11:32, December 1976, pp.3–23.
     Also published separately (Preston: Akros Publications, 1977).
     Reviewed by K.E. Smith, *Anglo-Welsh Review* 62, 1978, pp.129–31.

D8   With George Rosie. 'Glasgow: a suitable case for treatment'. *Radio Times*
     23–9 July 1977, pp.12–13.
     Article based on interview.

D9   With Cüneyt Ayral. 'Ozan E. Morgan ile Söyleşi'. *Dünya* (Ankara) 22
     April 1979.

D10 With Mick Lamont. *Glasgow English Magazine* 3:2, Spring 1981, pp.14–
     19.

D11 With Marshall Walker. *Seven Poets* (Glasgow: Third Eye Centre, March
     1981), pp.78–83.
     Edited version of interview videotaped on 20 September 1980.

D12 With William 'Buzz' Barr. *English Ayr* 7, [March 1982], pp.21–39.

D13 With Raymond J. Ross. 'Edwin Morgan: a poet who speaks for his
     community'. *Weekend Scotsman* 28 August 1982, p.3.
     Article based on interview. Photograph of EM by Brian Stewart.

D14 With John Duffy. 'Edwin Morgan Some Kind of Romantic'. *Glasgow
     University Magazine* [1], 28 October 1982, pp.1, 4 (Part One); *GUM* 2,
     9 December 1982, p.6 (Part Two).
     GUM published as an insert in *Glasgow University Guardian* of same
     dates.

D15 With Terje Johanssen. 'Strandhugg i britisk poesi'. *Poesi Magasin* 2,
     1984, pp.16–19.
     Report of interviews with Michael Longley, Gillian Clarke and EM at
     the British Council in Glasgow 6 December 1983. Photograph of
     poets.

D16 With W.N. Herbert. 'An Alphabet of Morgan'. *The Gairfish* 1:2,
     Autumn 1984, pp.57–61.
     Conducted by post, but EM tried to make his replies as spontaneous as
     possible. Only part of interview published.

D17 With Lesley Duncan. 'Poet's place for looking out at the universe'.
     Glasgow Herald 1 December 1984, p.7 (Weekender p.1).
     Article based on interview about *Sonnets from Scotland*. Photograph.

D18 With Michael Schmidt. On *Edwin Morgan: Selected Poems*. Bournemouth/
     Manchester: Canto Publications/Carcanet Press, 1985. Audio cassette
     CPS002.
     Reviewed by Hamish Whyte, *Prospice* 18, [July] 1986, p.148.

D19   With Robert Crawford. *Verse* 5:1, February 1988, pp.27–42.

D20   With Kevin McCarra. 'And One to Go!' *Scottish Field* July 1987, p.60.
      Article based on interview.

D21   With Kevin Paterson. 'One of the Glasgow Boys'. *Glasgow University
      Guardian* 31 October 1988, pp.8–9.
      Photograph.

D22   With Audrey Gillan. 'A poet with rhyme and good reason'. *Observer
      Scotland* 23 April 1989, p.7.
      Article based on interview. Photograph by Alan Donaldson.

E

EPHEMERA

Reprintings of poems in various forms.

E1   Siesta of a Hungarian Snake. Highlands, North Carolina: Jonathan
      Williams, 1971. (Jargon 65)
      Card printed in green tipped into folded sheet of paper, 28 × 20 cm;
      issued in envelope.

E2   ay but can ye (transl. from Mayakovsky). Toronto: Imprimerie droma-
      daire, October 1975.
      Broadside, printed by Glen Golushka.

E3   Grendel. Glasgow: The Mariscat Press, 1982.
      Folded card, 21 × 15 cm, printed in red and black; illustration by
      Peter Harrison on front. Printed in an edition of 300 on Heritage Book
      White 300 g., handset by Stephen Gill at the Arran Gallery Press.
      Reviewed briefly in *Private Library* 6:2, Summer 1983, p.95.

E4   The Subway Giraffe. Glasgow: National Book League Scotland, 1983.
      Printed on A5 flyer for *Glasgow Poster Poems*.

E5   Dona Ema Brazil April 1982. Glasgow: The Mariscat Press, 1983.
      Printed on A5 flyer for *Grafts/Takes*.

E6   Glasgow October 1982. Glasgow: The Mariscat Press, 1983.
      Printed on A5 invitation card to launch of *Grafts/Takes* at Third Eye
      Centre, Glasgow, 15 June 1983.

E7   By the Preaching of the Word. Glasgow: Third Eye Centre / Glasgow
      District Libraries Publications Board, 1983.
      Art card, 15 × 21 cm. with photograph by Oscar Marzaroli, 'Glasgow
      graffiti', on front. One of series of twelve, incorporating poems and
      visual images from *Noise and Smoky Breath*, ed. Hamish Whyte
      (Glasgow: Third Eye Centre/GDLPB, 1983).

E8   The Loch Ness Monster's Song. London: Poems on the Underground,
      1986.
      White poster, 25.5 × 60.5 cm, printed in black. Published as a poster
      in September 1986: 200 in London Underground October–December
      1986, 600 in schools, libraries, community centres and prisons. See
      Guardian 30 September 1986, p.1 and *Poetry Review* 76:4, December
      1986, pp.68–9: 'Tunnel Vision'.

F

ODDS AND ENDS

Out-of-the-way and association items.

F1   Philip Larkin, *The Less Deceived* (Hessle: Marvell Press, 1955).
     EM listed in 'Subscribers Before Publication', p.[44].

F2   Geoffrey Handley-Taylor, *John Masefield, O.M.: A Bibliography and Eighty-
     First Birthday Tribute* (London: Cranbrook Tower Press, 1960).
     Acknowledgement to EM for assistance is made on p.6.

F3   'Modern Drama (with special reference to the Theatre of the Absurd)'.
     Paper given by EM to the Word and Image Conference, Edinburgh
     University, 1972; seven page typescript duplicated and issued to those
     attending.

F4   Julian Glover, *Beowulf* (1982).
     EM's translation of *Beowulf* drawn on for Julian Glover's rendering at
     Edinburgh Festival, 31 August-2 September 1982. Reviewed by Mary
     Brennan, *Glasgow Herald* 1 September 1982, p.4.

F5   Alan Spence, *A View of Things* (1984).
     Television play, BBC 1, 22 August 1984; title taken from EM's poem of
     same name; includes classroom scene in which pupils discuss the poem.

G

MANUSCRIPTS

G1   BBC Written Archives Centre, Reading
     Correspondence with members of BBC staff, 1954–1962. (Radio
     Contributors. Talks, file 1)
     Correspondence with members of BBC staff, 1955–1962. (Radio
     Contributors. Scriptwriters, file 1 and Copyright, file 1)

G2   Brynmor Jones Library, University of Hull
     Poems for *Wave* 1, with correspondence. (DP/158/1)
     Correspondence with Philip Larkin about contribution to 1974
     Christmas Poetry Supplement of Poetry Book Society; with TS and
     proofs of poems included. (In DX/73/4(b))
     Letter and postcard to E. Tarling, with poem 'Warhol'. (DP/158/9) 3
     letters to Harry Chambers, 1973, 1975. (DP/162/6, 21, 7/2)

G3   Edinburgh University Library
     TS poem, 'For the International Poetry Incarnation', 1965. (Gen.
     767/28/1, fol. 12)

G4   Glasgow University Library
     Notebook (including short story, 'Dr Tampelius'; poem, 'The Whit-
     trick'; and essays). (MS. Morgan 918)
     Poems and translations (c. 350 translations), 1936–1980. (MS.
     Morgan 1–916)
     Scrapbooks, 1931–1966 (3646pp.). (MS. Morgan 917/1–16)

G5   John Rylands University Library of Manchester
     Essays: TS, proofs and correspondence.

From Glasgow to Saturn: proofs and correspondence.
The New Divan: TS and proofs.
TS and proofs of poems, including '10 Theatre Poems'; *Rites of Passage*;
and *Wi the Haill Voice*.
TS of poems ['Grafts'] by EM and Michael Schmidt.
Correspondence with Michael Schmidt, 1974–1980. With corre-
spondence with Tom Buchan about EM's translations from Montale.
(All in the Carcanet Press Archive)

G6   Lockwood Library, State University of New York at Buffalo
     Collection of letters and manuscripts.

G7   Mitchell Library, Glasgow
     Poems, translations, short story, plays (including *Beowulf* and 'Byron
     at Sixty-Five'), 1940–1987; miscellaneous correspondence; colour
     slides, 1955–1966; drawings, etchings and surrealist table mats,
     1932–1943; photographs; annotated books; and other material
     including transcripts of interviews with EM and criticism on EM.
     (MS.220, Edwin Morgan Collection)

G8   National Library of Scotland, Edinburgh
     Gnomes: TS and proofs. (In Acc. 7125)
     the horseman's word: TS. (In Acc. 7125)
     Drafts of nine poems (including 'King Billy'). (Acc. 4532)
     Drafts of translations from Mayakovsky (21 items). (Acc. 4535)
     Two poems, 1968. (Acc. 5604)
     Sealwear, 1966. (Acc. 4625)
     The Whittrick: TS. (In Acc. 7125)
     Letters in J.B. Caird's in-mail (on deposit). (Dep. 262)
     Correspondence with Duncan Glen of Akros Publications, 1966–
     1975.
     (Acc. 7125, box 10)

G9   National Library of Wales, Aberystwyth
     Two TS letters, 1969 (on deposit). (NLW *Poetry Wales* Archive)
     Letter to Ned Thomas, 1971 (on deposit). (NLW *Planet* Archive,
     1977 deposit)

G10 Newcastle upon Tyne Literary and Philosophical Society
     Four letters to Tom Pickard, 1964–1965. (Northern Arts Manuscript
     Collection: Morden Tower Correspondence)

G11 Reading University Library
     Poems translated from Eugenio Montale, with correspondence, 1959.
     (MS219)
     Translations from Tasso: autograph and TS, with letter. (MS878)
     'The Wanderer' (translated from Anglo-Saxon), with letter. (MS203)
     Four letters to Ian Fletcher, 1950–1955, with six TS poems. (MS276)
     Letters to Ian Fletcher, 1951–1974. (MSS798, 1433, 1472, 1650–
     51, 1681, 2002)

G12 University College, London
     Sixteen letters to Cavan McCarthy of *Tlaloc* magazine, 1964–1968.
     (*Tlaloc* Papers, Box 4)

H

RECORDINGS

H1   *A Double Scotch: Edwin Morgan and Alexander Scott read their own poetry.*
Claddagh Records, 1971. 12 inch disc. Stereo CCA5.
Edwin Morgan reads: The Apple Song [sic] – Afterwards – The White
Rhinoceros – In Glasgow – Starryveldt – Canedolia – King Billy –
Strawberries – Glasgow Green – One Cigarette – The Old Man and
the Sea – A View of Things – Che – Tropic – After the Party – Off
Course.
Recorded in the School of Scottish Studies, Edinburgh, January
1971 by Ioan Allen. Sleeve notes by Norman MacCaig. Reviewed
by Anne Stevenson, *Lines Review* 54, September 1975, pp.38–9.

H2   *Poems of William Dunbar.* Selected by Edwin Morgan. Introduction by
Edwin Morgan. Readers: Edwin Morgan, Robert Garioch, Alexander
Scott, Jack Aitken, Eleanor Aitken, Barbara Douglas, and Carol Ann
Crawford. Glasgow: Scotsoun, 1975. (Scotsoun Makars Series) Audio
cassette. SSC PWD 020.
Recorded for the First International Conference on Scottish Language
and Literature, Medieval and Renaissance, promoted by the Associa-
tion for Scottish Literary Studies, Edinburgh, September 1975.

H3   *Poems of Hugh MacDiarmid.* Selected by Kenneth Buthlay. Introduction
and linking commentary by Kenneth Buthlay. Poems in Scots read by
Kenneth Buthlay, Sandy Rose, and Eleanor Aitken. Poems in English
read by Edwin Morgan. Glasgow: Scotsoun, 1976. (Scotsoun Makars
Series) Two audio cassettes. SSC CMG 028–9.
Released on Hugh MacDiarmid's 84th birthday, 11 August 1976.

H4   *Robert Garioch: Poems.* Selected by Edwin Morgan. Commentary written
and read by Edwin Morgan. Readers: Robert Garioch, Norman Mac-
Caig, and Edwin Morgan. Glasgow: Scotsoun, 1978. (Scotsoun Makars
Series) Audio cassette. SSC 045.

H5   *In Mind o a Makar: Robert Garioch 1909–1981.* Comments and recollec-
tions by Alexander Scott, David Murison, James Caird, Norman
MacCaig, Jack Aitken, Sorley MacLean, J.K. Annand, Albert D.
Mackie, Edwin Morgan and the voice of Robert Garioch Sutherland
reading from his own works and those of Dunbar, Fergusson and
Ramsay. Glasgow: Scotsoun, 1981. (A Scotsoun Tribute) Audio cassette. SSC 061.

H6   *Edwin Morgan: Selected Poems.* Interview with Michael Schmidt. Bourne-
mouth: Canto Publications (in association with Carcanet Press,
Manchester), 1985. Audio cassette. CPS002.
EM reads: Night Pillion – Verses for a Christmas Card – Starryveldt –
The Computer's First Christmas Card – The Death of Marilyn Monroe
– Aberdeen Train – King Billy – In the Snack-Bar – Trio –
Strawberries – From the Domain of Arnheim – Columba's Song – In
Glasgow – The Apple's Song – The Loch Ness Monster's Song –
Afterwards – The First Men on Mercury – Shaker Shaken – Resurrec-
tions – Cinquevalli – from an Alphabet of Goddesses: Circe –
Oreithyia – Xenaea – Zeuxippe.

H7   *17 Poems by Edwin Morgan*. A commentary by Dr Roderick Watson with
      readings by Edwin Morgan. [Glasgow:] Association for Scottish Literary
      Studies in association with Scotsoun, 1986. Audio Cassette. (ASLS
      Commentary 8)
          EM reads: To Joan Eardley – In the Snack-Bar – Trio – For Bonfires –
          Instamatic Poems (Glasgow 5 March 1971 – Bangaon India July 1971
          – Leatherhead Surrey September 1971) – One Cigarette – Strawberries
          – Hyena – The Mummy – The Archaeopteryx's Song – From the
          Domain of Arnheim – The Computer's First Christmas Card –
          Message Clear – The Loch Ness Monster's Song – In Sobieski's Shield.

H8   *Nineteen Poems of Norman MacCaig: A Commentary*. With readings by
      Norman MacCaig. Glasgow: Association for Scottish Literary Studies,
      1987. (ASLS Commentary 9) Audio cassette. Recorded by Scotsoun
      Productions.

EM has also made archive recordings:

H9   *Edwin Morgan*. British Council, Recorded Sound Section, London.
      Contemporary Poets reading their own poems.
          EM reads: King Billy – Trio – Good Friday – In the Snack-Bar – Drift
          – Aberdeen Train – The Old Man and the Sea – Frontier Story – A
          View of Things – In Sobieski's Shield – Floating off to Timor – For
          Bonfires. (No. 1655)
          'Edwin Morgan talks to Joy Hatwood'. (No. 1656)
              Recorded 6 April 1970. Copy sent to the Harvard Poetry Room.

H10   In March 1977 EM recorded thirteen poems for the Poetry Room at
      Leeds University: The Old Man and the Sea – Trio – Opening the Cage –
      Strawberries – From the Domain of Arnheim – The Apple's Song – For
      Bonfires – The Loch Ness Monster's Song – Afterwards – Thoughts of a
      Module – The First Men on Mercury – Resurrections – Shaker Shaken.

H11   National Sound Archive
          Recordings of readings from his own works, 1970–1982 (including
          items from: BBC Radio 3 'The Living Poet' and 'Poetry Now' series;
          National Poetry Centre 'Festival of Scottish Poetry'; Eighth Interna-
          tional Festival of Sound Poetry).
          Recordings of talks by EM, 1965–1981.

H12   A version of 'The Loch Ness Monster's Song' is included by the Barrow
      Poets on their LP *Magic Egg*, 1971 (Argo Stereo ZSW.511).

H13   An excerpt from 'The Second Life' read by the Rev. William Morris at a
      service of Thanksgiving in Glasgow Cathedral is included on *Scrapbook of
      1977*, 1978 (BBC Records Stereo/Mono REC 303; Cassette ZCM 303).

I

MUSICAL SETTINGS

I1   *The Charcoal Burner*. Opera by Thomas Wilson. Libretto by Edwin
      Morgan. 1969.
          Performed BBC Radio. See interview with EM and TW, *Scottish
          International* 6, April 1969, pp. 15–17.

I2 Poems 'From a City Balcony' and 'To Joan Eardley' set and sung by Archie Fisher on *Orfeo*, Decca SKL 5057. 1970.

I3 Poem 'Blackbird Marigolds' (from *Twelve Songs*) set by John Kelsall. 1974.

I4 *Valentine*. Music by George Newson. Words by Edwin Morgan. 1976. Performed Glasgow University 1976; Queen's University, Belfast, 1979. Broadcast 14 February 1982 BBC Radio 3. Two of the poems, 'Chicago North Side' and 'Cook in Hawaii' were published in *Words Broadsheet* 25, 1976.

I5 *Coll for the Hazel: A Spell for Four Voices*. Music by Martin Dalby. Words by Edwin Morgan. 1979.

I6 *Columba*. Opera by Kenneth Leighton. Libretto by Edwin Morgan. 1981. Performed Glasgow June 1981 by the Opera Class of the RSAMD; Glasgow Cathedral 1986.

I7 *Five Sonnets from Scotland* (Matthew Paris – Colloquy in Glasgow – The Picts – Caledonian Antisyzygy – The Summons). Set by Martin Dalby. 1985. Commissioned by Neil Mackie and Kathleen Livingstone as a tribute to Sir Peter Pears on his seventy-fifth birthday.

I8 *20 Attila József Fragments for Solo Voice*. Translations by Edwin Morgan set by György Kurtágh. 1986. Performed Edinburgh 1986.

I9 *Three becomings for chamber choir*. Poems 'clydesdale', 'The Computer's First Christmas Card', 'centaur' set by Derek Taylor. 1986.

J
CRITICAL AND BIOGRAPHICAL

Items are listed chronologically by year and alphabetically within each year.

J0 'Thunder, heart-beats and a dustbin bring space into sound'. *Glasgow Herald* 9 June 1966, p.8. On recording EM's poems for radio. Photograph.

J1 Nicholas Zurbrugg, 'Shortest Poem' (letter). *Times Literary Supplement* 5 December 1968, p.1385. On one-letter poems by EM ('Phantom Beaver') and Ian Hamilton Finlay.

J2 Robin Fulton, 'Two Scottish Poets: Edwin Morgan and Iain Crichton Smith'. *Stand* 10:4, 1969, pp.60–68.

J3 Maurice Lindsay, [Essay] in *Contemporary Poets of the English Language*, edited by Rosalie Murphy (Chicago and London: St James Press, 1970), pp.776–7. Slightly updated for *Contemporary Poets*, Second Edition (London: St James Press / New York: St Martin's Press, 1975), pp.1078–80; and rewritten for *Contemporary Poets*, Third Edition (London: Macmillan Press, 1980), pp.1068–9.

J4 Norman MacCaig, 'Edwin Morgan' [sleeve notes for] *A Double Scotch*, Claddagh Records CCA5, 1971.

J5   Jonathan Raban, [discussion of EM's work] in *The Society of the Poem*
     (London: Harrap, 1971), pp.38–9, 85, 92–3, 102–4, 110–11.

J6   Alexander Scott, 'Literature' in *Whither Scotland?*, edited by Duncan Glan
     (London: Gollancz, 1971), pp.200–01.

J7   Robin Fulton, 'Edwin Morgan' in *Contemporary Scottish Poetry: Individuals
     and Contexts* (Edinburgh: Macdonald, 1974), pp.13–40.

J8   John Kease, 'Some comments on "The Computer's First Code Poem" by a
     machine employed by Mr Edwin Morgan'. *Poetry Nation* 2, 1974,
     pp.135–7.

J9   David Black, 'Scottish Poetry in the Sixties'. *Akros* 10:28, August 1975,
     pp.91, 92, 93, 98–9.

J10 Alexander Scott, 'Scottish Poetry in the Seventies'. *Akros* 10:28, August
     1975, pp.107–8.

J11 Maurice Lindsay, 'The Scottish Renaissance' in *History of Scottish Literature*
     (London: Robert Hale, 1977), pp.406–7.

J12 Radoslav Nenadál, 'K návštěvě skotského básníka' ('A visit of the Scottish
     poet'). *Světova Literatura* 24:1, 1979, p.246.

J13 Michael Schmidt, 'Edwin Morgan' in *An Introduction to Fifty Modern
     British Poets* (London: Pan Books, 1979), pp.314–20 (also as *A Reader's
     Guide to Fifty Modern British Poets* (London: Heinemann / New York:
     Barnes and Noble, 1979).

J14 'Edwin Morgan and his Poetry' in *Time to Think* (Glasgow: Scottish
     Television, 1979), pp.37–42.
     Teachers' handbook for series of ten programmes for English O and H
     Grade Literature; deals mainly with Glasgow poems.

J15 Raymond Gardner, 'Glasgow's galactic bard'. *Glasgow Herald* 26 April
     1980, p.9 (Weekender p.3).

J16 Robin Hamilton, 'The Poetry of Edwin Morgan: Translator of Reality'.
     Akros 15:43, April 1980, pp.23–39.

J17 Carl MacDougall, 'Edwin Morgan' in Programme for EM's 60th Birthday
     Celebration (Glasgow: Third Eye Centre, 27 April 1980), p.[3].

J18 Hayden Murphy, 'The Unstaunched Wound: Scottish Poetry Today
     through Irish Eyes'. *New Poetry* 48, Spring 1980, pp.6–7.

J19 Alan Young, 'Three "Neo-Moderns": Ian Hamilton Finlay, Edwin
     Morgan, Christopher Middleton' in *British Poetry Since 1970: A Critical
     Survey*, edited by Peter Jones and Michael Schmidt (Manchester: Carcanet
     New Press, 1980), pp.112–24 (U.S.A. edition published by Persea
     Books, 1980).

J20 'Professor Edwin Morgan' [presentation of EM for degree of Doctor of
     Letters, *honoris causa*, at Loughborough University, by the Public Orator,
     Professor P. Harvard-Williams]. *Loughborough University of Technology
     Gazette* 65, September 1981, pp.15–16.

J21 'Academy to premiere opera at Theatre Royal'. *Scottish Opera News* 56,
     May 1981, p.3.
     Preview of *Columba*. Photograph of EM and Kenneth Leighton.

J22 Neil Ascherson, 'Edwin Morgan' in *Seven Poets* (Glasgow: Third Eye Centre, 1981), pp.30–31.

J23 Andrew Greig, 'Poets on the Limerick trail'. *Scotsman* 21 September 1981, p.7.
Diary of reading tour of Ireland by EM and AG.

J24 Harry Blamires, 'Post-modern reassessment: The 1950s and 1960s' in *Twentieth Century English Literature* (London: Macmillan, 1982), p.248.
Mainly on *The Second Life*.

J25 Robin Hamilton, 'Edwin Morgan: Translator of Reality' in *Science & Psychodrama: The Poetry of Edwin Morgan and David Black* (Frome, Somerset: Bran's Head Books, 1982), pp.31–51.
Revised version of essay in *Akros* 15:43, April 1980.

J26 Kevin McCarra, 'Taking the Middle Ground: The Poetry of Edwin Morgan', June 1982.
Unpublished typescript; original in Mitchell Library, Glasgow, with notes and MS draft.

J27 R.S. Edgecombe, 'The Poetry of Edwin Morgan'. *Dalhousie Review* 62, 1982–83, pp.668–79.

J28 Alan Bold, 'Conversing in English: Lindsay to Morgan' in *Modern Scottish Literature* (London: Longman, 1983), pp.78–80.

J29 Mohammed Darweesh, 'A Report from Scotland: introductory notes on the Scottish poet Edwin Morgan'. *Al-Aqram* (Iraq) 18:2, February 1983, p.113.

J30 Jim Gilchrist, 'When Scots vernacular went for a song'. *Scotsman* 21 November 1983, p.6.
Report of paper by EM on the 'muckle sangs' at conference, *The Scots Language in Song*, Glasgow University, 19 November 1983.

J31 'Glasgow For Him'. *Sunday Post* 11 December 1983, p.7.
In 'Have You Heard?' column: 'Edwin Morgan is hard at work on a new collection'.

J32 Duncan Lunan, 'Taming the Giants' in *Man and the Planets: The Resources of the Solar System* (Bath: Ashgrove Press, 1983), Chapter 11.
Makes 'The Moons of Jupiter' a feature of the argument.

J33 Caroline Macafee, *Glasgow* (Amsterdam/Philadelphia: John Benjamins, 1983), p.138.
Uses 'The Porter' (Text 64) from 'Stobhill' to illustrate Glasgow speech.

J34 Roderick Watson, 'Edwin Morgan's "Glasgow Green"'. *Akros* 17:51, October 1983, pp.38–40.

J35 [Tom Leonard], 'EDWIN MORGAN'. Note on poster for POET-SOUND '84, Third Eye Centre, Glasgow, 23–5 March 1984.

J36 Roderick Watson, 'Edwin Morgan' in *The Literature of Scotland* (London: Macmillan, 1984), pp.439–41.

J37 Alan Young, 'Edwin Morgan' in *Poets of Great Britain and Ireland, 1945–1960*, edited by Vincent B. Sherry, Jr. (Detroit: Gale Research Company,

1984 [Dictionary of Literary Biography, Vol.27]), pp.247–53.
Includes photograph of EM by Jessie Ann Matthew and of the
worksheet of 'The Poet in the City' (from *Sonnets from Scotland*).

J38   Susan Cox, 'The Gentle Giant'. *Glasgow University Guardian* 21 Novem-
ber 1985, p.10.
Report of reading by EM at GU Literary Society, 13 November 1985.
Photograph.

J39   Erik Frykman, 'En skotsk poet: Edwin Morgan'. *Artes* 11:5, 1985,
pp.53–67.

J40   'Edwin (George) Morgan' in *Contemporary Literary Criticism*, Volume 31,
edited by Jean C. Stine and Daniel G. Marowski (Detroit: Gale Research
Company, 1985), pp.272–7.
Collects excerpts from reviews of *The Second Life, Glasgow Sonnets, From
Glasgow to Saturn, The New Divan* and *Poems of Thirty Years* and from
essays by Michael Schmidt and Alan Young.

J41   Kevin McCarra, 'Morgan's "Cinquevalli"'. *Scottish Literary Journal* 12:2,
November 1985, pp.69–75.

J42   Geoffrey Soar, [Essay] in *Contemporary Poets*, fourth edition, edited by
James Vinson and D.L. Kirkpatrick (London and Chicago: St James
Press, 1985), pp.593–4.

J43   John Blackburn, 'Edwin Morgan' in *Hardy to Heaney: Twentieth Century
Poets: Introductions and Explanations*, edited by John Blackburn (Edinburgh: Oliver & Boyd, 1986), pp.133–44.

J44   R.D.S. Jack, *Scottish Literature's Debt to Italy* (Edinburgh: Edinburgh
University Press, 1986), pp.49–54, 59.
Deals with EM's translations from Italian.

J45   Geddes Thomson, *The Poetry of Edwin Morgan*. Aberdeen: Association for
Scottish Literary Studies, 1986. (Scotnotes Number 2)
Reviewed by Simon Berry, *Artwork* 20, June/July 1986, p.3; by Beth
Dickson, *Books in Scotland* 22, Autumn 1986, pp.14–15; and by Ian
Campbell, *Books in Scotland* 28, Summer 1988, p.14.

J46   Robert Crawford, 'Recent Scottish poetry and the Scottish tradition'.
Krino 3, Spring 1987, pp.19, 21–3, 24, 25.

J47   Roderick Forsyth, 'Case of Irina and Morgan the refusenik: . . . why
Edwin Morgan refused to share a platform in Scotland with Russian
dissident poet Irina Ratushinskaya'. *Glasgow Herald* 17 March 1987, p.4.

J48   Brian McCabe, 'The Poetry of Edwin Morgan: Society Observed by the
Humane Eye'. *Radical Scotland* 25, February/March 1987, pp.38–9.

J49   Roderick Watson, 'Internationalising Scottish Poetry' in *The History of
Scottish Literature*, volume 4, edited by Cairns Craig (Aberdeen: Aberdeen
University Press, 1987), pp.322–5.

J50   Barry Wood, 'Scots, Poets and the City' in *The History of Scottish
Literature*, volume 4, edited by Cairns Craig (Aberdeen: Aberdeen
University Press, 1987), pp.340, 342–5.

J51 'Extra reading for five authors'. *Glasgow Herald* 29 April 1988, p.11.
Report of presentation of SAC Book Awards by EM at John Smith's
bookshop, Glasgow, 28 April 1988.

J52 Violeta Khristovka, 'A Scottish Bard: Edwin Morgan and his Poetry'.
Delos 74 (Shtip, Yugoslavia) XV:1–2, January–April 1988, pp.74–88.
In Macedonian.

J53 Willis Pickard, 'Forsyth summoned in "crusade" against poet'. *Times
Educational Supplement* 8 April 1988, p.1.
Complaint to Education Minister by Rev. David Randall about his son
being given 'At Central Station' for Higher English. See also article in
Scotsman 24 May 1988, p.8 and ensuing correspondence, 4 June, p.8
and 11 June, p.8; and letter from Rev. and Mrs D. Randall, *Life and
Work*, June 1989, p.33.

J54 Duncan Glen, 'European poetry translated in Scotland'. *Scottish Poetry
Library Newsletter* 13, Summer 1989, p.[3].
Comment on EM's translations.

J55 Michael Hamburger, 'Translation as Affinity' in *Testimonies: Selected Shorter
Prose 1950–1987* (Manchester: Carcanet Press, 1989), pp.266–7.

J56 Ian Gregson, 'Edwin Morgan's Metamorphoses'. *Bête Noir* 7, Spring
[December] 1989, pp.6–16.

Poems, parodies and cartoons about, or dedicated to, Edwin Morgan

J57 Peter Finch, 'silt koup list', poem for EM in *Whitesung* (Shirley, Solihull:
Aquila Publishing Company, 1972), p.[10]

J58 'Merry Organ', 'The First Men on the Bus', parody in *Scotia Review* 8,
December 1974, p.36.

J59 Liz Lochhead, 'The People's Poet', poem for EM in *Aquarius* 11, 1979,
pp.42–4; reprinted in her *Dreaming Frankenstein & Collected Poems* .
(Edinburgh: Polygon, 1984), pp.17–20.

J60 Robin Hamilton, 'Katacat, or the Encounter', poem for EM in *Lines
Review* 76, March 1981, pp.11–12.

J61 Alexander Scott, 'Space Opera', poem for EM in *Akros* 16:46, April 1981,
p.5.

J62 Hamish Whyte, 'Gasometer Follies', poem for EM in *Cencrastus* 8, Spring
1982, p.8; reprinted in *Noise and Smoky Breath: An Illustrated Anthology of
Glasgow Poems* (Glasgow: Third Eye Centre/Glasgow District Libraries,
1983), p.152.

J63 'M.D.', Cartoon of child asking teacher for EM's Mayakovsky translations
in *English Ayr* 7, [March 1982], p.9.

J64 Kay Bourne, 'After the Poetry Class', poem based on 'In the Snack-bar' in
Graffiti 6, [September 1982], p.9.

J65 Maud Devine, 'A Sonnet for Edwin Morgan', poem in *Original Prints III*
(Edinburgh: Polygon, 1989), p.25.

About the Contributors

ROBERT CRAWFORD is Lecturer in Modern Scottish Literature in the Department of English, University of St Andrews, and an editor of *Verse*. His books include *The Savage and the City in the Work of T.S. Eliot* (OUP, 1987) and *A Scottish Assembly* (Chatto, 1990).

DOUGLAS DUNN is Writer in Residence at the University of St Andrews and editor of the new *Faber Book of Twentieth Century Scottish Verse*. His *Elegies* (Faber, 1985) won the Whitbread Book of the Year award. His *Selected Poems* (Faber, 1986) were followed by *Northlight* (Faber, 1988).

ROBIN HAMILTON lectures in English Literature at Loughborough University, is author of a short study of Edwin Morgan, and has a special interest in Glasgow writing.

W.N. HERBERT is completing a doctorate on Hugh MacDiarmid at Oxford University. His experimental poetry in Scots and English has brought him favourable mention in the *London Review of Books* and the *Times Literary Supplement*.

PETER MCCAREY studied Russian at Oxford and Scottish Literature at Glasgow University. He is author of *Hugh MacDiarmid and the Russians* (Scottish Academic Press, 1988) and works as a professional translator in Geneva.

KEVIN MCCARRA is Football Correspondent for *Scotland on Sunday*. He was a co-editor of *The Glasgow Magazine*, has published articles on Edwin Morgan, and has received a grant from the Scottish Arts Council to work on a critical study of Morgan's poetry. He is the author of *Scottish Football: A Pictorial History* (1984).

ROBYN MARSACK is author of a study of Louis MacNeice, *The Cave of Making* (OUP, 1982) and has been an editor of *PN Review*. Having been a Junior Research Fellow at Wolfson College, Oxford, she now works as a freelance editor, translator, and critic.

JOHN A.M. RILLIE teaches in the Department of English Literature, University of Glasgow, and has published on various aspects of twentieth-century literature, including Edwin Morgan's prose and mid-century intellectual life in Glasgow.

IAIN CRICHTON SMITH is a bilingual (Gaelic/English) poet, critic, and novelist. His most recent collection of poems is *The Village* (Carcanet, 1989). His critical essays, *Towards the Human*, were published by Lines Review Editions in 1986.

GEDDES THOMSON, Principal Teacher of English at Shawlands Academy, is author of *The Poetry of Edwin Morgan* (ASLS Scotnotes No. 2, 1986) and has considerable experience of teaching Morgan's work to secondary school pupils.

MARSHALL WALKER is Professor of English at the University of Waikato, New Zealand, and author of various critical books including *Robert Penn Warren: A Vision Earned* (Edinburgh, 1979) and *The Literature of the United States* (Macmillan, 1983).

HAMISH WHYTE is editor of the anthology of Glasgow poems, paintings and photographs, *Noise and Smoky Breath*, and co-editor (with Moira Burgess) of *Streets of Gold: Contemporary Glasgow Short Stories* (Mainstream, 1989). He works in the Department of Language and Literature at The Mitchell Library, Glasgow, and has been instrumental in developing the Mitchell's collections of modern Scottish literary manuscripts.

Index to Works Discussed